THE LIFE OF
THEMISTOCLES

TH

THE LIFE OF
EMISTOCLES

A CRITICAL SURVEY OF
THE LITERARY AND
ARCHAEOLOGICAL EVIDENCE

A. J. PODLECKI

McGILL – QUEEN'S
UNIVERSITY PRESS
MONTREAL & LONDON 1975

© MCGILL–QUEEN'S UNIVERSITY PRESS 1975

INTERNATIONAL STANDARD BOOK NUMBER 0-7735-0185-1

LIBRARY OF CONGRESS CATALOG CARD NUMBER 73-93001

LEGAL DEPOSIT FIRST QUARTER 1975

BIBLIOTHÈQUE NATIONALE DU QUÉBEC

DESIGNED BY SUSAN MCPHEE

PRINTED IN CANADA BY T. H. BEST PRINTING COMPANY

Uxori Carissimae
Hoc Pignus Fidei

CONTENTS

ILLUSTRATIONS

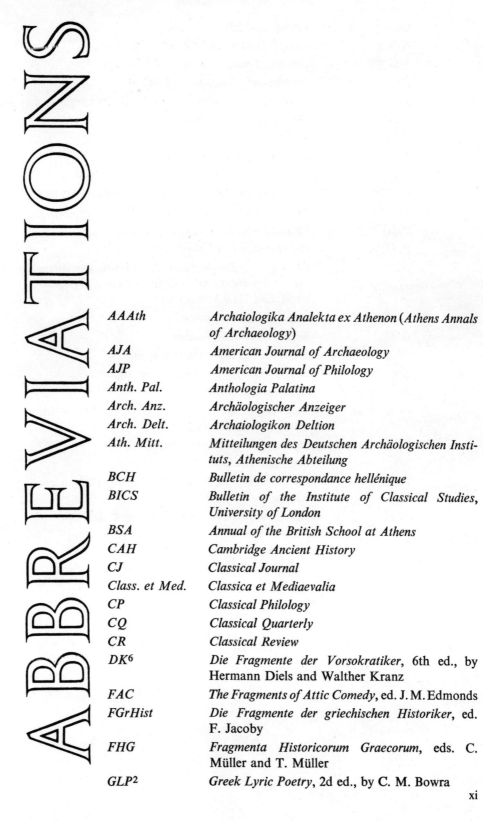

ABBREVIATIONS

AAAth	*Archaiologika Analekta ex Athenon* (*Athens Annals of Archaeology*)
AJA	*American Journal of Archaeology*
AJP	*American Journal of Philology*
Anth. Pal.	*Anthologia Palatina*
Arch. Anz.	*Archäologischer Anzeiger*
Arch. Delt.	*Archaiologikon Deltion*
Ath. Mitt.	*Mitteilungen des Deutschen Archäologischen Instituts, Athenische Abteilung*
BCH	*Bulletin de correspondance hellénique*
BICS	*Bulletin of the Institute of Classical Studies, University of London*
BSA	*Annual of the British School at Athens*
CAH	*Cambridge Ancient History*
CJ	*Classical Journal*
Class. et Med.	*Classica et Mediaevalia*
CP	*Classical Philology*
CQ	*Classical Quarterly*
CR	*Classical Review*
DK[6]	*Die Fragmente der Vorsokratiker*, 6th ed., by Hermann Diels and Walther Kranz
FAC	*The Fragments of Attic Comedy*, ed. J. M. Edmonds
FGrHist	*Die Fragmente der griechischen Historiker*, ed. F. Jacoby
FHG	*Fragmenta Historicorum Graecorum*, eds. C. Müller and T. Müller
GLP[2]	*Greek Lyric Poetry*, 2d ed., by C. M. Bowra

G&R	*Greece and Rome*
GRBS	*Greek, Roman, and Byzantine Studies*
HSCP	*Harvard Studies in Classical Philology*
IG	*Inscriptiones Graecae*
JDAI	*Jahrbuch des Deutschen Archäologischen Instituts*
JHS	*Journal of Hellenic Studies*
Mus. Helv.	*Museum Helveticum*
OCD	*Oxford Classical Dictionary*
PA	*Prosopographia Attica*, by Johannes Kirchner
PCPhS	*Proceedings of the Cambridge Philological Society*
PLG	*Poetae Lyrici Graeci*, ed. T. Bergk
PMG	*Poetae Melici Graeci*, ed. D. L. Page
P. Oxy.	*The Oxyrhynchus Papyri*
RE	*Pauly's Real-Encyclopädie der classischen Altertumswissenschaft*, eds. Georg Wissowa, Wilhelm Kroll, and Karl Mittelhaus
REA	*Revue des études anciennes*
REG	*Revue des études grecques*
Rh. Mus.	*Rheinisches Museum für Philologie*
Riv. di fil.	*Rivista di filologia e di istruzione classica*
Riv. stor. ital.	*Rivista storica italiana*
Röm. Mitt.	*Mitteilungen des Deutschen Archäologischen Instituts, Römische Abteilung*
SEG	*Supplementum Epigraphicum Graecum*
SO	*Symbolae Osloenses*
TAPA	*Transactions of the American Philological Association*
TGF^2	*Tragicorum Graecorum Fragmenta*, 2d ed., by August Nauck

PREFACE

WHEN I BEGAN to do serious research into early fifth century Athenian history, I was struck by the absence of a thorough modern study of the evidence, both literary and archaeological, touching upon the important figure of Themistocles, the man who had (or so at least it seemed to me) single-handedly altered the course of Greek, and thus also of world, history. Although Adolf Bauer's monograph of 1881 offers a survey of the main literary testimony, it does not deal with the archaeological material at all and is in any case virtually unobtainable. More recent studies, such as Labarbe's *La loi navale de Thémistocle*, F. J. Frost's expanded edition of Bauer's 1884 edition of Plutarch's *Themistocles*, with its useful collection of parallel passages and testimonia, and the vast outpouring of scholarly articles on the Troizen Decree, deal only with certain aspects of Themistocles' career or of the tradition concerning it. It seemed to me in 1965, when I began to collect material and visit the sites, that a comprehensive review of all the evidence might be of use. In spite of some recent glimmerings of interest in specific Themistoclean topics, I believe that the need for a thorough survey of all the main material has not yet been satisfied.

At the same time, it became increasingly clear as I progressed that the main lines risked getting lost in a fragmentation of scholarly controversy on specific items in the tradition; the general reader seemed to me to deserve a reasonably full narrative account. Part I, therefore, attempts to provide such a continuous narrative. Whether I have succeeded in my purpose to provide both the general and the scholarly reader with a reasonably convincing, and yet at the same time critical, reconstruction of the tradition regarding this truly remarkable individual rests with others than myself to decide.

I wish to express my thanks to several institutions for grants-in-aid. Northwestern University awarded me a travel grant for a visit to Ionia in the summer of 1965, and the Pennsylvania State University has contributed towards defraying secretarial and other research expenses, as well as freeing me from teaching and administrative duties for several terms, one of which was spent on the hospitable premises of Wolfson College, Oxford.

The individuals to whom I owe general or specific gratitude are many (names omitted in the following list are due to a lapse of memory, not intention): E. Badian, L. Bliquez, O. Broneer, G. L. Cawkwell, G. Daux and the École française d'Athènes, Mrs. P. Demoulini and the staff of the American School of Classical Studies at Athens, F. Eckstein and the Deutsches Archäologisches Institut in Rome, Miss Alison Frantz, H. Gundert, A. J. Holladay, Colin Kraay, D. M. Lewis, H. B. Mattingly, A. Momigliano, A. E. Raubitschek, J. D. Smart, H. Strasburger, J. Traill, J. Travlos, E. Vanderpool, Paul Wallace, and R. E. Wycherley. Russell Meiggs lent encouragement at a crucial stage; he read the typescript and helped me prune it to a more manageable size. Special thanks are due to my colleagues and students for their friendly interest during the years when this study was taking shape. My wife, for the unfailing encouragement on which I came to rely ever more heavily as time went on, deserves much more by way of return than a mere dedication.

I
THE LIFE OF
THEMISTOCLES

THEMISTOCLES, son of Neokles, of Phrearrhioi, was born about 523 B.C.[1] Of his father nothing whatever is known, but his name, which means "New Fame," at least suggests that he was not of the old, landed aristocracy. That the family was in a technical sense "noble" seems to be shown by the fact that Themistocles claimed membership in the *genos*, or clan, of the Lykomidai, which had its main locus in the deme of Phlya to the northeast of Athens. This deme was a cult centre of some importance, and the Lykomid clan, which traced its descent from a son of Pandion, retained the function of singing certain hymns (said to have been composed by Musaeus or Orpheus) at the Eleusinian Mysteries. What is not clear is what evidence there was, over and above Themistocles' own claim, which he advertised by rebuilding the clan's initiation house after the Persians had departed, that he really was a Lykomid. It is at least suspicious that his father's deme was in an outlying district in south Attica, and although later writers described him as *epieikes*, or *generosus*, this may be based on nothing more than the almost automatic assumption that all Athenian political leaders before Cleon were aristocrats. Whatever the technicalities of the case, the important point remains that, as Plutarch remarks at the beginning of his *Life*, Themistocles' origins were too obscure to give him much of a boost when he entered public life.

Of his mother much was conjectured, probably even invented, by later writers. The unreliable romanticizing tradition—or was this already among the slurs cast against Themistocles by his political enemies?—gave her a name and made her a slave from Caria or Thrace, but the Roman writer Cornelius Nepos asserts (without giving any evidence) that she was "an Acarnanian who enjoyed the rights of citizenship" (*Themistocles* 1. 2). This has as much, or as little, claim as any of the other conflicting versions to being true, and a grant of citizenship to such a "foreigner" would not have been rare under the Peisistratid tyrants, who were proud of, and took pains to foster, their

1. See Appendix A, "Chronology."

external connections. But perhaps certainty about her origins is unattainable and it is best to agree with a recent writer that "all that can safely be said is that she was probably not Athenian."[2] From Plutarch's mention of a nephew, Phrasikles (*Themistocles* 32. 3), it appears that Themistocles had a brother, about whom nothing more is known.

The location of the deme Phrearrhioi has now been settled: it lay in southern Attica some nine miles northwest of Cape Sunium, near to, but not quite within, the principal mining district of Laurium. What connection Themistocles' family may have had with the mining industry is unknown. Although the period of the mines' greatest productivity lay some years ahead, silver had been mined in the area from Mycenaean times, and it may be that the family had settled in the district originally because of the opportunities for work which it offered.[3]

Stories were told, with a wealth of unsavoury detail, of Themistocles' youthful debaucheries: he was said to have consorted freely with prostitutes, who pulled his chariot into the marketplace when it was at its most crowded, and later writers even produced their names—which is as much as to say that it is all sheer invention. His wantonness furthermore was said to have driven his father to disinheriting him (palpably untrue, in view of his official designation by patronymic on the ostraka) and his mother to suicide; again, the lurid details give the story away as a fiction.

Exactly when Themistocles came to Athens is unknown. His official identification as "of Phrearrhioi" shows that his father at least was still living there at the time of Cleisthenes' reorganization of 508. When Themistocles did take up residence in Athens, perhaps soon after 500, he lived in the deme of Melite to the southwest of the Cerameicus, or Potters' Quarter, which was for the most part a commercial and industrial area.[4] Plutarch comments (*Themistocles* 22. 2) that his house stood near the road which led out through the Hangman's Gate to the Barathron, where the bodies of criminals and suicides were disposed of—an unprepossessing location, but presumably for one with an eye on a political career a city residence was preferable to the obvious alternative, settling in the rural deme of Phlya with his kinsmen, the Lykomidai.

What Themistocles found when he came to Athens was a political setting in which a man's chances of success depended principally on two things: who his father was and what his family's connections were. Themistocles' endowments in these two respects were, as he must have been quick to realize, small, and it may have been in part to compensate for his rather dim background that he married, at an unknown date, Archippe, daughter of Lysandros, of Alopeke. Her name and place of residence show the family to have been aristocrats; Alopeke was one of several pockets of Alcmeonid influence, and this marriage may point to the fact that Themistocles was starting up the ladder of public prominence by the old technique of contracting an alliance with one of the influential houses.[5] Themistocles would now have to face competition from

2. J. K. Davies, *Athenian Propertied Families, 600–300 B.C.*, where this question and others relating to Themistocles' family are discussed.

3. For the location of Phrearrhioi, see E. Vanderpool, *Hesperia* 39 (1970), 50 ff. A possible connection of the family with the mines is suggested by F. J. Frost, *Calif. Studies Class. Ant.* 1 (1968), 113, with n.4.

4. For Melite, see Rodney Young in *Hesperia* 20 (1951), 140–43.

5. For a concentration of nobles, especially Alcmeonids, at Alopeke, see P. J. Bicknell, *Studies in Athenian Politics and Genealogy*, 56 ff., 62–63, who sees in the marriage Themistocles "seeking a point d'appui in an Alkmeonid 'constituency'" (62).

men whose very names advertised their racing stables, whose family trees sent branches to the semidivine past (Miltiades, for example, traced his descent from the hero Aeacus), and, above all, whose long exercise of power had imparted a confidence in their own abilities, an easiness of manner which the son of a Neokles must have found rather daunting.

At the beginning of the *Life*, Plutarch tells a story of how Themistocles persuaded some well-born young men to go with him and train at the gymnasium of Cynosarges,[6] which was situated on the south bank of the Ilissus and which was reserved for those of more or less impure birth (blue bloods were expected to use the other two gymnasia, the Academy and Lyceum); "by this ingenious social manoeuvre he is believed to have done away with the discrimination between pure Athenians and those of mixed descent" (Ian Scott-Kilvert's translation of *Themistocles* 1. 3). However little foundation in fact the story may have, it throws a good deal of light on what can be inferred about Themistocles' attitude to social distinctions.

The sources tell us nothing about Themistocles' early education, but an anecdote told by his near-contemporary Ion of Chios suggests that he later felt himself deficient in those literary and musical skills that, at least to a moderate degree of accomplishment, were considered a primary aim of an aristocrat's education: he "had not learned how to sing or play the lyre but," Themistocles added defiantly, "knew how to make a city great." At a later stage he may have attended lectures by some natural philosopher or mathematician, but Stesimbrotus' report that he was a pupil of Anaxagoras and Melissus of Samos is, as even Plutarch realized (*Themistocles* 2. 5), implausible. Plutarch himself preferred the version that had Themistocles taking lessons in political wisdom from his fellow demesman Mnesiphilus, but this seems to be only a more elaborate version of the story Herodotus tells of how Themistocles took over the plan to fight at Salamis from Mnesiphilus. The commoner tradition held up Themistocles as an outstanding example of one whose achievements rested on natural ability, not formal education, which may be nearer to the truth.

To a young man in Themistocles' position, without the money or family background to launch him into politics, there had recently been opened another avenue of approach, which significantly modified the rules under which the aristocrats had operated. When, in 514, two noblemen of the somewhat undistinguished *genos* of the Gephyraioi failed in their attempt on the life of the tyrant Hippias, Peisistratus' eldest son, and succeeded in murdering only Hipparchus, Hippias' brother, a chain reaction of events was set off that culminated in the constitutional reforms of Cleisthenes (508/7). After the murder of his brother, Hippias purged those nobles he considered to be the most serious threats, but before long the Alcmeonids (who may in fact have already been in exile), using as their base Leipsydrion, on a ridge of Mount Parnes north of Athens, were looking for an opportunity to return. They enlisted the support of Delphi (Herodotus retails the story that Cleisthenes himself had bribed the priestess, 5. 66), and

---

6. For Cynosarges, see J. Delorme, *Gymnasion*, 45 ff., who doubts Plutarch's story. Its location has now been fixed by J. Travlos, *AAAth* 3 (1970), 6 ff.; idem, *Pictorial Dictionary* *of Ancient Athens*, 341–42. The gymnasium appears to have been restored some time after 480 B.C., perhaps by Themistocles; see P. Rodeck in *BSA* 3 (1896/97), 103.

the personnel of the shrine were soon putting pressure on Sparta to "liberate Athens" of her Peisistratid oppressors, a request which the Spartans were glad to heed if it meant they could set up in Athens a ruler compliant to themselves. The first Spartan attack on Athens by sea was unsuccessful, but in 511/10 they sent a land army under Cleomenes, one of their two kings. With the assistance of some Athenians who responded to the Spartans' claim that they were "bringing freedom" to Athens, they blockaded the Peisistratids and their families on the northern part of the Acropolis. The siege was finally successful when the Peisistratid children were intercepted during their attempt to escape secretly from the country.

Herodotus records his view (5. 66) that the expulsion of the tyrants marked the beginning of Athen's leap forward to greatness, but it was also the signal for a return to the old style of politics by family groupings, which had prevailed before Peisistratus had gained firm control. The main contender was the head of the Alcmeonid clan, Cleisthenes. His chief opponent Isagoras had struck up a friendship with the Spartan king Cleomenes during the siege (rumour later had it that his wife had slept with the Spartan king), so he now tried to enlist Spartan help. To counter this appeal, Cleisthenes turned to a new element in the political game, the people, whose physical needs and aesthetic and religious impulses had been looked after by the tyrants, but who had begun to develop political aspirations as well. Cleisthenes, Herodotus tells us, "took the people into his political club," which, though it may be put in anachronistic terms, nevertheless well points up what Cleisthenes' game was: "The Athenian commons," Herodotus remarks, "which had formerly been excluded, he now thoroughly incorporated into his own faction" (5. 69). Cleisthenes' plan, which he was not able to put into effect until the Athenians rallied to his support, expelling Cleomenes and the Spartans and putting to death his Athenian supporters, called for a redivision of the population into ten new tribes, which replaced the four old Ionian tribes. Each of the new tribes was to be composed of three smaller units, which would be assigned in such a way as to ensure the breakup of the old geographical groupings that had fostered a client relationship between the ordinary citizen and his aristocratic local "protector." (There is insufficient evidence to support the current view that Cleisthenes' technique of assigning the constituent divisions was impartial to all save the Alcmeonids, whose former pockets of influence were allegedly left untouched.) The Aristotelian *Constitution of Athens* (21. 2) records that "those wishing to scrutinize the *gene* [presumably to validate the citizen-rolls] were told not to investigate the tribes" and that a citizen's official designation was henceforth to be by demotic. It appears that an Athenian citizen's most important associations were no longer with his *phrateres* (phratries were religious "brotherhood groups" which, however, Cleisthenes did not abolish) but with his demesmen; the result, writes W. G. Forrest, was a totally new emphasis on "the unity of the deme and the equality of all its members *qua* members."[7] Another important effect of Cleisthenes' reforms was in the military sphere. Athenians served in the army in regiments which were tribal and would, under circumstances of training and the even more critical conditions of actual warfare,

7. *The Emergence of Greek Democracy*, 195.   reforms by A. Andrewes, *The Greeks*, 182 ff.
There is a good, brief discussion of Cleisthenes'

meet men who came from other parts of Attica, which they had perhaps heard of but may never have visited, and yet who were *Athenians*. In this way a true sense of national identity, which transcended local boundaries, could not help but be fostered. At the same time, the important duties of political administration were to rest with a new Council of Five Hundred, which was also organized on tribal, that is to say, national, lines.

Themistocles may have been just old enough for the events of 510 and after to make a direct impression on him. In any case he would certainly have heard later the accounts of those who had themselves participated in these unexpected developments: how Cleisthenes the Alcmeonid had radically altered the shape of Athenian politics by interjecting into it a force which had had little attention paid to it until now, the common people.

When in power, Peisistratus' son and successor, Hippias, had been careful to keep his international contacts in good repair. He had, for example, married one of his daughters to the son of the tyrant of Lampsacus precisely because, as the later tradition had it, of the family's influence with Darius. As a result, when Hippias was driven from Athens in 510, the Thessalians, whose cavalry had successfully beaten back the first Spartan invading force, if not the second, offered him a refuge. The Macedonians did likewise, but Hippias chose instead to settle in Sigeum near the site of Troy, which had long been an invaluable Athenian foothold in the northeast. Within just a few years he was summoned to Sparta by Cleomenes, who offered to restore him to power in Athens in return for a pledge of noninterference with Sparta's plans to expand her own influence; Sparta's strongest allies, the Corinthians, however, objected to the forcible restoration of Hippias, perhaps because they realized that in the long term a complaisant Athens, which allowed Sparta her head, would not be in their own interests, and Sparta's other allies followed Corinth's lead. Hippias retired again to Sigeum, to return only with the Persian invaders at Marathon in 490. Members of the family who were less directly related to Hippias seem not to have been expelled, for a certain Hipparchus, whose name suggests that he was connected with the Peisistratids (he was perhaps the Hipparchus who was later to be the first victim of ostracism), was elected archon in 496/5. This need not betoken the re-emergence of a "Tyrant's Party," although not even so much can be confidently asserted, given the almost total silence of the sources. The only external event recorded for this period is Athens' temporary involvement in the abortive Ionian uprising of which Herodotus gives a detailed narrative (5. 99–6. 32). When Aristagoras, tyrant of Miletus, in concert with his cousin Histiaeus, decided to bring the Milesians and as many other Ionians as would follow him out of the Persian orbit, he sought help from King Cleomenes of Sparta but, being refused by him, turned next to Athens. The Athenians, responding to Aristagoras' appeal that they aid their "descendants" (popular Athenian belief had it that Athens was the city from which the migration of peoples from the mainland to Ionia had set out in about 1100 B.C.), sent a force of twenty ships, accompanied by five from Eretria, under the command of a certain Melanthius. The allied Ionian-Athenian force marched from Ephesus on the coast inland against Sardis, which they burnt, but they were then disastrously defeated in a battle against the defending Persians near Ephesus. Athenian aid was withdrawn, and further messages of appeal from Aristagoras were disregarded. The Ionians were left to confront, and ultimately capitulate to, the Persians on their own.

It is difficult to know what the implications of these bare facts may be. The original force of twenty Athenian ships probably represents a substantial portion of what must have been, at that time, a relatively small Athenian navy; original support for their Ionian "kinsmen" does not therefore seem to have been halfhearted. On the other hand, withdrawal after one defeat, albeit a serious one, does seem to represent a change in policy. It cannot now be ascertained whether this resulted from simple calculation of their own interest on the part of the Athenians, or whether it is to be taken as a sign of something deeper—an attempt, for example, to define two separate spheres of influence, a Persian and a Greek. Nor do we know which group was politically effective enough to instigate the volte-face. Although the chronology is not quite fixed, Sardis was burnt probably in the summer of 498, and within two years the Athenians would elect as eponymous archon a relative of their former tyrant Hippias, who had probably already begun negotiations with Darius of Persia. It may be that at least some of those who elected Hipparchus did so because they felt that the power in the East ought to be appeased. Some years earlier (Herodotus 5. 96–97 seems to synchronize it with Aristagoras' embassy to Athens in winter 500/499), an Athenian embassy was sent to Artaphrenes, Darius' brother and viceroy in Sardis, to try to undo the harm that Hippias was known to be causing by his slanders. The price demanded by Artaphrenes for Persian friendship, restoration of Hippias, proved too high, and there were some at Athens who felt that hostilities were now inevitable.

The first event in Themistocles' career for which we have a firm date is his archonship of 493/2.[8] The post gave a man with political aspirations not only a great deal of actual power during his year of office, but continuing influence as life-member thereafter of Athens' most venerable council, the Areopagus. This proved to be an eventful year. One of the archon's first official acts upon taking up his office was to appoint three choregi, or dramatic producers, for next spring's festival and "grant a chorus" to the dramatists who wanted to compete, that is, in effect, choose which three would be allowed a place on the programme at the most important Athenian dramatic festival, the City Dionysia, held in March of each year. One of the leading dramatists of the day, Phrynichus, who had been competing since about 510 B.C. but who had previously written plays on traditional subjects, turned to a recent event for the theme of his *Capture of Miletus*. Late in 494 that city had been laid siege to and captured by the Persians as the last crushing defeat of the Ionians on land (they had shortly before been beaten decisively at sea); the men of Miletus were for the most part slain and their women and children made captives. Athens reacted with a shudder of shock and remorse, and there must have been many Athenians who regretted their earlier failure to support the Ionians. It is an inference, but a safe enough one, from the fact that Phrynichus' play was performed in Themistocles' year as archon, that Themistocles was in sympathy with its theme.[9] His later policy of resistance to the

8. See Appendix A for a discussion of the date.

9. Herodotus (6. 21) does not specify the year in which Phrynichus' play was performed,

Persian menace also suggests that he felt Athens had acted wrongly in abandoning the Ionians. What Themistocles could not do was gauge the effect Phrynichus' play would have on the audience; deeply touched by the spectacle of their kinsmen's sufferings, the Athenians—perhaps at the urging of those who continued to favour a soft line towards Persia—fined the dramatist the relatively large sum of 1,000 drachmae and forbade that his play should ever be acted again, a reaction whose harshness is without parallel in the history of the ancient Athenian stage.

Themistocles' main activity during his year as archon was to begin the fortification of the Peiraeus, whose three natural harbours he discerned would be much more serviceable as the port of Athens than the relatively open Bay of Phaleron to the southeast, which the Athenians had been using since their earliest days of seafaring. Particularly the large northern harbour, called Kantharos because of its shape like an inverted cup, he saw could be sufficiently fortified to withstand attacks from the enemy, foreign or Greek, and the further possibility may have occurred to him of linking the whole harbour complex with the upper city by a narrow, walled corridor, although this was not actually achieved until the fifties of the century. How much of the work was in fact done at this early stage is unknown; perhaps no more than the surveying and planning, for just at this time the younger Miltiades returned to Athens, driven out of his ancestral kingdom in the Chersonese by the gradual Persian take-over of the area. Scion of one of the old families, a former archon, and now a successful imperialist who had added the islands of Lemnos and Imbros to the Athenian sphere of influence, Miltiades put himself forward as the natural leader of the resistance to the invasion which could not long be delayed now that Darius' armies were overrunning the Greek cities in Ionia and the Hellespont. Miltiades' claim to the leadership was challenged; he was put on trial on the charge of having set himself up as a "tyrant" in the Chersonese but was acquitted. What part Themistocles took in the trial, if, indeed, he interfered at all, is not known. The people's confidence in Miltiades' hoplite policy was apparently unshaken, for he was re-elected to the generalship continuously from 492 to 489. In the event, Miltiades' policy proved successful, at least temporarily; the Persian invaders, with the ageing former tyrant Hippias in tow, were defeated at Marathon in the autumn of 490.

There is no record of any other specific acts by Themistocles during his year as archon, but Plutarch retails stories of how he showed favouritism to his friends, perhaps in rendering such judicial decisions as fell to the archon's court (*Aristeides* 2. 5,

but since Miletus did not fall until late in 494, "there wasn't much time to write a play for March 493," as W. G. Forrest has pointed out to me. See Bruno Snell, *Tragicorum Graecorum Fragmenta*, I, 74, n.4b. For Phrynichus and Themistocles, see E. Meyer, *Geschichte des Altertums*[3], IV. 1, 294 ff.; A. von Blumenthal, "Phrynichos," *RE* 20. 1 (1941), col. 914; Graf Alexander S. von Stauffenberg, "Themistokles," in his collected essays *Macht und Geist*, 128 ff. E. Badian has recently argued that the production must have been separated from the fall of Miletus by a considerable interval, on grounds that Herodotus says Phrynichus "reminded" the audience of the occurrence: "You can remind people of what they may be presumed to have forgotten, and it would take longer than a few months to forget the destruction of one of the greatest cities in the Greek world, if one felt ties of kinship with it" ("Archons and *Strategoi*," *Antichthon* 5 [1971], 15–16, n.44). But a dramatist can also remind an audience of an event which they knew perfectly well had happened in real life, but may have preferred to forget.

Moralia 807 A–B). There are, however, several events in which he was involved, which, although they can be given no fixed date, seem to have occurred early in his career. He is known to have held the office of *Epistates Hydaton*, or water commissioner, which involved supervising the public water supply from the Cephisus River and the smaller streams in Attica to ensure that no private individuals infringed the rights of the rest by drawing off more water than they were entitled to or by diverting public water to their own personal uses. To commemorate his tenure of that office, which he may have held as a stepping-stone to the archonship or in some year after it, Plutarch tells how Themistocles set up a bronze statue of a female water-carrier over three feet high, which he paid for out of the money he had collected in fines for infringements of the water regulations (*Themistocles* 31. 1). Also from this period in the nineties may date Themistocles' friendship, which was to be close and long, with the poet Simonides. This man, an incredibly versatile writer and one of the leading composers of victory songs for athletes and of epigrams of his day, had come to Athens first at the invitation of Hippias' brother Hipparchus, who had played the role of patron of the arts at the Peisistratid court. With the fall of the tyranny, Simonides went to Thessaly. Exactly when he returned to Athens is unknown, but it may well have been at this period in the nineties, early in Themistocles' career. It may have been at this period, too, when he was about thirty, the normal age for a Greek man to marry, that Themistocles entered into his first marriage, which has already been mentioned. From the union issued the five sons and probably also three of the five daughters whom Plutarch names in *Themistocles* 32.

Marathon was a stunning, and indeed completely unexpected, victory. It was Miltiades' hour, and Themistocles' name does not occur as a colleague of Miltiades in the generalship. There can be little doubt, however, that as an able-bodied Athenian of military age he fought in the battle, although later reports like those of Plutarch (*Aristeides* 5. 4) and Justin (2. 9. 15), which record an exchange between Themistocles and Aristeides, are nothing more than the inevitable association of great names with great events. The people may have been prompted by Miltiades' success to grant his somewhat unusual request in the following year for a squadron of seventy ships for a purpose unspecified. When his plan, to extort money from the island of Paros on the pretext of the Parians' collaboration with Darius, failed miserably, he returned home and was made to stand trial on charges of having "deceived the people." (He had in fact promised to enrich the state treasury.) The defence successfully resisted a demand for the death penalty and had it reduced instead to a fine of fifty talents, which, when Miltiades, still in prison, died from gangrene of a wound he had received during the siege of Paros, his son Cimon had to pay.

The only one of his prosecutors to be identified by name is Xanthippus, who had married a niece of the Alcmeonid Cleisthenes (a marriage of which Pericles had recently been born), and it may have been as a counterattack that the story was spread that the Alcmeonids had used a polished shield to signal the Persians at Marathon about an appropriate time to sail around Sunium and launch a surprise attack on Athens. No source mentions Themistocles among Miltiades' accusers, but he cannot have regretted the discomfiture of so potent a political rival. There are later accounts of how Themistocles was kept awake at night thinking of Miltiades' trophy after Marathon and wondering how he could match that victory. So far from being the end of the war with Persia, Themistocles, according to Plutarch, "believed that it was only the prelude to a far greater struggle, and he prepared, as it were, to anoint himself for this and come forward as the champion of all Greece" (*Themistocles* 3. 5, Scott-Kilvert's translation).

In the spring of 487 (or, with less likelihood, 486), the Athenians for the first time applied the mechanism known as ostracism, which they counted among the enactments of Cleisthenes, although its date and original purpose are alike uncertain. As it was used in succeeding years it became a powerful weapon in the hands of a politician to secure temporary removal of an opponent so that his own proposals might proceed unobstructed. It was a relatively innocuous penalty, which did not involve confiscation of property or loss of citizen rights, whereby the loser in the final vote, held in about March, had to leave Athens for ten years—geographical limits within which the ostracized persons could not come were defined at a later date—and there is some evidence that a similar arrangement was also in effect in other Greek states, which may have adopted it from Athens. The ancient sources are in disagreement whether 6,000 votes had to be marshalled against the unsuccessful individual, or whether 6,000 was merely the quorum, a simple majority of which sufficed to ostracize, but in either case it is obvious that an ostracism did not just happen; votes had to be canvassed by a man's opponents who saw to it that a sufficient number of citizens turned up to vote against him on ostracism day. In fact, a surprisingly large number of what appear to be prefabricated ostraka with Themistocles' name carefully inscribed on them have been unearthed to show that he himself was a near victim some time in the 480s.[10]

A certain amount of information about the victims of the early ostracisms is provided by the *Constitution of Athens*, ascribed to Aristotle. The first man removed, Hipparchus, whose name connects him with the tyrants' family and who may be identical with the Hipparchus whose name is given as the archon for 496/5, is described as "leader and chief of the 'friends of the tyrants'" (22. 4). In the following year, 486, the Athenians removed Megacles, son of Hippocrates, leader of the Alcmeonids; a "provisional" count of over 4,600 ostraka with Megacles' name have recently come to light in the Cerameicus excavations, together with over 1,600 against Themistocles, which suggests that these two were locked in a political combat which Megacles ultimately lost. (The Cerameicus finds have also revealed, interestingly enough, that the young Cimon was a candidate in this year, for his name joins those of Megacles and Themistocles on fragments of a black-figure vase of distinctive decoration.) "For three years," the *Constitution* continues, "they ostracized the friends of the tyrants"; the third victim, who is not named, may have been Hippocrates, son of Alcmeonides, whose name occurs on 125 of the ostraka found in the Agora (one adds the curse "Vengeance on him!"), or possibly an otherwise unknown Kallias, son of Kratios, of Alopeke, whose name occurs on 760 of the new Cerameicus ostraka, on 11 of which he is described as "the Mede."

10. Ostracism and the discoveries of ostraka are discussed more fully in chapter 11.

It seems, then, that a well-organized campaign was being run against these public figures, who either were Alcmeonids themselves or were allied to that family; the propaganda against them probably involved reviving the story that one of their group had tried to assist the Persians at Marathon in their avowed purpose to restore Hippias to power at Athens, a charge which, whether true or not, would have caused deep apprehension among the people. The Alcmeonids, their enemies could maintain, were therefore "friends of the tyrants," and one ostrakon from the large number cast against the Alcmeonid Kallixenos, son of Aristonymos, even describes him as "traitor." Who was it who was organizing this well-planned, smoothly executed campaign? The whole series of ostracisms in the eighties shows signs of manipulation by an expert's hand, and there can be little doubt that it was Themistocles', against whom the Alcmeonids were later to lodge a charge of treason. The sources assign to him responsibility for the ostracism of Aristeides later in the decade (whom one ostrakon accuses of Persian sympathies by calling him, with somewhat heavy-handed irony, the "brother of Datis"), and the inference that he was also behind the earlier ostracisms seems inevitable.

The year 487/6 also brought a constitutional change: the nine archons, previously elected, were from now on to be chosen by lot from a panel of pre-elected candidates. The effect of the law was certainly to weaken the status of the archons and concomitantly to increase that of the ten generals, who had been elected annually on a tribal basis since 501 (*Constitution of Athens* 22. 2), but we have no indication of whether this was also the purpose of the law, or who proposed it. Although the precise statutory relationship between the generals and Callimachus, the *archon polemarchos*, at Marathon is a matter of continuing debate among scholars, he is the last archon of whom we hear in a specifically military connection; from now on the generals become the chief elective officers in Athens and it is the generalship to which men of ability could hope to be re-elected—witness Pericles' phenomenal fifteen generalships later. It has been maintained that this constitutional change in the year of Telesinus may not have had any special significance, but once again, as with the series of ostracisms, constitutional innovations (even if they are recorded by only a solitary source such as the *Constitution of Athens*) are unlikely to have occurred without some individual, or some group, pressing for them and mustering popular support to ensure their passage. When we ask who this may have been, the answer again suggests itself—although perhaps not so compellingly as with the ostracisms—Themistocles.[11]

In the spring of 484 Xanthippus was ostracized. Xerxes had recently succeeded his father, Darius, as the Persian king, and there were many at the court at Susa who urged him to requite the insult Darius had suffered at Marathon. Xanthippus' earlier prosecution of Miltiades, the man who had defeated the Persians there, may have been

11. The extremes of scepticism and credulity in the matter of Themistocles' part in the reform are represented by Badian, *Antichthon* 5 (1971), 1–34, and C. Hignett, *A History of the Athenian Constitution*, 187–89. The bill may have been intended to curtail an "undemocratic" and potentially dangerous power of the archons if A. Rosenberg is right in suggesting that as part of the reform the presidency of the Boule was transferred from the archon to a daily rotating *epistates ton prytanon* ("Die Parteistellung des Themistokles," *Hermes* 53 [1918], 308 ff., esp. 314–16).

made to count against him. The *Constitution of Athens* (22. 6) remarks that Xanthip-pus was the "first of those not connected with the tyranny" to be ostracized, but his marriage into the Alcmeonid family could not have helped him on this occasion (it may be this which one ostrakon was alluding to in calling him "accursed"). Did Themistocles contribute any of his political influence in removing Xanthippus? We simply do not know, although he certainly would not have been sorry to see a potential rival go.

Themistocles' purpose in eliminating his opponents one by one was the realization of a scheme he had cherished at least since his archonship, the transformation of Athens from a second-rate land power to the leading maritime state in Greece. Just at this time chance placed into his hands the wherewithal to fulfil his ambitions. Some years previously a new vein had been struck in the state silver mines at Laurium close to his family seat, and silver was now coming out of the ground in vastly increased quantities. A proposal for distributing it as a kind of dole, ten drachmae to each adult Athenian male, was brought before the Assembly—we have no information about the proposer—but Themistocles, realizing that here at last was the opportunity he had been looking for to expand Athens' navy, brought forward the counterproposal that the city's new wealth should not be disbursed but turned rather to the building and outfitting of a fleet. Although the ancient sources are vague on the details of his plan, it seems to have called for an initial outlay of 100 talents to build 100 triremes, with regular increments thereafter to a total of 200.[12] The reason he gave the people for requesting the additional ships was that Athens had to have a fleet to settle matters with Aegina once and for all, for hostilities had been dragging on with this formidable seafaring neighbour for over twenty years.

For Themistocles to have persuaded the Athenians to adopt his proposal was a brilliant achievement. Ten years before, the Athenians had been able to muster only 50 seaworthy ships of their own against Aegina, and 70 were available for Miltiades' Parian venture (Herodotus 6. 89 and 132); in the combined Greek fleet that was to face Xerxes' no less than 200 vessels were Athenian. Themistocles had at a stroke succeeded in turning "steadfast hoplites into sailors and seamen," as the conservative Plato was later to remark. His persuasive abilities are well captured by Plutarch: "Little by little he coaxed the city along and made her go down to the sea, by telling them that they, who before had not been a match for their neighbours in land fighting, would be able, with the strength their ships gave them, both to beat back the barbar-ians and to exercise control over Greece" (*Themistocles* 4. 4). Thucydides, too, credits Themistocles with the foresight to see that naval supremacy would lead to empire. Whether he had foreseen this possibility as early as 493 when, as archon, he began fortifying the Peiraeus it is impossible to be certain; still, his family's connections with the mining district, as well as the fact that in the 490s the Thasians had used the income from their gold mines to build a fleet and strengthen their walls (Herodotus 6. 46), may have given him a suggestion of the direction from which help might come. (It is worth remarking that it is unknown when exactly the rich third contact at the Maroneia

12. Themistocles' Naval Bill is discussed in Appendix B.

district in Laurium was struck; the mines may have been producing in increased quantities for a considerable time before the proposal was made to distribute the money among the citizens.) This discovery was what the Greeks called a *hermaion*, a piece of luck which they ascribed to the goodwill of the god Hermes. But it took a man of Themistocles' imagination and courage (the term is used of him in this connection by both Thucydides and Plutarch) to come forward with the unpopular proposal that immediate personal gain be sacrificed to the possible long-term advantages that might accrue to Athens as a nation. He repeatedly told his countrymen, in phrases which Pericles was later to echo, that if they wanted to be superior to their enemies—and he did not mean merely the Persians—they would have to "hold onto the sea."

The chief obstacle to the fulfilment of Themistocles' plans for an Athenian navy was Aristeides. What later generations had done to heighten, and so probably distort, the contrast between the two is summed up by Plutarch: their "rivalry quickly revealed their respective natures, Themistocles' being resourceful, daring, unscrupulous, and ready to dash impetuously into any undertaking, while Aristeides' was founded upon a steadfast character, which was intent on justice and incapable of any falsehood, vulgarity, or trickery even in jest" (*Aristeides* 2. 2, Scott-Kilvert's translation). The bad feelings between them were supposed to go back to their school days, and later Peripatetic writers like Ariston of Ceos added the detail that they had both been enamoured of the same pretty boy. When allowances have been made for romantic embellishment, the fact remains that these two individuals were very different in ability and temperament. Aristeides' background was aristocratic and conservative, and his residence in Alopeke brought him into contact with others like himself; these natural affinities were enhanced when a kinsman of his, the wealthy Callias, married Cimon's sister Elpinike. On all these counts he will have incurred the hostility of Themistocles, which Aristeides was no doubt quite willing to reciprocate.

How early their latent antagonism to one another burst into open flame we do not know. Plutarch tells a tale of the period preceding Aristeides' ostracism of how Themistocles spread the story that Aristeides had "done away with the law courts by judging everything in private and had, imperceptibly, all but established an unarmed monarchy" (*Aristeides* 7. 1). If this has any truth in it, the charge must apply to a period when Aristeides was in a position to hear lawsuits, that is, when he was archon.[13] But an aura of the fictitious surrounds later accounts like Idomeneus' story of how they brought charge and countercharge against one another: Aristeides maintaining that Themistocles had embezzled public funds while holding some unspecified office, Themistocles countering with a prosecution of Aristeides at his audits after holding some magistracy, again unspecified. There may be some truth, and even more point, in the comment that Plutarch says Aristeides made upon leaving the Assembly after a particularly heated exchange between himself and Themistocles: "The Athenians would do well to throw us both into the prisoners' pit" (*Aristeides* 3. 2; it should be recalled that Themistocles' house stood near the road which led out to this spot).

13. The date of 489/8 for Aristeides' archonship seems clearly to be the correct one (see Plutarch, *Aristeides* 1), in spite of Demetrius of Phaleron, and the doubts of P. J. Bicknell, *Riv. di fil.* 100 (1972), 164–72.

Athens, Aristeides meant, and many of his fellow Athenians would have agreed, was not big enough for them both. To prevent interference with the buildup of Athens' fleet, which had already begun, Aristeides was ostracized, probably in the spring of 482.

The Persians in their turn had been requisitioning ships from their maritime subjects, principally Phoenicia, Egypt, and Cyprus. They began preparations for an invasion by both land and sea by cutting a canal through the Athos peninsula (Xerxes could not risk a recurrence of the disaster which had befallen Mardonius' fleet in 492) and by arranging for bridges to be built across the Strymon River in Thrace and the Hellespont. Xerxes ordered a muster of his land army at Critalla in Cappadocia (perhaps modern Ereğli in Turkey) in the autumn of 481, and from there the army set out for Sardis in the Lydian satrapy.

It is at this point that Themistocles makes his first appearance in Herodotus' pages. The Athenians had sent an official embassy of inquiry to Delphi to ask for Apollo's advice in the face of the impending invasion, but the twelve-line hexameter response given by the priestess (whose name Herodotus records at 7. 140, along with that of another member of the temple staff; he thus had this part of the story from official sources) was not encouraging.

Leave your houses and city and flee to the ends of the earth...
Against the city press fire and sharp Ares...
Leave the shrine; bestrew your heart with ills.

So bleak and comfortless, indeed, was the oracle that Herodotus remarks that "the Athenians considered it a disaster. They were encouraged...to apply to the oracle again, and so they appealed to Apollo to respect their supplication and give them some better response for the fatherland." In the second twelve-line response were the more hopeful words

Wide-seeing Zeus grants to Athena, Triton-born, that
The wooden wall alone remain unsacked...
O divine Salamis! You shall destroy the children of women
When Demeter is scattered or gathered.

(7. 141)

When the responses were brought back from Delphi, the Athenians were in considerable doubt as to the meaning of certain cryptic phrases in the oracle. What precisely was the "wooden wall"? Why had the God singled out Salamis? And who were the "children of women" who would die there? One group (Herodotus calls them "older men") maintained that the wooden wall was a suitably riddling oracular reference to the Acropolis, which in times long past was said to have been fenced round with a thorn hedge. Another group (including, as will appear shortly, Themistocles) insisted that Apollo had meant the ships, and that the Athenians were being instructed to meet the Persian invaders at sea. The reference to Salamis, however, they found extremely puzzling, for the professional oracle interpreters contended that if the wooden wall were taken as signifying the fleet, mention of Salamis must indicate that their navy would be defeated there (7. 142).

Themistocles stepped in to break the deadlock (and perhaps earned for himself the epithet Pythian, which is assigned to him in the later tradition); the professionals were wrong, he said, for, if the purport of the oracle were hostile to the Greeks, Apollo would not have called Salamis "divine," but would have used some harsher term such as "hateful" or "destructive." The phrase must indicate, he maintained, that it was the *enemy's* sons who would perish at Salamis. He advised the Athenians accordingly to prepare for a naval battle and put their trust in the ships, the wooden wall which Apollo had said would save them (7. 143). It has been suggested in modern times that Themistocles' treatment of the oracles went beyond simple interpretation; he may have adjusted certain details in them, or even fabricated the whole of the second oracle to suit his plans for Athens' defence.[14] The deceit was then, according to this interpretation, connived at by the Delphic priests after the war to cover up their own collaborationist posture. Although the theory appears plausible, there is nothing in the ancient sources to support it. The date at which Herodotus implies the Athenian embassy went to Delphi, summer of 481, has also fallen under suspicion, especially in light of the specific reference to Salamis in the second oracle. Some would bring it down to the spring of 480, after the abortive expedition to Tempe, but no good grounds have been brought forward for "correcting" Herodotus in this way.[15]

News of Xerxes' mustering of troops in Cappadocia would have reached Athens at about this time, late autumn of 481. Although the king's plans were not yet known in detail, an invasion was expected, probably within the year. Preparations for the resistance had therefore to be made, and so Themistocles introduced in the Assembly a decree calling for total mobilization of Athens' forces. The decree itself was a conditional one: "When the barbarian marched on Greece, the Athenian people would face him, in their ships, *en masse*, in conformity with the God's instructions, together with any other Greeks willing to take part." This is Herodotus' summary (7. 144); later in his narrative (8. 41), Herodotus notes a "proclamation" (*kerygma*), made probably by the generals, that the conditions envisaged by the mobilization decree of the preceding autumn were now fulfilled, as Xerxes' army had invaded Greece, and that evacuation of the city should begin forthwith. The controversial Troizen Decree, about which too many problems of interpretation have clustered for its terms to be accepted unequivocally, may represent a later, literary reworking and conflation of the two measures which Herodotus mentions. Plutarch cites another decree, which he says Themistocles proposed, which made provision for the recall of those who had previously been ostracized so that they might "in action and word serve Greece to the best of their abilities, along with the rest of the citizens" (*Themistocles* 11. 1). The date of this decree of return of the exiles is given by the *Constitution of Athens* (22. 8) as the archonship of Hypsichides, 481/80. Although it is possible that the decree was

14. Thus Reginald W. Macan suggested that Themistocles "contrived, by one means or another, to adjust the wires at Delphi" (*Herodotus, the Seventh, Eighth and Ninth Books,* I. 1, 189; hereafter cited as *Herodotus, Books VII–IX).* For a more extreme view, that Themistocles fabricated both oracles, see R. Crahay, *La littérature oraculaire chez Hérodote,* 301–2.

15. See A. R. Hands, "On Strategy and Oracles 480/79," *JHS* 85 (1965), 59–61. The chronological problems are discussed by C. Hignett, *Xerxes' Invasion of Greece,* App. 13, pp. 441 ff.

passed late in the archon year, for example, in the spring of 480 (as seems to be implied by Plutarch's vague synchronism of the decree with "Xerxes' march through Thessaly and Boeotia," *Aristeides* 8. 1), it makes more sense to place it in the preceding autumn, along with the initial mobilization decree, and to see it as part of Athens'—that is to say, Themistocles'—preliminary response to the threat of invasion. Once the decision had been taken to withstand the invaders, it was only common sense to summon all available resources of manpower, particularly those political leaders who had been temporarily removed for partisan reasons. Of those who were recalled, Xanthippus and Aristeides took an active part in the fighting. Both men probably joined Themistocles on the board of generals elected in the spring of 480, which shows that, in spite of the fact that the status of the exiles appears to be left unresolved by the closing, mutilated clauses of the Troizen inscription, they were almost certainly recalled early in the archon year, perhaps as early as the autumn of 481.[16]

The next step was to mobilize resistance among the other Greek states. A congress was called to meet at the Isthmus of Corinth,[17] to which delegates were to be sent by those states that, in Herodotus' phrase (7. 145), "had better intentions for Greece," that is, were prepared to help the Athenians ward off the Persian threat. When the delegates assembled late in 481, their first order of business was to try to resolve the feuds and intermittent armed hostilities which had wracked Greece in the past and which, if they were not settled, would make a Persian take-over that much easier. Most troublesome of all was the cancerous war between Athens and Aegina, which had provided Themistocles with the reason he needed to expand Athens' navy. According to later tradition, it was Themistocles himself who laid to rest these inter-necine rivalries and reconciled the bickering Greek cities, "persuading them," Plutarch reports, "to defer their hostilities on account of the war" (*Themistocles* 6, fin.), but intrusion of his name into the account is perhaps nothing more than a plausible inference from Herodotus' narrative, where no names are mentioned.[18] It may have been at this first meeting at the Isthmus, too, that there was broached the question of who was to lead the united Greek force. Herodotus is rather vague about when this important matter was discussed, remarking simply that it was "even before they sent the embassy to Sicily" (8. 3), the last decision which he records as having been taken by the Greeks assembled at the Isthmus. (At *Themistocles* 7. 3–4, Plutarch brings the whole debate down to the eve of the battle of Artemisium and makes it a personal issue between Themistocles and the Spartan Eurybiades.) But whenever the actual

16. For a possible connection between the decree of recall and the end of the Troizen Decree, see Michael H. Jameson, "A Decree of Themistokles from Troizen," *Hesperia* 29 (1960), 221–22; A. E. Raubitschek in *Studi in onore di Luisa Banti*, 285–87. Recently Stanley M. Burstein has examined the issues anew and believes that the final clauses of the Troizen inscription show that "the ostracized are in fact included in a plan for evacuating Athens and not being recalled" (*Calif. Studies Class. Ant.* 4 [1971], 103).

17. The first meeting was probably not held at Sparta, in spite of Pausanias (3. 12. 6), who is merely reporting one of two late explanations of the name Hellenion (Hignett, *Xerxes' Invasion*, 98, with n.1, against P. A. Brunt in *Historia* 2 [1953/54], 148).

18. It should be noted in favour of Plutarch's statement, which is taken over by Aelius Aristeides (II, 248 Dindorf [1829, rpt. 1964]), that the person he mentions as Themistocles' agent, an Arcadian named Cheileon, is not a figment (he is called Chileos of Tegea by Herodotus, 9. 9); see Hignett, *Xerxes' Invasion*, 96–98.

discussions are to be dated, it is perfectly clear that such a dispute must have arisen and would have to have been settled if a united resistance were to be undertaken. Athenian claims were based on the fact that they were providing and manning almost more ships than all the others combined; Sparta countered by pointing out that her claims to leadership of a united Greek force were supported even by the tradition of Agamemnon's headship over the Greeks at Troy. In the end Athens thought it prudent to defer to Spartan insistence, "because they considered it of utmost importance," Herodotus remarks, "that Greece survive, and they realized that, if there was a dispute over the leadership, Greece would perish" (8. 3).

News was brought to the Greek delegates at the Isthmus that Xerxes and his army were at Sardis. The sessions were cut short with a vote to send ships to Asia to try to get more definite information about Xerxes' plans for the invasion, and ambassadors to Argos, Corcyra, and Crete to urge them to join their fellow Greeks in the alliance, as well as to Gelon in Sicily, the most powerful of the western Greek princes (the embassy to Gelon has been unjustly thought by some to be a fabrication). Argos, Gelon, and Crete rejected the appeal; Corcyra promised to send a contingent of sixty ships, which, if they were ever sent, never arrived.

During the winter that followed, Xerxes sent from Sardis messengers to all the Greek cities except Athens and Sparta to demand earth and water as a symbolic act of submission to him. Early the next spring his army set out for Abydos on the Helles-pont, where the Egyptians and Phoenicians had built two pontoon bridges across to the European side. Another meeting was called for the Isthmus (Herodotus' wording at 7. 121. 1 implies that he thought of this as a continuous session with the previous meeting, although this seems unlikely), and the delegates heard envoys from those Thessalian tribes that remained loyal to the Greek cause, one of the ruling families of Thessaly, the Aleuadae, and their followers having long since cast in their lot with the Persians. They requested that the Greeks from the south send troops to guard the pass between the mountains of Olympus and Ossa in the valley of Tempe. A force of about ten thousand armed men was sent north, the Spartan contingent under the command of Euainetos and the Athenian under Themistocles. The expedition in fact remained in Thessaly only a few days, which puzzled Herodotus who says that they were dis-concerted to learn from Alexander, king of Macedon, of the true size of Xerxes' arma-ment; they may also have been dismayed, Herodotus suggests (7. 173. 4), by the dis-covery of an alternate route into Thessaly, the one which the Persians in fact used. Perhaps also Themistocles discovered for himself that the Thessalians were unwilling to put up a unified defence against the Persians and that Alexander and his Mace-donians were unlikely to offer any substantive assistance to the Greek cause.[19] "The Greeks got into their ships and went back to the Isthmus," Herodotus reports (7. 174), and with their departure Thessalian resistance collapsed. A new plan therefore had to be formed, and the Greeks at the Isthmus, after discussing various proposals, decided to try to block the Persians' advance at the pass of Thermopylae on the mainland opposite the northwest tip of Euboea. The allied navy was to meet the Persian fleet

19. See Macan, *Herodotus, Books VII–IX*, I. 1, 253–54; Hignett, *Xerxes' Invasion*, 103.

off Artemisium on Euboea's northern coast, from where, if the Persian navy had secured a landing, all of Euboea and from there central Greece could have been overrun.

The Persian land army, meanwhile, had marched through Thrace and Macedonia and made a prearranged contact with the fleet at the town of Therma, near modern Thessaloniki. News reached the Greeks at the Isthmus that Xerxes, with an advance contingent of his land army, was already in the Pierian district of Macedonia, where he had received tokens of submission from most of the northern Greek states as far as Thebes. A decision was taken that an attempt should be made to stop the Persians by having a land force, numbering between three and four thousand men under the Spartan king of the Agiad house, Leonidas, march overland to Thermopylae, while the Greek fleet, consisting of 271 triremes, sailed to Artemisium. The fleet was under the command of Eurybiades, the Spartan, but the 127 ships (later reinforced by an additional 53 ships) provided by Athens and led by Themistocles were bound to give Athens an important voice in the allied war councils.

The main body of the Persian fleet set sail from Therma eleven days after Xerxes and his land army had set out from there, and the ships put in at Cape Sepias on the mainland opposite Artemisium. At dawn the following day a strong wind brewed up a storm which did considerable damage to the Persian ships, although the later account that it lasted three days and wrecked 400 of the enemy's vessels seems to be an exaggeration. The Athenians later maintained that they had been advised by an oracle to pray to their "son-in-law," the wind god Boreas, who, according to a local legend, had carried off Oreithyia, the daughter of Erechtheus, an early king of Attica. After the Persian threat had passed, the Athenians acknowledged the help of the wind by erecting a shrine in honour of Boreas on the banks of the river Ilissus, and the Boreas-Oreithyia legend became a favourite theme with Athenian vase painters. When the storm subsided, the Persian fleet sailed south and west along the coast of Magnesia and took up a new position on the Gulf of Pagasai. According to Herodotus (8. 4), the Greek forces at Artemisium were dismayed at the sight of the Persian ships and contemplated withdrawal. The Euboeans asked the Spartan commander Eurybiades to wait until they could get their children and household goods away to safety, but Eurybiades refused, so they went to Themistocles and offered him a bribe of thirty talents, five of which he allegedly passed on to Eurybiades and three to Adeimantus, the Corinthian admiral (8. 4–5). The story may be true, but the probabilities are against it. Themistocles did not have to be "persuaded" to stay at Artemisium by the Euboeans or anyone else, and if lines 41–42 of the Troizen Decree are authentic, he had projected Artemisium in advance as a possible site for a naval encounter with the enemy. As for the corruptibility of the other two commanders, it may be nothing more than the fabrication of a hostile Athenian tradition. On the other hand, there are grounds for suspecting that something lies just beneath the surface of Herodotus' narrative. It may be that there was agitation among some of the national contingents (chiefly perhaps the Peloponnesians) for returning south and drawing a line of defence closer to home, in the vicinity of the Isthmus, where, according to Herodotus (8. 71), a wall was being built to withstand the invaders. In that case, Themistocles would have had to use all his persuasive powers to secure maintenance of the northern line.

Plutarch (*Themistocles* 7. 3) reports that dissatisfaction had broken out among the Athenian troops, who felt that supreme command belonged to themselves, since they were providing most of the ships; again Themistocles had to do his best to smooth his men's ruffled pride, urging them to fight bravely even though they were taking orders from Eurybiades.

The three separate encounters off Artemisium were indecisive or, worse, had gone against the Greeks; in the third battle they were "badly mauled" and half the Athenian contingent of 200 ships was damaged (Herodotus 8. 18). Nevertheless the Athenians claimed it as a victory: Pindar would later call Artemisium the place where "the sons of the Athenians laid the shining foundations of freedom" (fragment 65 Bowra), and Plutarch records that thank-offerings were set up in a temple of Artemis on the coast with an inscription that told of how "the sons of the Athenians once conquered in these waters motley hordes of men from Asia" (*Themistocles* 8. 5). Individual honours for valour were awarded to a certain Lykomedes, son of Aischraios, to judge from his name a fellow clansman of Themistocles, and to Cleinias, son of Alcibiades (Herodotus 8. 11, 17).

When the two sides parted after the battle, the Greeks collected their corpses and wreckage without interference. Themistocles had devised a plan for dislodging the Ionian and Carian contingents from the enemy's fleet, which he was just beginning to put into effect when news arrived from Thermopylae, carried by one of Themistocles' trusted agents, a certain Habronichus, that the Greek force under Leonidas had been wiped out. The northern line was no longer defensible, and the fleet would have to draw back southward immediately. Themistocles instructed the other commanders to have their men slaughter the cattle grazing near the shore to prevent them from falling into the Persians' hands, and also light fires which would serve both to cook the meat and, with luck, to give the enemy the impression that they were planning a leisurely withdrawal. Something of his original plan for shaking the Ionians loose from Xerxes' fleet might yet be salvaged, in spite of the pressing need for quick withdrawal. At places along the shore where the Persians were likely to stop for provisions and drinking water, Themistocles and his men scratched on the rocks messages to the Ionians, Carians, and other Greeks, appealing to them as kinsmen and urging them to come over to the allied side, or at least to fight halfheartedly in the next encounter. "Remember," the gist of the messages ran, "you are descended from us and right from the beginning you were the source of our quarrel with the barbarians"—an allusion to Athenian support at the beginning of the Ionian revolt. Themistocles' reasoning, according to Herodotus (8. 22), was that either the Ionians would respond to the appeal to their Greek loyalties and change sides, or at the very least Xerxes would begin to feel doubts about them and keep them out of battle thereafter.

The fighting at Thermopylae and Artemisium had taken place during the last days of August. Xerxes and his men marched south, overrunning northern Euboea, advancing through Doris, Phocis, and Boeotia to the very outskirts of Athens. The Greek fleet collected again at Salamis not, as Herodotus' narrative implies (8. 40), by a last-minute and desperate change of plan, but as part of a prearranged second front. It was reasonably obvious that a last-ditch defence of the city itself would be to no avail before the Persian advance. A proclamation was therefore made which activated the mobilization decree of the previous autumn: the city was to be evacuated and each Athenian was to save his wife, children, and household goods as best as he could. The ships were to assist in the evacuation, and the refugees would be deposited for safe-keeping in Troizen, Aegina, and Salamis itself. Haste was essential. Those who still clung to their hope in the Acropolis had to be coaxed into putting their scruples behind them: they were not in fact abandoning their city, but merely "turning it over to its mistress, Athena, and to the other gods, for safekeeping." A new and more sinister omen was offered to them in the refusal of the sacred snake, which was lodged in Athena's temple, to touch the monthly honey cake which was offered to it by the priestess (Herodotus 8. 41). The suggestion that this portent was really manufactured by Themistocles is given some support by Plutarch's mention of the "omen of the viper" immediately after he has remarked that "Themistocles, despairing of bringing the multitude over to his views by any human reasonings, set machinery, as it were, to introduce the gods to them, as a theatrical manager for a tragedy, and brought to bear upon them signs from heaven and oracles" (*Themistocles* 10. 1, B. Perrin's trans-lation).[20] It was Themistocles, Plutarch asserts, who "put the interpretation into the mouth" of the priests that the snake's refusal to touch its food showed that Athena had left the Acropolis and was leading her people down to the sea. The evacuation of the city, already under way, was completed with greater dispatch because of this allegedly supernatural occurrence. Each man who was to serve in the crews was given a sum of money equivalent to twenty-four days' regular pay. The *Constitution of Athens* (23. 1) attributes this special subvention to the initiative of the Areopagus, whereas Cleidemus is reported by Plutarch (*Themistocles* 10. 6) as assigning credit for it to Themistocles. It may be that both these versions are mere figments of fourth-century doctrinaire polemic: the one representing a conservative, the other, a demo-cratic, answer to the question then being debated, Who was most responsible for saving Greece at Salamis?

The departure scene is described by Plutarch in vivid and pathetic terms. The people of Athens could hardly believe that such a bold, indeed unparalleled, step was being taken, that they must now send their loved ones and possessions to an uncertain fate and leave behind the aged, infirm, and their household pets. And there were still some who refused to leave; they would lodge themselves with the priests and temple per-sonnel on the Acropolis and die if necessary, rather than yield their belief that this was what Apollo had meant when he mentioned Athens' wooden wall.

The Persians took up a position on the Areopagus Hill to the northwest and shot flaming arrows into the barricade which the defenders had erected. The terms offered by the turncoat Peisistratids, now acting as mouthpieces for Xerxes, were rejected. Finally, Xerxes' men discovered a secret ascent to the Acropolis by way of the shrine of Aglaurus, daughter of one of Athens' early mythical kings, Cecrops, and Xerxes ordered the Athenian fugitives in his party to offer the customary sacrifices in the temples; but not even so was he to propitiate the Greek gods, who, it was later

20. R. Crahay, *La littérature oraculaire chez Hérodote*, 301.

believed, showed their continuing support for Athens' survival by causing the sacred olive tree in Erechtheus' shrine, which the Persians had burnt the day before, miraculously to bloom again.

When news that the citadel had fallen reached the troops at Salamis, panic swept through them. Some of the commanders called for immediate departure and the proposal to withdraw to the Isthmus was once again bruited. The crisis had been reached. Themistocles knew that once the ships withdrew, the various national contingents would disperse, each to its own city, and the cause would be lost. The navy had to be held together long enough to force an engagement with the enemy fleet, which had sailed around Attica some days before and was now anchored in Phaleron Bay. The straits of Salamis seemed to offer a site for a sea battle which would work to the advantage of a smaller, and therefore more manoeuvrable, fleet; the difficulty was in getting the king to offer battle in the straits before the Greeks panicked and fled.

Themistocles crossed in a boat to Eurybiades' flagship, presented the case for holding on where they were and trying to provoke the enemy, and asked to be allowed to speak first when the council of admirals reconvened the next morning. When he addressed them at that meeting, Themistocles made no mention of the disastrous results of a withdrawal, nor of his fears that once the ships left Salamis they could probably never again be rallied. He had spoken of these fears privately to Eurybiades the evening before, and there was nothing to be gained now from imputing ignoble motives and thus possibly antagonizing the men further. Instead, Themistocles took a more positive tack. Herodotus preserves the substance of his speech, if not the actual words he used.

You now have it in your hands to save Greece. If you engage the enemy off the Isthmus, you will be fighting in open waters, which is least to our advantage since our ships are heavier and fewer than the enemy's. Moreover you will lose Salamis, Megara, and Aegina, even if we are otherwise successful.

Do not think that in withdrawing to the Isthmus you will be taking steps to defend it; the enemy's land army will follow with his fleet, and so you will actually be leading them to the Peloponnese and endangering all the rest of Greece. If, on the other hand, you follow my advice to stay and fight here, the chances of success are high, for my plan has the following advantages.

First, if we engage here in the straits, even though we are outnumbered, we stand a chance of winning, if what usually happens in such a case should occur. For a sea fight in confined waters is to the advantage of the smaller fleet, since the larger does not have room to manoeuvre. Secondly, Salamis is saved (and this is particularly important for us Athenians, since our wives and children are here). Third, by staying here you will, as I have said, be fighting for the Peloponnese just as effectively as if you were to go to the Isthmus and, what is more, you won't be leading them there.

Finally, if it turns out as I hope and we win a battle at sea, the Persians will not attack again at the Isthmus; they will have advanced no farther than Attica and will retreat in total disorder. We shall profit by the survival of Megara,

Aegina, and Salamis, where an oracle says we are to get the better of our enemies. Things turn out for the most part successfully for men who make reasonable plans, while for those who don't—not even God will compensate for human miscalculation. (8. 60)

The Corinthian admiral Adeimantus had told Themistocles at the beginning of his speech that those competitors in the games who started before the signal were flogged, to which Themistocles had retorted that "those who started too late won no crowns" (8. 59, a traditional anecdote, which recurs frequently in later accounts). Now, after Themistocles had finished speaking, Adeimantus ordered him to be silent on the grounds that with the abandonment of Athens he no longer had a country of his own. Themistocles' response was a torrent of abuse which he capped with his famous brag, "The Athenians have a city and a country greater even than Corinth, as long as they have 200 ships full of men; no Greeks could beat them off if they chose to attack" (8. 61). Themistocles then made some additional remarks to Eurybiades:

If you stay here you will be a hero; if not, you will destroy Greece, for our ships bear the whole burden of the war. If you don't follow my advice, we will pack up our households and sail off to Siris in Italy, which was ours from very ancient times, where there are oracles that we must found a colony. When the allies have abandoned you, you will remember my words. (8. 62)

Themistocles' threat to sail to Italy is a curious one, but there may have been some substance to it; the fact that two of his daughters were named Italia and Sybaris shows that at some stage of his life the West was very much on his mind and that his plans for Athens' greatness, like Alcibiades' schemes later, extended as far as an Athenian foothold in Magna Graecia.[21]

When the matter was put to a vote, Themistocles' suggestion was carried. According to Diodorus (11. 16), Themistocles and Eurybiades then made the rounds of the ships' crews and did what they could to rouse the men's spirits. The Peloponnesians especially had let the death of their king at Thermopylae and the smoke they could see rising over Athens gnaw away at their resolve. In spite of Eurybiades' efforts, Themistocles could see that the men's patience was at the breaking point, and they were once more pressing for a new line of defence behind the Isthmus wall. He did not have much time left to precipitate an action with the Persian fleet.

At dawn the next day an earthquake occurred. To counter the renewed panic among the troops who took it as a bad omen, the Greek commanders sent to Aegina for the images of the hero Aeacus and his sons, from whom some supernatural help might be expected, a move which may have had Themistocles' support as it would effectively silence those who kept harking back to Marathon and Miltiades: the Greeks would

21. On Themistocles' western policy, see Macan, *Herodotus, Books VII–IX*, I. 2, 451b–52a. G. E. M. de Ste Croix has recently remarked that Themistocles' threat at Herodotus 8. 62 "would make particularly good sense if Themistocles was known to have advocated the founding of an Athenian colony in the neighbourhood of Siris....Themistocles may certainly have seen the West as a useful source of supply of the two basic commodities Athens most needed to import: corn and timber" (*The Origins of the Peloponnesian War*, 379).

now have, if not Miltiades, the heroic ancestor from whom he claimed descent.[22] Later writers follow Herodotus (8. 65) in recording the tale of Dikaios, an Athenian exile in Xerxes' army who, on the eve of the battle, saw a cloud of dust "as of some 30,000 men" coming from Eleusis. His vision was taken by both sides as signalling the gods' displeasure at the occupation of Attica, which had prevented the Athenians from holding their annual celebration of the Eleusinian procession; the story also helps to date the battle, around the end of September, when the Eleusinian festival was normally celebrated.

The Persian admirals, too, knew that the issue at sea would have to be decided here if their land army was to proceed against the Greeks at the Isthmus unmolested. Accordingly a council was called and it was decided, although over the objections of some, to risk an engagement. The hope was that the Greek ships would fight in the open waters outside the mouth of Salamis strait, where the Persians' vastly superior numbers would give them the advantage. Late in the afternoon the Persian ships put out from Phaleron and arranged themselves in formation along the coast as far as Peiraeus. When the challenge was not answered by the Greeks and evening came on, the Persians returned to their base.

Herodotus' narrative shifts to Salamis. The Greeks were in (the same or a new?) assembly. Panic had once more broken out; a last-minute run for it was again winning adherents, but the Athenians, Aeginetans, and Megarians were pleading with them to stay and fight. At this juncture Themistocles left the assembly unnoticed and dispatched Sicinnus, his slave and tutor of his children, to the Persian camp with a message for the king. This individual is fortunately more than a name, for Herodotus adds in a parenthesis that Themistocles later made him wealthy and a citizen of Thespiai, which had been burnt by Xerxes' troops for remaining loyal to the Greek cause. Inscriptional evidence reveals that about 447 B.C. four Thespian citizens, one of them named Athenaios, were made Athenian *proxenoi*, the equivalent of consular representatives, and the name Themistocles is recorded in a late third century B.C. decree from Thespiai. It is tempting to speculate that Sicinnus' descendants may have been active in the town's later history.[23] Sicinnus, Herodotus continues, went in a boat to the generals of the barbarians and spoke as follows:

> The general of the Athenians sent me without the knowledge of the other Greeks (for he is on your side and wants you rather than the Greeks to win) to say that they are afraid and are planning to run for it. You can now achieve a brilliant *coup*, if you don't sit by and watch them run. They are not in agreement among themselves and so will not oppose you; their naval battle, as you will see, will be against each other, those on your side and those not. (8. 75)

A simpler version of Themistocles' message is given by Aeschylus in *The Persians*, lines 355–60, where the most significant divergence from Herodotus' account is the

22. See Crahay, *La littérature oraculaire chez Hérodote*, 276, 304.

23. The inscriptions are *IG* I², 36 (*c.* 447 B.C.) and *SEG* 23 (1968), 271, line 85 (late third century); see A. W. Gomme, *A Historical Commentary on Thucydides*, I, 339, and M. B. Wallace, *Phoenix* 24 (1970), 203, with n.18.

absence of secrecy and of any implication of disharmony among the Greek forces, or of medism by Themistocles himself. In fact, Herodotus' additions to the plain message look like later embellishments, designed to enhance the Themistocles mystique, a schemer so wily that he outwitted even his fellow Greeks. It seems certain that, the uneasiness of some modern historians notwithstanding, a private communication of some sort was sent by Themistocles via his slave, although details of its exact content and some of the circumstances of its delivery may be uncertain; as George Grote remarked, "What surprises us the most is, that after having reaped signal honour from it in the eyes of the Greeks as a stratagem, Themistokles lived to take credit for it, during the exile of his latter days, as a capital service rendered to the Persian monarch."[24]

Xerxes reacted to Themistocles' message by ordering his captains to wait until after nightfall, then have their sailors embark and divide the fleet into three squadrons, whose instructions were to close all the escape routes from Salamis. A select band of soldiers, which later tradition numbered at 400, was to be landed on the small island of Psyttaleia (probably modern Lipsokoutali), there to lie in wait for any Greek sailors who might swim to the island for safety and to render assistance to their own shipwrecked crews. Xerxes' commanders obeyed and gave their crews orders to keep at their oars and be on the lookout for the Greek ships. All night they waited. Finally, just as dawn was breaking, the Persians heard a sound from Salamis: not, however, the confused hubbub of men running for their lives, but a strong, even a joyful, challenge to battle. The Persians had been cheated of what they hoped would be an easy prey, and their men, weary from a long night of rowing, now had to face a full-scale engagement with fresh Greek crews. It must have been a disheartening prospect.

What had happened on the Greek side was this. Well after midnight a ship from the island of Tenos deserted from the Persian fleet and reported to the Greek camp that the Persian fleet was on the move and seemed in fact to have blocked the main exits from the Salamis channel (the version recorded by Herodotus at 8. 79 that Aristeides coming from Aegina brought this information can be disregarded as unhistorical). Themistocles was delighted that Xerxes seemed to be taking his bait. The marines who would be fighting from the decks were summoned to an assembly, and Themistocles addressed them in a speech, which Herodotus summarizes (8. 33): speaking as befitted the situation, he pointed out what they stood to gain or lose, according to how they responded to the promptings of the better elements in man's nature, the will to freedom and the instinct protective of homeland and family, or the worse, passive acceptance of what might seem inevitable defeat in the face of superior numbers; he urged them to choose the better and embark without delay.

The Persians, then, heard the Greek war cry, the blare of the military trumpet, the splash of measured oar strokes churning up the sea; next they saw the Greek line of battle, the Spartan contingent leading on the right wing. At this moment came the last exhortation to bravery, which Aeschylus records in *The Persians*:

Sons of Greeks, forward!
Bring freedom to your fatherland, bring freedom

24. *A History of Greece* (New York ed., 1883), II, 305. The chief modern doubter is   Hignett, *Xerxes' Invasion*, App. 9a, pp. 403–8.

to your children, wives, your gods' ancestral shrines,
your forefathers' graves. Now the struggle is for all!

(lines 402–5)

And with that the opposing lines were upon one another.

None of the eyewitnesses could have given a clear, coherent account of the stages through which the battle passed to its conclusion, but two things mainly contributed to the Greek victory: the Persian sailors, who had been kept at their oars all night, were taken off guard by the sudden, orderly, and precise advance of the Greek ships; and the narrow waters cramped their ability to manoeuvre. In fact, their swollen numbers (an almost uniform tradition gave the incredibly high figure of 1,207 ships) were a liability. As the Persians streamed into the narrows in response to the Greek challenge, they began to be constricted through lack of space. The ships in front had little enough room in which to fight, but when those in the rear ranks kept continually pushing forward, freedom of motion was completely taken away from all. The Greek ships, slightly broader and heavier, rammed their enemy's ships broadsides or head on, and in this way a significant portion of the Persian navy was disabled early in the action; the gods had indeed, as the Greeks were later to maintain, equalized the opposing forces by drastically reducing the number of seaworthy Persian ships. These also did themselves a good deal of damage; squeezed closer together, they were not able to maintain order but even accidentally rammed one another and broke off the pennage of their oars as they scraped each other's sides. At some stage in the action it seems that the Greeks took advantage of the confusion by forming a line which encircled and compressed the Persian ships even more tightly together. Ships' hulls capsized; bits of wrecked ships and bodies covered the surface of the water and were washed up onshore along the coast of Salamis and the mainland. (An anecdote, probably without foundation in fact, was later told of Themistocles' surveying the corpses along the shore after the battle and showily refusing to help himself to the gold jewellery with which they were adorned.) Persian survivors, who tried to save themselves by swimming or holding onto pieces of flotsam, were dispatched by the Greek sailors with poles and broken oars. Finally, the Persians had no other recourse but to signal retreat and try to extricate the ships that survived from the choking confines of the channel. The carnage continued throughout the day and was brought to a halt only with the onset of dusk. The Greeks towed what hulls they thought they could salvage to Salamis and made ready to renew the fighting on the following day.

Two important episodes occurred at some undetermined point in the course of the battle. The Athenians somehow found out about the picked force of Persians which had been detailed to Psyttaleia to assist any of their own side who might swim there and to hamper any Greeks who might try to do the same. Aristeides with a special detachment of Athenian hoplites sailed across from Salamis and turned the tables on the Persians, killing them all to a man. The contingent of thirty Aeginetan ships, whose movements had been closely coordinated with those of the Athenians throughout the fighting, performed various acts of daring and seem to have been of particular service in pursuing enemy ships, which tried to escape out of the channel to Phaleron. When one of their commanders, Polycritus, who was pursuing a Sidonian ship, saw that he was within range of Themistocles' ship, whose ensign he recognized, he shouted out, "Here's medism for you!"—meaning that the charge of favouring the Persian side which had been levelled against the Aeginetans preliminary to the campaign of Marathon ten years earlier (Themistocles had perhaps been among those who had insisted that Aegina be dealt with firmly) received its most effective refutation in the courage now being shown by the Aeginetans. It is doubtful how successful Themistocles had been in his strategy of trying to appeal to the Greek affinities of Xerxes' Ionian contingents. Later reports were conflicting, some maintaining that certain Ionian ships (those of Samos received particular mention in this regard) fought only halfheartedly and gave the Phoenicians a chance to impugn their loyalty to Xerxes, others that few, if any, Ionian ships had held back during the battle.

Although night fell on the Greeks' expecting their enemies to give battle again the following morning, Xerxes saw that his forces had been dealt a death blow. He himself had watched from a special seat on the slopes of Mount Aegaleos overlooking the straits as the grim panorama of defeat unfolded before him. His half-brother Ariabignes, who had led the Ionian and Carian contingents, had fallen, and, in spite of the outstanding performances of some of his commanders, such as Artemisia, queen of Halicarnassus, and her five ships, it was clear that not only the strength, but the spirit to resist, of most of his men had been shattered. Xerxes had no choice but to withdraw, and he passed the word that the army was to prepare for an immediate retreat. In their haste and eagerness to return, the Persians left to their would-be victims several choice items of booty, including Xerxes' special seat, golden but with silver feet, which was long afterward proudly displayed on the Acropolis, and the royal tent, which was thought to have served as a model for the music hall which Pericles later built near the theatre.[25] But to save face and also, if possible, win a victory by land, Xerxes left behind with his general Mardonius a land force for which the tradition recorded the again inflated figure of 300,000 men. The Greeks on the other hand were to be kept in ignorance of Xerxes' plans as long as possible, for there was fear that otherwise their fleet might get the start on the retreating Persians, sail to the Hellespont, and burn the pontoon bridges before Xerxes' men could cross into Asia. Accordingly, on the following day an advance force of ships was sent ahead to guard the bridges and a false show was made by the Persian side of preparing for another battle.

Herodotus' account of the sequel is riddled with difficulties. In his version, when the Greeks saw that the Persian ships were gone, they pursued them as far as Andros, but finding that the Persians had eluded them, they decided to hold a council before proceeding any further. A dispute arose among the commanders as to the best plan of action. Themistocles, according to Herodotus (8. 108), maintained that they should "set their course through the islands and sail in pursuit of the ships straight for the Hellespont to destroy the bridges," whereas Eurybiades, whose vigorous opposition on this occasion is perhaps merely part of the stock picture of the two men at continual loggerheads, pointed out that the best thing would be for Xerxes' army to get out of

25. Attempts to connect Themistocles' name with this Odeion, or an early theatre building, are purely speculative; see further discussion in chapter 10, pp. 173–74.

Europe as quickly as possible; so far from cutting off Xerxes' escape route, they would do well to do everything they could to hasten his retreat. When Themistocles saw that the other Peloponnesian generals were siding with Eurybiades, he made a virtue of necessity, changed sides, and tried to dampen the enthusiasm of his own men who were all for pursuing the Persians. At this point in his narrative (8. 110), Herodotus relates how Themistocles sent a second message to Xerxes, who was apparently still in Attica, by the agency of "men whose silence he could trust," including Sicinnus, the purport of which was that he, Themistocles, had done the king a good service by restraining the Greeks from pursuing the Persians' ships and destroying the Hellespontine bridges; Xerxes' retreat, Themistocles assured him, could therefore be a leisurely one.

A substantially different version of these proceedings is given by Plutarch (*Themistocles* 16 and, in a slightly abridged form, *Aristeides* 9), who may be drawing, either directly or through an intermediary source, on the fourth-century historian Ctesias.[26] In Plutarch the council takes place "after the sea battle," apparently while the fleet is still at Salamis (although the locale is not specified), and Themistocles puts his proposal, not to Eurybiades, but to Aristeides, "just to try him out" (*apopeiromenos*). When Aristeides points out that it would be more advantageous, so far from destroying the bridge, to build yet another in order to hasten Xerxes' retreat, Themistocles responds, "Then we must all see to it and contrive [*mechanasthai*] that he get out of Greece by the quickest way." The affair is managed "through the prudent planning of Themistocles and Aristeides." Themistocles dispatches, not Sicinnus, but one of the royal eunuchs whom he had found among the Persian captives, an individual named Arnakes, and the purport of the message is quite different from that which Herodotus records: not "take your time," but "hurry and cross as quickly as you can, I don't know how much longer I can restrain the Greek fleet."

In fact modern scholarship condemns this second message altogether; how could Xerxes be stupid enough to fall for this trick a second time? Surely the whole thing was made up by Themistocles himself *post eventum* after he arrived in Persia, when he was dealing, not with Xerxes, but his son Artaxerxes, and was casting around for extra and unjustified claims to the king's gratitude. The difficulty with this theory is that at the royal court of Persia of all places records were kept and messages recorded almost obsessively, and it seems unlikely that Themistocles could have succeeded with an utterly fabricated second message, although it is perfectly possible that he was less than ingenuous about his motives; what had originally been a ruse, *mechane*, to speed Xerxes' departure from Greece could have become in his retelling of it for the benefit of Xerxes' son and successor an additional, incredible beau geste by which he had hoped to store up an extra deposit of gratitude with the Persian king, if he should ever stand in need of assistance from that quarter ("which is exactly what happened," is Herodotus' naïve but illuminating comment on the whole incident, 8. 109. 5). And those who would write off the second message as a complete hoax must contend with

---

26. I base this suggestion on the similarity of wording between Plutarch, *Themistocles* 16. 6, ἡ Θεμιστοκλέους καὶ Ἀριστείδου φρόνησις, and Ctesias, *Persika*, FGrHist 688 F 13 (30), φεύγει Ξέρξης βουλῇ πάλιν καὶ τέχνῃ Ἀριστείδου καὶ Θεμιστοκλέους.

the apparent mention of it by Thucydides, although his reference to it at 1. 137. 4 is somewhat obscurely worded and its meaning has been disputed.

In any case, what does seem to be credible in the later memory of the allied council, whether at Salamis or Andros, is Themistocles' address to the Athenian troops, who, having set out from Salamis in hot pursuit of the enemy, now, in view of the change of plan, had to have their enthusiasm dampened. Herodotus gives the following report of Themistocles' words.

> A defeated man, when driven into a corner, often renews the struggle and recoups his former loss. We have recovered ourselves and Greece, a lucky stroke. Let us not pursue the very men whom we have, in fact, just succeeded in driving away. For not we, but the gods and heroes have achieved this. They begrudged one man the kingship of both Asia and Europe, especially a man who was himself so wicked and godless, who trampled upon sacred and profane alike, burning and over-turning the gods' statues; who flogged the sea and let down chains into it.
>
> We are well situated for the time being. So let us now stay in Greece, take thought of ourselves and our families. Let each man rebuild his house and look to the sowing, since he has succeeded in utterly driving off the barbarian. In the spring let us sail to the Hellespont and Ionia. (8. 109. 2–4)

The Greek fleet then besieged Andros in an effort to extract war reparations from this medizer. To Themistocles' demand that they yield to the pressure exerted by two powerful new "gods," Persuasion and Necessity, which the Athenians had on their side, the Andrians countered that they had two divinities long enshrined in folk poetry, Want and Resourcelessness.[27] Similar demands for money were also made on Paros and Carystus, and the Parians yielded to the threat of a siege such as Andros was experiencing, while Carystus refused and was devastated. It is almost inevitable that the tradition followed by Herodotus (8. 112) saw these demands from the medizing island states as motivated by personal greed on Themistocles' part.

Mardonius meanwhile escorted Xerxes' army as far as Thessaly and there selected the troops which were to be left with him for next season's campaign. The main body arrived at the Hellespont after a forty-five-day march beset by starvation, dysentery, plague, only to find that the bridge cables had been loosened by a storm. Herodotus preserves two versions of the crossing (8. 117–18); he prefers that according to which the king and his troops crossed over to Abydos in ships, but an alternate version had it that Xerxes and a select band of nobles left the main body with Hydarnes at Eion on the Strymon River and crossed from there back to Asia by ship.

Their siege of Andros a failure, the Greeks ravaged Carystus and returned to Salamis. There the spoil was divided and various dedications decreed in thanksgiving for the victory. The late travel writer Pausanias gives a suspiciously detailed account of an unsuccessful attempt by Themistocles to deliver personally to Delphi part of the Persian booty (10. 14. 5–6), but the reason Pausanias suggests why Themistocles was

27. Herodotus 8. 111; see Hesiod, *Works and Days* 496–97; Alcaeus, fragment 364 Lobel-Page; Theognis 384–85.

rebuffed, that Apollo foresaw that he would one day become a suppliant of the Persian king and did not want to hurt his chances, seems to discredit the whole episode.

From Salamis the Greeks sailed to the Isthmus to determine who should receive the prize for valour shown during the battle. The story which Herodotus tells, of how each general voted for himself first and put Themistocles in second place (8. 123), may be apocryphal, since an almost identical one is told by Pliny the Elder of the sculptor Polyclitus (*Natural History* 34. 53). This failure to award the prize to Themistocles was in any case forgotten by later writers, and Justin and Aelius Aristeides say simply that he did receive it. The award in fact seems to have gone to Ameinias, perhaps a brother of Aeschylus; according to the author of the eleventh of the "Themistocles Epistles" (page 751 Hercher), Ameinias received the prize through the good offices of Themistocles. In spite of this failure to obtain the prize, "Themistocles' name," Herodotus reports, "was on everyone's lips and his reputation swelled throughout Greece as by far the wisest of the Greeks" (8. 124). He went to Sparta (a hostile tradition, which Herodotus records, had it that it was to compensate for his failure to receive honours at the Isthmus) and there received an extraordinary reception: an olive crown for "wisdom and cleverness" was awarded to him similar to that which the Spartans gave their own general Eurybiades. In addition, he was escorted to the border in a magnificent chariot and accompanied by 300 chosen Spartiates, the "Knights." Herodotus remarks that Themistocles was the only man he knew of to be so honoured (8. 124).

When he returned to Athens, Themistocles was attacked by a certain Timodemus of Aphidna, whom Herodotus, the first to recount what was to become the most famous of all Themistoclean anecdotes, calls "one of Themistocles' enemies" (8. 125), although it is uncertain whether there was any evidence for the assertion beyond the tenor of the man's remarks. "Crazed with jealousy Timodemus reproached him, saying that he had his honours because of Athens, not through his own merits." "Sir, you are right," Themistocles retorted acidly. "I should not have been honoured had I come from Belbina [a small, rocky island off the south coast of Attica], nor would you, though you are an Athenian."

Herodotus reports a set of speeches as having been made by the Athenians to delegations from Xerxes' general Mardonius and from the Spartans who came to Athens in the following spring, 479, to argue the one side for yielding to, the other, for rejecting, Mardonius' demands that Athens desert the Greek alliance. "We shall go out to defend ourselves against Xerxes," the Athenians told Mardonius' envoy Alexander of Macedon, "relying on the gods who are our allies and the heroes whose temples and statues he irreverently burnt." To the Spartans they replied, "You need not worry: there is nowhere on earth enough gold to make us medize and enslave Greece. There are many reasons why we should not even wish to do so—the most important being the gods' statues and temples which have been burnt and destroyed... second, the ideal of a united Greece, composed of men of one blood and one tongue, and sanctuaries of the gods and sacrifices and ways of life which are common to us all, of which the Athenians could not well be betrayers" (8. 143. 2–144. 2). Who the Athenian spokesmen were on this occasion Herodotus does not tell us, and Plutarch's mention (*Aristeides* 10) of Aristeides may be only a guess. In any case the similarity of motif between these speeches and Themistocles' address on Andros, and indeed the whole ideal of a Greece united in its determination to resist the barbarian invaders, suggests that the sentiments, if not dictated by Themistocles, were at least thoroughly consonant with his policy of resistance.

The last great battle of the campaign was fought at Cape Mycale opposite Samos in the autumn of 479, and it was here that Themistocles' Ionian policy at last bore fruit. The allied commander Leotychidas appealed to the Ionian contingents in the Persian fleet with the same arguments and for the same reason as Themistocles had done at Artemisium (Herodotus 9. 98). The Samians, who had some weeks before secretly sent a delegation to the Greek fleet, which was then stationed at Delos, to promise cooperation, had already fallen under suspicion and were disarmed by the Persians; in the battle itself they turned on their oppressors and their lead was followed by the Milesians. The result was a stunning victory for the Greeks and, in Herodotus' phrase, "the second revolt of Ionia from the Persians" (9. 104). It was popularly believed that the battle of Mycale was fought on the same day as that on which Mardonius and his troops were decisively defeated at Plataea near Thebes in a long-fought struggle in which the allied Greek land army had been led to victory by the Spartan regent Pausanias.

Bolstered by their victory at Mycale, the Spartans and their allies proposed the abandonment of Ionia to the Persians, on grounds that it would be difficult to garrison, and the resettlement of the loyal Greeks from there to the mainland on land which was to be confiscated from those states that had medized. The Athenians objected that the Peloponnesians had no business making deliberations about their own colonists (a convenient fiction which it was in Athens' interests to foster; the Dark Age Ionian migration was supposed to have started from there). It is difficult to determine how much truth there is in the story as Herodotus tells it (9. 106), but it is suspiciously similar to Plutarch's account of an Amphictyonic League assembly (which he does not date), at which a Spartan proposal to expel the cities that had medized from the league was vociferously opposed by Themistocles, who thereby allegedly incurred the Spartans' undying hatred (*Themistocles* 20. 3–4). Although Plutarch's narrative contains several theatrical elements, it is not in itself implausible and many scholars accept its historicity, at least in essence.[28]

What is of greatest interest in the whole affair is that the Athenian speaker, whom Herodotus does not name but who must have been Xanthippus, leader of Athens' forces at Mycale, is seen to be supporting Themistocles' contention at Artemisium that Athens had a right to count on the loyalty of the Ionian Greeks and (by implication, at least) also a corresponding obligation to look after their interests. For it was this feeling of affinity and mutual dependence that later provided the bond between Athens and her allies in the Delian League. In fact, as Herodotus makes clear, it was

28. H. Bengtson, "Themistokles und die del-phische Amphiktyonie," *Eranos* 49 (1951), 85–92, suggests Theopompus as the source, and dates the Amphictyonic League meeting to autumn 479 or spring 478 (p. 92; further refs. at Frost, *Calif. Studies Class. Ant.* 1 [1968], 120, n.71).

immediately after the battle at Mycale that Samos, Chios, Lesbos, and "the other islanders" joined the Greek alliance, thus anticipating by well over a year the similar treaty that Aristeides administered in 478/7 (*Constitution of Athens* 23. 5). The allied Greek fleet then sailed to the Hellespont, where it expected to find the Persian bridges intact, but on discovering that the bridges had been destroyed by a storm, it dispersed: Leotychidas and the Peloponnesians back home, and the Athenians under Xanthippus to the Chersonese, where they laid siege to Sestos, a Persian stronghold filled with refugees (Herodotus 9. 114–15).

The names of the two Athenian commanders in the campaigns of 479 are preserved, Xanthippus and Aristeides. Themistocles is conspicuously absent. Diodorus asserted that the Athenians, angered by Themistocles' acceptance of the extraordinary honours at Sparta late in 480, removed him from the generalship and replaced him with Xanthippus (11. 27. 3, presumably from Ephorus). But why would they have reacted so violently to honours in which they clearly had a share themselves? Although it is possible that Themistocles was not re-elected general in the spring of 479, it seems highly unlikely in view of the remarkable success of Salamis. He was probably a member of the board of generals along with Aristeides and Xanthippus, although he may have opposed a confrontation with Mardonius' force by land; certainly in the later tradition Plataea was remembered as Aristeides' victory. On the other hand, if some breach had already occurred between Themistocles and his colleagues, we have no evidence for determining how serious it was in these early stages.

When it became clear that the Persian threat had been finally repelled, the Athenians began to bring back their families and household goods from Salamis, Aegina, and Troizen and prepared to rebuild their city and the walls, which for the most part lay in ruins. On learning of the plan to rebuild, the Spartans sent an embassy which attempted to persuade the Athenians not only to leave their own walls unrestored, but also to join in dismantling the city walls left standing in the rest of Greece outside the Peloponnese. It offered the rather lame pretext that possible fortified bases would be eliminated should the Persians invade again, but Thucydides indicates that its real reason was the fear which Sparta and her allies felt of Athens' growing power. To meet the situation Themistocles devised a scheme, whose unfolding Thucydides recounts with a wealth of detail.

> At Themistocles' prompting the Athenians replied that they would send an embassy to discuss the proposals; then he told them to send him with all haste to Sparta, to choose other ambassadors in addition and send them, too, but not immediately—rather, they were to be held back until the walls had been raised to a height sufficient to ward off an attack.... These were Themistocles' instructions and, when he had added that he would attend to the rest at Sparta, he departed. (1. 90. 3–4)

It seems likely that Themistocles was counting on the honours bestowed on him at Sparta after Salamis to gain for him a period of grace; he could probably draw out the negotiations for some time without having his hosts suspect any treachery. As his fellow ambassadors the people chose (no doubt with his approval) Habronichus, who had brought news of the disaster at Thermopylae to the troops at Artemisium, and Aristeides, whose selection would convince the Spartans both of the importance of the mission and of the unanimity of Athenian public opinion about its objectives. Thucydides' account continues:

When he arrived in Sparta, he did not approach the magistrates, but kept delaying and making excuses [later writers said he pretended to have fallen ill en route]. Whenever anyone of those in authority [that is, presumably, the ephors] asked him why he did not come before the Assembly, he said he was waiting for his colleagues, who must have been detained by some business, but he was expecting them to arrive shortly and was surprised that they had not yet done so. When they heard his explanation, they believed Themistocles because of their friendship for him [at *Themistocles* 19. 1 Plutarch cites Theopompus for the detail that Themistocles bribed the ephors—the usual slur], but others came from Athens [Plutarch names a certain Polyarchus of Aegina, otherwise unknown] with clear reports that the walls were building and had already reached quite a height, so the Spartans could no longer close their eyes to it.

When Themistocles realized what had happened, he told the Spartans not to be deceived by rumours, but to send from their own number reputable men whom they could trust [three ex-ephors, according to Nepos (*Themistocles* 7), but this may only be an inference from Thucydides' statement] who were to observe the facts and report back to them. So the delegation was sent and Themistocles for his part sent a secret message to the Athenians at home to detain the envoys in the least obvious manner [again, later writers like Diodorus (11. 40) turn this into an order to imprison the ambassadors], and not let them leave until the original Athenian embassy—for Themistocles' two fellow envoys had since joined him, bringing the news that the wall was of a sufficient height—had returned; for he was afraid that the Spartans would not let them go once they had got clear evidence about the wall.

The Athenians detained the Spartan ambassadors just as they had been told to do and Themistocles came before the Spartan Assembly and said quite openly, then, that their city was walled sufficiently to safeguard its inhabitants and, if the Spartans or their allies wished to send an embassy to the Athenians, they would be going to men who could determine in advance[29] what was in their own interests and the common interests of all. For when the decree was passed that it was preferable to abandon the city and embark on the ships, the decision had been reached and the daring deed done without the Spartans' help; later, in the matters which they had deliberated in common with the Spartans, they themselves had appeared second to none in good judgement. So it seemed to them preferable now that their city should have a wall, and it would prove to be more beneficial both to the individual good of their own citizens and to the common good of all the allies; for an equal voice in the councils of war was impossible for

29. The MSS. have *prodiagignoskontas*, which is retained by K. A. Laskaris, *Phos eis to* *Thoukidideion Erebos*, A', 73–77, whose suggestion to improve the text I have translated above.

those whose ability to fight was not on an equal footing. Either all the members of the alliance, he said, should be unfortified, or it should be considered right for them to have fortifications. (1. 90. 5–91)

Themistocles, while all the time observing the diplomatic niceties, left the Spartans in no doubt that from now on the Athenians intended to challenge Sparta's traditional position of leadership over the other Greeks; he was pointing out quite unmistakably that since Athens' walls were now a reality, her voice would have to be listened to at least equally with Sparta's in any collective decisions. In his narrative of what followed, Thucydides indicates that, for all the calm correctness of their response, the Spartans were furious at being so completely outmanoeuvred by Themistocles.

When the Spartans heard this reply, they did not become openly angry with the Athenians (for they had sent their embassy, they said, not to prevent the construction, but simply to give advice for the common good; at the same time they happened to be on especially friendly terms with the Athenians because of their prosecution of the war against the Persians); nevertheless, because they had not got their way, they were secretly vexed. Both embassies returned home without being summoned back. (1. 92)

The Spartan disavowal of wishing to interfere with the building of the wall must easily have been seen for what it was: a face-saving, but ultimately unconvincing, excuse. Themistocles had been willing to sacrifice all the credit he had been storing up at Sparta as the victor of Salamis for the long-term gain to his plan for Athenian supremacy in Greece, which the rebuilt walls would afford; and Thucydides leaves us in no doubt that Spartan animosity towards Themistocles dates from this occasion.

As to the walls themselves we have some information. Themistocles, before he went to Sparta, had left instructions that "the whole populace, including women and children, were to join in the wall building, sparing no private or public structure which might assist the work, but dismantling them all" (1. 90. 3), and Thucydides remarks that even in his own day it was evident how hastily the walls had been built. The accuracy of his observation has been strikingly confirmed by excavations in modern times.[30]

Thucydides proceeds with an account of Themistocles' fortification of Peiraeus, but before we consider it, notice must be taken of certain events at Sparta which were to affect Themistocles' later career. Leotychidas, the Spartan king in the Eurypontid line, had returned from the Hellespont late in the autumn of 479, and the following spring Pausanias, the young regent of the Agiad house and hero of Plataea, pressed for energetically renewing the war against the Persians in the Aegean. Pausanias was agitating for renewal of the war at the very time that Themistocles was playing for time at Sparta, and although no ancient authority mentions direct contact between them on this occasion, it seems likely that they would have met, if only casually, and it may have been this meeting that later gave their respective enemies grounds for the charges of collusion between them.

30. The archaeological evidence for the Themistoclean fortifications is presented in chapter 10.

Some time in the winter or early spring of 479/8, the Athenian ambassadors returned home, in time for Aristeides to take a contingent of thirty Athenian ships to join the allied fleet under Pausanias for an assault on Cyprus and later Byzantium. It appears from Plutarch (*Aristeides* 23. 1, *Cimon* 6. 1) that Aristeides was joined on the board of generals by Cimon, of whom nothing has been heard in the sources since he had paid the fine of his father, Miltiades, in 489 (Herodotus 6. 136), save for the trivial story of his dedicating his horse's bridle, the aristocrat's emblem, on the Acropolis before Salamis as a sign of national unity (Plutarch, *Cimon* 5. 2–3). Whether or not Xanthippus also took part in the expedition against Cyprus is uncertain; he had been in charge of the Athenian and Ionian forces besieging Sestos, which, according to Herodotus (9. 117), had turned into an unexpectedly lengthy affair, but these troops had no doubt already returned home by the spring of 478. What is important about this campaign is that it marks the first successes of the cooperative venture which was soon to be formalized as the Delian League. Most of Cyprus was conquered (although it subsequently went over to the Persian side again, for we hear of Athenian expeditions there later, in about 460 and 450 B.C.), and Byzantium was captured from the Persian force which held it. It was during this campaign that a rift appeared in the allied ranks. Disaffection with Pausanias' leadership set in, and the other Greek contingents, especially the Ionian, asked the Athenians as kinsmen of theirs to take over the leadership; the Athenians for their part "welcomed the proposals," according to Thucydides, and "took thought how to arrange matters as appeared to them to be best" (1. 95. 2). The author of the *Constitution of Athens* is a little more explicit: "Aristeides was the one who encouraged the Ionians to withdraw from the alliance with the Spartans, by watching for the charges brought against them on account of Pausanias" (23. 4), and even Herodotus remarks that the Athenians "made Pausanias' arrogance a pretext for stripping the Spartans of their leadership" (8. 3). When in the following year (478/7) oaths were finally sworn at Delos between Athens and her new allies, and the first contributions were assessed, Aristeides' hand is mentioned as being at the tiller of events.

What was Themistocles' position in all of this? We simply do not know, for he is left in Thucydides' narrative supervising the Peiraeus fortifications in the spring of 478. Thucydides writes:

> Themistocles persuaded them, too, to complete the Peiraeus fortifications which he had begun previously during the annual magistracy which he held in Athens,[31] because he believed that it was an ideal spot with its three natural harbours, and that if they became a maritime nation it would greatly contribute to the acquisition of power.... And they built the wall to the thickness which his plan called for.... Its height, however, was only one-half of what he had originally intended. For he had wanted to fend off enemy attacks by the walls' very size and thickness, and he thought that a small number of men unfit for service would suffice to defend it while the rest embarked on the ships. For he was especially insistent upon the ships because he saw, as I believe, that the king's army could attack more

31. Evidently the eponymous archonship of 493/2; see Appendix A for full discussion.

easily by sea than by land, and he considered the Peiraeus to be more serviceable than the upper city. Again and again he exhorted the Athenians, if they were ever hard pressed by land, to go down to Peiraeus and oppose all their enemies with their ships. (1. 93. 3–7)

Completion of the Peiraeus walls represents fulfilment of the organic plan which Themistocles began when he was archon and carried to its next logical stage when he used the Aeginetan threat to force the expansion of the fleet. Impregnable walls, which could be defended by the young and old and those otherwise unfit for active service, would allow the rest to embark on the ships and meet their enemies at sea (the phrasing "all their enemies" is calculatedly ambiguous and could include Greeks as well as Persians). Athens would thus gain a military superiority which, if the policy were followed consistently, no one else could match. When, on the eve of the Peloponnesian War, Pericles told the Athenians, "It is not homes and fields which acquire men, but the reverse, and if I thought I could persuade you, I would be advising you to devastate them yourselves and thus show that you do not intend to become slaves for their sakes" (Thucydides 1. 143. 5), he was merely echoing Themistocles.

In the summer and autumn of 478, then, Themistocles was in Athens, supervising the reconstruction of the city walls and the completion of the harbour walls; Aristeides and Cimon were off winning friends for Athens among the island cities and in Ionia. What Themistocles may have felt about their successes in the Aegean is unknown, for the tradition at this point becomes heavily anecdotal. At *Aristeides* 24. 6 Plutarch tells a foolish story of Themistocles' response to the praise Aristeides was getting for the honesty of his tribute assessment; "that," sniffed Themistocles, "is praise fit more for a safe-deposit box than a man." But the sources give us no help in determining where Themistocles may have stood on the question of prosecuting the war against the Persians in the eastern Aegean, which was the avowed purpose for founding the league. It is perhaps legitimate to deduce that Themistocles' exposure to the Spartan mentality in 480, when he had had to deal with them as often unwilling allies, had convinced him that they, and not the Persians, presented the real obstacle to Athens' greatness. Xerxes had been trounced, and however protective he might turn out to be of his interests in Ionia, he was unlikely ever again to launch a full-scale attack on the Greek mainland. The Spartans, on the other hand, were bound to look with suspicion and fear at any challenge to their supremacy, and there are hints that even her surrender of the naval command to Athens was only decided on after a bitter debate.[32]

One thing is certain: from this period dates the beginning of Themistocles' steady decline in popularity, which was matched by the increasingly rapid rise to public favour of Cimon, one of the staunchest Athenian friends Sparta was to have in the whole course of her history. Accounts of personal rivalry between the two are probably without factual basis (the story Plutarch tells of how Themistocles disgraced himself at Olympia by trying to emulate Cimon, one of his social superiors, sounds

32. The Spartan assembly meeting reported by Diodorus (11. 50), and dated by him to 475, perhaps really occurred a few years earlier; see G. L. Cawkwell, "The Fall of Themistocles," in *Auckland Classical Essays Presented to E. M. Blaiklock*, 46, and n.14.

like pure fiction).[33] Better authenticated are the statements that Cimon's position at Athens was purposely enhanced by the Spartans as a counterpoise to Themistocles (Plutarch, *Themistocles* 20. 4, *Cimon* 16. 2). Cimon's family had been active in public affairs since the days of the tyranny when his grand-uncle Miltiades had led a colony to the Chersonese; his father had been the hero of Marathon. The family's fortunes were assured by the marriage of his sister to the notoriously wealthy Callias, and he had himself played at dynastic politics by marrying a grand-niece of the Alcmeonid reformer Cleisthenes (Plutarch, *Cimon* 4. 10). Of this marriage was born a son, at just about this time to judge from the fact that he served as hipparch *c.* 446;[34] as if to commemorate his deepest sympathies, Cimon named the boy Lakedaimonios.

Equally ominous for Themistocles' future was the fact that Cimon found a political ally in Aristeides, who was a kinsman of Cimon's brother-in-law Callias (Plutarch, *Aristeides* 25. 4, 6). Twice in the *Life of Cimon* Plutarch comments that Aristeides and Cimon cooperated against Themistocles. At *Cimon* 10. 8 it is implied that Aristeides found Cimon's "aristocratic and Laconian" leanings more sympathetic than Themistocles' exaltation of the common people, and at 5. 6 Plutarch remarks that Aristeides did most to further Cimon's early political career and "made him, as it were, a foil to the cleverness and daring of Themistocles" (Perrin's translation). It is perhaps not pure coincidence that Plutarch uses the same word here, *antipalon*, as he had at *Themistocles* 20. 4 to account for the Spartans' support of Cimon.

When Cimon and Aristeides set out to join the allied fleet in the summer of 478, their action may have been intended in part at least as a blow to the policy of Themistocles who was emphasizing the need to take steps against Athens' rivals closer to home; conversely, the early successes of the combined league forces probably contributed towards the undermining of Themistocles' position in Athens. Why were the Peiraeus walls finished to only half the height Themistocles had originally intended? May it not have been that after the capture of Eion, a Persian outpost on the Strymon River—a feat, by the way, for which Cimon could make the astounding claim that here the Greeks "*first* brought their enemies to an impasse"[35]—Cimon was able to argue that such an excessively high wall was unnecessary in view of the success with which the enemy was being flushed from his hiding places in the Aegean, his strongholds captured, and their inhabitants enslaved? The Athenians cannot have needed much persuading to abandon a task which was difficult, time-consuming, and expensive.

How Themistocles may have tried to refute Cimon's contentions we can only guess, but the measures he took to try to stop his skid from popularity have left some traces in the sources. Plutarch remarks that he "would often remind the Assembly of his own achievements," which in fact simply annoyed the people more (*Themistocles*

33. Plutarch, *Themistocles* 5. 4 (cf. *Eudemian Ethics* 1233 b 10), perhaps from Ion of Chios, who is cited elsewhere for a similar story (*Cimon* 9. 1; cf. *Themistocles* 2. 4).

34. *IG* I², 400. He was one of the three generals in command of the Athenian naval force sent to Corcyra in the summer of 433 (Thucydides 1. 45. 2; Plutarch, *Pericles* 29).

Cimon's attempts at playing dynastic politics through marriage alliances have recently been examined by Bicknell, "Isodike," in *Studies in Athenian Politics and Genealogy*, 89–95.

35. Aeschines 3. 184; Plutarch, *Cimon* 7. 4, line 4 (my italics). On these controversial epigrams see Gomme, *Commentary*, I, 288; Felix Jacoby, *Hesperia* 14 (1945), 185 ff.

22. 1). He went back to his contributions at Salamis not only verbally, but visually. At the theatrical festival held in honour of Dionysus in March of 476, the tragedian Phrynichus, whose *Capture of Miletus* had earlier created such a stir, presented a new play with Themistocles as choregus. This was almost certainly *The Phoenician Women*, of which we know little more than that in it a chorus composed of the wives of the Sidonian sailors in the Persian fleet reacted with violent grief to the news of Xerxes' defeat. From its similarity to Aeschylus' *Persians* (an ancient critic said that Aeschylus' play was "taken over" from Phrynichus'), it may be inferred that it, too, highlighted Themistocles' role in the events of 480. What more appropriate time for Themistocles to turn to a writer, with whom he had probably worked earlier, to commission a play which would remind the Athenians of how much they were in his debt than now when his enemies were beginning to undermine his popularity?

In this same year Simonides, Themistocles' publicist in 480, won a victory with a dithyrambic chorus and was commissioned to compose the dedicatory epigram for a new monument honouring the so-called tyrannicides, Harmodius and Aristogeiton, to be cast in bronze by the sculptors Critius and Nesiotes as a replacement for the original group by Antenor which Xerxes' men had carried back to Susa. As the dedication seems to have been intended primarily to put forward claims rivalling those of the family which had really expelled the tyrants, Themistocles' old political enemies the Alcmeonids, it seems reasonable to detect his guiding hand behind the whole proceeding.[36] If there is any truth to the story told by later writers of Themistocles' creating a stir when he went to Olympia for the festival games (probably those of 476), it may point to the fact that his reputation in Greece still remained high, although his stock at Athens had perhaps already begun to drop.[37]

At about this time Themistocles also had a hand in the building of two structures, the second of which, unfortunately, had the opposite effect from that which he intended. After the invaders withdrew, he undertook to reconstruct and redecorate at his own expense the initiation place of his clan, the Lykomidai, in the deme of Phlya. Although Plutarch leaves the date vague, he cites Simonides for the dedication recording Themistocles' benefaction (*Themistocles* 1. 4). He also built a small temple to the goddess Artemis near his house in the deme of Melite, but Plutarch comments that he overstepped the mark and affronted people's sensibilities by applying to her the title Aristoboule, "Best Counsellor," "on grounds that he had given the best counsel to the city and the Greeks" (*Themistocles* 22. 2). It is difficult to know whether to credit Plutarch's analysis of the cause of Themistocles' fall from favour, for his narrative here is full of anecdotes. Even if Themistocles did not actually say to the people, who, Plutarch says, were by now weary of his self-praise, "Why do you grow tired of being done good to repeatedly by the same people?" or really utter the witticism put into his mouth by Aelian, "I have no time for such men, who use the same vessel as a wine-jug and a chamber-pot," it is clear that his steady decline in

36. For details, see my article "The Political Significance of the Athenian 'Tyrannicide-' Cult," *Historia* 15 (1966), 129–41.

37. Pausanias 8. 50. 3; Aelian, *Varia Historia* 13. 43. Plutarch's version is the fullest and

Themistocles' response may be significant: "He acknowledged that he was now reaping in full the fruit due to him for his labours in behalf of Greece" (*Themistocles* 17. 4, H. A. Holden's translation).

popularity must have surprised and troubled him. He compared himself, in one anecdote, to a plane tree under whose broad branches the Athenians ran for shelter in a storm, but in fine weather they pulled off his limbs and abused him. In another tale which Plutarch tells, also in the heavily anecdotal chapter 18 of his *Themistocles*, he silenced the boasting of another general with the fable of the Two-Day Feast. The First Day, on which preparations were made and much trouble taken setting up booths and organizing the procession, was being abused by the Day After, which asserted that it provided the people with an opportunity for leisurely enjoyment without work; "True," said Day One, "but if I had not come first, you would not have come at all." Themistocles then drew the obvious moral: "If I had not come first," he said to his critic (Cimon? or Aristeides?), "where would you and your colleagues be now?"

So long as the Aegean policy of Cimon and Aristeides continued to bring success, Themistocles could do little to restore his plummeting favour. Cimon had clearly set out to erase the memory of Salamis, and this he very nearly succeeded in doing when, in response to a Delphic oracle to restore Theseus' bones, he used the forces of the league to besiege and capture the island of Skyros northeast of Euboea, which lay on the route to Thrace and the Hellespont. "Theseus' bones" were located there, dug up, and returned to Athens, where they were ceremoniously and richly enshrined, and as part of the celebration a new annual feast was instituted in Theseus' honour; Skyros itself was subjected to an influx of Athenian settlers. Now it was commonly believed by the people that Cimon's father, Miltiades, had been assisted by an apparition of Theseus at Marathon; the restoration of Theseus' remains thus seems to have been intended to mark the replacement of Salamis by Marathon as the victory par excellence against the Persians. Theseus in coming home was giving heroic blessing to Cimon's policy and showing disapproval of Themistocles'. The whole episode was a masterstroke in the propaganda duel being waged between the two men at this time in Athens.[38]

As a first move against him, Themistocles' enemies tried to muster the negative votes necessary to ostracize him. His defence was again a poetic one: in the spring of 472 Aeschylus presented his drama *The Persians*, with Pericles as choregus and the victory of Salamis at centre stage. In it Aeschylus attempted to call the Athenians to their senses, to remind them again, as Phrynichus had done four years earlier, of the debt they owed to the Saviour of Salamis. Although the tetralogy of which the play formed the first part won the prize, Themistocles, paradoxically, was ostracized nonetheless. He took up residence in Argos and began to make trips around the Peloponnese. What he was doing no ancient source reports, but it has been conjectured that he was engaged in stirring up opposition to Sparta in the smaller states of the Peloponnese, and it is unlikely to be a mere coincidence that there occurred political changes to a more democratic form of government in Elis and Mantineia at about this time.[39]

The Spartans could not long tolerate this threat to their own conservative dominance

38. The date is uncertain, but may be *c.* 474; for further details, see my article "Cimon, Skyros and 'Theseus' Bones,'" *JHS* 91 (1971), 141–43.

39. See A. Andrewes, *Phoenix* 6 (1952), 1–5; W. G. Forrest, *CQ*, n.s. 10 (1960), 229–32.

in the area, and so they began to look for a way to engineer a more complete overthrow of Themistocles than that provided by the relatively honourable penalty of
ostracism. Sparta's Athenian friends, chief among them Cimon, who also happened
to be Themistocles' enemies, agreed to cooperate, and an expedient against him was
soon found. The flamboyant figure of their own regent Pausanias could be sacrificed;
the story which the ephors gave out after his death was that certain of his private
papers had been discovered in which Themistocles was implicated in what the Spartans
alleged were Pausanias' dealings with the Persian king. This melancholy episode in
Themistocles' story is related by Thucydides.

> The Spartans sent ambassadors to Athens and accused Themistocles, too, of a
> share in the medism of Pausanias; they said they had found it out from their own
> investigations of Pausanias, and they asked the Athenians to punish him for it.
> The latter believed the Spartans (Themistocles happened to have been ostracized
> and now was living in Argos, although he was also visiting the rest of the Pelo-
> ponnese) and sent men along with them who were ready to join in the pursuit;
> their orders were to bring him back from wherever they happened to find him.
>
> Themistocles got advance word of it and fled from the Peloponnese to Corcyra,
> whose benefactor he was. When the Corcyraeans said that they were afraid that
> by sheltering him they might incur the enmity of the Spartans and Athenians,
> they conveyed him to the mainland opposite. As he was being pursued by the
> men assigned to the task, according to the information given them of his move-
> ments, he was forced because of a difficulty to break his journey and take refuge
> with Admetus, king of the Molossi, who was not friendly to him. The king was
> not there, but Themistocles became a suppliant of his wife and was instructed by
> her to hold their child and take up a position at the hearth. When, not much later,
> Admetus returned, Themistocles explained who he was and asked him, even if
> he himself had opposed some request the king had made of the Athenians, not
> to take vengeance on him now that he was in exile: for, in that case, he would be
> much weaker than the one who was treating him ill,[40] and it was the noble thing
> to revenge oneself on equals only on terms of equality. At the same time, he
> continued, he had opposed him only in some minor request, not in a life-and-
> death matter, whereas the king, if he should surrender him (he explained who was
> pursuing him and why) would be depriving him of the chance to save his life.
>
> When the king heard him, he told him to rise with his son (for he had taken
> up his position with the boy in his arms, and this was a powerful suppliant appeal)
> and soon afterwards, when the Spartans and Athenians came and delivered a
> long speech, Admetus did not surrender him but, as he wanted to be conveyed
> to the Persian king, had him transported overland to the other sea [that is, east-
> wards to the Thermaic Gulf], to Pydna in Alexander's kingdom. There he chanced
> upon a merchant-vessel which was setting off for Ionia. He went on board but
> was carried off course by a storm to the Athenian forces which were besieging

---

40. Reading, at Thucydides 1. 136. 4, *asthenesteros* or *asthenesteron*, for the better manuscripts'
asthenesterou.

Naxos. In terror he told the captain who he was (for he was unknown to those aboard the ship) and why he was trying to escape; if the man refused to save him, Themistocles said he would tell the Athenians that he had taken a bribe to transport him. Their only chance of safety was for no one to debark until the voyage was resumed; if the captain agreed, he would remember him with a worthy reward.

The captain did what he was told and, after riding out the swell for a day and a night near the Athenian camp, later came to Ephesus. Themistocles took care of the man with a grant of money (for money which he had deposited was sent to him later from his friends in Athens and from Argos), and, after he had journeyed inland with one of the Persians from the coast, he sent a letter to King Artaxerxes, son of Xerxes, who had recently ascended the throne. (Thucydides 1. 135–37. 3)

Can anything be added to Thucydides' sparse narrative? The account of Themistocles' condemnation is given in much greater detail by Diodorus, in whose version we hear of an early trial *and acquittal*, but this may be based on nothing more than a confusion with the proceedings for ostracism. Diodorus' mention of an early approach by Pausanias made to Themistocles but rejected by him is repeated by Plutarch, who further remarks that at his trial Themistocles had to "defend himself in writing, making use of earlier accusations against himself" (*Themistocles* 23. 3–4). This reference to earlier accusations may also point to an earlier trial, or, again, may represent nothing but Plutarch's attempt to harmonize the versions of Thucydides and Ephorus, Diodorus' source. In the same chapter, however, Plutarch adds the valuable piece of information that the charge of treason was brought by Leobotes, son of Alcmeon, of Agryle (whose full identification suggests that Plutarch may have been using an official source). At *Aristeides* 25. 10 Plutarch remarks that "Alcmeon [perhaps the same individual as Leobotes, son of Alcmeon; an Alcmeonides is known from the 'Themistocles Epistles' and ostraka] and Cimon attacked and brought accusations" against Themistocles, and the author of the Epistles adds several other names, but it is uncertain what evidence he may have had for them.[41] Aristeides' position in the attacks is unclear; Plutarch, in the passage just cited, maintains that when others were attacking Themistocles, Aristeides "alone did not do or say anything base, nor took advantage of an enemy in distress," but this is contradicted by Lucian, who, in his essay *On Slander* (27), comments that for all his probity even Aristeides "sided against Themistocles and joined in whetting the people's anger against him." Curiously, both

41. For a discussion of the possible connections among Themistocles' accusers, see Bicknell, "Leobotes Alkmeonos and Alkmeon Aristonymou," in *Studies in Athenian Politics and Genealogy*, 54 ff. W. R. Connor has recently defended the testimony of the Byzantine writer Theodorus Metochites that Themistocles' clansman Lykomedes was among his accusers ("Lycomedes against Themistocles? A Note on Intra-genos Rivalry," *Historia* 21 [1972], 569–74). I find it difficult to believe that such a sensational piece of information lay hidden from the view of all historians to be unearthed only by a Byzantine essayist *c.* A.D. 1300. It seems easier to suppose that Theodorus was "confused and misreported what he read" (a possibility Connor entertains, but rejects, on p. 571 of his article); the name in Theodorus' source might, for example, have been Lykon, who is mentioned in one of the as yet unpublished Cerameicus ostraka, and who may be the historical individual posing as the "Lykos" who is said to have ostracized Theseus (schol. Aristophanes, *Plutus* 627; I hope to develop this suggestion elsewhere).

traditions are represented in the Epistles, numbers 3 and 18 portraying Aristeides as Themistocles' friend, and 8 placing him among his enemies.

How Themistocles got word of his condemnation while in Argos is unknown. Thucydides says merely "learning in advance [*proaisthomenos*] he escaped"; a secret message from friends in Athens is an easy conjecture. In this connection it is unclear what, if anything, is to be made of the detail in Epistle 1 that Themistocles' friendly reception at Argos was due to the fact that his father, Neokles, had lived there for a long time. In any case, the friendly feelings of the Argives towards him (and Nepos remarks that he lived at Argos *magna cum dignitate* [*Themistocles* 8. 2]) would obviously have been strained by his change of circumstances. The Argives could hardly have refused to surrender him in the face of a combined Atheno-Spartan demand such as was soon to be made on Admetus, and so, perceiving his position to be untenable, Themistocles left.

The first stop on his escape route, Corcyra, is geographically a most unlikely place for a fugitive who was to end in Asia. Plutarch (*Themistocles* 24. 4) quotes from Stesimbrotus the story, which even Plutarch realized was ridiculous, that Themistocles fled to Sicily and demanded in marriage the daughter of the tyrant Hieron of Syracuse. Although Themistocles seems to have had the West very much on his mind at least since Salamis, the detail about Hieron's daughter is merely the usual romantic complication, and an implausible one at that. Themistocles never reached Sicily, although it has been suggested that he was heading for Sicily as his first choice of refuge, but that when he arrived at Corcyra off the west coast of Greece, he changed his plans, perhaps because news reached him there of Hieron's recent death.[42] Thucydides mentions simply that Themistocles had performed some good service for Corcyra, and an ancient note on the passage remarks that he had prevented the allied Greek forces from punishing her for her neutrality in the war with Persia, while Plutarch (*Themistocles* 24. 1) offers the explanation that he had once arbitrated a dispute between Corcyra and Corinth in favour of the former. Of the two suggestions Plutarch's sounds the more convincing, but both may be mere guesswork.

The next act in the drama of pursuit takes place in Epirus, in Admetus' kingdom of the Molossi. This part of Thucydides' narrative has been accused of being theatrical in the worst sense, and its similarity with the plot of Euripides' *Telephus*, so far as the latter can be reconstructed, is indeed too close to be ignored. But parallels, which are in any case imperfect (Themistocles did not threaten the child with death, as Telephus had done to the infant Orestes), are hardly sufficient grounds for condemning Thucydides' account. It is possible that Euripides, and perhaps Aeschylus before him, based their dramatic versions on an historical incident in the life of Themistocles.[43]

42. Gomme, *Commentary*, I, 400, n.1; but although Corcyra was a likely stopover in a coasting voyage to Sicily (Thucydides 1. 36. 2 and 44. 3), if Themistocles were fleeing for his life would he not have made directly for Sicily across open sea? M. E. White has noted that "the route up the west coast was no doubt the safest " since the Athenian navy controlled the Aegean (*JHS* 84 [1964], 147, n.29).

43. Gomme, *Commentary*, I, 439, cites N. Wecklein, *SB könig. Bayer. Akad.*, 18–19; cf. Louis Séchan, *Études sur la tragédie grecque* (rpt. 1967), 124, with the vase illustrated on p. 126. Themistocles' visit to the court of Admetus is discussed (and apparently treated as historical) by N. G. L. Hammond, *Epirus* (Oxford: Clarendon Press, 1967), 492–93.

There remain several obscurities in Thucydides' narrative. He mentions a prior request by Admetus to the Athenians, which Themistocles had opposed, but we hear nothing elsewhere of what this may have been. How long Themistocles stayed with Admetus is likewise unknown. A good deal of embroidery is added to Thucydides' account by later writers. Although Thucydides says specifically that Admetus was "not in the land" when Themistocles arrived, Diodorus has the king "welcome him in friendly fashion" and "tell him to take heart" (11. 56). Thucydides has the joint embassy of Athenians and Spartans come to Admetus and "say much," only to be met with a refusal to surrender Themistocles; in Diodorus the embassy calls Themistocles the "betrayer and defiler of all Greece," and threatens to "make war on the king with all the Greeks" if he refuses to surrender the fugitive. The king, thoroughly affrighted, pays Themistocles' travel expenses and provides two Lyncestian youths as an escort. Plutarch names the queen Phthia, Nepos turns the prince into a daughter, the "Themistocles Epistles" call the queen Cratesipolis and the lad Arybbas (which was an hereditary Epirote name). At *Themistocles* 24. 6 Plutarch cites Stesimbrotus for the plausible detail that Themistocles' wife and children joined him before he left the Molossians. The additional item, for which Stesimbrotus is also cited, that it was a certain Epikrates of Acharnae who arranged to get Themistocles' wife and children out of Athens, and that he was later prosecuted for it by Cimon and condemned to death, may be based on the decree of condemnation.

Thucydides' account of the journey from Pydna to Ephesus, with the close escape from the Athenian fleet involved in the siege of Naxos, is preferable to the alternate version preserved by Plutarch (*Themistocles* 25. 2, 26. 1) that Themistocles' encounter was with the Athenian fleet besieging Thasos and that the ship made the Asian coast at Cyme, although it remains possible that both versions are ultimately nothing but ancient conjectures.[44]

The last part of the story, Themistocles in Asia, encouraged writers, including the usually level-headed Thucydides, to discard historical reporting for romantic fantasy. Plutarch (*Themistocles* 25. 3) quotes Theopompus to the effect that the money discovered and confiscated after Themistocles' condemnation amounted to 100 talents, while Theophrastus makes the figure 80. The man who conveyed him into the interior was, according to Thucydides, "a certain Persian living along the coast"; Diodorus and Plutarch made him a Greek, named Lysitheides (Diodorus) or Nikogenes (Plutarch), and both tell a fantastic story of how Themistocles travelled incognito, hidden in a covered wagon like some Oriental courtesan. The most that can safely be said is that Themistocles travelled inland from the coast by a method unknown, and that when he reached Sardis and learnt that Xerxes had recently been succeeded by his son Artaxerxes (an event which can be dated from eastern sources to late in 465), he decided to risk an approach. Thucydides says that the first contact was by a letter in which Themistocles mentioned both the message before Salamis and a second one "regarding the bridges"; there were also broad hints of a greater service he might render to the new king, which is made out by later writers to have been a promise to

44. See P. J. Rhodes, "Thucydides on Pausanias and Themistocles," *Historia* 19 (1970), 394. For the possible chronological implications of the two versions, see Appendix A.

lead another invading force against Greece. After this first contact Themistocles spent a year preparing for the meeting, and when he thought he had become sufficiently fluent in the vernacular to deal without interpreters, he finally approached Artaxerxes at Susa in person.

"When he arrived after the year was up," Thucydides reports (1. 138. 1), "he was held in great esteem at court, more so, in fact, than any other Greek had ever achieved [the Peripatetic Phanias later reported that a Cretan named Entimos went to Arta- xerxes 'in emulation of Themistocles' and was treated royally by the king (fragment 27 Wehrli)], because of his former reputation and the hope he kept holding out of enslaving the Greek world to the king, but mostly because of the manifest proofs he gave of his intelligence." Artaxerxes' response was generous: he turned over to Themistocles the revenues of at least three cities, in the largest of which, Magnesia, Themistocles decided to settle. There he took an interest in the civic cults and did much to foster devotion to his patroness Artemis, under her title Leukophryene, "Goddess of the Gleaming Brow." He also established a female relative, his daughter or wife, as priestess in a temple which he constructed to honour the Great Mother under her surname Dindymene. An historian of Magnesia named Possis reports that Themistocles held an annual magistracy there, and introduced two typically Athenian festivals, the Panathenaea and Festival of Pitchers in honour of Dionysus.[45] Although the detail of Themistocles' holding the office of *Stephanephoros* is probably an anachron- ism, it seems likely enough that he held some public office in Magnesia, perhaps that of *prytanis*. His transference of the typically Athenian festivals of Panathenaea and Choës should likewise not be doubted; it bespeaks a continuing loyalty, or at least a sentimental attachment, to the city which had dealt with him so ungratefully.

As dynast in Magnesia, which Thucydides says brought him fifty talents a year, Themistocles issued his personal coinage, a usual practice for Persian satraps with troops under their commands. Two recently discovered examples of coins of small denomination bearing his initials may plausibly be seen as money issued by him to pay troops in his private employ. It is not so clear what control Themistocles exercised over the other two cities Thucydides mentions: "Lampsacus for wine and Myus for salt." It is generally assumed that Myus, near Miletus on the Ionian coast, and Lampsacus, on the Hellespont, had already been recaptured from Persia by the Greeks; if that were so, they could hardly have formed part of a real benefice from the king. It has therefore been suggested that they were but "empty show" (A. W. Gomme's phrase), or that the king was in fact encouraging Themistocles to seize these cities from the Greeks and bring them again into the Persian empire. The correct solution to the problem remains to be found, but it should be pointed out that it is unknown exactly when Myus and Lampsacus joined Athens' league; furthermore, a parallel may exist in other cities bestowed by Xerxes upon the Spartan Demaratus and Gongylus the Eretrian, cities which were held by their descendants as late as 399 B.C. but which were also members of the Delian League.[46]

45. *FGrHist* 480 F 1; from Athenaeus 12. 533 D–E.

46. Russell Meiggs remarks that it would be "surprising, but not impossible" if Lampsacus had remained outside the league as late as the 460s (*The Athenian Empire*, 54).

The circumstances, and even the exact year, of Themistocles' death are uncertain. Although Thucydides reports the contrary view that "his death was self-inflicted, by poison, when he thought himself incapable of fulfilling his promises to the king" (1. 138. 4), the historian insists that his death was due to an illness. The more melodramatic version that he committed suicide by drinking the blood of a bull which he was in the act of sacrificing was prevalent at least from 424 B.C., when Aristophanes alludes to it in *Knights* (lines 83–84) and Plutarch works it into a full-scale drama (*Themistocles* 31), following, one suspects, some late novelistic account like that of Phanias or Phylarchus. In this version, in which there occurs the potentially valuable synchronism with the revolt of Egypt from Persia *c.* 460, Artaxerxes kept insisting that Themistocles "make good his promises" (Thucydides at 1. 138. 2 also alludes to "the hope which he held out of enslaving Greece"), and Themistocles, unable or at least unwilling to oblige the king, chooses the nobler way out. Plutarch offers several reasons for Themistocles' scruple: despair of being able to compete with Cimon's successes (a motive which is repeated at *Cimon* 18. 6–7), or "out of respect for the reputation of his deeds and the trophies he had won" (*Themistocles* 31. 5), but both suggested reasons are suspicious. The detail of rivalry with Cimon was a conventional one, and is in any case inapplicable to Themistocles' last years, for by now Cimon's brilliant victories at the Eurymedon River and elsewhere had given way to the long, expensive, and unpopular siege of Thasos (465–463) and the fiasco of having the Spartans rebuff the Athenian relief force which he had struggled to secure at the time of the earthquake. The conservatives at Athens had found themselves displaced by politicians of a more liberal cut, and Cimon himself was ostracized *c.* 461. As for the twinge of patriotic feeling which Themistocles in Plutarch feels at the last, this too smacks of romance: the archtraitor and enemy of his country undergoing an eleventh-hour conversion! "By his death he left the fairest defence," remarks Diodorus piously, "that he had managed fairly the political interests of Greece" (11. 58. 3); an end too literally good to be true. The whole thing reads more like Restoration drama— Themistocles' story did, in fact, find its way onto the English stage in the early eighteenth century—than sober history, and we should probably accept Thucydides' verdict that his death was a natural one.

There was also great uncertainty about where his body was buried. Thucydides refers to a "memorial" to him in the marketplace of Magnesia, which is also mentioned by several later writers, but this may have been merely a cenotaph, for Thucydides records a rumour that "his relatives brought his bones back home following his instructions, and that he was buried secretly in Attica" (1. 138. 6). It is this version which may underlie an anonymous account quoted in an ancient note on Aristophanes' *Knights* 84: "When the Athenians were suffering from a plague, the God [that is, Apollo] told them to bring back Themistocles' bones. The Magnesians did not agree, so they asked to be able to sacrifice at the grave after 30 days, pitched their tents all about the place, dug up the bones secretly, and brought them home." What appears to be yet a different story is ascribed by Plutarch to the orator Andocides, who is quoted as having said that "the Athenians secretly stole his remains [from Magnesia? from his grave in Attica?] and dispersed them" (*Themistocles* 32. 4).

Whatever the truth of the matter, it is certain that there existed in Athens at a later date a structure, apparently referred to as the "Themistokleion," which was thought to be either his tomb or his cenotaph.[47]

What impressed Thucydides most about Themistocles was his inventiveness, his ability to extemporize a solution to a problem on the spot, without great amounts of advance preparation. What perhaps impresses a modern even more is his skilful manipulation of the means at his disposal at any given time to achieve both his country's advantage and his own glory. From an unpromising beginning as an outsider and newcomer into a situation where birth and breeding, marriage and money, meant everything, and where individual worth counted for little, he borrowed his rivals' weapons and used devices, such as ostracism, in ways that their authors could not have foreseen; he was thus able to get rid of his opponents and secure his countrymen's confidence during that crucial decade which was climaxed by the most serious threat that Athens had yet to face, and it was thanks almost single-handedly to his military genius and strategic cunning that she had been able to repel that threat.

Themistocles' foresight may also have extended to the directions which Athenian politics were to take in the succeeding years. He rode the tide of a growing demand for broader participation in public affairs and, in creating Athens' navy, forged a weapon which gave his countrymen virtual impregnability against their enemies for almost the rest of the century. But with the fickleness which also characterized the Athenian populace at other periods in its history, his fellow Athenians forgot what he had done to make them great and—worse—failed to see through the machinations of his enemies who took over from him the dream of empire and wielded against him some of his own political weapons. He was forced into increasingly offensive self-glorification and was finally ostracized and condemned on the ludicrously implausible charge of treason.

What his enemies could not see was that the trend of events was on his side; their own day, based as it was on an archaic standard of aristocratic conservatism, was bound to be brief. The full blossoming of Athenian democracy, when it came, was possible only because Themistocles had planted the seeds.

47. Possible identifications of this structure are discussed in chapter 10.

II

THE LITERARY AND
ARCHAEOLOGICAL EVIDENCE

1 THE EARLIEST LITERARY EVIDENCE

IT MAY BE SOMEWHAT surprising that the earliest surviving written evidence for Themistocles' life and career is found in three poets who were his contemporaries: Aeschylus, Simonides, and Timocreon of Rhodes. Born in 525/4, probably just a few years before Themistocles himself,[1] the tragic poet Aeschylus began to exhibit plays in the dramatic competitions at the Great Dionysia at Athens about 500 B.C. but did not win his first victory until 484. Ancient testimony connects his name with the battles of the Persian Wars: Marathon, Salamis, and (though this may be inference or mere guesswork) Artemisium and Plataea.[2] The first play of his that is still extant, *The Persians*, was produced in 472 B.C. and deals extensively with the battle of Salamis, its antecedents, and the actual encounter in the straits between the Persians and Greeks. I have argued elsewhere[3] that Aeschylus was moved to write his play, probably modelled to some degree on Phrynichus' *Phoenician Women* of 476 B.C., for which Themistocles himself served as choregus,[4] by the precarious political position in which the hero of Salamis found himself in the late 470s; part of Aeschylus' motive was to remind his fellow Athenians of the debt which they, and all Greece, owed to Themi-

1. The Parian Marble (*FGrHist* 239) Ep. 48 makes Aeschylus thirty-five in the year of Marathon (490 B.C.). For Themistocles' birth date, see Appendix A.

2. The evidence is discussed in my study *The Political Background of Aeschylean Tragedy*, 4–5, with notes.

3. *Political Background*, chap. 2, and, more recently, the Introduction to my translation of *The Persians*, 10–11, from which the translations of *The Persians* in this chapter are drawn.

4. This is the almost inescapable inference, made first by Bentley (*Dissertations upon the Epistles of Phalaris*, Bohn Library ed. [London, 1883], 281), from Plutarch, *Them.* 5. 5, where a commemorative inscription is cited for a

victory of Phrynichus, with Themistocles as choregus, in the archonship of Adeimantus (477/6). The Hypothesis to *The Persians*, citing the shadowy Glaucus of Rhegium, makes it clear that Aeschylus drew heavily on Phrynichus for content as well as for the opening line; in other words that Salamis was the reported defeat to which the chorus of Sidonian women violently reacted (A. Nauck, *TGF²*, p. 723, fr. 11; the remaining fragments tell us next to nothing). Against the implausibilities of F. Marx (*Rh. Mus.*, n.s. 77 [1928], 357 ff.) and F. Stoessl (*Mus. Helv.* 2 [1945], 158–59), who refer the battle to Mycale, see M. Pohlenz, *Griech. Trag.²*, Erläut., p. 24, and G. Nenci. *Parola del Passato* 5 (1950), 216, n.1.

stocles. Even if this view of the play's motivation not be accepted, it is undeniable that at a central position of prominence within the play stands the victory of Salamis. From the moment when the messenger begins his account to the Persian queen and elders with the words

> The one that started the whole disaster, lady, was
> Some Curse or Evil Spirit which appeared from somewhere.
> For a man, a Greek, arrived from the Athenian camp
> And spoke to your son Xerxes words to this effect...
>
> (Pers. 353 ff.)

the audience's attention must inevitably have been concentrated on Themistocles and his hand in the victory. The account which the messenger proceeds to give of the information which "a Greek" brings to Xerxes,

> That once the darkness and the black of night should come,
> The Greeks would not remain, but to their rowers' seats
> Would leap in disarray, each man for himself,
> And run away in secret flight to save their lives.
>
> (Pers. 357–60)

is substantially the same as Herodotus' version, with a single, but crucial, difference. Herodotus makes it quite clear that Themistocles sent one of his slaves, a certain Sicinnus, with the message by which the Persians were lured into the trap (8. 75). This individual is conveniently omitted in the Aeschylean account, with the effect of throwing additional emphasis on Themistocles as not only the author but even, for dramatic purposes, the deliverer of the message.

Aeschylus' whole account of the effects of the message on Xerxes' forces and the events which took place at daybreak must be given their due weight in any reconstruction of the battle, for he is an eyewitness and is writing for an audience many of whom would themselves have taken part in the fighting. He is writing drama, true, but it seems unlikely that he could have radically falsified the history of those events. In fact, more than mere lip service must be paid to Aeschylus' lines as being among the primary evidence for this incident in the Persian Wars.[5] When, for example, Aeschylus has the messenger say

> [The Greeks'] right wing first, in order just as they had been
> Arranged, led off, and next the whole remaining force
> Came out to the attack, and with the sight we heard
> A loud voice of command: "O sons of Greeks, go on,
> Bring freedom to your fatherland, bring freedom to
> Your children, wives, and seats of your ancestral gods,
> And your forbears' graves; now the struggle is for all."
>
> (Pers. 399–405)

he is writing as one who was there and *knows*; the words of the battle cry may be altered slightly or in part misremembered, but the gist must be genuine.

A more controversial case has been made for Aeschylus' *Suppliants*, presented

---

5. I have argued this point at greater length, and compared the accounts of Aeschylus and Herodotus, in Appendix A of *Political Background*, pp. 131–41.

sometime in the 460s, as portraying a mythico-dramatic paradigm for Themistocles' own position as a refugee at Argos some years before the date of production. Whether or not this theory be accepted,[6] the honorific position given to the victory of Salamis and Themistocles' contribution to it in *The Persians* is enough to justify the view that Aeschylus was taking sides *for* Themistocles in March 472 B.C. when many of his fellow Athenians had forgotten their debt to him and were seriously considering (or perhaps had already voted for) his ostracism.[7]

The direct evidence for personal friendship between Themistocles and the poet Simonides is, though not abundant, clear enough. Plutarch records a slightly acerb exchange between the two men. Simonides had requested Themistocles to use his office (probably the archonship) for some less than honest purpose, but Themistocles cut him off with the comment that he, Simonides, would not be a good poet if he sang out of tune nor he, Themistocles, a good magistrate if he ruled out of tune, in which a pun on the word *nomos*, "law" or "tune" (and so synonymous with *melos*), is involved.[8] The context in which Plutarch tells the anecdote in the *Themistocles* (5. 6) is curious: "He was a man of the people," Plutarch has just remarked, "and in fact knew the names of each of the citizens by heart," that is, he had a good memory for faces.[9] Now another dialogue between Simonides and Themistocles is recorded by Cicero, based on Simonides' reputation in antiquity as the inventor of a system of memory strengthening, or mnemonics;[10] what he needed, Themistocles told the poet, was not a system for remembering, but a system for forgetting (*de Fin.* 2. 32. 104). The transition of thought in Plutarch *Themistocles* 5. 6, from Themistocles' superior memory to the exchange with Simonides, clearly has the same basis. Plutarch continues with another anecdote. On a different occasion Themistocles jocularly (*episkopton*) told Simonides that it was foolish of him to abuse the Corinthians, who inhabited a great city, while he himself had portrait statues made, even though he was so ugly. Underlying this story is a reference by Simonides, in what poem we cannot tell, to the fact that "Troy had no fault to find with the Corinthians for fighting against her, since her great Lycian ally, Glaucus, was of ancient Corinthian lineage."[11]

Whether or not these anecdotes have any historical truth to them matters little. The impression they give is of an easy familiarity between the statesman and the poet, an impression which is confirmed by Plutarch's mention elsewhere in the *Themistocles* of two of Simonides' works which specifically involved Themistocles. At the end of chapter 15 of the *Life*, Plutarch, after describing the first successful encounter of a Greek with a Persian ship at Salamis, continues:

6. See W. G. Forrest, "Themistokles and Argos," *CQ*, n.s. 10 (1960), 221–41; Podlecki, *Political Background*, chap. 4, pp. 42 ff.; Christina Gülke, *Mythos und Zeitgeschichte bei Aischylos*, 58 ff.

7. On the possible connection between the date of *The Persians* and the date of Themistocles' ostracism, see Appendix A.

8. *Them.* 5. 6. The story is told by Plutarch also at *Mor.* 185 D, 534 E, and 807 C (the context of 807 B–C, as well as Themistocles' reply, suggests he was then archon; στρατηγοῦντος at *Them.* 5. 6 seems to be a mere slip).

9. Before Plutarch, the point had already been made by Cicero (*de Sen.* 7. 21) and Valerius Maximus (8. 7, ext. 15).

10. See H. Blum, *Die Antike Mnemotechnik*, 41–46 (p. 46 for Simonides and Themistocles).

11. B. Perrin (*Plutarch's 'Themistocles' and 'Aristeides,'* 190), explaining Simonides fr. 572 Page (cited, or paraphrased, by Aristotle, *Rhet.* I. 6, 1363 a; Plutarch, *Dionys.* 1. 2; schol. Pindar, *Ol.* 13. 78b, I. 374 Drachm.). See T. Bergk, *PLG*, III, 412, and H. A. Holden, *Plutarch's 'Life of Themistocles'*[3], 82–83.

Then the rest, put on an equality in numbers with their foes, because the barbarians had to attack them by detachments in the narrow strait and so ran foul
of one another, routed them, though they resisted till the evening drew on, and
thus "bore away," as Simonides says, "that fair and notorious victory, than
which no more brilliant exploit was ever performed upon the sea, either by
Hellenes or Barbarians, through the manly valour and common ardour of all
who fought their ships, but through the clever judgment of Themistocles." (*Them.*
15. 4, trans. B. Perrin)

The passage is a paraphrase of what must have been the central section of the elegiac
poem by Simonides, *The Sea-fight at Salamis* (fr. 536 Page), which seems to have been
known under the alternate title *Xerxes' Sea-fight.* Our chief source of information
about it is this citation by Plutarch, who testifies to the prominence in it of Themistocles and his *deinotes*—the word suggests, perhaps, that Simonides recounted
the ruse of Themistocles' false message to Xerxes in another part of the poem. At the
beginning of the *Life*, Plutarch records that after the war Themistocles paid for the
restoration and redecoration with murals of the initiation place of the Lykomid clan
at Phlya northeast of Athens, "as Simonides has related" (*Them.* 1. 4 = fr. 627 Page).
This may have been in a separate dedicatory epigram which Plutarch could have seen
inside the building or (less plausibly), as Perrin suggested, "perhaps in the great
Salamis-hymn."[12] Wherever it occurred, it is additional evidence of the strongest kind
for a personal link between Themistocles and Simonides.

There was a poem from Simonides' pen, too, *The Sea-fight off Artemisium*, about
which slightly more is known. Boreas was called upon, perhaps in his capacity as
"kin by marriage" to the Athenian people; the story of his rape of Erechtheus' daughter
Oreithyia was probably narrated at some length (see fr. 534 Page). On the basis of two
passages by Himerius, an orator of the fourth century A.D., it has been conjectured
that the chorus which sang the poem referred at some point to a "gentle breeze
spreading over the waves" and a "prow cleaving the purple waves."[13] Now, among
the antecedents of the battles off Cape Artemisium in northern Euboea, Herodotus
mentions oracles, one to the Delphians to "pray to the winds" (7. 178), another to
the Athenians to "call upon their son-in-law," whom the Athenians identified as
"Boreas" (7. 189). A large part of the Persian fleet was destroyed by a sudden storm
at sea (7. 188; there is a further—or perhaps alternate version of the same—storm at
8. 13), and Herodotus reports that "when the Athenians returned home [presumably
from Artemisium], they constructed a shrine to Boreas along the banks of the Ilissus
river" (7. 189. 3). It was suggested long ago by Wilamowitz that Simonides' poem
was the "official" hymn sung at the dedication ceremonies,[14] and if that is correct (as
seems likely), we may have here another example of a poem "commissioned" by

12. *Plutarch's 'Themistocles,'* 176.
13. Himerius, Or. 12. 32 and 47. 14 (Colonna).
14. *Sappho und Simonides*, 206–8. It may be
significant that representations of the Boreas-
Oreithyia story become more frequent on Attic
vases after 480; see W. J. Agard, "Boreas at
Athens," *CJ* 61 (1966), 241–46, and Erika
Simon, "Boreas und Oreithyia auf dem sil-

bernen Rhyton in Triest," *Antike und Abendland*
13 (1967), 101–26, esp. 107 ff. (At p. 118 she
makes the interesting suggestion that Aeschylus'
Oreithyia was "weder ein Satyrspiel noch eine
reine Tragödie..., sondern...ein Festspiel
[like *Women of Aetna*] aufgeführt zur Gründung
des Boreaskults am Ilissos.")

Themistocles to celebrate one of the victories of 480 in which he had a guiding hand. In the temple of "Dawn-facing" Artemis at Artemisium, the Athenians set up a four-line dedication in thanksgiving, which Plutarch records (*Them.* 8. 5, *de mal. Her.* 867 F) and which, though not ascribed to Simonides by any ancient author, has been assigned to him in modern times.[15] Whether or not this guess should prove to be correct, there is more than enough evidence to support C. M. Bowra's contention that "the connexion between [Simonides] and Themistocles must be an historical fact.... His poetical activities in [480] and succeeding years are best explained by a personal attachment to the statesman."[16]

A relationship of a far different sort existed between Themistocles and another contemporary poet, Timocreon of Rhodes. This individual would have been nothing but a name were it not for a running feud he seems to have carried on with Themistocles, a feud which Plutarch mentions, recording in passing fairly extensive passages of Timocreon's poetry. From what Bowra aptly calls "a curious little hymn of hate" comes the following:

> But if you, sir, praise Pausanias, and you, sir, Xanthippus,
> and you, sir, Leotychidas, I praise Aristides,
> who was the best man to come from holy Athens, when
> Lato formed a hatred for Themistocles,
>
> liar, unjust, traitor, who in obedience to
> ill-gotten bribes did not bring his guest-friend Timocreon
> to his land of Ialysus, but took three talents
> of silver and went sailing to the devil,
>
> bringing some unjustly home, persecuting others, killing others,
> and, gorged with silver, kept ridiculous hospitality at the Isthmus,
> providing cold meats. They ate, praying
> that no attention be paid to Themistocles.[17]

The poem presents difficulties of interpretation which cannot be totally resolved in the present state of the evidence. Taking a very old lyric formula, whereby a poet lists several items, or, in this case, persons, who might find favour with others, rejects them, and substitutes his own preference,[18] Timocreon turns it into a political diatribe against Themistocles, who, he says, was bribed "not to bring his guest-friend home" to Rhodes. There is a clear implication that Themistocles had thus violated an agreement between the two men, but the occasion on which this breach of trust might have occurred is obscure. It has been maintained that a possible context would be the events immediately following the Greek victory at Salamis when, according to Herodotus, Themistocles sailed with the Athenian fleet to Andros, Carystus (on the south coast of Euboea), and Paros to extort money from them.[19] "He sent threatening

15. By Schneidewin; see Diehl at Simonides fr. 109.

16. *GLP²*, 342. I have examined the evidence for connections between the two men, and Simonides' Themistoclean poems, in *Historia* 17 (1968), 257–74, and *Historia* 18 (1969), 251. At *Historia* 15 (1966), 129 ff., I suggest that they collaborated in 477/6 to resuscitate the claims of Harmodius and Aristogeiton against the Alcmeonids.

17. Plut. *Them.* 21. 4 = fr. 727 Page. The translation and line division are Bowra's (*GLP²*, 351).

18. Tyrtaeus 9 (Diehl), Sappho 16 (Lobel-Page), Pindar, *Ol.* 1, imitated by Horace, *Odes* I. 1 and 7.

19. Hdt. 8. 111–12; Plut. *Them.* 21. 1.

messages to the other islands to demand money," Herodotus remarks; "if others of the islanders also gave him money, I cannot say—my impression is that they did" (8. 112. 2). According to Wilamowitz, "Themistocles had encouraged Timocreon to think that the fleet would sail to Rhodes, and Timocreon was furious when it came back from Paros to the Isthmus."[20] The difficulty with this theory, as C. Fornara has pointed out, is that the Herodotus passage does not support an inference to activity by the Greek fleet (or even by Themistocles' spokesmen, one of whom, if Herodotus is to be taken literally, was Sicinnus) farther east than Paros;[21] rather the reverse, for Herodotus says that "the Greeks, after an unsuccessful siege of Andros, betook themselves to Carystus and ravaged their land, and then returned to Salamis" (8. 121. 1), and it will hardly do to maintain "that on his further voyages Themistokles took only a small detachment."[22] It seems improbable that Themistocles, with however small a Greek contingent, would have been able to sail freely to the eastern Mediterranean and the vicinity of Rhodes before the Greek victory over the Persians at Mycale in the following autumn, and Timocreon's mention of Pausanias, Leotychidas, and Xanthippus as *possible* preferences suggests that the victories of 479 have already taken place.[23] It would be possible, then, to see Timocreon's allusion to events on Rhodes as referring to a subsidiary generalship held by Themistocles in 479/8;[24] the difficulty with this interpretation is that there is no evidence for Themistocles' having held a generalship after Salamis.

Although some of the events to which Timocreon's poem refers may have taken place as early as 480, the objections to such an early date for composition of the poem as a whole seem insuperable. Bowra proposed dating it later in the 470s on grounds of what he believes to be the specific implication of line 4, "Lato formed a hatred for Themistocles." Since Delos was the sacred island where Lato (or, to give her non-Doric form, Leto) had borne Apollo and Artemis, Bowra argues that "the mention of Lato would suggest Delos to anyone in Timocreon's company. So, when he ranks her first in the downfall of Themistocles, we may infer that the poem was inspired by events in Delos." Bowra attempts to pin down the date more precisely: "The prominence which Timocreon gives to Aristides means that Aristides has replaced Themistocles in power and popularity, and the date of this may be placed at the foundation of the Delian League in 478–477."[25] It is an ingenious argument, and almost persuasive; but how can we be sure that by 478/7 Aristeides had already replaced Themistocles in power and popularity? If lines 3–4 seem to point incontrovertibly to Aristeides' organization of the Delian League and "just" assessment of tribute in 478/7, all we are entitled to conclude is that the poem was written *after* that date; in

20. *Aristoteles und Athen*, I, 138, quoted by Bowra, *GLP*[2], 352.

21. "Some Aspects of the Career of Pausanias of Sparta," *Historia* 15 (1966), 259.

22. B. D. Meritt, H. T. Wade-Gery, and M. F. McGregor, *The Athenian Tribute Lists*, III, 185, n.10, rightly rejected by Fornara, *Historia* 15 (1966), 259, n.10.

23. So Fornara, *Historia* 15 (1966), 257, n.2.

24. See Russell Meiggs, *Athenian Empire*, endnote 2, "Timocreon on Themistocles," pp.

414–15. Meiggs suggests that "while Pausanias sailed to Byzantium in 478, Themistocles was sent to consolidate the Greek cause in Rhodes and other islands" (415).

25. This and the preceding quotation are from *GLP*[2], 354. A date "at the earliest in summer 477, probably first in one of the following years," had already been maintained on other grounds by K. J. Beloch, *Griech. Gesch.*[2], II. 2, 145 n.

other words, Bowra's shrewd observations give us a new, and somewhat lower, *terminus post quem.* (The same would apply to the reference in lines 10–11, Themistocles' "ridiculous hospitality at the Isthmus / providing cold meats," which has been taken—in my opinion, rightly—to refer to Themistocles' failure to obtain first prize for valour at the Assembly at the Isthmus in the autumn of 480, which Herodotus mentions at 8. 123.)[26] The prominent position assumed by Pausanias has also been taken as a hint of when the poem might have been composed. Some scholars have placed it earlier rather than later in the 470s on grounds that Pausanias would not have been held up as an object of praise after the Athenians expelled him from Byzantium (*c.* 477 and in any case no later than 471). But this is to misunderstand the point of introducing him as a war hero. Timocreon is saying in effect, "Some think Plataea is the most significant victory against the Persians, others Mycale, while yet others are misguided enough to laud Themistocles' performance at Salamis; let me tell you what Themistocles was really like...."

Whatever the truth to Timocreon's charges and whenever the events to which they refer took place, insufficient attention has been paid to his phrasing in another line which may help to specify more precisely the date at which the poem was written. In line 5 he accuses Themistocles of being a "liar, unjust, traitor," and the word he uses for the last charge, *prodotan,* has overtones which have escaped most commentators. Timocreon may mean nothing more than "traitor [to his promises to me]," but we know that a technical charge of *prodosia,* "high treason," was brought against Themistocles while he was already in exile in Argos after his ostracism in the late 470s.[27] Timocreon's use of the term would have much more point if Themistocles were already under indictment, or even had already been condemned, for treason at Athens. In that case, the lines may have been written by Timocreon at a time nearer to that at which he composed another poem against Themistocles (also quoted by Plutarch), which alludes to Themistocles' presence in Persia:

> Muse, spread the fame of this song
> among the Hellenes,
> as is fit and right
> . . . .
> Not only Timocreon, it seems,
> swears oaths with the Medes.
> There are other blackguards, too.
> I am not the only curtail.
> There are other vixens, too.
>   (frs. 728, 729 Page, trans. C. M. Bowra)

Plutarch says that the lines were aimed specifically at Themistocles after he had been charged with medism, although it is unclear how much trust is to be put in his further comment, "It is said that Timocreon was exiled for medism, and that Themistocles joined in the vote of condemnation" (*Them.* 21. 7). An occasion for the passage has

26. So, among others, *Athenian Tribute Lists,* III, 185, *pace* Paul Maas, "Timokreon," *RE* 6.A (1937), col. 1271, and Fornara, *Historia* 15 (1966), 259, n.9.

27. Plut. *Them.* 23. 1, confirmed by Thuc. 1. 138. 6.

been sought in some of the joint activities of Athens and her partners in the Delian League in the mid-470s, but other scholars have condemned it as intrusive in Plutarch's text.[28] Timocreon's presence at the Persian court as a guest of the Great King is vouched for by the fifth-century Sophistic writer Thrasymachus of Chalcedon.[29] The comment in Plutarch may be based on this fact, combined with a misinterpretation of the line quoted above in which Timocreon refers to himself as a "curtail," since the term he uses, *kolouris*, means "animal with a tail," apparently a slang name for fox, and can, but need not, have the further implication "that has lost its tail," that is, one who has been caught doing wrong.[30]

If we can believe the ascriptions of authorship in certain ancient, but not always trustworthy, sources, it seems that Timocreon also carried out something like a poetic vendetta against Themistocles and his poetic ally Simonides. What is apparently a mock epitaph on Timocreon, which records his great capacity at drinking, eating, and verbal abuse, is ascribed to Simonides by the *Palatine Anthology* (7. 348); this is in turn answered by a two-line reply from Timocreon referring to the "Cean nonsense" (obviously an unflattering reference to Simonides) and in a poetic form which makes fun of a form of composition in which the words of the first line occur in a different order in the second, a device which may have been used originally by Simonides and is here being parodied—again, if the ascriptions are genuine.[31] Finally, a further verbal attack on Themistocles has been detected by Bergk in the unflattering, if obscure, line quoted by the late metrician Hephaestion from Timocreon's *Epigrams*: "With whom to plot the mind stands ready though the hands hold off."[32]

Potential prose sources for Themistocles' career are two writers who dealt with events of the Persian Wars, but whose accounts have all but disappeared. To a certain Xanthus, who seems to have been an older contemporary of Herodotus, are ascribed four books of *Lydiaka*, or "Matters pertaining to Lydia," in which he apparently dealt with early mythical history (for example, an account of the accession of Gyges which differed from Herodotus'), but mentioned as well events which had occurred within his own lifetime (according to Strabo [1. C 49], Xanthus described a great drought which had afflicted Asia Minor in the reign of Artaxerxes). None of the extant fragments indicates that he dealt in any way with Xerxes' invasion of Greece, much less with Themistocles' part in the Persian Wars or the later history of Themistocles.[33] Charon of Lampsacus also lived and wrote during the fifth century, but whether he was older or younger than Herodotus cannot be determined. There were ascribed to him in antiquity, among other titles, four books of *Hellenika* and two of *Persika*. It is certain that he mentioned Themistocles' later career from a comment in

28. The comment is condemned by Maas, *RE* 6.A (1937), col. 1272; for a less sceptical interpretation, see A. Kirchhoff, *Hermes* 11 (1876), 47–48.

29. An amusing anecdote of Timocreon at the Persian court is recorded on Thrasymachus' authority by Athenaeus 10. 416 A.

30. See Holden, *Plutarch's 'Life of Themistocles'*³, 139 (note on *Them.* 21, fin.).

31. *Anth. Pal.* 13. 30 and 31, discussed fully

by Bowra, *GLP*², 356 ff.

32. Edmonds' translation of fr. 9 Bergk; see Bergk, *PLG*, III, 540–41.

33. For the fragments of Xanthus, see Jacoby, *FGrHist* III C, 765; discussion by Lionel Pearson, *Early Ionian Historians*, chap. 3 (bibliography, pp. 137–38); K. von Fritz, *Die griech. Geschichtsschreibung*, I, "Anmerkungen," "Exkurs" II, pp. 348–77.

Plutarch's *Themistocles* (27. 1) that Charon agreed with Thucydides in bringing Themistocles before Artaxerxes, not his father, Xerxes. The fact could have been mentioned in either of Charon's above-named works or even in his work *On Lampsacus*, since Lampsacus was among the towns whose revenues the king assigned to Themistocles, and since there is inscriptional evidence for Themistocles' descendants present and active there as late as the third century B.C.[34] From other fragments it appears that Charon dealt, perhaps at length, with the Athenian expedition in aid of the Ionians and the attack on Sardis in 498 B.C., as well as the destruction of the Persian fleet under Mardonius off Mount Athos in 492 B.C.[35]

A prolific fifth-century writer was Ion, who was born on the island of Chios about 480 B.C., produced his first tragedy in about 450, and died in 422. Little of his works now remains, but he is said to have written dramatic works, lyric poems, elegies, as well as a prose account of the foundation of Chios and a book of memoirs that may be identical with a work entitled *Epidemiai*, or "Sojourns."[36] There are anecdotes which show Ion to have been on familiar terms with Aeschylus[37] and Cimon, whose physical characteristics he described and whose traits of character he compared with those of Pericles, to Pericles' detriment.[38] According to a story told by Plutarch, Ion related that "he was once a fellow-guest with Cimon at a dinner given by Laomedon, and that over the wine [Cimon] was invited to sing, and did sing very agreeably, and was praised by the guests as a cleverer man than Themistocles. That hero [Themistocles], they said, declared that he had not learned to sing, nor even to play the lyre, but knew how to make a city great and rich."[39] There is no reason to doubt the historicity of Ion's account, which may come from the *Epidemiai*, apparently a collection of stories related to "visits of Ion to Athens and other cities, chiefly of Greece proper, and visits of famous men to Chios."[40] Although the date of the dinner party in question is uncertain, Jacoby places it between 468 and 464 B.C. and maintains that "Ion had not met [Themistocles] personally, either in Athens or in Asia."[41] In another (now unknown) context Ion referred to Themistocles' daughter as an "Athenian foreigner" (F 11). Jacoby suggests that the reference may be to Themistocles' daughter Italia, who is known to have married a Chian named Panthoides. "Did [Ion] describe

34. The king gave Themistocles Lampsacus "for wine" (Thuc. 1. 138. 5; Plut. *Them.* 29. 11); honours for descendants of his son Cleophantus, H. G. Lolling, *Ath. Mitt.* 6 (1881), 103 ff.

35. *FGrHist* III C, 687 b, Ff 5, 1; discussion by Pearson, *Early Ionian Historians*, chap. 4; von Fritz, *Die griech. Geschichtsschreibung*, I, "Text," 519–22. According to Pearson, "One may reasonably suppose that Charon took the occasion of outlining the future career of Themistocles at some earlier stage in his account of the Persian Wars" (148).

36. Biographical data and prose fragments at *FGrHist* III B, 392, with commentary (discussion by Jacoby in *CQ* 41 [1947], 1–17); lyric fragments at Page, *PMG*, nos. 740–45. For the dramatic fragments, see Nauck, *TGF²*, pp. 732–46 (some sixty lines wholly or par-

tially preserved, from a total variously given in antiquity as twelve, thirty, or forty tragedies, including satyr plays; there is a fleeting reference at schol. Aristoph. *Peace* 835 to "comedies").

37. Plut. *Mor.* 79 E (cf. *Mor.* 29 F).

38. Plut. *Cim.* 5. 3, *Per.* 5. 3.

39. *Cim.* 9. 1; there is a variation of the same story as a retort of Themistocles', but without mentioning Ion, at *Them.* 2. 4.

40. Jacoby, *CQ* 41 (1947), 15; *FGrHist* III b, 193.

41. *CQ* 41 (1947), 12 (pp. 2–3, n.7, for Jacoby's arguments on the date; he remarks that "it is evident that Themistokles was not among the guests." There is not necessarily a contradiction between this view and the variation at *Them.* 2. 4 mentioned above in n.39).

the wedding?" Jacoby asks.[42] Ion's intimacy with Cimon may account for the tone of slight disparagement in his references to Themistocles and his family, who (even if Jacoby is not quite justified in arguing from Plutarch's failure to quote Ion in the *Themistocles* that "not much could be got from the Ἐπιδημίαι about Themistokles")[43] seem not to have formed one of Ion's main interests.

The case is far different with Stesimbrotus of Thasos, a contemporary of Ion, who lived at Athens during the time of Cimon and Pericles and acquired wide influence as a teacher among members of the next generation of poets (Niceratus and Antimachus of Colophon are mentioned specifically as his "pupils"). He was one of the first to compose a "scientific" study of Homer in which he attempted to discover biographical information about the poet and presented elucidations of difficult passages in the *Iliad*; there is also a work *On Initiation-ritual* ascribed to him, whose content seems to have been largely mythographical. But the book of Stesimbrotus from which most survives, and by far the most important for our purposes, is his *On Themistocles, Thucydides [son of Melesias] and Pericles*.[44] It was known (at least indirectly) to Plutarch, who quotes from it three times in the *Themistocles* (chaps. 2. 5, 4. 5, 24. 5), four times in *Cimon* (4. 5, 14. 5, 16. 1, 16. 3), and four times again in the *Pericles* (8. 9, 13. 16, 26. 1, 36. 6). The tone of the citations makes clear that Stesimbrotus' work was not straightforward biography or military history, but what Jacoby terms "eine politische Tendenzschrift,"[45] or, as has more recently been maintained, an early example of a Sophistic treatise *On Demagogues*.[46] Plutarch himself, even while citing him, had doubts about the credibility of Stesimbrotus' testimony for details of Themistocles' life. He had said that "Themistocles was a pupil of Anaxagoras and a disciple of Melissus the Physicist" (*Them.* 2. 5 = F 1), but this, as Plutarch notes, seems chronologically impossible, for Melissus had fought opposite Pericles in the Samian War (that is, in 440 B.C.), and it was Pericles, who was "much younger than" Themistocles, with whom Anaxagoras had been on terms of intimacy. Schachermeyr argues that Stesimbrotus could have meant, not that Themistocles had been Melissus' pupil, but merely that he "took an interest in" his teachings, and that this could have been in Magnesia in the last part of Themistocles' life.[47] But the word Stesimbrotus uses, *spoudasai*, implies a more than casual interest, and the term with which he describes Themistocles' relations with Anaxagoras, *diakousai*, is the usual way of describing a teacher-pupil relationship;[48] it is in any case obvious from the context that this is the way Plutarch understood Stesimbrotus' phrase. The exact date of Anaxagoras' arrival in Athens is uncertain,[49] but on any of the suggested chronologies

42. Ibid., 12. (The reference in the Suda s.v. Ἀθηναίας is not to Diphilus' *Amastris, pace* Edmonds, *FAC*, IIIA, p. 102, for the Suda's text must be corrected from the Berlin Photius, as Jacoby points out.)

43. Ibid.; *FGrHist* III b. ii, 126, n.5.

44. *FGrHist* 107 F 1–11.

45. *FGrHist* II D, p. 343.

46. F. Schachermeyr, "Stesimbrotos und seine Schrift über die Staatsmänner," *SB Oester. Akad.*, phil.-hist. Kl. 247. 5, 20–21

("ein ganz respektabler Vorläufer der peripatetischen Charakterologie" [21]).

47. "Samos lag ja nicht weit von Magnesia" (ibid., 12).

48. See the passages collected by Holden at *Plutarch's 'Life of Themistocles'*[3], ad loc.

49. The choice is between a residence in Athens c. 480–450, based on the authorities cited by Diogenes Laertius 2. 7 (so A. E. Taylor, *CQ* 11 [1917], 81–87), or his removal from Athens in the face of anti-Periclean feeling

it seems impossible that he could have come there, set himself up as a teacher, and had Themistocles as a pupil (by implication, over a period of years)—all before Themistocles' exile *c*. 470. Again, the contact may have occurred in Ionia,[50] but it seems easier to believe, with Plutarch, that Stesimbrotus skipped a generation and confused Themistocles with Pericles, the politician who did come into contact with philosophers like Anaxagoras and Melissus. There may be nothing more to the conjunction of names than that Themistocles had exercised some sort of suzerainty over Lampsacus, where Anaxagoras settled after leaving Athens (it is mere coincidence that the honour accorded him there after his death paralleled Themistocles' at Magnesia).

Plutarch reports two items from what must have been a full account by Stesimbrotus of Themistocles' condemnation and escape from Greece. A certain Epikrates of Acharnae secretly got Themistocles' wife and children out of Athens after his condemnation (probably this wife was the unnamed woman Plutarch says he married after Archippe, Lysandros' daughter [*Them*. 32. 2]) and sent them to join Themistocles in Epirus, where he had taken up asylum with King Admetus of the Molossi. For this action Epikrates was subsequently prosecuted by Cimon and condemned to death.

Plutarch rightly questions another item that Stesimbrotus reported, namely, that Themistocles (after leaving Corcyra?) "sailed to Sicily and asked for the hand of the tyrant Hieron's daughter in marriage, and promised to make Greece subject to him" (F 3).[51] As Plutarch remarks, Stesimbrotus seems to have forgotten completely about the wife whom Epikrates has been spiriting out of Athens! Although a direct contact between Themistocles and Hieron before Hieron's death in 467 B.C. is not impossible, it is highly unlikely; as Plutarch further notes at the beginning of chapter 25, a story was told by Theophrastus which, even if not literally true, may point to animosity between the two men, which would have made an approach such as Stesimbrotus describes difficult in the extreme. We can only conclude that Stesimbrotus gave an alternate, and highly coloured, account of Themistocles' appeal to Hieron, an account that had him taking the same kind of calculated risk in throwing himself at the feet of a powerful enemy as he had in approaching Admetus, and making the same promise that he would subjugate his former fellow citizens as some said he was also to make to Artaxerxes. Schachermeyr believes that Stesimbrotus was writing in Athens in the 420s and that his testimony reflects what some people really thought regarding great men of the preceding generation. Nevertheless, in reporting these variant accounts as *fact*, we must agree that Stesimbrotus was "ein schlechter Historiker," and it may even have been his version of Themistocles' career which Thucydides had in mind when he censured his fellow Athenians for "taking over from others by hearsay accounts of past events—even their own history—without trying to verify them"

c. 432 (Plut. *Per*. 32). The evidence is discussed (somewhat inconclusively) by W. K. C. Guthrie, *A History of Greek Philosophy*, II, 322–23. See, most recently, Meiggs, *Athenian Empire*, endnote 20, pp. 435–36.

50. Schachermeyr, "Stesimbrotos," 14; Holden, *Plutarch's 'Life of Themistocles'*[3], 64.

51. For a possible bearing this version may have on Themistocles' chronology, see Appendix A.

(1. 20. 1) and which led him to investigate the end of Themistocles' career and to present the results in an excursus.[52]

The third "fact" for which Plutarch cites Stesimbrotus is the opposition to Themistocles' naval policy on the part of Miltiades (*Them.* 4. 5 = F 2). Although Plutarch places the detail in the context of Themistocles' Naval Bill and the building of the fleet, ostensibly for the war against Aegina, in the late 480s—a time at which Miltiades would have been dead for several years—it is just possible that Stesimbrotus' testimony may reflect an earlier naval policy by Themistocles and an earlier opponent to his plans. If so, a possible time would be the late 490s when Miltiades had returned from his overlordship of the Chersonese and Themistocles, in his year as archon, had begun to fortify the Peiraeus.[53] An alternate explanation might be that Stesimbrotus has here again merely confused Miltiades with Aristeides, whom we know to have been a vociferous opponent of Themistocles' plan to build a fleet in the eighties and who finally had to be removed by ostracism.[54]

The ancient anonymous *Life of Sophocles*, whose origins may lie in the Peripatetic school of literary criticism, remarks that the writers of comedy "did not even keep their hands off Themistocles."[55] Little is left of Athenian comedy to verify the statement, which suggests that Themistocles may have been as roughly handled on the comic stage as were Pericles and Cleon. What references remain are relatively innocuous. In his political satire *Prytaneis* (roughly, "Committeemen"), Telekleides described "life in the days of Themistocles" as "dainty" (fr. 22 Edmonds), which need not have been a compliment, although Telekleides may have had in mind a Golden Age, referred to by other writers as the Age of Cronos, which gave way to the harsher, more repressive reign of Zeus (who, in fact, often allegorically represents Pericles in Attic comedy). Cimon's generosity was called the Age of Cronos, according to Plutarch (*Cim.* 10. 7), who, although he does not cite a source, may be drawing upon Cratinus' *Archilochuses*, from which several lines are quoted earlier in the same chapter to illustrate Cimon's generosity. Is it possible that Telekleides, by transferring what appears to be the same allusion to Themistocles, is taking sides in a political controversy which had reached as far as the comic stage? In Cratinus' *Panoptai* ("See-alls," a satiric allusion to followers of the philosopher Hippon), there is a cryptic reference to "memory aids that forget," which is probably, as Edmonds suggests, to be interpreted in light of the story that Simonides once offered to teach Themistocles his technique for memory strengthening, but was rebuffed by Themistocles with the comment, "I would rather have a 'Tricks for Forgetting,' for I remember what I don't want to and can't forget what I do."[56]

52. 1. 135–36; see chapter 2. At 1. 97. 2 Thucydides censures Hellanicus for "chronological inaccuracy," but his strictures would apply equally well to Stesimbrotus. G. Busolt, *Griech. Gesch.*[2], III. 1, 11, n.1, suggested: "Vielleicht richtete Thukydides in seiner Charakteristik des Themistokles das ἐπιμαθών [1. 138. 3] gegen die Angabe des Stesimbrotos."

53. So Schachermeyr, "Stesimbrotos," 13. Stesimbrotus' testimony in this matter has recently been championed (unconvincingly, it seems to me) by E. S. Gruen, "Stesimbrotus on Miltiades and Themistocles," *Calif. Studies Class. Ant.* 3 (1970), 91–98.

54. Jacoby, *FGrHist* II D, p. 345; p. 203 below.

55. *Vita Sophoclis* 1; for a possible Peripatetic origin, see my article "The Peripatetics as Literary Critics," *Phoenix* 23 (1969), 134–35.

56. Cratinus fr. 154 Edmonds (Cicero relates the story at *de Fin.* 2. 32. 104).

Themistocles plays a comparatively large part in Aristophanes' *Knights*. In a bit of comic dialogue at the beginning, Nicias says that things have become so bad under the Paphlagonian (Cleon) that the only way out is death—"of the manliest kind... by drinking bull's blood; a Themistoclean death is to be preferred" (lines 81–84). The reference shows that the story that Themistocles had committed suicide by drinking bull's blood, told in full by Plutarch (*Them.* 31. 5–6), was current at least as early as 424 B.C. when the *Knights* was presented. A scholiast (ancient commentator) on the passage quotes two lines from Sophocles' lost play, *Demand for Helen*, in which suicide by drinking bull's blood is also mentioned, and then adds the comment, "Some say that Sophocles is referring to Themistocles," but this may be merely some ancient scholar's conjecture. In a sequence later in the *Knights*, Cleon claims that he has done more for the city than Themistocles (lines 811–12), to which the sausage seller replies:

O city of Argos! yourself would you match with mighty Themistocles, him
Who made of our city a bumper indeed, though he found her scarce filled to the brim,
Who, while she was lunching, Peiraeus threw in, as a dainty additional dish,
Who secured her the old, while providing untold the novel assortments of fish;
Whilst you, with your walls of partition forsooth, and the oracle-chants which you hatch,
Would dwarf and belittle the city again, who yourself with Themistocles match!
And *he* was an exile, but *you* upon crumbs Achillean your fingers are cleaning [that is, have free meals in the Prytaneion].

(lines 813–19, trans. B. B. Rogers)

There is no reason to doubt the implication that Cleon, after his unexpected success at Pylos in the summer of 425 B.C., did go around Athens claiming that he had done more for the city than Themistocles, just as (to judge from lines 1036 ff. of the *Knights*) he also compared himself with Pericles. Aristophanes' character, after what may be a significant reference to Argos, where Themistocles had spent time between his ostracism and his final condemnation for treason, retorts that Themistocles had "kneaded Peiraeus onto" the city of Athens, and while "taking away none of the old dishes had set before the Athenians new fish-delicacies," a witty reference to the greater variety of imports which Athens could enjoy once she had secure access to the sea as a result of the completion of the Long Walls. No matter that the building of the Long Walls, to which Aristophanes here seems to be cryptically alluding, actually occurred, according to Thucydides (1. 107. 1, 108. 3), some years after Themistocles had been forced out of Athens and was probably due to Pericles, who, in Thucydides' *Funeral Speech*, refers specifically to the volume and variety of Athenian imports.[57] The spirit of the measure was Themistoclean, and the contrast Aristophanes is underlining is one between the days of the great democrats of the past, Themistocles and Pericles, and the present period of diminished horizons and smaller men like Cleon. It can also be argued that Aristophanes has recognized that Pericles' building of the Long Walls in the early 450s was a logical completion of the plan of Themistocles, which he had initiated by beginning the fortification of Peiraeus during his year as archon.

57. Thuc. 2. 38. 2, which does not seem to me independent of *Knights* 816.

The reference in line 814 is rather more difficult to interpret: "finding the city *epicheile*, he made it full." The phrase was taken by the scholiast to mean "finding the city *without walls* [he then proceeded to build them]." In that case, the reference would be to the account of Themistocles' hasty rebuilding of the city fortifications in 479 after the invading armies had withdrawn. Thucydides tells the story fully and, presumably, accurately (1. 89. 3 ff.). It was inevitable that the story should grow more fanciful through the addition of romantic details, and it is this later version, with Themistocles' offering himself as a hostage in Sparta and secretly bidding the Athenians hold the Spartan ambassadors captive until he and his fellow ambassadors returned safely, that the scholiast on this passage in *Knights* recounts. It is suspiciously similar to the version in Diodorus and may go back ultimately to the fourth-century historian Ephorus. Modern commentators like Rogers prefer another simpler explanation of the term *epicheile*: since the *cheilos* of a Greek cup was a rim of some depth, to speak of it as being filled merely *up to* the rim means there is quite a lot remaining to be filled; hence the term means simply "[partially] empty."[58] Given the physical nature of the image and the mention of Peiraeus in the next line, the earlier, more specific, interpretation seems to me preferable.

That it was the Peiraeus for which Themistocles was remembered is clearly shown by the comment of Demos a few lines later when he refers to Themistocles and the "stratagem" (*sophon*) of the Peiraeus, but ludicrously prefers to it the tunic which the sausage seller offers him (*Knights* 884–86). Later, when the Paphlagonian and the sausage seller are competing for Demos' attentions by producing oracles, the Paphlagonian recites one which is a ridiculous jumble of the well-known dream which Pericles' mother was said by Herodotus (6. 131. 2) to have had on the eve of her giving birth to Pericles and the wooden wall which the audience would have recognized as an allusion to the Delphic oracle delivered to the Athenians before Salamis, whose ambiguity Themistocles turned to good account when he interpreted it as a reference to the ships which he had been largely instrumental in having built (Hdt. 7. 141). Some have seen an allusion to Themistocles, too, in the lines quoted from Aristophanes' first play, *Banqueters* (427 B.C.), where one character seems to be urging another to "spend money for the sort of things our ancestors spent theirs—triremes and walls."[59] There is a further brief but pointed allusion to Themistocles' Peiraeus wall in the *Birds*. "Your wall has been built," a messenger tells Peisthetairos,

> And a most grand, magnificent work it is.
> So broad, that on its top the Braggadocian
> Proxenides could pass Theagenes
> Each driving in his chariot, drawn by horses
> As bulky as the Trojan.
>   (lines 1125–29, trans. Rogers)

From Thucydides' fuller description of the way in which the Peiraeus circuit was built,

58. B. B. Rogers, *The 'Knights' of Aristophanes*, ad loc., following the lead of a scholiast on the passage and the ancient lexicographers.
59. Fr. 220 Edmonds (who, however, interprets the line differently). The suggestion of an allusion to Themistocles is made by Holden, *Plutarch's 'Life of Themistocles'*³, xlvii, n.115.

that "two wagons opposite one another [whatever that may mean] brought up the stones" (1. 93. 5), it appears likely that Aristophanes' audience in 414 B.C. would have recognized the allusion.

In chapter 32 of the *Themistocles*, Plutarch quotes four lines from the comic writer Plato, which he says the fourth-century writer Diodorus had interpreted as referring to a "tomb" of Themistocles which stood on a promontory overlooking the Great Harbour of Peiraeus:

> Thy tomb is mounded in a fair and sightly place;
> The merchantmen shall greet it from on every side;
> It shall behold those outward, and those inward bound,
> And view the emulous rivalry of racing ships.
> (fr. 183 Edmonds, trans. Perrin)

Although Diodorus seems to have been a careful author, who wrote the works *On Monuments* and *On the Dedications on the Acropolis*, something like early annotated guidebooks of the type more familiar to us from Pausanias, Plutarch is clearly sceptical of his testimony on this point. The question we must ask is, Was there more to the passage in Plato which would have guaranteed for Diodorus the reference "thy tomb" as being to that of Themistocles? It is a question which cannot, unfortunately, be answered; nor can the larger one, If this structure was somehow connected with Themistocles, what was it and when was it built?[60] As Gomme suggests, this structure may also be alluded to in a phrase from the comic writer Hermippus, which the source says comes, not from a comedy, but from his *Tetrameters*. As the quotation is textually corrupt and has not been satisfactorily emended, not much more can be obtained from it than a reference to a "promontory [*pron*] of Themistocles," which was said by Hermippus to be, or to be like, the bird known as a "red-cap."[61]

Two poets active during the last decades of the fifth century wrote about the Persian Wars. Among the works ascribed to Choirilus of Samos we find the titles *Barbarika*, *Medika*, *Persika*, which may be separate poems or alternate titles for the work called, in the entry under his name in the Suda lexicon, *The Victory of the Athenians against Xerxes* (that is, Salamis).[62] There we read also that he was "a Samian slave, of handsome appearance, who escaped from Samos, became a close companion of Herodotus the historian and became enamoured of his stories." Whatever its exact title, his poem on the Persian Wars began with the traditional invocation of the Muse:

60. For a discussion of the so-called tomb of Themistocles, see chapter 10.

61. Gomme, *Commentary*, I, 446, n.1, from a scholiast on Aristophanes, *Birds* 303. Interest in Themistocles as a dramatic figure revived in the Alexandrian period with Philiscus' *Themistocles* (see Nauck, *TGF²*, p. 819, and the discussion by Bruno Snell, *Tragicorum Graecorum Fragmenta*, I, 259, note on T.5 with refs. there) and Moschion's *Themistocles*, of which three lines survive (Nauck, *TGF²*, p. 812, fr. 1 [= p. 264 Snell]; I would also assign fragment 9 to this play, and hope to develop this sug-

gestion at length elsewhere; cf. A. Meineke in *SB Berlin Akad.* [1855], 102–14; E. Diehl, *RE* 16 [1935], cols. 345–47).

62. The biographical information and most of the fragments are collected by Jacoby, *FGrHist* 696 Ff 32–34 (several additional fragments may be found in G. Kinkel, *Epicorum Graecorum Fragmenta*, pp. 265–72). The data are discussed briefly by H. J. Mette in *Der kleine Pauly* 1 (1964), 1152–53, and more fully by G. L. Huxley, "Choirilos of Samos," *GRBS* 10 (1969), 12–29, esp. 14–24 for *Persika*

Lead on to a new story, how from Asia's land
Came to Europe a great war.

The poem contained an account of Xerxes' muster and review of his forces (perhaps at the Hellespont, as in Herodotus), in which the troops were compared to the "myriad swarms of bees" which swarmed around the fountain Arethusa; Choirilus then described how they crossed by the Hellespontine bridge. In what may have been a mythological digression within his account of the events preceding the battle of Artemisium, the poet narrated Boreas' rape of Oreithyia "as she was picking flowers near the waters of Cephisus."[63] A reference to "a swift-sailing Samian ship, shaped like a sow," may come, as Huxley suggests, from a description of the battle of Salamis, and three lines quoted by Athenaeus may come from a speech of Xerxes after the defeat, in which he compared the wrecks of ships washed up on the shore to so much broken crockery after a drinking party: "a shipwreck of feasting men."[64] If there was any specific mention of Themistocles or his exploits in connection with the battles, the lines which might serve as evidence have not been preserved.

A case has been made for Themistocles' holding a prominent position in the lyric poem entitled *The Persians* by Timotheus of Miletus. A fourth-century B.C. papyrus (and thus one of the earliest literary papyri so far discovered) was found at Abu Sir in Egypt in 1902, which contained some two hundred and forty lines of this celebrated but peculiar poem. Unfortunately, the papyrus is severely mutilated at the beginning, but the first section preserved in it appears to be an account of the closing incidents in the battle of Salamis.[65] What seems to emerge from the extremely battered early lines is a description of the way in which the Persian rowers had their oars sheared off (by their own or the Greeks' ships?) or broken as they were driven ashore; there seem to be anachronistic references to leaden ramming-weights known as "dolphins" and firedarts made of tarred tow. This section of the poem ends with the description of how "the furrow of the emerald-tressed sea grew crimson with enemies' blood...and a confused hubbub held sway."[66] The better-preserved sections of the poem consist of a series of threnodic laments (the work is technically classed as a *nomos*, or virtuoso piece performed by a singer accompanying himself on a zither), by Persians singly or in a group, culminating in the scene of Xerxes' rending his robes and bemoaning the destruction of his royal house and the loss of his army through the agency of the Greek ships (lines 174–95). The verbal echoes of Aeschylus, scattered throughout the poem, become particularly frequent here;[67] the picture of the king, almost maddened

63. *FGrHist* 696 F 34 g; see Huxley, *GRBS* 10 (1969), 21–22. The inference is based on a similar detail in Simonides' poem on Artemisium; see my article in *Historia* 17 (1968), esp. 262 ff.

64. Fr. 9 Kinkel; see Huxley, *GRBS* 10 (1969), 23–24.

65. *P. Berol.* 9865. The *editio princeps* is Wilamowitz' *Timotheus, Die Perser* (1903), most recently and conveniently available at Page, *PMG*, no. 791, whose text and line numeration I follow.

66. *PMG*, no. 791. 31–34; I accept Van Leeuwen's δαίοις for the MS.'s ναίοις in line 32.

67. Most of the Aeschylean reminiscences, too frequent to be accidental, are catalogued by M. Croiset in *REG* 16 (1903), 330–35. I would add that the ambiguity of νᾶες in Timotheus 791. 179 and 182 (Greek blending into Persian) is paralleled by Aeschylus' *Pers.* 560–63.

by grief, turning back from Salamis in defeat, is very similar in both authors. The narrative section ends with a surprisingly brief description of the Greeks' setting up a trophy to Zeus (on Salamis?) and singing and dancing a paean of thanksgiving (lines 196–201).

References to the poem known before the discovery of the papyrus make it clear that what survives on the papyrus is merely the finale, but how much of it has perished cannot be determined. This is a pity, for it is precisely in this first part that references to Themistocles would most likely have occurred. Plutarch preserves the opening line, from the prelude in dactylic hexameters, which Euripides is said to have helped Timotheus to compose:[68] "Fashioning for Greece the great and glorious ornament of freedom" (fr. 788 Page, trans. Edmonds). Plutarch relates that when the line was sung at the Nemean Games in 207 B.C., the audience turned and applauded Philopoemen, the man of the hour (*Phil.* 11). It has been argued that "this seems to mean that Philopoemen was hailed as a second Themistocles."[69] The tale, which is suspiciously similar to one told by Plutarch elsewhere regarding Aristeides (*Arist.* 3. 5), need not be literally true to sustain the inference that Timotheus' original reference was to a victorious general[70] who had been, in some sense, Philopoemen's predecessor. Plutarch elsewhere cites a line which he specifically says comes from the "exhortation to the Greeks": "Worship *Aidos*, the helpmate [*synergon*] of spear-battling Arete" (789 Page). Edmonds cites the passage in Herodotus in which we are told that, before embarking, the Greek forces at Salamis were harangued by Themistocles, who "contrasted all that is fine in human nature with its inferior impulses and urged them to choose the better course" (8. 83), and assigns this line to Timotheus' version of Themistocles' exhortation.[71] Another cryptic line which Plutarch quotes, "Ares is king; Greece fears no gold" (fr. 790 Page), is assigned by Bassett to this same address.[72] A four-line fragment quoted by Macrobius from Timotheus (but without naming the poem), in which the sun is addressed in the second person as Paean and called upon to "send a far-shot shaft from your bowstring against the enemy," has plausibly been assigned to the paean that Aeschylus says the Greek forces raised when they came in sight of the Persians.[73] It has been suggested that a line cited by Dionysius of Halicarnassus as an example of cretic rhythm may come from the beginning of the section which described the Greek attack.[74] Although Dionysius does not name the author, the identification carries some conviction in light of the occurrence of cretics in the papyrus (runs of three cretics at lines 116 and 118) and especially Timotheus' fondness

---

68. According to the Peripatetic Satyrus in his *Life of Euripides*, P. Oxy. 1176, fr. 39, xxii, lines 27 ff.

69. S. E. Bassett, *CP* 26 (1931), 155, following M. Croiset, *Hist. litt. grecque*², III, 650.

70. The nominative masculine particle τεύχων refers most probably to a single Athenian male rather than collectively to the Athenian λαός or δῆμος (S. Reinach suggested, rather implausibly, that the reference was to a contemporary, e.g., Lysander [*REG* 16 (1903), 66, n.1]).

71. *Lyra Graeca*, III, 307, n.4 (Loeb Classical

Library); this seems more probable than Bassett's theory that they belong to the "mighty shout" assigned by Herodotus (8. 84) to a "phantom woman."

72. *CP* 26 (1931), 155. Does the phrase χρυσὸν δ' Ἑλλὰς οὐ δέδοικεν show that the story of Themistocles and Arthmius of Zeleia (Plut. *Them.* 6. 4) had already become prevalent?

73. *Pers.* 393; see Edmonds, *Lyra Graeca*, III, 306–7, n.1, and Bassett, *CP* 26 (1931), 156.

74. Bassett, *CP* 26 (1931), 156, following Usener, Wilamowitz, and Edmonds.

for such overblown circumlocutions as that which the line quoted by Dionysius contains: "bronze-rammed floating chariots" = "ships."

When and where Timotheus presented his *Persians* remains uncertain. An ancient chronographic source, the Parian Marble, places Timotheus' death in the period 365 to 357 at the age of ninety; his birth date would then be approximately 455 to 447 B.C. In the concluding section of the poem (known technically as the *sphragis*, or "seal"), in which the poet speaks in his own person, he says he is "neither young nor old" (lines 213–14). It seems unlikely that a man who was younger than forty would refer to himself in this way, and that perhaps gives 415 as a rough *terminus post quem*. P. Maas combined the story of Euripides' helping Timotheus with the proem, and the resultant first place which Timotheus won, with the notice of his victory over his old teacher Phrynis, "which, because of the period of Phrynis' lifetime, cannot come long after 420 B.C."[75] Maas also felt that the period between 415 and 408 (when a section of the *Persians* seems to be echoed in Euripides' *Orestes* 1369 ff.) was ruled out by the praise of Sparta in lines 206 ff. It may be more than coincidental that the amusing (to us, but perhaps unintentionally) broken Ionic of the captive Persian from Celaenae at lines 150 ff. has close analogies with a scene from Aristophanes' *Acharnians* of 425 B.C. The story of Timotheus' victory with Euripides' assistance seems to point to Athens as the place of presentation,[76] but some scholars, perhaps putting too much emphasis on the absence of any mention of Athens (or, for that matter, of the Greeks), have suggested a Delphian or Ionian locale.[77]

The picture of Timotheus sitting at Herodotus' feet, perhaps even listening to the same informants about events in the Persian Wars, is a pleasant one but rests on no very secure evidence. In any case, since most of that part of the poem which dealt with events in which Themistocles had had a hand is now lost, how authentic the tradition which Timotheus followed might have been is not a very pressing question.

What emerges from this survey is that much of the earliest literary testimony about Themistocles was poetic. His friends Simonides, Phrynichus, and Aeschylus dealt in their poems with events in which he had been involved. How much of this work one chooses to call propagandistic is perhaps a matter of taste. The evidence presented by the contemporary but hostile Timocreon of Rhodes is valuable, but largely enigmatic. Of the prose accounts very little survives, and much of it is either tendentious (Ion's *Memoirs*) or downright erroneous (Stesimbrotus); what the Lydian Xanthus or Charon of Lampsacus (whom Thucydides may have drawn on) had to say about Themistocles cannot now be recovered.

75. *RE* 6.A (1937), col. 1332; this reconstruction is accepted by T. B. L. Webster, *The Tragedies of Euripides*, 17–18. The fragment in question is 802 Page.

76. So Maas, *RE* 6.A (1937), col. 1332; Bassett, *CP* 26 (1931), 157–58 (although too much weight should not be put on Zenobius' reference to the success of the poem *at Athens*).

77. Wilamowitz, *SB Berlin Akad.* (1906), 50, n.1, suggested Miletus. H. L. Ebeling (*AJP* 46 [1925], 318), following Aron, put forward Ephesus. M. Croiset, *REG* 16 (1903), 336–37, offers a choice from among a spring festival at Delphi, or, on the basis of the mention of the Achaeans at line 236, an Achaean city like Patras or Pellene, or an Achaean colony like Metapontum. The last word of the poem, *eunomia*, has naturally suggested Spartan oligarchy, but Bassett shows how this can be reconciled with an Athenian setting.

The casual references in Aristophanes show what elements in the Themistocles story had early become (not necessarily trustworthy) commonplaces: his wall building and his suicide. But for the accident of preservation, the fascinating if bizarre Timotheus might have had considerable light to shed. A continuous surviving narrative of an important chapter in Themistocles' life is not to be found until Herodotus' *Histories*.

2 HERODOTUS AND THUCYDIDES

SOME TIME AFTER 450 B.C. when the travels of the Halicarnassian Herodotus brought him to Athens and he formed the design to record the story of the war between the Greeks and Persians of a generation earlier, he began to make inquiries among men who had taken part in the fighting or were closely related to those who had done so. The main facts would have been known to all, at least in outline, and some details might have been kept alive by being retold whenever men gathered and reminisced about the miraculous escape they had had from all but certain defeat at the Persians' hands in 490 and again ten years later. No story of the latter engagement off the island of Salamis would have been complete without a mention in a more or less prominent position of Themistocles. There survive hints of a current controversy over Themistocles and his contribution to Greece's successful repulse of the invaders, but precise details of this debate are unfortunately lacking.

It would be helpful to know exactly when Herodotus penned his portrait of Themistocles. It is generally assumed that he began collecting his material for the early books before he came to Athens, that is, before his participation in the colony to Thurii in 444/3. At some later stage he seems to have conceived the plan to expand his traveller's *logoi* to embrace the great confrontation between the Greeks and Persians in 490 and 480, and there are indications that these last books were at least revised, if not actually written in the first place, in the decade between 430 and 420 B.C.[1] Athens was locked in another struggle, this time against other Greeks and her own former allies; men readily went back to those old, more glorious days, and stories which had been handed down from participants in the battles against Persia were remembered—or invented. Above all, the successors of those who had fought in the old *Parteikämpfe* tended, and may even have fanned, the flames of grievances which might otherwise have been forgotten.

1. See C. W. Fornara, *Herodotus*, 43, n.13, 86 ff.

Thucydides' Athenian speaker at Sparta in 432 B.C. refers in passing to "the annoyance caused by those who are always thrusting forward stories of the Persian Wars" (1. 73. 2—a slap at Herodotus' informants?). He then proceeds to justify the retention by the Athenians of their top position among the Greeks by doing exactly what he had condemned a moment before, returning yet again to the period of the resistance when "Greece's affairs lay in the ships" and Athens supplied "the three items which contributed most to victory: the most ships, the cleverest general, the most unhesitating drive: a little less than two-thirds of the almost 400 ships, Themistocles as general, who was most responsible for fighting the sea battle in the straits, which was most obviously the thing that saved the day (and you yourselves honoured him)" (1. 74). Thucydides thus makes it clear as early as this in his narrative where he stands on the issue of Themistocles. Where Herodotus (or his informants) stood emerges, if not in so sharp and straightforward a way, just as definitely from the insinuation and damaging innuendo with which he tells his version of the story. He lines up squarely on the side of those writers like Timocreon, Ion, and perhaps Stesimbrotus, who, although they could not ignore Themistocles in the events of 480, nevertheless did all they could to belittle his contribution and besmirch his name.[2]

In his narrative of the controversy over the wooden wall oracle and its interpretation, Herodotus introduces Themistocles with the description, "There was a certain Athenian who had recently come into prominence" (7. 143. 1). The implication of the words *es protous neosti parion* is that before this Themistocles was of no importance. Yet in the very next chapter Herodotus discusses "another motion of Themistocles which turned out for the best," his Naval Bill; in point of fact Themistocles had been eponymous archon, Athens' chief magistrate, some twelve years before.[3] It may be that Herodotus was ignorant of the fact, but he cannot both have known it and described Themistocles' entrance on the scene in 480 as he does, without laying himself open to the charge of unfairness in his use of the term *neosti*; for it cannot seriously be maintained, as a recent writer would have it, that "archons and junior Areopagites were not to be considered among the *protoi*."[4] Thucydides in his account seems consciously to be countering the charge that Themistocles did nothing during his year as archon by pointing out that it was in that year that he began fortification of the Peiraeus (1. 93. 3–4). Herodotus' use of *neosti* in the case of Themistocles has been defended by some who point out that he uses the term again within a few chapters, to describe Argos' defeat at the hands of the Spartan king Cleomenes, an event which had taken place fourteen years previously (7. 148. 2), but the parallel proves little, for the word is there put into the mouths of Argive speakers to whose advantage it is to minimize the interval of time. Fornara attempts to absolve Herodotus by emphasizing the first two words Herodotus uses, ἦν δὲ, and by noting that Themistocles' "name is withheld until the sentence runs to its end. Expectation, suspense and under-

2. This has been denied by K. Goldscheider, *Die Darstellung des Themistokles bei Herodot*, and Fornara, *Herodotus*, 66 ff., but their arguments are not compelling. I wish to express thanks to Profs. H. Strasburger and H. Gundert of Freiburg for supplying me with a copy of Goldscheider's work.

3. For the date, see Appendix A.

4. F. J. Frost, "Themistocles' Place in Athenian Politics," *Calif. Studies Class. Ant.* 1 (1968), 115.

statement: Herodotus has given Themistocles a drumoll."[5] This interpretation might have had a chance of being correct were it not for the term *neosti*, which Fornara passes over in silence. Furthermore, Herodotus identifies Themistocles' father by using the words, "He was called the son of Neokles," which may be intended, as G. L. Cawkwell has recently maintained, to "cast a slur on his origin."[6] In his glance back to Themistocles' Naval Bill, Herodotus tries, not altogether successfully, to deprive Themistocles of the credit for the victory made possible by the existence of an adequate Athenian fleet; Themistocles persuaded the Athenians to use the money to build ships for the war, "by which he meant," Herodotus continues, "the war against Aegina. For it was this war which, by breaking out, saved Greece on that occasion by forcing the Athenians to take to the sea" (7. 144). To this slur Thucydides seems to be taking explicit exception when, in his review of the growth of early Greek naval power in the introductory chapters of his first book, he comments that "Themistocles persuaded the Athenians who were waging war against the Aeginetans (and at the same time the barbarian invasion was expected) to build the ships with which they in fact fought their battles at sea" (1. 14. 3).

It was perhaps inevitable that accounts of the events which preceded the battles off Cape Artemisium should have been a good deal embroidered and embellished. What is not clear is why the motif of "bribery of the venal Themistocles" should have been introduced on this occasion, and not, say, earlier when the withdrawal of the Greek forces from Tempe would have offered an even better opportunity for such a slur on Themistocles, who led the Athenian contingent. According to Herodotus, when the Greeks at Artemisium saw the unexpectedly large number of Persian ships drawn up at Aphetai, they took fright and contemplated withdrawal. The Euboeans begged the Spartan commander Eurybiades for enough time to get their children and slaves out safely, and when he refused, they approached Themistocles with a thirty-talent bribe (an enormous sum) to fight at sea there. Themistocles handed over five talents to Eurybiades ("as if it were his own," Herodotus adds, 8. 5. 1) and sent the Corinthian Adeimantus three talents with the promise that he would "make him richer by staying than the Persian king would for leaving"; Themistocles "secretly kept the rest himself and so made a profit" (8. 5. 3). The story was too much for Plutarch, or whoever it was who wrote the essay *On the Malice of Herodotus*,[7] who objects that Herodotus' account turns the victory "into the fruit of bribery and deceit, and shows the Greeks fighting reluctantly, tricked by their corrupt commanders" (*Mor.* 867 C, trans. L. Pearson).

Perhaps Herodotus' most damaging slur against Themistocles is his introduction of a fellow demesman, Mnesiphilus, into the story of the antecedents of Salamis. When Themistocles told him that the commanders of the allied naval contingents were for leaving Salamis and sailing to the Isthmus, Mnesiphilus replied in horror, "Why in that case you won't fight for a single fatherland, because they will all scatter to their

5. *Herodotus*, 68

6. "The Fall of Themistocles," in *Auckland Classical Essays Presented to E. M. Blaiklock*, 40.

7. One of the reasons for doubting Plutarch's authorship is that he raises no objections to the story, which he tells in a slightly different form (but mentions Herodotus by name), at *Them.* 7. 3–4.

own cities. Hellas will perish through folly. If you can devise some way, go and undo what has been decided. Try to persuade Eurybiades to change his decision and remain here" (8. 57). Herodotus comments that "the advice was mightily pleasing to Themistocles...who reported to Eurybiades all that he had heard from Mnesiphilus, taking it over as his own and adding much else besides" (8. 58). Themistocles then delivered an impassioned speech in which the arguments were well ordered and persuasively expressed, and all mention of the danger of defection by the allies was diplomatically suppressed (8. 60). By the lame expedient of introducing a totally superfluous (but not fictitious) character, Herodotus seeks to suggest that, in Cawkwell's words, "Themistocles got the credit which did not really belong to him.... For Herodotus Themistocles is a cheat."[8]

Deceit is again imputed to Themistocles by Herodotus in his narrative of events following the battle. The Greek ships pursued the fleeing Persians as far as Andros and there held a council at which Themistocles advised that they "sail in pursuit of the ships straight for the Hellespont to destroy the bridges" (8. 108), but when he saw that he would be unable to persuade the majority, he changed sides and argued to his men that it was better for them to let the Persians go and return home to attend to rebuilding their houses and sowing next season's crops. Herodotus' comment is that "Themistocles said this in order to make a deposit of gratitude with the Persian king, so he would have a refuge if catastrophe ever should befall him—which is exactly what happened" (8. 109. 5). Herodotus' imputation of motive for Themistocles' volte-face is clearly an inference *post eventum* and can be dismissed. What in later writers is a second example of a patriotic "stratagem" (Diodorus' word, 11. 19, fin.) is for Herodotus nothing more than mendacious self-seeking.[9] Fornara's defence of the episode on grounds that "Herodotus' intent was to show Themistocles' great capacity for the clever ruse" is ingenious,[10] but unconvincing.

Themistocles' avarice is once more prominent in Herodotus' account of what followed the council of Andros. Cheated of their prey, the Greeks decided to lay siege to Andros, but the inhabitants, "the first islands from whom Themistocles demanded money" (8. 11. 2), refused to give him any (Herodotus here recounts a lively dialogue between them and Themistocles, whose two "gods," Persuasion and Necessity, are countered by the Andrian divinities, Poverty and Resourcelessness). Themistocles then ("for he never ceased being greedy," Herodotus adds) sent to the other islands the same messengers as to the king—Sicinnus again!—to threaten to reduce them if they did not contribute. Herodotus closes with another slap: "Using Andros as his base, Themistocles acquired money from the islanders without the other

8. "Fall of Themistocles," 41–42. Objections to Herodotus' version are as old as *de mal. Her.* 37 [Plut. *Mor.* 869 D–F]; see C. Hignett, *Xerxes' Invasion,* 204. Goldscheider's defence of the Mnesiphilus episode (*Themistokles bei Herodot,* 56–64) is ingenious but futile, nor am I convinced by Fornara's comment that Herodotus' introduction of Mnesiphilus "is calculated to give dramatic emphasis to the crucial moment at Salamis, not to deprive Themistocles of credit" (*Herodotus,* 72, n.19).

9. The story was famous in antiquity, occurring also in Ephorus, *FGrHist* 70 F 191. 1 8–13; Nepos, *Them.* 5. 1; Justin 2. 13. 5–7 Frontinus, *Strat.* 2. 6. 8; Polyaenus 1. 30. 4, and Aristodemus, *FGrHist* 104. 1 (7). The variants are analysed by L. Bodin, *REG* 30 (1917), 138 ff.

10. *Herodotus,* 71.

generals' knowledge" (8. 112. 3). When it comes to specifics, however, Herodotus is able to mention only Paros and Carystus, and here he unwittingly lets fall the comment that they contributed when they learned that Andros was being besieged *for medism.* Herodotus thus reveals the real motive behind Themistocles' collections: the money was clearly to be a kind of indemnity levied upon disloyal states to defray expenses of the fleet; in effect, tribute similar to that later exacted by Athens from her allies.[11]

Only three times does Herodotus allow himself an even faintly laudatory comment about Themistocles. He mentions the Naval Bill as "another proposal [that is, in addition to the interpretation of the wooden wall oracle] which turned out for the best" (7. 144. 1). Later, Herodotus remarks that Themistocles was able to persuade his men not to pursue the Persians to the Hellespont, "since, in addition to his previous reputation for wisdom, the true wisdom of his advice was manifest" (8. 110. 1). In the wake of the Salamis victory "Themistocles' name was on everyone's lips and he acquired the reputation throughout all of Greece of being by far the wisest of Greeks" (8. 124. 1), and he is then rewarded at Sparta for "wisdom and cleverness" with an honour guard "such as no other man we know of" (124. 3).

Why does Herodotus paint such an unflattering and, in some respects, positively untrue portrait of Themistocles? The answer usually suggested is the hatred felt by the Alcmeonids for their political adversary. The Alcmeonids get an exceedingly favourable press in Herodotus (see, for example, 6. 125. 1), and he even tries with considerable pains to exonerate them of the charge of treason at Marathon (6. 121 ff.).[12] On the other hand, the Alcmeonids themselves are not above criticism (for example, the charge of bribery of the Delphic priestess is alluded to at 5. 63. 1 and 66. 1), and perhaps we need not seek a unitary source for Herodotus' picture. By the time Herodotus began his inquiries, the Themistocles legend had been formed, and the black-and-white contrast between Themistocles, "all guile, restless, and democratic, and Aristeides, honest as the day, the dignified conservative" (Gomme's phrase, who rightly condemns it as a false contrast) could hardly have been avoided, even by so fair-minded an inquirer as Herodotus. Dishonesty in money matters had become a stock charge against Themistocles as early as Timocreon. Aristeides' honesty (especially, in view of the increasingly heavy price of membership in the Delian League, the relative fairness of the assessment of 477) had long since become proverbial. For Herodotus, Aristeides, although he appears but rarely in the *Inquiries,* was "the man whom I, as a result of investigation into his character, consider to have been the best and justest man in Athens" (8. 79. 1). (It is a pity he was not as discriminating about either of these two individuals as he could be about Pausanias; see 5. 32 where Herodotus expresses doubts about the story of Pausanias' dynastic marriage and tyrannical ambitions.) But by the time Herodotus wrote, a substantial portion of his audience was expecting Themistocles to be portrayed as a "fifth-century Odysseus" (Fornara's felicitous phrase);[13] also, by this time Themistocles had committed the

11. Cawkwell, "Fall of Themistocles," 41, who comments, "Out of these tentative efforts of 480 came the tribute of the Delian League."

12. The Alcmeonid source theory is sub-scribed to by, among others, W. W. How and J. Wells, *A Commentary on Herodotus,* I, 42–43; F. Jacoby, *RE,* supp. 2 (1939), cols. 413–14.

13. *Herodotus,* 72.

unpardonable offence, as Alcibiades was soon to do, of going over to the enemy. Because of the disgrace of Themistocles' last years, the majority of his countrymen had simply forgotten that Greece owed its very survival to him. It remained for Thucydides to remind them of the fact.

We are likewise unsure about when Thucydides composed his *Peloponnesian War*. He began to write, he tells us, as soon as the war began (1. 1), but it is clear that certain passages were written after 404 (2. 65. 12; 6. 15. 3). When the so-called excursus on Pausanias and Themistocles was written is unknown, but there are signs that it may have been early, perhaps in the very period Herodotus was publicly reciting his version.[14] Although Thucydides nowhere mentions Herodotus by name, he seems in several places to be correcting, or supplementing, his predecessor,[15] and it is hard to avoid the impression that his portrait of Themistocles is intended in part at least to counterbalance Herodotus' antipathetic portrayal.

Thucydides digresses from his narrative of events leading to the outbreak of war to explain that the Spartans, too, had a "curse" which they might well be ashamed of, and so were in no position to dredge up yet again the charge against Pericles that one of his ancestors, a Megacles who was archon in the latter part of the seventh century, had dealt impiously with religious suppliants. The Spartans' own more recent treatment of their regent Pausanias was no better. What immediately precipitated Themistocles' final condemnation was the Spartan claim that they had discovered in the course of their investigations evidence that implicated Themistocles in Pausanias' alleged dealings with the Persian king (what this so-called evidence was is nowhere specified in the sources), and they sent a delegation to Athens to demand Themistocles' removal. If we read between the lines of Thucydides' statement that Themistocles "happened already to have been ostracized and was living in Argos, but was also visiting other parts of the Peloponnese" (1. 135. 3), we can see that the Spartans had their own motives for wanting to get rid of Themistocles, who may have been stirring up trouble for Sparta among her dependent states. We in fact hear from other sources of democratic movements in two of these, Elis and Mantineia, at about this time. In any case Thucydides takes this opportunity to narrate the events of Themistocles' escape, first to Corcyra and then to the kingdom of Admetus in Epirus (1. 136), thence overland to Pydna in Macedon and via Naxos to Ephesus (137). Although certain details in this section of Thucydides' narrative have been questioned (for example, the authenticity of the scene in which Themistocles supplicates King Admetus) and later writers varied some of the details (an escape via Thasos and Cyme),[16] on the whole Thucydides' account rings true. Where he got his information we cannot

---

14. K. Ziegler, "Der Ursprung der Exkurse im Thukydides," *Rh. Mus.* 78 (1929), 58–67; F. E. Adcock, *Thucydides and His History*, 23–24; and, most recently, P. J. Rhodes in *Historia* 19 (1970), 399–400; cf. K. von Fritz, *Die griech. Geschichtsschreibung*, I, "Text," 616–17, and O. Luschnat, *RE*, supp. 12 (1970), col. 1107. Helmut Münsch, on the other hand, argues that it shows signs of being a late addition (*Studien zu den Exkursen des Thukydides*

[Heidelberg, 1935], esp. 27–33).

15. For example, 1. 20. 3, 22. 2; 2. 8. 3 and, in general, A. W. Gomme, *Commentary*, I, 148.

16. Thasos in MS. S (Seitenstettensis) of Plut. *Them.* 25. 2; ibid., 26. 1 for Cyme. See F. J. Frost in *CR*, n.s. 12 (1962), 15–16. Rhodes has recently argued that "Naxos and Thasos may represent not alternatives between which we must choose but rival embellishments of a less specific original" (*Historia* 19 [1970], 398).

tell, but the captain of the merchant vessel that bore Themistocles to Ephesus is mentioned several times (1. 137. 2, and at 137. 3 a comment on the "grant of money" with which Themistocles rewarded him for his services), and it may have been someone connected with this captain or his household who was Thucydides' source of information.

With Themistocles' arrival in Asia, an element of the fabulous enters into the story, although not to so great an extent as in later writers who were to rework and heighten Thucydides' account. How much credit are we to place in the letter which Themistocles sent to Artaxerxes, whose contents Thucydides reports at 1. 137. 4? Gomme was sceptical, and it must be admitted that it does not follow the expected form in such apparently invariable items as the prescript.[17] Thucydides' spare narrative of Themistocles' waiting a year to learn the vernacular "as best he could" contrasts with the overstatements of later accounts,[18] and a note of caution is introduced: "The king, as it is said, was amazed" (138. 1); but, for all that, the best that can be said for Thucydides' critical judgement is that he does not go to the lengths of his successors. Diodorus (11. 57) has a wild tale of court intrigue involving Darius' daughter Mandane, which reaches its climax with Themistocles' successfully pleading his case before a Persian jury in their own language. Thucydides is, however, in full control of his critical faculties once again in discussing the variant traditions regarding Themistocles' death and the uncertainty about where his body was buried (1. 138. 4 and 6, where Thucydides identifies his source with the phrase "his relatives say"). The historian closes his account with the comment that Pausanias and Themistocles were "the most famous Greeks of their time" (138. 6). This section, when taken together with the narrative of Themistocles' outwitting the Spartans in the matter of Athens' refortification and then going on to complete the walls of Peiraeus (1. 90–93), provides an invaluable, because early, and, on the whole, critical contribution to our knowledge of Themistocles' life. The importance of these chapters cannot be exaggerated: they constitute the earliest attempt known by one of his countrymen to gather evidence and sift facts about this gifted, if controversial, figure. Moreover, we have in Thucydides' account the earliest detailed and coherent narrative about an ancient figure which is motivated by an interest in the personality of the subject, by considerations, in short, which are primarily biographical.[19]

Thucydides' admiration for Themistocles comes out most forcefully in the section at the end of the excursus in which he tries to analyse the reasons for Themistocles' success.

> Themistocles was a man who showed most surely the force of natural ability [Thucydides thus makes clear where he stands on the nature/training debate

17. Gustav A. Gerhard, *Untersuchungen zur Geschichte des griechischen Briefes* (diss. Heidelberg: H. Laupp, 1903). What appears to be a more authentic formula is found at Thucydides 1. 129. 3, Xerxes' letter to Pausanias (Gerhard, 30, n.77).

18. "Better than a Persian," according to Nepos, *Them.* 10. 1; cf. Quint. *Inst. Orat.* 11. 2. 50 ("optime"). Plutarch, for all his embroideries, is in this detail close to Thucydides (*Them.* 29. 3).

19. F. Leo, *Die griech.-röm. Biographie*, 86. H. Homeyer attempts to discover a truly biographical interest in Herodotus ("Zu den Anfängen der griech. Biographie," *Philologus* 106 [1962], 75–85; cf. A. Momigliano, *The Development of Greek Biography*, 34), but this seems to me unsuccessful in the case of Themistocles (Homeyer, 81).

initiated perhaps by Stesimbrotus] and was, in a more outstanding way than anyone else, worthy of admiration in this respect. For by his own native intelligence, without depending on either advance or, subsequently, additional information, he was both the best judge of proposals which lay immediately before him with the least deliberation, and was also best at guessing about the future over the widest range of what was actually to come. Matters which he had himself in hand he could explain; in those of which he had no personal experience, he did not fall short of an adequate judgement; what was still hidden in the future —both better and worse—he foresaw most clearly. To sum up, through both strength of nature and brevity of rehearsal he was best at devising *extempore* what the situation called for. (1. 138. 3)[20]

For Thucydides, then, Themistocles' most outstanding characteristics were sheer intelligence, a purely natural insight into what the situation in hand called for, coupled with an amazing foresight as to the turn events might take in future. Others might learn through experience, through repeated exposure to similar sets of circumstances, even through advance planning and theoretical exercise; Themistocles was able to choose from among the various alternatives immediately offered, without antecedent deliberation or personal experience, and—the mark of the true statesman, though possessed by few mere politicians—*explain* the crucial factors in his decision to his colleagues or supporters who might not see matters as clearly as he. Thucydides sums it up by saying that through the force of his natural ability, with little or no time for rehearsal, he was able to improvise, or extemporize, a successful performance.

In only one other person, Pericles, are the qualities which Thucydides singles out for comment combined as they are in Themistocles. Three times in the famous evaluation Thucydides comments on Pericles' foresight (2. 65. 5, 6, 13), and Thucydides has him claim for himself that unique blend of intelligence and the capacity to explain (and so to influence others), which is the hallmark of the great leader: γνῶναί τε τὰ δέοντα καὶ ἑρμηνεῦσαι ταῦτα (2. 60. 5; compare 1. 138. 3). As the author of a recent study of Thucydides' psychological terminology shrewdly remarks, "It is certainly not by chance that the portrait of Themistocles is followed almost at once by the entry of Pericles onto the scene."[21]

Another characteristic high on Thucydides' list of admirable qualities is τόλμα, an energetic will-to-action (for which "daring" is too weak a term), which, without a cool calculation of the risks involved, could easily turn into mere foolhardy bravado. In this linguistic field, too, Themistocles not only epitomizes all that is best in Athens, but prefigures Pericles. Themistocles uses the term to describe the motive force behind the Athenian evacuation (1. 91. 5), as the Athenian speaker at Sparta will later (1. 74. 4; cf. 74. 2, προθυμίαν τολμηροτάτην),[22] and Thucydides applies it to Themi-

20. My own translation, although I have occasionally borrowed a phrase from Gomme.

21. P. Huart, *Le vocabulaire d'analyse psychologique dans l'œuvre de Thucydide*, 312. Huart notes the virtual identification of Themistocles and Pericles in respect of ξύνεσις (311–13), πρόνοια and its cognates (349, 352–53; sum-mary at 503–4), and the ability to persuade which is virtually the same as ἑρμηνεῦσαι/ ἐξηγήσασθαι (355, n.7, with refs. to Thuc. 1. 14. 3, 91. 1, 93. 3, and 137. 2).

22. This parallel was noted by Gomme (*Commentary*, I, 259).

stocles' whole naval policy (1. 93. 4). It is precisely this active thrust of their oppo
nents which the conservative Spartans had reason to fear (τὸ τολμηρόν, 1. 102. 3;
the Corinthians at 1. 70. 3 sting the Spartans by calling the Athenians τολμηταί).
This peculiar blend of energy and intellect had brought Athens to the pinnacle of
imperial success, and its possession by the majority of her citizens is one of Pericles'
proudest boasts in the *Funeral Speech*: "This is what singles us out from others, that
in all our undertakings we show a daring which is based on advance calculation
[τολμᾶν...καὶ...ἐκλογίζεσθαι], whereas others derive their boldness from ignorance: if they think, they can no longer act" (2. 40. 3). Pericles urges his hearers to
have the same resolute daring as the fallen soldiers being honoured on this occasion
(2. 43. 1), to base their love for Athens on the realization that her greatness was
achieved through the honourable deeds of their forefathers, who "both knew and
dared to do their duty" (τολμῶντες καὶ γιγνώσκοντες τὰ δέοντα). Thucydides has
Pericles in his last speech gather up some of these linguistic strands to which the historian attached such importance: "Intelligence [ξύνεσις], provided that fortune is
equal, makes boldness [τόλμαν] also much stronger: for it does not trust to hope, but
to reason based on facts, whose foresight [πρόνοια] is much more reliable" (2. 62. 5,
Gomme's translation). This concatenation of terms which have all previously been
applied to Themistocles, coming now from his great successor, can hardly be
accidental.

Gomme remarks that Thucydides' analysis is concerned only with intellectual
qualities: "He ignores that astonishing power and energy which enabled Themistokles
to impose his will on his colleagues at Salamis, as well as his skill as a tactician."[23]
Still less do we hear of any reference to, or defence of, his moral character. But this
need not surprise us. Thucydides was struck, captivated, by a quality which Themistocles possessed to an immeasurably higher degree than any of Thucydides' own
contemporaries among the successors of Pericles: raw intelligence which could be
applied to both present and future. His remaining virtues such as generalship and
willpower he shared with others, who may even have surpassed him in these respects.
His faults, for example, what Gomme calls his "weakness in money matters," had had
their press in gossip and anecdote and were being retailed by Herodotus for the
delectation of his audiences. In Thucydides' opinion they deserved no place in sober
history. As for what most people believed to be Themistocles' greatest, all-but-
unforgivable sin, defection from his country to her most hated enemy, Thucydides
had a more recent and more melancholy example in Alcibiades, and so did nothing
more than record the fact, without blame or rancour, and leave it to lesser minds to
make moral judgements upon.

23. Ibid., 443–44.

3 THE PHILOSOPHICAL AND RHETORICAL SCHOOLS

THE INTEREST IN Themistocles in philosophical circles seems to have originated with Socrates. In Xenophon's *Symposium*, Socrates tells Critias to become worthy of the affection of his friend Autolycus by "seeking into the kind of knowledge which made Themistocles able to bring freedom to Greece" (8. 39). Critias himself is known to have contrasted Themistocles' poverty at the beginning of his public life with the 100-talent fortune which came to light when his goods were confiscated after his condemnation.[1] The type of discussion in which Themistocles' name may have come up is illustrated by several stories told by Xenophon in the *Memorabilia*. For the benefit of Euthydemus, Socrates instigates a lesson on the best form of education by having one of his companions ask, "Themistocles' pre-eminent position among his fellow citizens, so much so that the city looked to him whenever it needed an outstanding man—was this due to converse with some wise man or to natural ability?" (4. 2. 2); in other words, the debate over nature versus education, of which we caught glimpses in Stesimbrotus' treatment,[2] had already begun. Elsewhere, Critobulus asks Socrates, "How did Themistocles make the city love him?" and Socrates replies, "Not by spells and incantations, but by attaching some good amulet to it," that is, by providing useful appendages like the walls and harbour (2. 6. 13). In a section which expands on the theme of the statesman as the man who performs beneficial services to the city, Socrates tells Plato's brother Glaukon that if he persists in his ambition to become the "leading man" in the city, he will "make a name for himself first in the city, then in Greece, then perhaps—like Themistocles—among the barbarians as well" (3. 6. 2). The legend of the Greek who made good in the land of the enemy is already fully

1. *DK*[6], 88 fr. 45 (= Ael. *V.H.* 10. 17). The same set of figures (3 talents at the beginning, 100 at the end, of his career) is quoted by Plutarch from Theopompus. Theophrastus said the amount at the end was 80 talents (*Them.* 25. 3).

2. The connection with Stesimbrotus is drawn by O. Gigon in his commentary on Xen. *Mem.* 2. 6. 13 (1956), p. 138, where there is also a brief discussion of the other Xenophon passages.

formed, and there no longer seems to be any odium attached to Themistocles' name for having betrayed his country.

One of Socrates' admirers, Aeschines of Sphettus, wrote dialogues that featured Socrates expounding his teachings for the benefit of various interlocutors. One of these, *Alcibiades*, seems to have been given over in large part to a discussion of the character of Themistocles.[3] It is of interest that a member of Socrates' circle drew the connection between the characters and careers of Themistocles and Alcibiades; certain characteristics will be shared by the two in Plutarch's treatment of them later. Socrates in the dialogue tantalizes Alcibiades and reduces him to tears by the thought that, for all his emulation of Themistocles, he will not surpass Themistocles in fame or achievements.[4] When Xerxes, "one man who ruled a country the size of Asia," invaded, the Athenians in panic fled to Salamis and "entrusted their affairs to Themistocles to do with as he pleased"; in him lay their one hope of safety. Themistocles for his part realized that it was a matter, not of sheer numbers, but of strategy and, more important, excellence of leadership.

> [Themistocles'] conviction was that success falls as a rule to the side whose affairs are directed by the better man.... The King felt his situation the weaker from the very day that he encountered a better man than himself.

The story is then told of Themistocles' failure, after the victory, to persuade the troops to burn the Hellespontine bridges and of Themistocles' about-face, by which he pretended that he had done the king a service in preventing the Greeks from burning the bridges.

> Hence it is not merely ourselves and the Greek world who regard Themistocles as the author of our deliverance; the very King whom he defeated believed that he owed his preservation to him, and to him alone, such was his pre-eminence in intelligence.[5]

Socrates underlines the moral that even though Themistocles surpassed Xerxes in intelligence, he had not the true knowledge (*episteme*) to avoid falling from popular favour. Socrates asks Alcibiades:

> Who has a better claim, then, to be considered the most powerful man of his age than Themistocles, the generalissimo of the Greeks, and conqueror of a king whose dominions reach from sunrise to sunset? And yet...all his service was not enough to save him from exile and disfranchisement at the hands of the city, but proved too little.[6]

3. This dialogue is quoted extensively by Aelius Aristeides in his Oration 46 (*For the Four*), Dindorf's edition, vol. II, pp. 292 ff. and 369 ff., and further fragments were discovered in a second-century papyrus, *P. Oxy*. XIII (1909), 1608. (Text and numbering of the earlier fragments by H. Krauss [Teubner, 1911]; discussion by H. Dittmar, *Aischines von Sphettos*; translation and discussion by A. E. Taylor in his *Philosophical Studies*, chap. 1, esp. pp. 10 ff., 16–19; see also E. G. Berry in *TAPA* 81 [1950], 1–8.)

4. Ael. Arist. Or. 46, II, 369 Dind.; cf. Cic. *Tusc*. 3. 77, Plut. *Mor*. 69 F.

5. Taylor argues that this use of *phronein* in the sense of "to be wise" is Ionian and goes back to Socrates' teacher Archelaus; it is thus "one echo of the actual phraseology of Socrates" (*Philosophical Studies*, 17).

6. Ael. Arist. II, 292–94 Dind.; part of this section is also preserved on the papyrus (*P. Oxy*. 1608, lines 85–136). (This and the preceding translation are by A. E. Taylor.)

In another part of the dialogue, preserved on the papyrus, Socrates alludes to the story of Themistocles' unfilial treatment of his parents and to the alleged disinheritance of Themistocles by his father.[7] This tale Alcibiades refuses to countenance on grounds that "such conduct betokens a mean character and reaches the height of folly."[8] In another fragment we have the remains of what appears to have been a discussion of whether Themistocles achieved pre-eminence through his natural ability or through training.[9]

Plato's discussion of Themistocles' character takes a different tack. In the *Gorgias* Socrates argues that Gorgias' far-flung claims for the results which rhetoric can achieve must be limited to the extent that when there is call for technical knowledge, as in the building of the walls or harbours or dockyards, it is the craftsman's advice which is sought, not the rhetorician's. To this Gorgias retorts that the shipyards, walls, and harbours would never have been built except on the advice (that is, the persuasive ability) of Themistocles or Pericles (455 B–E). Socrates insists that the true orator should aim at improving the citizens, at making them better *men*, and he flings back Callias' objection that Themistocles is spoken of by the people as a "good man," along with Cimon, Miltiades, and Pericles, by observing that this reduces "goodness" to the mere technique of satisfying one's own desires and those of others (503 C). Judged by the standard of the extent to which they improved the characters of their fellow citizens, the Four were not "good statesmen," otherwise they would not have been thrown over by the people, ostracized, and sent into exile, as Themistocles was (516 D). Socrates' criterion of true statesmanship is a lofty one: the provisioning of the city, not with "harbours and shipyards, walls and tribute and such nonsense," but with "temperance and justice" (519 A).

Plato returns to the subject in the *Meno*, in a passage which, according to E. R. Dodds, "looks like a conscious retreat from the extreme position adopted in the *Gorgias*."[10] Popular opinion had it that Themistocles was a "good and wise man," and yet, if he and the other statesmen of the past had had true *arete*, why could they not teach it to their sons? The only knowledge that Themistocles managed to impart to his son Cleophantus was horsemanship, how to ride and throw the lance from a standing position.[11] At the end of the dialogue Socrates remarks that Themistocles and the other famous men of the past "could not make others like themselves, because it was not through knowledge" that they themselves were "good" or "virtuous," but through "true opinion"; in other words, *political* virtue and wisdom are misnomers (99 B). There may be some relation between the disparagement of Themistocles in these two Platonic dialogues and the more flattering portrait in Aeschines' *Alcibiades*, but the exact relationship among these works must remain a matter for speculation.[12]

7. *P. Oxy.* 1608, lines 1–5 and 38 ff. Cf. also Plut. *Them.* 2; Ael. *V.H.* 2. 12; Nepos, *Them.* 1.

8. *P. Oxy.* 1608, lines 40–42, trans. B. P. Grenfell and A. S. Hunt.

9. Fr. 1, lines 7–15, with the note of Grenfell and Hunt ad loc.

10. *Plato's 'Gorgias'* (Oxford: Clarendon Press, 1959), 360.

11. *Meno* 93 B–E. The argument and the illustration are repeated in the pseudo-Platonic *de Virtute* 376–77.

12. R. S. Bluck, *Plato's 'Meno'* (Cambridge: Cambridge University Press, 1961), 368. The most plausible suggestion seems to be that the attack in the *Gorgias* was answered by a defence

There is a passing allusion to Themistocles' famous retort to a detractor, found in a different version in Herodotus (8. 125), in the *Republic* (329 E–330 A), with Seriphus becoming the critic's place of origin instead of the even more obscure Belbina; it was this version—which probably Plato did not himself originate—that later held the field.[13]

In his last work, *The Laws*, Plato shifted the ground of his attack somewhat: it was not the battle of Salamis which "saved Greece," as people usually said, but rather Marathon was the beginning, and Plataea the end, of salvation of Greece, for these battles made the Greeks "better" and the victories of Salamis and Artemisium did not (707 B–D). Plataea and Marathon are chosen as land battles which inculcated conservative hoplite virtues, as against the degeneracy which Plato believed ensued when the naval "mobs" got the upper hand. Although he does not mention Themistocles by name, it seems clear (as Plutarch, who quotes the passage at *Themistocles* 4. 4, saw) that he had him in mind earlier in the dialogue when the Athenian remarks that the Athenians should never have taken to the sea in an effort to "become like" their enemies, a process which began back in the days of Minos: "It would have been better for many times more than seven youths to have perished [the legendary tribute to Minos] instead of having men turned from steadfast hoplites into sailors, constantly leaping from their ships and then dashing back to them again" (706 B–C).

Apart from the factual material in the *Constitution of Athens*, Aristotle's comments on Themistocles are few and serve only to illustrate certain points he is making. In the *Eudemian Ethics*, as an illustration of entertainments which do not befit their agent, the official embassy which Themistocles made to Olympia is given as an example; it was "not fitting for him, because of his former low station, but would have been for Cimon" (1233 b 10, trans. H. Rackham). The reference shows that the stories of Themistocles' humble origins and of his attempt to outdo Cimon's lavish entertaining at Olympia were already current in the fourth century.[14] The famous wooden wall oracle is alluded to in the *Rhetoric* (I. 15, 1376 a 1). A passing mention in the *Sophistical Refutations* (176 a 1), "What is the difference between asking whether Callias and Themistocles are musical?", seems to be a survival of the earlier philosophical debate over whether the great men of the past owed their attainments to natural disposition or training.[15] There is, in addition, an obscure reference to a "Themistokleion," or monument to Themistocles, in the treatise *History of Animals*,

of Themistocles in the dialogue *Accusation of Socrates*, now no longer extant, by the rhetorician Polycrates (on which see E. R. Dodds, '*Gorgias*,' 28–29), which in turn led to the modified view of Themistocles in *Meno*. The laudatory tones of Aeschines' dialogue may be explained either as an attempt "to undo the harm done to Socrates' memory by his unkind handling of the great democratic statesman in the *Gorgias*" (Dodds, '*Gorgias*,' 30) or "to counter the effect of *both* the *Gorgias and the Meno*" (Bluck, *Plato's 'Meno*,' 118, n.2). When so little remains of Aeschines' and nothing of Polycrates' dialogues, it would be unwise to

dogmatize; P. Natorp suggests that Aeschines' views complement, rather than contradict, Plato's (*Philologus* 51 [1892], 499–500), a view elaborated by Taylor.

13. See, for example, Cicero, *de Sen.* 3. 8.

14. A more extended account is given by Plutarch, *Them.* 5. 4.

15. This debate, over whether Themistocles was musical or not, has also left traces in Aeschines' dialogue *Alcibiades* (*P. Oxy.* XIII, 1608, fr. 1, lines 9–11) and in an anecdote which Plutarch twice relates (*Them.* 2. 4 and *Cim.* 9. 1).

where Aristotle lists it among sites which he describes as "sheltered and marshy...
when after a spell of fine weather the ground is getting warmer."[16]

Aristotle's successor Theophrastus is cited by Plutarch for two details: the size of
Themistocles' fortune at the end of his career, eighty talents (*Them.* 25. 3),[17] and the
story, ascribed to the treatise *On Kingship* (about whose authorship there were doubts
in antiquity), of Themistocles' denunciation of Hieron at the Olympic Games and his
attempt to stir up the spectators to tear the Sicilian tyrant's tent to pieces (25. 1).
A papyrus, containing what appears to be a treatise on literary criticism of the Roman
period, refers to Theophrastus' essay *Peri Kairon*, "On [Political] Occasions," for the
detail left vague by Thucydides that Themistocles had been a "benefactor" of the
Corcyraeans (1. 136. 1): "The Corcyraeans had a quarrel with the Corinthians, and
Themistocles being made arbiter decided that the people of Corinth should pay to the
Corcyraeans twenty talents."[18] The story in fact occurs again in Plutarch (*Them.*
24. 1), where the additional information is given that the dispute had brewed up
over the colony of Leukas; Plutarch, however, fails to name Theophrastus as his
source.[19]

As for the philosopher Epicurus, Plutarch notes his scorn of political men:
"Epicurus spurns under his feet the achievements of Themistocles and Miltiades, and
makes them cheap."[20] Neokles, the name of Themistocles' father and first son, was
also held by several members of Epicurus' family,[21] a circumstance which gave the
writer of an epigram, mistakenly assigned to Menander, the opportunity to pen the
following playful lines:

Hail, twin offspring of Neokles, you of whom
One saved your country from slavery, the other from folly.
(*Palatine Anthology*, 7. 72)

The names of Marathon and Salamis, Miltiades and Themistocles, all the glories
of Athens' past, echo again and again through the oratorical literature of the fourth
century. But it is doubtful how much *new* and trustworthy information we are likely
to find here, for the fact of the matter is that the orators were not scholars, men
interested in delving into their city's past and verifying the facts; for them, it was more
a matter of turning familiar examples to good rhetorical effect. Jacoby's scathing
condemnation of the "truly astonishing ignorance of most of the Attic orators and

16. *Hist. Anim.* 6. 15, 569 b 12, trans. D'Arcy
W. Thompson.

17. Plutarch does not name the work in
which Theophrastus mentioned this detail, but
it may have been the same as that in which
there occurred a discussion of the distinction
drawn by Aristeides between private and public
justice (Plut. *Arist.* 25. 2–3, continuing the
citation down to διετέλεσε with Wimmer,
Theophrasti Eresii Opera, 448, fr. 136). Theophrastus may thus have contrasted Themistocles and Aristeides in respect of *personal*
honesty.

18. *P. Oxy.* 1012, fr. 9, ii, lines 28–33, trans.
A. S. Hunt (*P. Oxy.* VIII [1910], p. 99).

19. Plutarch wrote a work, now lost, on
Theophrastus' *On [Political] Occasions* (no. 53
in the Lamprias catalogue). On Theophrastus'
historical works, see F. Dümmler, "Zu den
historischen Arbeiten der ältesten Peripate-
tiker," *Rh. Mus.*, n.F. 42 (1881), 179 ff.; O.
Regenbogen, "Theophrastos," *RE*, supp. 7
(1940), cols. 1516–21. An attempt to reconstruct
Theophrastus' account of ostracism has been
made by A. E. Raubitschek in *Class. et Med.*
19 (1958), 73 ff.

20. Usener, *Epicurea*, fr. 559, p. 329, lines
13 ff. = Plut. *Mor.* 1097 C.

21. J. Kirchner, *PA*, 10640, 10641.

the little use they made of the history of their city" seems to be largely justified.[22] The first of the orators whom we know to have referred specifically to Themistocles is Andocides, whose speech, or perhaps pamphlet, *To his Club-members*, Plutarch quotes (only to condemn) for the story that "the Athenians stole away his remains [probably from the 'spendid' tomb' in Magnesia, just mentioned by Plutarch, or from a secret burial place in Attica (Thuc. 1. 138. 6)] and scattered them abroad."[23] "Andocides is worthy of no attention," Plutarch comments, "...for he is trying by his lies to incite the oligarchs against the people" (*Them.* 32. 4, trans. Perrin). The context in which the reference occurred, and its date, are unknown.[24]

The orators chose freely from the stock of patriotic motifs from their city's past, and the examples in which Themistocles' name most frequently comes up are those glorious feats with which he was almost invariably associated: the repulse of Xerxes at Salamis and the rebuilding of the city's walls. Lysias turns the example to good effect in the speech *Against Eratosthenes*, who, he says, "if he had been a political associate of Themistocles, would be making a great show of working for the construction of the walls—just as he is now doing of working with Theramenes to take them down!" Lysias then drives the contrast home: "The one built the walls against the Spartans' wishes, the other destroyed them only after deceiving his fellow citizens" (Or. 12. 63). In the speech *Against Nicomachus*, who was charged with illegally prolonging his appointment as *anagrapheus*, or "transcriber," of Solon's laws, the position which he had been assigned after the "Four Hundred" were deposed in 411 B.C., the jury is asked to contrast men like Teisamenus and Nicomachus with "the lawgivers whom your forefathers chose, Solon, Themistocles, and Pericles, because they believed that the laws would be of the same character as the lawgiver" (30. 28). Themistocles' name figures rather strangely in a catalogue of *Nomothetai*, and if this is not merely a selection from among famous men of the past for the expected rhetorical triad, it may be suggested that what is lurking here is a memory (correct or not) of the evacuation and mobilization decree before Salamis, or perhaps the decree for recall of the exiles. In the *Epitaphios*, or "Funeral Oration," which is generally thought not to be by Lysias on stylistic grounds, the events of the Persian Wars (along with the attack of the Amazons) naturally figure among the "travails of our ancestors" successfully overcome. The sea battle at Artemisium is a "victory" for Athens (2. 31); the description of Salamis and the terrors felt before the actual attack by Xerxes' fleet (2. 37–40) is a highly charged, if somewhat overwrought, description in the manner of Thucydides:

Beyond all compare did those men in their valour surpass all mankind, whether in their counsels [*bouleumasi*] or in the perils of that war.... They made the fullest and fairest contribution in aid of the freedom of the Greeks by providing Themistocles as commander, most competent to speak and decide [*gnonai*] and

22. *FGrHist* III b (Supp.) i. 95; "I include Isokrates," he adds in vol. ii, n.84.

23. Andocides fr. 4 (Blass) = Plut. *Them.* 32. 4, trans. Perrin. See D. Macdowell, *Andokides 'On the Mysteries'* (Oxford: Clarendon

Press, 1962), 191.

24. H. A. Holden, *Plutarch's 'Life of Themistocles'*[3], 177, quotes authorities for 411 or 420–418 B.C. (Jebb).

act, and ships more numerous than those of all their allies, and men of the greatest experience. For indeed who among the rest of the Greeks could have vied with these in decision [gnomei], in number and in valour?[25]

The tone is very much that of the Athenian speaker at Sparta in Thucydides (1. 74), where Themistocles is also mentioned, and the section in the *Epitaphios* may even be modelled directly upon the earlier speech.

Isocrates, a teacher of rhetoric and a "political publicist,"[26] rather than an orator and statesman, lived almost a full century from 436 to 338 B.C. His political message was simple and unswerving throughout his long career: Greece must unite under a strong leader—even, if need be, a Macedonian—and the threat (real or magnified) to Hellenism posed by Persia must be beaten back. Obviously, the great victories against Persia of an earlier generation, which had been won only through more or less united action, were a useful example and contrast with the contemporary period, and so references to the Persian Wars dot Isocrates' pages. The first of these great calls to unity is the *Panegyricus* of about 388 B.C. Athens' claim to leadership against the barbarian is supported by the usual examples of her past successes; the Amazons (as in Lysias' *Epitaphios* 4) share the stage with Darius and Xerxes (Or. 4. 68–71, 89–98). Although in this section of the speech the victory of Salamis is given climactic emphasis as constituting the winning of the whole war (98), Themistocles is not mentioned by name. His name occurs only in passing later to illustrate the persistent spinelessness of the Persians: although he had defeated them severely at Salamis, "they thought him worthy of the greatest gifts" (154). It may be worth remarking here on Isocrates' comment, a little further on in the speech, that the "Athenians while away their most pleasant hours with stories [mythoi] of the Trojan and Persian Wars" (157), surely an indication of how some of the fanciful tales surrounding Themistocles' career may have originated.

From the period of the Social War date two of Isocrates' political works, the *Areopagiticus* and *On the Peace*.[27] The *Areopagiticus* forcefully expresses that conservative philosophy which, as we shall see later, can be detected in the historical writings of some of Isocrates' pupils: Androtion and perhaps Theopompus. What can re-establish Athens in a position of moral strength at home and leadership abroad is a return to an aristocratic state under the guidance of her oldest Council, the Areopagus. Naturally, the name of Themistocles, that archdemocrat, is missing, and the achievements against the Persians are passed over with the merest mention (Or. 7. 75). The end of Athens' war with her allies in 355 occasioned a speech in which Isocrates urged his city to abandon all thoughts of empire and to adopt a policy of true independence for her allies, as in the early years of the Delian League. In it, contemporary demagogues (Aristophon and Eubulus are probably meant) are put in the

---

25. Or. 2. 40, 42, trans. W. R. M. Lamb (Loeb Classical Library). There is a slight echo in Isocrates, *Panegyricus* (Or. 4. 98), and an ironical summary of these patriotic motifs in the Platonic *Menexenus* (241 B–C, with its mocking echoes of Thucydides).

26. Jacoby's phrase, *FGrHist* III b (Supp.) i. 90.

27. Jacoby dates the *Areopagiticus* to "early in the time of the Social War" and *On the Peace* to "during its latter part or even immediately after it" (*FGrHist* III b (Supp.) ii. 85 n.54).

same class as Hyperbolus and Cleophon, and contrasted with Aristeides, Themistocles, and Miltiades—of course to the disadvantage of the former (Or. 8. 75). Themistocles' achievements are twice alluded to in the *Antidosis* (about 354 B.C.), and in the first of these passages he is named in a catalogue of past worthies along with Solon, Cleisthenes, and Pericles. On the basis of his ability to persuade the Athenians to swallow so unpalatable a remedy as abandoning the city, he must have been an orator of no mean skill.[28] Another such listing of great men of the past, with a description of Miltiades replacing that of Solon in the earlier triad, occurs later in the speech; Isocrates asks, "Who was the man who, after Miltiades, freed the Greeks and led our ancestors forward to the leadership and supremacy they held? Saw clearly the natural excellence of the Peiraeus and encircled the city with a wall against the Spartans' wishes?" (*Antid.* 307).

Towards the end of his long life Isocrates wrote the *Panathenaicus*, "a last testimonial to the glory of Athens."[29] The theme of unity is here abandoned for a straightforward encomium on Athens' past accomplishments, and in surveying the period of the Persian Wars Isocrates draws a sharp contrast between Athenian and Spartan reaction to the barbarian threat:

> The Lacedaemonians contributed to this battle [Salamis] the leadership of Eurybiades, who, had he carried into effect what he intended to do, could have been prevented by nothing in the world from bringing destruction upon the Hellenes, whereas the Athenians furnished Themistocles, who, by the common assent of all, was credited with being responsible for the victorious outcome of that battle as well as for all the other successes which were achieved during that time.[30]

It should be noted that Isocrates here reflects a very different tradition from that followed by his pupil Ephorus, who, as can be inferred from the account of Diodorus, seems to have glossed over the tensions between Themistocles and Eurybiades and portrayed them as working together in harmonious understanding.[31] Indeed, there is a glaring discrepancy between the chauvinistic tone of Isocrates' last speech and the "panhellenic" slant he gives to Atheno-Spartan relations in the *Panegyricus*.[32] And the ascription to Themistocles of almost single-handed responsibility for the victory of Salamis and "other successes" is in noticeable conflict with the conservative view as reflected by Isocrates himself in the *Areopagiticus*.

We may turn now to the greatest of the Attic orators, Demosthenes. In the first of the speeches delivered in his own name on a public matter, *Against Leptines* (354 B.C.), he summarizes the Thucydidean version of the story of Themistocles' duping the Spartans while Athens' walls were being rebuilt. He contrasts Themistocles' duplicity

28. Or. 15. 233. The rhetorical point is made here, as at *Archidamus* 43, that, in exchange for a few days of being without their own possessions, "they became masters of others' for many years." (Themistocles is not named but the splendid phrase occurs that the Athenians, in abandoning Athens, "made freedom their fatherland.")

29. G. Norlin, in the Introduction to his Loeb translation (*Isocrates*, II, p. 368).

30. Or. 5. 51, trans. Norlin.

31. Ephorus' account is discussed in the following chapter.

32. Cf. especially Or. 4, secs. 85 ff.

with the openness of Conon, who defeated the Spartans in battle and then rebuilt Athens' walls, and Themistocles comes off the worse for the comparison (Or. 20. 73–74). In another of Demosthenes' early political speeches, *Against Aristocrates* (352 B.C.), he contrasts the relatively restrained honours which the Athenians bestowed on their great generals of the Persian Wars with the excessiveness (as Demosthenes considered it) of their response to Charidemus. Miltiades and Themistocles, he says, were not memorialized with bronze statues erected in their honour by their country- men, and yet the respect in which they were held was no less real. Then he adds the interesting comment that, contrary to current usage, the victories of Marathon and Salamis were not spoken of as "Miltiades' victory" or "Themistocles' victory," but "the city's."[33] Somewhat later in the speech, he draws the opposite moral: our ances- tors could also punish men who acted wrongly. "When they caught Themistocles presumptuously setting himself above the people, they banished him from Athens, and found him guilty of siding with the Medes."[34] Demosthenes' wording here should not be pressed for accuracy of detail, chronological or otherwise, for in the next sentence he illustrates his point with a reference that shows that he has confused the ostracism of Cimon with the earlier condemnation of his father, Miltiades. Themi- stocles' name occurs one final time in the speech, again with Miltiades', when the modesty of their scale of life, and in particular the humble nature of their private houses, are contrasted with what Demosthenes believes to be the tasteless ostentation of the leading men of his own day.[35]

The political oratory of the 340s was a most opportune time, for men on both sides of the question of what stance should be taken towards Philip, to recall to the Assembly examples from Athens' past. The first reference that we can trace to the evacuation decree before Salamis, under the identification the "Themistocles Decree," occurred in a speech made by Aeschines in his anti-Philip period, "apparently in the second half of 348."[36] Allusion to this is made by Demosthenes in his speech *On the False Embassy*, delivered in 343 B.C.: "Who harangued you with those long and fine speeches, reading out the decrees of Miltiades and Themistocles...? Was it not Aeschines?"[37] In his reply Aeschines charges Demosthenes with having insulted Philocrates, through whom the peace treaty with Philip had been concluded, "as if he [Demosthenes] were passing judgement on Alcibiades or Themistocles, those men who stood out among the Greeks in reputation" (Or. 2. 9). In his later attack on Demosthenes in the speech *Against Ctesiphon*, Aeschines pointedly asks the jurors, "Does Themistocles seem to you to be the better man, your general when you won over the Persian in the sea fight at Salamis—or Demosthenes, who recently left his battle station?" (Or. 3. 181). In

33. *Against Aristocrates* 196–98. The refer- ence in 196 has been thought to have some bearing on the question of the authenticity of the Ostia bust (see below, p. 145, n.7). These themes of the absence of a statue and the refusal to call the victories Miltiades' or Themi- stocles' are copied almost directly in the forged or plagiarized speech *On Organization*, secs. 21–22.

34. *Against Aristocrates* 205, trans. J. H. Vince (Loeb Classical Library).

35. Ibid., 207. (Cf. *On Organization* 29, where Themistocles' undistinguished house joins com- pany with those of Cimon and Aristeides.)

36. C. Hignett, *Xerxes' Invasion*, 459.

37. *On the False Embassy* 303. The Greek text reads "the Miltiades-and-Themistocles decree," but this is generally emended to "the decree of Miltiades and [the one] of Themi- stocles"; the scholiast's note on the passage clearly understands two separate evacuation decrees to have been intended.

the emotional peroration of the speech Aeschines summons up the shades of Solon and Aristeides, "Themistocles and the dead of Marathon and Plataea, and the very graves of our forefathers," who, he says, will groan aloud if Demosthenes is crowned (3. 257–59). In his equally impassioned rebuttal, Demosthenes, too, invokes the name of Themistocles as an example of Athenian love of freedom and *arete*, and asks, "Who would not exult in the valour of those famous men who, rather than yield to a conqueror's behests, left city and country and made the war-galleys their home; who chose Themistocles, the man who gave them that counsel, as their commander, and stoned Cyrsilus to death for advising obedient submission?"[38] Aeschines had ended his speech by summoning up the heroes of the past, and Demosthenes counters with an oath by the victors of "Marathon and Plataea, Salamis and Artemisium, and the many other good men who lie buried in tombs which the state provides" (Or. 18. 208).

Of the minor orators, Dinarchus in his speech *Against Demosthenes*, delivered in 323 B.C., gives brief mention to "Aristeides and Themistocles, men who built the city's walls and brought tribute up to the Acropolis from the willing and eager Greek allies" (Or. 1. 37). And, at about the same time, Hypereides, in his *Funeral Oration* for the heroes of the Lamian War, compares the fallen Leosthenes with "Miltiades and Themistocles and the others who, in freeing Greece, made their country honoured and their own lives famous"; "Leosthenes," he continues, "so far surpassed them in courage and intelligence [*phronesei*] that, although they fought off the barbarian force when it attacked, he prevented it from attacking at all" (Or. 6. 37–38).

By the fourth century Themistocles had taken his place among the other great names of Athens' past. As F. J. Frost has observed, "In general, the memory of the great man was such that all factions within the fourth-century democracy evoked his name to support their arguments."[39] For the orators, he provided a useful *exemplum* of how the city had made good her claims to superiority over the barbarians in a more vigorous age; Themistocles keeps company with Miltiades, Aristeides, and Cimon, and the animosities between them are all but forgotten. When any specific accomplishments are alluded to, it is invariably Salamis and the walls that are mentioned. Themistocles is compared to fourth-century counterparts like Conon for intelligence (or, if the comparison is an unfavourable one, guile). His defection to Persia is forgotten, or at least forgiven.[40] More than once he finds himself in the venerable company of Solon. The philosophers, on the other hand, probably taking their lead from Socrates, were primarily interested in his character. What was it in his personal make-up that enabled him to achieve greatness? How corruptible was he? Was he possessed of true knowledge? Virtue? Parallels between his career and that of Alcibiades could not fail to suggest themselves. Plato, although he was concerned to remove the great

38. *De Corona* 204, trans. C. A. Vince and J. H. Vince (Loeb Classical Library). The reference to Cyrsilus is apparently to the same incident as that related by Herodotus (9. 5) regarding Lycides (cf. also Lycurgus, *Against Leocrates* 122).

39. "Themistocles' Place in Athenian Poli-

tics," *Calif. Studies Class. Ant.* 1 (1968), 109.

40. R. W. Macan remarked that "the *Rettung* by Thucydides, the diminished horror of Medism, and the re-adjustment of the perspective, due to mere lapse of time, have brought justice to the memory of the 'Liberator of Hellas'" (*Herodotus, Books VII–IX*, II, 32).

military men of the past from their heroic pedestals, seems to have penetrated more deeply into Themistocles' true excellence.[41]

It is the historical writers as such who might have had the greatest contribution to make, but unfortunately this potential, as will be seen in the next chapter, is not realized in the surviving fragments.

41. "Of all the heroes of the war," notes Macan, "Themistokles stands highest [in Plato's writings], his name occurs most frequently" (ibid., 50).

4 FOURTH-CENTURY HISTORIANS

The Atthidographers

HELLANICUS, born at Mytilene on the island of Lesbos, is the first writer we know of to have composed a prose history of Athens, or *Atthis*, to give it the somewhat artificial label which was apparently devised by the librarians at Alexandria.[1] These works seem generally to have been year-by-year accounts of events from the earliest period, that of the (mythical) kings, to the writers' own day. A discussion of Themistocles' career would have been inevitable in an *Atthis*; unfortunately, there is not a phrase in the fragments specifically assigned to Hellanicus (which appeared not earlier than 406 B.C.)[2] which seems to have any bearing upon it. Hellanicus also wrote a *Persika* in at least two books which, like the *Atthis*, began with mythical times and continued at least as far as the Persian Wars. We learn from a reference in the treatise *On the Malice of Herodotus* that Hellanicus said that the Naxians had come over from the Persian to the Greek side before Salamis with six ships (Herodotus' figure is four); from this single, though quite secure, bit of evidence it can be inferred that his *Persika* contained an account of the battle of Salamis, but there is nothing in the extant remains to suggest how extensive Themistocles' role might have been.

The first native Athenian to write an *Atthis* was Cleidemus, whose book was published shortly before 350 B.C.[3] All we have left of his account of Themistocles is the stratagem by which Themistocles was said to have provisioned the crews of the ships who embarked before the battle of Salamis.

> When the Athenians were going down to the Peiraeus and abandoning their city, the Gorgon's head was lost from the image of the goddess; and then Themi-

1. *FGrHist* 323 a (see also F. Jacoby, *Atthis*, 68–69); L. Pearson, *Early Ionian Historians*, chap. 5.
2. 323 a F 25 records the freeing of the slaves who had fought at Arginusae in 406 B.C.
3. See W. G. Forrest, *GRBS* 10 (1969), 277, and n.1.

stocles, pretending to search for it, and ransacking everything, thereby discovered
an abundance of money hidden away in the baggage, which had only to be confiscated, and the crews of the ships were well provided with rations and wages.
(Plut. *Them.* 10. 6–7 = *FGrHist* 323 F 21)

We know from the same chapter in Plutarch and a similar reference in the Aristotelian *Constitution of Athens* (23. 1) that there was another version of this incident,
according to which the Council of the Areopagus was "most responsible" for manning
the ships.

> When the generals were at a loss at the turn events had taken, and had issued a
> proclamation that each man was to save himself as best he could, the Areopagus
> provided and distributed eight drachmae per man and effected the embarka-
> tion.

It is possible to detect here the results of a contemporary debate over the question,
Who was mainly responsible for the victory of Salamis, and so the salvation of
Greece? Cleidemus maintained that it was Themistocles; the other side (and some
have wished to give to the anonymous source the name of Androtion) championed
the claims of the Areopagus.[4] It has recently been suggested that Cleidemus' *Atthis*
was the source of the evacuation decree mentioned by Plutarch at *Themistocles* 10. 4,
a fuller version of which was discovered on an inscription from Troizen.[5]

Apart from the assumed polemic with Cleidemus, no source directly connects any
detail in Androtion's *Atthis* with the name of Themistocles, who must, however, have
been mentioned in view of the fact that Androtion discussed ostracism at some length.[6]
If those scholars are correct who ascribe the historical sections of the *Constitution of
Athens* to Androtion,[7] his few nuggets of factual information about Themistocles were
deeply buried in a great deal of fanciful theorizing. Chapter 23 of the *Constitution*
continues with a contrast of Themistocles and Aristeides—the motif can be traced as
far back as Herodotus 8. 79—both of whom are termed "leaders of the people" during
the period following the battle of Salamis.

> The latter [Themistocles] had the greatest renown for military skill, while the
> former [Aristeides] was famous as a statesman and as the most upright man of
> his time. For this reason they used the one as a general, the other as a counsellor.
> Though they were political rivals, they collaborated in the reconstruction of the
> walls of the city. (23. 3–4)[8]

The contrast between the two types of leaders, the general who "practised military
affairs" and the politician who counselled the citizens on the best course of action,

4. The ideological polemic between Cleidemus and Androtion is developed to implausible
lengths by J. H. Schreiner, *Aristotle and
Perikles, SO,* supp. 21 (1968), 54 ff.

5. G. L. Huxley, "Kleidemos and the 'Themistocles Decree,'" *GRBS* 9 (1968), 313–18.

6. *FGrHist* 324 F 6, discussed more fully in
chapter 11, pp. 185–86.

7. Jacoby, *Atthis,* 74, with n.22; J. Day and
M. Chambers, *Aristotle's History of Athenian
Democracy,* 7–11. Other influences have also
been detected: Gomme saw Theopompus
"behind" chapters 24. 1, 26, and 28. 3.

8. This and the following translation are by
K. von Fritz and E. Kapp, *Aristotle's 'Constitution of Athens' and Related Texts.*

became a commonplace in the fourth century,[9] and finds its way into Plutarch, who has Aristeides distinguish between "you [Themistocles], a magistrate and a general, and me, an assistant and counsellor" (*Arist.* 8. 3). A similar distinction also lies behind Plutarch's comment that Cimon "did not take second place to Miltiades in daring, nor to Themistocles in intelligence"; he equalled both men in military virtues, but surpassed them in political ones (*Cim.* 5. 1). In chapter 25 the *Constitution* traces the breakdown of the old "leadership of the Areopagus," which is said to have lasted for seventeen years after the battle of Salamis. Ephialtes brought indictments against individual Areopagites for misconduct in office, "with the assistance of Themistocles, who was himself a member of the Areopagus and was about to be tried for treasonable collaboration with Persia" (25. 3). There follows an elaborate account of Themistocles' playing a devious game as double agent between the Areopagus and Ephialtes, and it concludes, "At the next meeting of the Council of the Five Hundred, and later, before the Assembly of the People, Ephialtes and Themistocles denounced the Areopagitae again and again until they succeeded in depriving the Areopagus of its power" (25. 4). Wherever its author got his information connecting Themistocles with Ephialtes' attack on the Areopagus of 462/1 B.C., whether from Androtion or some other writer, it is almost certainly misinformation; on any reasonable reconstruction, Themistocles had long since been in Persia at the time of Ephialtes' reforms.[10] In the quick survey of the "leaders" (*prostatai*) of the opposing factions of "democrats and aristocrats" in chapter 28, the treatise once again (as at 23. 3) lists Themistocles and Aristeides as joint leaders of the *demos*, which provides a useful corrective to the oversimplified scheme according to which Themistocles and Aristeides were always on opposing sides, the former as leader of the people and the latter, almost by default, as representative of the old aristocracy.[11]

The *Atthis* of Phanodemus, who was an orator and director of public finance at Athens in the 330s, is specifically cited for the location of Xerxes' vantage point for the battle of Salamis, "above the Herakleion, where only a narrow passage separates the island [that is, Salamis] from Attica" (*FGrHist* 325 F 24). According to other ancient authors, this sanctuary of Heracles was at the narrowest point of the Salamis straits, and it was from here that Xerxes intended to build a causeway to the island, a plan he never carried to fulfilment.[12] The only other citations from Phanodemus' treatment of events in this period touch the career of Cimon (Ff 22, 23). Although certainty in this matter is impossible, it may be that Phanodemus' testimony lies behind Plutarch's apparent synchronism of Cimon's last campaign to Cyprus and Themistocles' death.[13]

9. J. E. Sandys (*Aristotle's 'Constitution of Athens'*[2], 99) cites Aristotle, *Politics* 1309 a 39, and Isocrates, *Panathenaicus* 143.

10. See Appendix A. There is an unsuccessful defence of this strange account by P. N. Ure, "When Was Themistocles Last in Athens?" *JHS* 41 (1921), 165–78. A similar story is found in an abridged form in a late Hypothesis to Isocrates' *Areopagiticus* in which Ephialtes and Themistocles are said to have joined forces "because they owed money to the State and knew that, if they were brought to trial by the Areopagites, they would pay it all back."

11. See, in general, the remarks of F. J. Frost, "Themistocles' Place in Athenian Politics," *Calif. Studies Class. Ant.* 1 (1968), 111–12.

12. Ctesias, *FGrHist* 688 F 13 (30); Aristodemus, *FGrHist* 104 F 1 (2).

13. Plut. *Them.* 31. 4–7; *Cim.* 18. 6–7. For a discussion of this synchronism, see Appendix A.

Of the account of Themistocles by Philochorus, the last of the Atthidographers, almost nothing remains. The merest traces of his treatment of Themistocles' fortification of Peiraeus survive. He mentioned the *krepis* of some construction in the harbour complex and discussed the name Kantharos given to the largest of the three harbours (328 Ff 201, 203). Although the term *krepis* might refer to the quay of the new harbour (cf. Pollux 9. 28), Photius, the source of the quotation, goes on to explain it as a "place in Athens." Jacoby therefore suggested that Philochorus had referred to the so-called tomb of Themistocles, which was described by a writer of about the same period, Diodorus, as a *krepis eumegethes*, "of goodly size," with an altar-like structure upon it. Another possibility may be that Philochorus' reference is to the trophy said by Pausanias (1. 36. 1) to have been erected by the Athenians on Salamis, which the late "Themistocles Epistle" 12 describes as "of stone and very large" (*eumegethes*, p. 752 Hercher). The severely abbreviated citation makes a decision difficult, but it seems safe enough to conclude, with Jacoby, that the description occurred "in the third book of the *Atthis* which must have recorded the building of the Peiraeus harbour and which contained also what Ph[ilochorus] had to say about Themistocles."[14] It is also possible that a two-line epigram cited from Philochorus by Harpocration was quoted by Philochorus in connection with the Themistoclean fortification of 493.[15]

"Universal" Historians

Ephorus of Cyme, who lived *c*. 405 to 330 B.C. and became a pupil of Isocrates at Athens, wrote a *History* from the Dorian invasion to Philip's siege of Perinthos in 341 B.C. The period which coincided with Themistocles' career was treated in books 9 to 11, book 10 in particular being devoted to the Persian Wars. Although ancient authors cite Ephorus himself directly only a few times for this important period, it is now generally agreed that in book 11 of his *Bibliotheca* Diodorus of Sicily, writing in the first century B.C., was using Ephorus as his main source for affairs in Greece. A case in point is the discussion of relations between Themistocles and Pausanias. The author of the essay *On the Malice of Herodotus*, which is ascribed to Plutarch, quotes Ephorus directly: "Ephorus, in writing about Themistocles, says he knew of the treachery of Pausanias and his negotiations with the King's generals; 'but,' he says, 'when Pausanias told him about it and invited him to share in the expected rewards, he was not persuaded to accept the offer.'"[16] The similarity of wording in Diodorus is quite striking and cannot be accounted for on any hypothesis other than that Ephorus was Diodorus' immediate source. (Whether the chronological implausibilities and generally disconnected nature of Diodorus' narrative are to be laid at Ephorus' door is another matter.)

According to Plutarch (*Them.* 27. 1), Ephorus took the majority view, against Thucydides and Charon of Lampsacus, in bringing Themistocles face to face, not

14. *FGrHist* III b (Supp.) i. 571.
15. This epigram is discussed in chapter 10.

16. *De mal. Her.* 855 F, trans. Pearson (= *FGrHist* 70 F 189).

with the son Artaxerxes, but with Xerxes himself. As far as Ephorus can be detected behind Diodorus' account of Themistocles' escape from Greece, Ephorus' version apparently followed Thucydides' narrative closely but, as Jacoby points out, abbreviated it somewhat (Thucydides records stops at Corcyra and Pydna which Diodorus omits), made changes in certain details (Themistocles' journey overland through the land of the Molossi to the coast, Diodorus 11. 56. 3), and coloured the story of Themistocles' adventures in Asia through the addition of numerous romantic details, probably from a *Persika*.[17] The last part of Ephorus' narrative of Themistocles' flight seems to be preserved, in an abbreviated form, in some papyrus fragments of *c*. A.D. 200: "It is necessary to (return?) to what (happened) then concerning Themistocles. Some say that he [sc. Themistocles] reminded him [presumably Xerxes] of his warnings about both the sea-fight and the bridge; but with regard to the sea-fight...."[18] The reference seems to be, as the original editors Grenfell and Hunt observe, to Themistocles' reception at the court of Xerxes, and there is an allusion to a disagreement among the ancient accounts ("some say")—about what we are not told, but the context suggests that the disagreement involved the *content* of Themistocles' speech.[19] This excerpt and the fuller version of the story in Diodorus (11. 58) make clear that Ephorus had Themistocles make his defence before the king in person, not, as in Thucydides (1. 137), by letter. But in one detail the phrases used by the two authors are strikingly similar: Thucydides has Themistocles remind the king of his good services, mentioning "the advance information of the withdrawal from Salamis and of the bridges"; in our fragment, Ephorus says Themistocles "gave advance information about the naval battle and the bridge." The account in Ephorus apparently continued, as it does in Diodorus (11. 58. 4–59), with an excursus on the character of Themistocles and the Athenians' ingratitude to him: "that while he was dishonoured by the city, the city owing to his achievements was held by the Greeks to be worthy of the highest honour which (city founded)...a great empire...(the city) which was the wisest and justest became the most...and severe to him...."[20] The gist of the passage is clear and the gaps can be filled by reference to Diodorus (11. 59. 3), who presents a verbatim echo. There is mention in a later fragment (fr. 31) of a "gift of land," which may refer, as the editors suggest, to the king's "gifts" to Themistocles of several Asian cities.

It seems to be legitimate to try to fill out these directly attested fragments by going to Diodorus' account; the assumption, based on the observed correspondence between Diodorus and Ephorus elsewhere, will be that Ephorus' treatment of these events lies not far beneath the surface. Ephorus may have treated Themistocles' early life and career in view of the anecdote preserved among the fragments of book 10 of Diodorus. When Themistocles was asked by a man where he could find a wealthy son-in-law, he replied, "Look for a man without money rather than money without the man" (10, fr. 32). This *bon mot* is preserved in several later authors, but Ephorus gave it a

17. *FGrHist* II C, p. 90. See Jacoby's comments at *FGrHist* II C, pp. 31, 90.

18. *P. Oxy.* XIII, 1610, fr. 1, lines 4–13, trans. Grenfell and Hunt.

19. So Jacoby, *FGrHist* III C, p. 90.

20. *P. Oxy.* 1610, frs. 3–5, lines 18–31, trans. Grenfell and Hunt.

new twist, for in the version which Diodorus followed, Themistocles proceeds to advise his interlocutor to marry his daughter to Cimon, "and this was the way that Cimon became wealthy,[21] secured his release from prison, called the magistrates who had imprisoned him to turn in their 'accounts' and secured their condemnation." The incident has all the odour of a fabrication—the more since, in historical fact, Cimon's bride was an Alcmeonid, a granddaughter of Megacles (Plut. *Cim.* 4. 10). Themistocles' helpful advice to Cimon seems to represent Ephorus' attempt to reconcile and smooth over the differences between Themistocles and his political rivals which the earlier, Herodotean tradition had been at pains to emphasize and even exaggerate.

The same motive can be seen to be at work in Diodorus' narrative of the engagements of 480 B.C. There is none of the acrimonious wrangling between Themistocles and his fellow generals, none of the "wise duplicity" exercised by Themistocles on his fellow generals to secure his own way; in Diodorus all Themistocles' dealings with his fellow Greeks are harmonious, and his stratagems are reserved for the Persians (and, later, the Spartans). Thus, in describing the locale and size of the Greek fleet before the engagements off Cape Artemisium, Diodorus comments, "Their admiral [*nauarchos*] was Eurybiades, but it was Themistocles who managed the affairs of the fleet, for he, by reason of his sagacity and skill as a general, enjoyed great favour not only with the Greeks throughout the fleet but also with Eurybiades himself, and all men looked to him and hearkened to him eagerly."[22] This is a far cry from the intrigues involving the two commanders in Herodotus' account (8. 4–5). Later, Themistocles counselled that the confrontation with the Persian fleet take place at Salamis, "and by presenting...many other facts pertinent to the occasion he persuaded all present to cast their votes with him for the plan he recommended."[23] Not a word about Mnesiphilus! Before the battle itself "Eurybiades, accompanied by Themistocles, undertook to encourage the crews and incite them to face the impending struggle" (11. 16. 1). Themistocles' ruse by which he lures the Persian fleet into the straits is tactfully motivated: he sent the message to Xerxes "because he perceived that the admiral, Eurybiades, was unable to overcome the mood of his forces" (11. 17. 1; contrast Herodotus 8. 74–75). And protocol is observed by having the Samian swimmer bring news of the king's reactions to Eurybiades (11. 17. 4). As battle is about to be joined, the Greeks are arranged in battle formation by "staff-members of Eurybiades and Themistocles" (11. 18. 1). Whichever of the two extremes, Ephorus' harmony or Herodotus' acerbity between the generals, is more correct—and in this, as in most matters, the truest answer probably lies somewhere in the middle—the reason behind Ephorus' roseate picture is not far to seek: it is an inheritance from Isocrates, whose world view was both panhellenic and anti-Persian.[24]

21. Alternatively, gossip had it that Cimon enriched himself by marrying his sister Elpinike to the millionaire Callias (Plut. *Cim.* 4. 8; further embellishments at Nepos, *Cim.* 1).

22. 11. 12. 4. In the last part of the citation I have taken over the translation of C. H. Oldfather (*Diodorus of Sicily*, IV, Loeb Classical Library).

23. 11. 15. 4, fin.; this and the following translation are those of Oldfather.

24. According to J. F. Dobson, "[Isocrates] saw no way to establish peace and unity unless some common cause could teach the Greeks to regard themselves as a nation. He suggested that Sparta and Athens should make a compromise in their claims to leadership and head a union of all States in a national war against Persia" (art. "Isocrates" in *OCD*[1], 460).

A more serious problem exists in trying to evaluate Diodorus' (that is, on the above assumption, Ephorus') treatment of several episodes in Themistocles' career. Ephorus apparently gave a slant to the prize-giving ceremonies after the battle of Salamis, which differed considerably from the relatively factual account of Herodotus. According to Diodorus it was the Spartans who, by virtue of their *charis* and because they "foresaw the impending contest for hegemony and were eager to humble Athenian pride," caused the first prize for valour to be given to the Aeginetan contingent. Diodorus continues:

> And when the Athenians showed their anger at this undeserved humiliation, the Lacedaemonians, fearful lest Themistocles should be displeased at the outcome and should devise some great evil against them and the Greeks, honoured him with double the number of gifts awarded to those who had received the prize of valour. And when Themistocles accepted the gifts, the Athenians in assembly removed him from the generalship and bestowed the office upon Xanthippus the son of Ariphron.[25]

The interference of the Spartans in the prize-giving and the base motive assigned to their special honour to Themistocles can safely be ignored. But what of the statement that Themistocles was deposed from the generalship and replaced by Xanthippus? (Whether or not the motive assigned for the Athenians' action is correct is of secondary importance.) Diodorus is the only ancient writer to comment specifically on Themistocles' tenure of the generalship, but this may be nothing more than Ephorus' attempt to answer the question, which has troubled many modern scholars as well, Was Themistocles general in 479/8, and, if not, why not? On the basis of the silence of our sources, the view held by most scholars (even those who disbelieve Diodorus-Ephorus on this point) is that he was not.[26] Diodorus recounts under the year 478 (the annalistic chronography may be his own rather than Ephorus') Themistocles' stratagem of refortifying Athens against the wishes, and indeed under the very noses, of the Spartans. The factual outlines and many of the details of the narrative are straight from Thucydides.[27] The embellishments added by Ephorus tend to reinforce the conspiratorial aspects of the story, which are already present to a less extent in Thucydides: thus, "he told the Council in confidence" that he would lead an embassy to Sparta (11. 39. 5; the other ambassadors, whom Diodorus does not name, set out with Themistocles and do not, as in Thucydides, come later); Themistocles allows himself

---

25. 11. 27. 2–3, trans. Oldfather. Compare Herodotus 8. 123 (which is also anecdotal regarding Themistocles) and 124 (a factual account, save for the comment, which Herodotus lets fall almost unawares, that Themistocles was "the only man I know" to have received a special escort from the Spartans).

26. See C. Hignett, *Xerxes' Invasion*, 275–78, for full discussion, with the views of earlier scholars. I am not convinced by Hignett's suggestion that "if Themistocles was still general in 479, his inactivity may perhaps be explained by his disapproval of the strategy now in favour

in Athens" (278).

27. Diod. 11. 39–40 ~ Thuc. 1. 89. 3–93. 2. Even the pretext given by the Spartans in attempting to deter the Athenians is the same in both (Diod. 11. 39. 3 = Thuc. 1. 90. 2). There is an abbreviated, though substantially the same, version in Plutarch, *Them.* 19. 1–3 (the detail of Polyarchus, the Aeginetan informer, may be from Theopompus, whom Plutarch cites at the beginning of the chapter for the detail, found nowhere else, that Themistocles *bribed* the Spartan ephors).

to be put under guard as a guarantee of his story. Then the Spartan ambassadors are imprisoned at Athens and a reciprocal release is effected (11. 40. 3), while in Thucydides this detention of the Spartans is to be done "in the least obvious manner possible" (1. 91. 3), that is, no formal arrest took place. But the implication of Thucydides' narrative is exactly as Diodorus specifies: "The Spartans were outgeneralled...by Themistocles' stratagem" (11. 40. 5). Both Thucydides and Diodorus continue their accounts with the fortification of the Peiraeus,[28] and once again Diodorus, presumably following Ephorus, adds romantic, but probably untrustworthy, material to enhance the undercover aspect of the story. Although Thucydides remarks that this constituted a resumption of the fortification which "Themistocles had begun during his year as archon" (1. 93. 3), Ephorus seems to have introduced it as a totally new theme (again, Diodorus' year, 477/6, is not necessarily from Ephorus). Themistocles, who is, somewhat contradictorily, both "held in esteem" by his fellow citizens and the object of their suspicions (11. 41. 4), is given a committee of two others, Aristeides and Xanthippus, to whom he communicates his intention to fortify the Peiraeus. Secrecy is maintained to avoid interference from the Spartans (11. 42. 1), and the Assembly, told that the secret plan is "important, beneficial to the city, and possible," finally approves, but only after the entire Boule also vouches for it. Themistocles devises, we are told, another stratagem, which turns out to be nothing more subtle than a second embassy to Sparta to explain that "it was to the advantage of the common interests of Greece that it should possess a first-rate harbour in view of the expedition which was to be expected on the part of the Persians."[29]

None of this need be any more than imaginative embroidery on the Thucydidean framework, but two details may be singled out for special attention. At the end of chapter 43 Diodorus reports that "Themistocles persuaded the people each year to construct and add twenty triremes to the fleet they already possessed, and also to remove the tax upon metics and artisans, in order that great crowds of people might stream into the city from every quarter and that the Athenians might easily procure labour for a greater number of crafts" (11. 43. 3). It would be interesting to know what evidence Ephorus—if he was the source—had for the detail, which is in fact accepted by some scholars.[30] In assigning motives for Themistocles' eagerness to secure mastery at sea for Athens (a motif already present in Thucydides' account, 1. 93. 6–7), Diodorus introduces as a reason the desire to "liberate the Ionians their kinsmen and the other Greeks in Asia" (11. 41. 4), which fits in well with the story told by Herodotus of Themistocles' appeal to the Ionian contingent in Xerxes' fleet

---

28. Thuc. 1. 93. 3–7 ~ Diod. 11. 41–43.

29. Diod. 11. 43. 1–2. The words in quotations are from Oldfather's translation. It should be noted that, whether or not there is any truth to the story, the reason given would have been far more plausible *before* the original invasion, that is, at the (apparently) Thucydidean date of 493/2 (cf. especially Thuc. 1. 93. 7). P. J. Rhodes classes this among stories which "have a suspicious ring" because, as he remarks, "the boule is entrusted with the kind of decision which we should expect the ecclesia [Assembly] to reserve for itself" (*The Athenian Boule*, 40–41).

30. See J. S. Morrison and R. T. Williams, *Greek Oared Ships, 900–322 B.C.*, 225; D. Blackman in *GRBS* 10 (1969), 203–4, who remarks, "The only problem is that we do not know how long this annual rate remained standard" (203).

after the battles off Artemisium.[31] Freedom, *eleutheria*, was to be the watchword, not only for the original repulse of the barbarian, but for the continuing operations in Asia which resulted in the formation and early successes of the Delian League.

The final section of Diodorus' narrative which concerns us is Themistocles' trial(s), condemnation, escape, and last years in Asia (11. 54–59). All this material Diodorus narrates under the year 471/70, but it is generally recognized that, in so doing, he has drastically cut up and perhaps even rearranged his source.[32] In the background certainly stands Thucydides' narrative, but Diodorus' account is much more circumstantial. The Spartans, dejected over the treason of their own general Pausanias, and the good repute of Athens, none of whose citizens had been condemned on similar charges, and

> eager to involve Athens in similar discreditable charges, accused [Themistocles] of treason, maintaining that he had been a close friend of Pausanias and had agreed with him that together they would betray Greece to Xerxes. They also carried on conversations with the enemies of Themistocles, inciting them to lodge an accusation against him, and gave them money; and they explained that, when Pausanias decided to betray the Greeks, he disclosed the plan he had to Themistocles and urged him to participate in the project, and that Themistocles neither agreed to the request nor decided that it was his duty to accuse a man who was his friend.[33]

The naïve motive ascribed to the Spartans for initiating the charges may safely be ignored, but the detail that they entered into a conspiracy with Themistocles' enemies at Athens may well be true. It will be picked up by Plutarch, who, in this section of his *Life of Themistocles*, chapters 22–23, follows Diodorus (or more probably, the latter's source, Ephorus) closely and adds the name of Themistocles' accuser, Leobotes, son of Alcmeon. Diodorus next relates that a charge of treason (*prodosia*) was laid against Themistocles, and he was tried, but *acquitted*; there follows an account of his ostracism, with a digression on the technique and significance of ostracism (this section is drastically abbreviated, but, again, has verbal echoes in Plutarch, *Themistocles* 22. 5). After this Diodorus recounts a Spartan demand that Themistocles be tried *again*, this time before the *Koinon Synedrion*, or "General Congress," of the Greeks (11. 55. 4). Diodorus then digresses to explain why Themistocles believed he could not get a fair trial before the Synedrion—the Athenians had, after all, been deprived of first prize for valour through Spartan jealousy (11. 27. 2)—and he adds,

> It was from the speech in his own defence which Themistocles had made in Athens on the former occasion that the Lacedaemonians had got the basis for the accusation they afterwards made. For in that defence Themistocles had acknowledged that Pausanias had sent letters to him, urging him to share in the act of treason, and using this as the strongest piece of evidence in his behalf, he

31. Hdt. 8. 22; cf. 9. 98 where Leotychidas is specifically paralleled with Themistocles.
32. Jacoby, *FGrHist* II C, p. 89.

33. 11. 54. 2–4, trans. Oldfather (direct quotations in the succeeding sections are likewise taken from Oldfather's translation).

had established that Pausanias would not have urged him, unless he had opposed his first request. (11. 55. 7–8, trans. C. H. Oldfather)

What chance is there that any of this is true? It is hardly sufficient to remark that the first trial and acquittal are not mentioned by Thucydides, for Thucydides' narrative makes no pretence to completeness; he begins this portion of Themistocles' story only at the point at which Themistocles is already in exile following his ostracism (1. 135. 2–3). Gomme's verdict, "nothing that is in Diodorus and is not in Thucydides is of any value,"[34] seems unnecessarily severe. The detail of the *Koinon Synedrion* likewise has been doubted; but a trial before all the Greeks does not seem to be an impossible, or even an implausible, demand for the Spartans to have made.[35] A priori notions about the relative merits of Thucydides and Ephorus apart, what emerges from Diodorus' narrative is a coherent account: a trial at Athens instigated by the Spartans and Themistocles' Athenian enemies; a speech in his own defence in which Themistocles apparently produced a letter from Pausanias in which he was urged by the Spartan regent to join him in his treasonable designs—this invitation Themistocles turned to his favour by arguing that Pausanias would not have had to urge him if he had not previously shown his unwillingness to accede to the Spartan's requests; a subsequent ostracism; a proposed second trial before the *Koinon Synedrion*, demanded by the Spartans on grounds of the admissions made by Themistocles at his first trial. (Diodorus' narrative implies that the Spartans felt Themistocles would not get off as easily as he had at his earlier trial in Athens, and it was because Themistocles realized this that he fled from Argos.) Almost the weakest of all grounds on which to evaluate ancient evidence is that of internal coherence, but on this criterion, at least, Diodorus' (that is, Ephorus') account may deserve more credence than modern historians like Gomme usually give it.[36]

For the last part of Themistocles' journey Ephorus followed the account of Thucydides, but added to it details of a romantic, even sensational, cast from a *Persika*. Jacoby suggested that this may have been the work by Ctesias of Cnidus (c. 400 B.C.) directly, or through—perhaps in addition to—some such intermediary as Heracleides of Cyme, a closer contemporary and fellow citizen of Ephorus, with whom, according to Plutarch (*Them.* 27. 1), he agreed on Themistocles' encounter, not with Artaxerxes, but Xerxes. From the summary of Ctesias by Photius comes a passage in which Themistocles is twice mentioned by name: "Through the plan of the Athenian Themistocles and Aristeides, Cretan archers were summoned and were at hand.... [After the Greek victory] Xerxes fled, through the plan and contrivance again [*boulei palin kai technei*] of Aristeides and Themistocles."[37] Not much can be inferred from

34. *Commentary*, I, 437. Gomme was preceded by the treatise *On the Malice of Herodotus*: "Thucydides has tacitly condemned the story [told by Ephorus F 189 = Diod. 11. 54. 4 and 55. 8] by leaving it out altogether" (*Mor.* 855 F, trans. Pearson). So, for example, K. B. J. Herbert, "The former [set of charges brought before Themistocles' ostracism] is the invention of [Ephorus] to give Themistocles the opportunity to repel the accusations at least once" ("Ephorus in Plutarch's *Lives*," 64–65).

35. For a defence of the Synedrion and this detail in Diodorus, cf. J. A. O. Larsen in *CP* 28 (1933), 264.

36. Jacoby, *FGrHist* II C, pp. 89–90, seems more optimistic, though cautiously so.

37. *FGrHist* 688 F 13 (30).

this meagre abbreviation. It is doubtful even whether an inference could be justified that Ctesias either was unaware of, or consciously chose to ignore, the tradition of hostility between Themistocles and Aristeides. Diodorus' highly coloured account of the charges brought against Themistocles by Xerxes' sister Mandane, the trial held before a specially summoned court of the noblest Persians (it was for this trial that Themistocles learned Persian, a detail mentioned in another context by Thucydides [1. 138. 1]), and Themistocles' acquittal, if these events figured in Ephorus' narrative, may suggest that Ephorus was here, too, drawing on Ctesias as he had done for the tale full of intrigue regarding Xerxes' death at the hands of Artabanus.[38]

Theopompus of Chios, who came to Athens about 360 B.C. and like Ephorus entered the rhetorical school of Isocrates (whose most distinguished pupil he was later said to have been),[39] continued Thucydides' *History* to 394 B.C. in twelve books and composed, in addition, a fifty-eight book *Philippika*, or "History of Philip." The work was notorious, even in antiquity, for its discursiveness, and book 10 contained a lengthy digression, "On Athenian Demagogues." The "demagogues" treated in this excursus seem to have been, so far as can be inferred from the fragments, Themistocles, Cimon, Thucydides son of Melesias, Pericles, Cleon, Hyperbolus, and, in Theopompus' own period, Callistratus and Eubulus. Theopompus is cited three times in Plutarch's *Life of Themistocles*, and it is generally assumed that the citations all come from book 10 of the *Philippika*. Theopompus diverged from the Thucydidean version of how Themistocles had engineered the rebuilding of Athens' fortifications after Salamis in maintaining that Themistocles had bribed, rather than outwitted, the Spartan ephors.[40] After his escape to Asia and condemnation in absentia, Themistocles' property was confiscated and turned over to the public treasury; "although he had been worth less than 3 talents when he entered public life, the sum confiscated was 100 talents" (Theophrastus said 80). Lastly, Plutarch cites Theopompus only to contradict him for the detail that Themistocles "wandered about Asia" during his last years, whereas Plutarch insists, probably following Thucydides, that he had a house in Magnesia and, by implication, had settled there.[41] It seems clear, even from these meagre remains, that Theopompus' picture of Themistocles was not complimentary, and in that respect formed a contrast to his treatment of Cimon.[42] What access he may have had to new material is unclear; among his sources have been

38. *FGrHist* 688 F 13 (32–33) ~ Diod. 11. 69 (Ctesias had given the name of the eunuch accomplice as Aspamitros; in Diodorus it is Mithridates).

39. Dionysius of Halicarnassus, *Epistle to Pompey* 6; evaluations of Theopompus by Gomme, *Commentary*, I, 46 ff., and W. R. Connor, *Theopompus and Fifth-Century Athens*, chap. 6.

40. Plut. *Them.* 19. 1 = *FGrHist* 115 F 85. The detail of the bribe is given some slight support, as Gomme (*Commentary*, I, 260) notes, by Andocides (3. 38), who remarks that the Spartans were "bought [i.e., bribed] not to seek

redress" for the stealthy rebuilding of the walls.

41. The citations are from Plutarch, *Them.* 25. 3, 31. 3 (= *FGrHist* 115 Ff 86, 87).

42. *FGrHist* 115 F 88 (Cimon's recall from exile five years early, "because the people believed that through his intervention peace could be most easily concluded"); F 89 (the tale of Cimon's benefactions, quoted at length by Athenaeus 12. 533 A–C). The latter story is repeated in the *Constitution of Athens* (27. 3, with Sandys' note ad loc.), and both details reappear, unacknowledged, in Plutarch (*Cim.* 17. 8–9, 10. 1).

suggested the earlier political pamphlets by Stesimbrotus and Critias.[43] Similarities have been noted between Theopompus and certain passages in Old Comedy; fragment 86, regarding Themistocles' enrichment while in public office, has been seen as a pseudohistorical echo of the allusion in a comic line which Plutarch referred—on what evidence is unclear—to Themistocles.[44] At the other end of the tradition, it is idle to speculate how much (or little) of Theopompus may have filtered down to Pompeius Trogus' *Philippics*, which is preserved only in an abridged form by Justin.[45]

Compilations, Annotated Guides, and Other Treatises

We turn now to the various collections, guidebooks, and treatises on specialized subjects which began to appear in the fourth century and which may have made useful contributions to the Themistocles tradition. In addition to Philochorus' *Epigrammata Attika* (of which nothing remains but the title), we hear of a *Collection of Decrees* by the Macedonian writer Craterus, whose exact dates are uncertain, but who seems to have been active around 300 B.C. This work was, according to Jacoby, "a publication of documents with an accompanying or connecting text,"[46] and Craterus is quoted specifically for the name of Themistocles' accuser, "Leobotes, son of Alcmeon, of Agryle," as contained in the decree of impeachment, or *eisangelia* (*FGrHist* 342 F 11). With reference to this passage Jacoby notes that "the fragment of Krateros does furnish documentary evidence that the charge against Themistokles was brought in the form of *eisangelia*, but we do not learn whether it was brought before the Areopagos or before the people (or the Council)."[47] The normal procedure, however, was for an *eisangelia* to be brought before the Council, which determined by a preliminary hearing whether the case was serious enough to go before the Assembly or a Heliastic court for trial,[48] but there is reason to suppose that this procedure was not followed in the charge against Themistocles.[49] One other preserved fragment of Craterus touches on an incident in the career of Themistocles, but only indirectly; the decree against Arthmius of Zeleia, who was said to have "brought the Medes' gold to the

43. Gomme, *Commentary*, I, 46 and 48. The figures for Themistocles' wealth in F 86 are, as Jacoby points out, the same as those for which Aelian (*V.H.* 10. 17) cites Critias. H. T. Wade-Gery suggested that Critias was "a major source for [Theopompus'] *Philippika X*" (*AJP* 59 [1938], 133, n.9 = *Essays in Greek History*, 236, n.3).

44. Connor, *Theopompus*, 104–5 (the line was assigned to Eupolis by Wilamowitz). Theopompus' errors can hardly be excused by saying, as Connor does, that "Theopompus' luck was bad; in every case he seems to have preferred the less accurate account" (ibid., 176, n.4).

45. Jacoby issued a similar caveat for Ephorus as a source for Justin-Trogus (*RE* 11 [1922], col. 2068).

46. *Atthis*, 204.

47. *FGrHist* III b (Supp.) ii. 453 n.9 (on

Philochorus 328 F 199). Themistocles' exile was also mentioned by Craterus in connection with the later career of Aristeides (*FGrHist* 342 F 12 = Plut. *Arist.* 26).

48. G. Gilbert, *Constitutional Antiquities of Sparta and Athens*, 281; G. Busolt and H. Swoboda, *Griech. Staatskunde*, II, 1007 ff., with 1007, n.2; G. Busolt, *Griech. Gesch.²*, III. 1, 125, n.4; Rhodes, *Athenian Boule*, 162 ff. (199 ff. for Themistocles' trial). The stages in Themistocles' trial and condemnation are reconstructed by M. de Koutorga in *Acad. des inscr. et des belles-lettres*, 1st ser. 6 (1860), 374 ff.

49. Rhodes suggests that "the strange story in *A.P.* 25. iii–iv [Themistocles' association with Ephialtes in attacking the Areopagus] might lend some support to the view that this charge was an εἰσαγγελία heard by the Areopagus" (*Athenian Boule*, 201).

Greeks," and whose condemnation became a favourite rhetorical talking-point in the fourth century, is said by Plutarch (*Them.* 6. 4) to have been moved by Themistocles, while Craterus is cited for the ascription of the decree to Cimon.[50] Although there is no direct evidence to support such a theory, it has often been suggested that the decrees summarized in Plutarch, *Themistocles* 10. 4–5, regarding the evacuation of the Athenians from Attica and their reception at Troizen, were recorded in, and derived by Plutarch or his source from, Craterus' *Collection*, which Plutarch cites at *Aristeides* 26. 1 and *Cimon* 13. 5.

The class of "periegetic" or guidebook literature is best represented by Diodorus who wrote, some time after 300 B.C., a work *On Monuments* in at least three books. Plutarch cites it directly for information regarding the so-called tomb of Themistocles: "Near the large harbour of the Peiraeus a sort of elbow juts out from the promontory opposite Alcimus,...as you round this and come inside, where the water of the sea is still, there is a basement [*krepis*] of goodly size,...the altar-like structure upon this is the Tomb of Themistocles" (*FGrHist* 372 F 35 = Plut. *Them.* 32. 5, trans. Perrin). According to Plutarch, Diodorus cited in support of his view some lines of the comic writer Plato, which have already been discussed,[51] and Plutarch himself was sceptical, for he remarks that Diodorus' account comes "more from conjecture than from actual knowledge." But Gomme thought the passage was "a careful citation of the reliable Diodorus Periegetes,"[52] and since we do not know on what evidence Diodorus based his inference (what Plutarch calls his *hyponoia*), it would be unwise to reject his testimony out of hand, although exactly what the structure Diodorus described may have been remains uncertain.

Writers of local histories of Attica could hardly have excluded the events of 500 to 470, but these could be, and probably were, interpreted to suit the political bent of the author or his circle. Philochorus' comments on the Peiraeus rebuilding provide only a tantalizing glimpse of what his full account might have offered. So little in any case remains of any of these works (except the *Constitution of Athens*) that they are hardly worth speculating about. The "universal" histories promised more, and with less bias, but here again what is left disappoints. The credulity of Ephorus is visible for all to see in Diodorus. Only Theopompus, whom Gomme called "a more learned man, and a much more industrious worker" than Ephorus,[53] may have added something of value to the inherited stock of material about Themistocles. Unfortunately, however, in those particulars where his version can be checked against that of Thucydides (Themistocles' approach to the ephors, his residence in Asia), Theopompus' reputation is not enhanced by the comparison. Those who will may speculate on his possible influence on later writers like Nepos and Justin.

50. *FGrHist* 342 F 14: "Craterus (said) the inscribing of the decree was Cimon's doing, while [Aelius] Aristeides says it was Themistocles'," reports the scholiast on Aelius Aristeides, *For the Four* (II, 287 Dind.). Aristeides' text does not actually say this, but the scholiast clearly had in mind the tradition which Plutarch followed. See M. Cary, *CQ* 29 (1935), 177 ff.; R. Meiggs, *Athenian Empire*, App. 10c,

pp. 508 ff. R. J. Lenardon accepts the historicity of the incident, but dates it before Marathon (*Historia* 5 [1956], 110–11). M. B. Wallace argues for a date of 466 or 465, but assigns the decree, with Craterus, to Cimon (*Phoenix* 24 [1970], 200–202, esp. 200, n.15).

51. See chapter 1, p. 61.
52. *Commentary*, I, 62.
53. Ibid., 46.

Surprisingly, accounts written later than the fourth century have much more new material to offer, some of which probably goes back to a genuine early tradition; only, as the thread connecting the events with the record grows ever thinner with time, the credibility of that record diminishes, and the situation is not improved by the almost total anonymity of the original sources.

5 LATE ACCOUNTS

IT WILL BE of interest, and some possible use, to trace the development of the Themistocles legend in later writers down to the Roman period.[1] The testimonies will be of widely differing extent and value, and the authors of very disparate genres. A serviceable division may be as follows: history and biography proper by writers who treated Themistocles' story either for itself, or as an excursus to an account of the Persian Wars or to some other period with which they were more directly concerned; passing references to the deeds of, or tales about, Themistocles by writers who were not primarily historians (for example, orators, geographers); material in late collections or compilations of stratagems, anecdotes; and a catch-all category of miscellaneous information.

Late Historians and Biographers

Significant accretions to the Themistocles story began in the period immediately following the death of Aristotle among members of his school, the so-called Peripatetics. The development of special interest in the lives and deeds of outstanding men is understandable enough in light of the Aristotelian emphasis on *ethos*, "character," as manifested in action;[2] what is not so easily comprehended is why Peripatetic biography should have taken the romanticizing and even sensational turn it did. The outstanding example (outstanding both because his work is best known thanks to Plutarch's use of it and because the vices of the literary form are so manifest in it) is Phanias of Eresus on Lesbos, a contemporary and friend of Theophrastus, who is

1. There is an informative account of the changing fortunes of the Persian War traditions in later ages, with much useful material concerning Themistocles, in R. W. Macan, *Herodotus, Books VII–IX*, vol. II, App. 1.

2. See A. Dihle, *Studien zur griechischen Biographie*, Abh. Akad. Wiss. Göttingen, phil.-hist. Kl., 3. Folge 37 (1956), chap. 4, esp. pp. 62 ff.

cited five times in Plutarch's *Themistocles* and whose influence has been suspected elsewhere in Plutarch's account. In spite of the description of him by Plutarch as "a philosopher who was not unfamiliar with historical writings" (*Them.* 13. 5), he is clearly a writer to whom it would be rash to go for *credible* new material concerning Themistocles. Plutarch quotes him for an alternate version of Themistocles' mother's name and place of origin (a Carian named Euterpe); for the silly story that Themistocles, in an effort to forestall disaffection among the crew of the official Athenian galley before the battle of Artemisium, sent a bribe of one talent in the bottom of a dinner pail to the commander Architeles; for the histrionic story of Themistocles' sacrifice of three "most beautiful" young men of the royal family to Dionysus Omestes (roughly, "Cannibalic"); for Themistocles' long but inconclusive interview with the Persian chiliarch Artabanus; and, finally, for the additional two cities of Perkote and Palaiskepsis as part of the Persian king's "gift" to Themistocles.[3] The general character of Phanias' account can be discerned in these citations. It must have been full of bizarre and even hair-raising detail—we are told, for example, that "at one and the same moment a great and glaring flame shot up from the sacrificial victims and a sneeze gave forth its good omen on the right"[4] before the sacrifice of the Persian youths; proper names abounded (the victims' parents, the seer Euphrantides); details were invented to give the semblance, rather than the substance, of truth. The extent to which Plutarch may have been indebted to Phanias' work, indeed the very name and nature of the composition, cannot now be determined. It has been suggested that the story of Themistocles may have been handled chronographically in Phanias' *Magistrates of Eresus*;[5] but another candidate among the known titles would be the work *On Tyrants*, or *On the Sicilian Tyrants*, in which Themistocles' story might have been brought into some sort of connection with the account of Gelon and Hieron.[6] Some scholars believe that, in large portions of the account of Themistocles' adventures at the end of the *Life*, Plutarch's unacknowledged source is Phanias.[7] Another of Aristotle's pupils, Clearchus of Soli, showed an interest in Themistocles. Athenaeus (12. 533 E) cites the first book of Clearchus' work *On Friendship* for the story of how Themistocles had built himself a very lovely *triclinium*, or intimate dining room, and then remarked that he "would have liked to have friends to fill it" (fr. 17 W).

Roughly contemporary is Idomeneus of Lampsacus, friend and student of Epicurus, who wrote a work entitled *On Athenian Demagogues*, the preserved fragments of which show it to have dealt extensively with the careers of Aristeides and Themistocles. It heavily underlined the rivalry between the two men: Aristeides, when elected super-

3. Frs. 23 Wehrli (*Die Schule des Aristoteles*, IX) = Plut. *Them.* 1. 2; 24W = *Them.* 7. 6–7; 25W = *Them.* 13. 2–5 (alluded to also at *Arist.* 9. 2 and *Pelop.* 21. 3); 26W = *Them.* 27; 28W = *Them.* 29. 11.

4. Plut. *Them.* 13. 3, trans. B. Perrin.

5. Philip Smith, art. "Phanias," in *William Smith's Dictionary of Greek and Roman Biography and Mythology*, III, 237.

6. Fr. 11W. Plutarch rejects an item connecting Themistocles and Hieron retailed by

Stesimbrotus (*Them.* 24. 7).

7. H. A. Holden, *Plutarch's 'Life of Themistocles'*[3], xliii, n.99, citing Fr. Blass and M. Mohr. The theory of Plutarch's dependence upon Phanias for chapters 26 to 29 of the *Themistocles* is worked out in detail by L. Bodin, "Histoire et biographie: Phanias d' Erèse," *REG* 28 (1915), 251–81; 30 (1917), 117–57; followed by R. Laqueur, "Phainias," *RE* 19 (1938), col. 1567 ff.

visor of public revenue, accused Themistocles of playing fast and loose with public monies, and Themistocles, in turn, obtained an indictment against Aristeides at the audit of the latter's accounts after his year of office.[8] Idomeneus' narrative of Themistocles' condemnation came in the second book of the work and is summarized as follows: "The Athenians condemned him and his family to perpetual banishment for treason against Greece and confiscated his property."[9] The matter-of-fact tone and straightforward reportage contrast with the detail (presumably from an early stage of Themistocles' career), for which Idomeneus is also quoted, that Themistocles made a show of driving through the Cerameicus, when it was most crowded, with four *hetairai* (whose names Idomeneus supplied), if not yoked to and drawing his chariot— for that was the story other writers told—at least riding alongside him.[10] It should, however, be noted (with Jacoby) to Idomeneus' credit that he was in the minority of writers, along with Charon of Lampsacus and Thucydides, who, correctly, brought Themistocles face to face, not with Xerxes, but Artaxerxes.[11]

In chapter 27 of his *Life of Themistocles*, Plutarch names the writers who took sides in the controversy over whether Themistocles, when he made his way to Susa, found Xerxes or Artaxerxes on the throne. Among those who maintained it had been Xerxes were (besides Ephorus, the shadowy Heracleides,[12] and, according to Plutarch, many others) Deinon and Cleitarchus, father and son, the first of whom wrote a *Persika*, or "History of Persia," the second, a *History of Alexander*, in which the account of Themistocles must have occurred in a digression.[13] Deinon received the dubious accolade of a compliment by Cornelius Nepos,[14] while Cicero mentions Cleitarchus, along with the otherwise all but unknown Stratokles,[15] as examples of "rhetoricians [who] distort history in order to give more point to their narrative."[16] From Cicero's criticism, it appears that these writers told of Themistocles' suicide by drinking the blood of a bull which he had been sacrificing, the "kind of a death that gave them the chance for rhetorical and tragic treatment."[17]

Twice in the *Themistocles*, both times in connection with Phanias, Plutarch mentions a detail as deriving from a certain Neanthes, a rhetorician of Cyzicus and pupil of the rhetorician Philiscus of Miletus, who was himself a pupil of Isocrates: "the only dated

8. *FGrHist* 338 F 7 (= Plut. *Arist.* 4. 3–4); Jacoby sees Idomeneus in the tradition of Stesimbrotus and Theopompus, but doubts the authenticity of this whole episode.

9. 338 F 1 (= schol. Aristoph. *Wasps* 947, where F. Clinton saw that the reference was not to Thucydides, son of Melesias, but to Themistocles [*Fasti Hellenici*², 500 n.]).

10. 338 F 4; Athenaeus (576 C); the source of the citation uses Idomeneus to correct the account, quoted from a work entitled *On Famous Men* by a certain Amphicrates, that Themistocles' mother had been a courtesan named Habrotonon.

11. *FGrHist* III b, Text, p. 86, on the basis of 338 F 1.

12. *FGrHist* 689. Placed by Jacoby *c.* 350 B.C., Heracleides was a native of Cyme (and so perhaps an influence upon Ephorus) and wrote

a *Persika* in five books (Diogenes Laertius 5. 93).

13. Deinon, *FGrHist* 690 (see L. Pearson, *Lost Histories of Alexander the Great*, 226–27); Cleitarchus, *FGrHist* 137 (Pearson, *Lost Histories*, chap. 8).

14. "cui nos plurimum de Persicis rebus credimus," *Conon* 5. 4.

15. Stratokles may be the same as the fourth-century orator and politician who prosecuted Demosthenes in the Harpalus affair and later was a supporter of Demetrius of Phaleron (see A. E. Douglas' note on *Cicero, Brutus* 43).

16. *Brutus* 42, trans. G. L. Hendrickson (Loeb Classical Library).

17. Ibid., 43, trans. Hendrickson. Cleitarchus is mentioned disparagingly by Cicero again at *de Legibus* 1. 2. 7 and by Quintilian, *Inst. Orat.* 10. 1. 74.

event in [Philiscus'] life is that Delphic honours were decreed to him *ca.* 287."[18] To Phanias' statement that Themistocles' mother was a Carian woman named Euterpe, Neanthes added that she had come from Halicarnassus, and Neanthes and Phanias are both mentioned as having said that the Persian king's gifts to Themistocles included, in addition to the cities mentioned by Thucydides (Magnesia, Lampsacus, Myus), "Perkote and Palaiskepsis as well, for bedding and clothing."[19] Neanthes appears to have been a voluminous writer; among other titles ascribed to him is a work entitled *On Famous Men*, but from a reference in Athenaeus it appears that the material on Themistocles was presented "in the third and fourth books of his *History of Greece*."[20] Approximately contemporary with Neanthes was Ariston of Ceos, who succeeded to the headship of the Peripatetic school about 230 B.C. He is cited by Plutarch twice for the detail that the political rivalry between Themistocles and Aristeides originated in their mutual attachment to a handsome Cean youth named Stesilaos.[21] Plutarch also mentions Ariston's pupil Eratosthenes, the famous polymath who succeeded Callimachus as head of the Library at Alexandria, for an item from the last part of Themistocles' career. The preliminary interview between Themistocles and the Persian chiliarch Artabanus is narrated in chapter 27 of the *Life* (Themistocles dramatically refuses to divulge his name to anyone but the king), mainly, Plutarch says, on the authority of Phanias; then he adds the detail, from Eratosthenes' treatise *On Wealth*, that the interview had been arranged in the first place by Artabanus' Eretrian wife,[22] who had perhaps been among the captives taken by Datis and Artaphrenes before Marathon and resettled, according to Herodotus (6. 119), some thirty miles from Susa in the district known as Cissia.

In the latter part of the third century, Phylarchus, who worked at Athens and wrote *Histories* which covered the period from 272 to 220 B.C. in twenty-eight books, treated the subject of Themistocles, probably in an excursus to his main story. He is known to have mentioned the guardian snake which was said to have abandoned its post in the temple of Athena Polias on the Acropolis as a presage of disaster when the Persian invaders were approaching. The omen is narrated in straightforward fashion by Herodotus (8. 41); Plutarch expands the simpler version into an intentional manipulation of *semeia daimonia* by Themistocles, who thus hoped to reinforce his interpretation of the wooden wall oracle that the city was to be abandoned (*Them.* 10. 1). On the basis of Plutarch's comment in describing the event, that Themistocles "got his machinery ready, as if for a production of tragedy," and a similar comment which he makes about Phylarchus himself later in the *Life*, Jacoby suggested that the mention

18. F. Solmsen, "Philiskos," *RE* 19 (1938), col. 2385; cf. *FGrHist* 84 T 2.

19. Plut. *Them.* 1. 2; 29. 11 (= *FGrHist* 84 Ff 2b, 17a; Jacoby's comment on the latter fragment: "That N[eanthes] cited or used Phainias (F 2) naturally does not turn him into a Peripatetic").

20. 13. 576 D, cf. Clinton, *Fasti Hellenici*[2], 526–27, n.i.

21. *Them.* 3. 2, *Arist.* 2. 3–4 (= frs. 19,

20 Wehrli), apparently from the work whose title is given elsewhere as *Erotic Likenesses*. Cicero criticizes Ariston's lack of *gravitas* and *auctoritas* (*de Fin.* 5. 5. 13).

22. *Them.* 27. 8 (= *FGrHist* 241 F 27). Artabanus' special role under Xerxes shows, as Jacoby *ad loc.* remarks, that Eratosthenes followed the majority view (Plut. *Them.* 27, init.) in bringing Themistocles into the presence of Xerxes.

of the snake belongs to Phylarchus' "Themistocles excursus."[23] This may be correct, but it should be pointed out that the context in which Phylarchus mentioned it (if he indeed did)[24] is completely unknown, and to proceed upon this tenuous basis to a suggestion that Plutarch derived other parts of chapter 10 of the *Themistocles* from Phylarchus is unwarranted.[25] Certainly Plutarch's later verdict of him is unflattering: "that he all but raised his theatrical machinery for a tragedy and brought onstage a certain Neokles and Demopolis, sons of Themistocles, wishing to stir up a show of feeling—and even a layman could tell it was fabricated."[26] Plutarch had just reported that Neokles, the eldest son, died in childhood as the result of a horse's bite; Demopolis is not elsewhere mentioned, but may be nothing more than an invention on the basis of his father's democratic leanings and on the analogy of the better-authenticated name of Themistocles' daughter Mnesiptolema. How Themistocles' sons were thus brought into the story is unknown, but the context in which Plutarch places his reference, the story told by Andocides (which Plutarch soundly rejects) that the Athenians secretly stole Themistocles' remains from his tomb in Magnesia, suggests that Phylarchus may have had the boys in some way attempt to interfere with this planned savagery; one thinks perhaps of an embassy to the Magnesians, with Themistocles' sons' trying to counter the Athenian ambassadors' demands.[27] In book 10 of his *Histories*, Phylarchus told how Demaratus, the exiled Spartan king, had asked of Xerxes the special privilege of being allowed to enter Sardis wearing his tiara upright in the fashion of the king himself, and Plutarch recounts how the king's anger with Demaratus for making a request which he considered to be an affront had to be assuaged, and the two men reconciled, by Themistocles. Although there are some difficulties in the citation from Phylarchus, which again (like the snake on the Acropolis) occurs only in an abbreviated entry in Photius' *Lexicon*, it seems a safe enough inference that the longer version given by Plutarch (*Them.* 29. 7–8, where no source is cited) ultimately derives from Phylarchus;[28] if so, his poor showing on other matters pertaining to Themistocles reinforces the doubts already felt about the intrinsic plausibility of the story.

From what must have been a valuable and authoritative account of Themistocles' activities after he had taken up residence in Magnesia, *The History of Magnesia* by a certain Possis, but one quotation survives, to the effect that "Themistocles, after

23. *FGrHist* 81 F 72, with commentary.

24. The citation from Photius appears to be corrupt; Jacoby cites Lucht for the conjecture Philochorus.

25. Thus, one must treat with suspicion such an assertion as that "Phylarchus is a probable source through 10. 6 [of Plutarch's *Themistocles*]" (T. W. Africa, *Phoenix* 14 [1960], 226, n.39).

26. *FGrHist* 81 F 76 (= Plut. *Them.* 32. 4). This accords with (and may simply have been taken over from) the unfavourable verdict of Polybius on Phylarchus (II. 56 = *FGrHist* 81 T 3).

27. Compare the story told by a scholiast on Aristophanes, *Knights* 84 (which Jacoby calls "offenbar erschwindelte Geschichte" and ascribes to Possis) that "when the Athenians were suffering from a plague, the god [sc. of Delphi] told them to bring back the bones of Themistocles. When the Magnesians did not agree to it, they asked to make sacrifices at the grave after 30 days, pitched tents about the place, dug up the bones secretly, and brought them home."

28. *FGrHist* 81 F 22. Photius' entry implies (although does not say) that the king in question was Xerxes, which will show which side Phylarchus took in the controversy over whether Themistocles found Xerxes or Artaxerxes on the throne (Plut. *Them.* 27, init.).

assuming the office in Magnesia which carried with it the right to wear a crown, made sacrifices to Athena, calling the festival Panathenaea, and again after sacrificing to Dionysus the Pitcher-Drinker [*Choöpotes*] he instituted there the festival of Pitchers."[29] Possis' date is unfortunately unknown; Jacoby places him around 200 B.C., and remarks that the fact that the account of Themistocles is said by Athenaeus to have occurred in the third book of the *Magnetika* shows that Possis probably began his narrative with the foundation of the city.[30] Although the detail of Themistocles' having held the office of *Stephanephoros*, or "crown-bearer," seems to be an anachronism, there is no reason to doubt that Themistocles did, indeed, hold a magistracy in his adoptive city (perhaps as *prytanis*), or that he transferred to it the celebration of the Athenian festivals of Panathenaea and Choës; this is just the kind of detail that a local historian—of whatever period—can be expected to have recorded from an authentic local tradition.

The renewed interest in their past, which educated Greeks of the first century B.C. began to feel, was quickly transferred to Rome by those writers who turned to Athens for inspiration or even studied there. Cornelius Nepos, "the friend of Catullus, of Varro, of Atticus, and of Cicero,"[31] wrote extensively in the field of history and biography; what remains is a work *de Viris Illustribus* (a Latin translation of Amphicrates' title), which includes the lives of Miltiades, Themistocles, Aristeides, and Pausanias. According to Macan, they "add little of substance and less of value to the materials for the history of the Persian War."[32] This judgement seems rather harsh. There are some egregious errors to be sure: in chapter 2 of his *Themistocles* Nepos refers repeatedly to the "war with the Corcyraeans" as the occasion which enabled Themistocles to persuade the Athenians to expand their fleet; if Nepos had bothered to read Herodotus' account, he would have found repeated references to a war against Aegina. Nepos does not see the glaring internal inconsistency of then bringing Themistocles to Corcyra on his way to Asia (chap. 8). Nepos, following what earlier authority we cannot tell, gives the figures for the time consumed in Xerxes' invasion as six months for the journey from Asia to Greece, less than thirty days for the return, "by the same route."[33] His sense of geography is lamentably lacking; Artemisium is vaguely described as "between Euboea and the mainland," and Nepos' next comment that "Themistocles was looking for a narrow place so he wouldn't be surrounded by superior numbers" (chap. 3) is simply transferred from Salamis. And certain items, though new, seem to be mere inferences, or conventional motifs, quite obviously based on nothing that could be called evidence. Themistocles' new fleet gives him the wherewithal to "make the high seas safe by hunting down pirates" (chap. 2), and the

29. Athenaeus 12. 533 D–E, trans. C. B. Gulick (Loeb Classical Library) = *FGrHist* 480 F 1.

30. Jacoby suggests that Possis' "official" *History of Magnesia* may have somehow been connected with the reorganization of the festival of Artemis Leukophryene as a panhellenic cult in 221 B.C. (see *FGrHist* 482 Anhang, F 2, and Jacoby's comments in vol. III b, Kommentar-Text [1955], pp. 384–86).

31. Macan, *Herodotus, Books VII–IX*, II, 82; cf. T. A. Dorey, ed., *Latin Biography*, chap. 1.

32. Ibid. Edna Jenkinson, in *Latin Biography*, comments: "The *Life of Themistocles* shows the same fine indifference to dates, times and distances [as the *Life of Miltiades*]" (p. 10).

33. "...seque [sc. Xerxes] a Themistocle non superatum, sed conservatum," Nepos adds (*Them.* 1); the motif is at least as old as Aeschines the Socratic in the fourth century.

Spartan embassy sent to Athens on Themistocles' urging to investigate reports about the walls consists of "three men who had held the main magistracy" (that is, former ephors), three being a regular number for ambassadors.

This much credit should be allowed Nepos for historical judgement: he had the sense to follow Thucydides, the only source so singled out, for that part of Themistocles' story that had been treated by the earlier historian. Nepos cites him by name three times in *Themistocles*. From him he takes over the famous character analysis,[34] wisely sides with Thucydides in having Themistocles make his approaches to Artaxerxes—on the unimpeachable grounds that Thucydides was "most nearly contemporary" with the subject he treated (chap. 9)—and mentions him one final time in preferring his account of how Themistocles died (chap. 10). In fact, chapters 6 and 7 of Nepos' *Life* are virtually a translation and synopsis of Thucydides' account in book 1, chapters 90–92; the few divergences (for example, Nepos has Themistocles send back his two fellow ambassadors with the second Spartan delegation) seem to be mere slips of the pen, or innocent rhetorical flourishes: Themistocles tells the Spartans in his last speech after the walls have been completed that Athens "was like a fortress [*propugnaculum*] in the path of the barbarians, and upon it the king's fleets had already twice suffered shipwreck."[35] The account of Themistocles' escape in chapters 8 to 10 likewise follows Thucydides, though less closely. Nepos allows a few discrepancies to creep in: Themistocles is described as being on terms of *hospitium* with King Admetus;[36] the child by whom Themistocles makes his supplication Nepos calls a girl, Thucydides a boy. The route via Naxos is Thucydidean, but Nepos adds the romantic detail that the captain of the escape ship was "seized with pity for so famous a man" (chap. 8). Themistocles' letter to Artaxerxes is expanded, but not to unreasonable lengths. The obscure phrase by which Thucydides seems to allude to the "second message" is legitimately filled out along lines which most modern scholars believe Thucydides himself to have intended, and, in a neat turn of phrase, Nepos has Themistocles say that he will be "as good a friend [of Artaxerxes], as he was a brave enemy" of his father (chap. 9). In only one detail does Nepos heavy-handedly spoil his model: Thucydides has Themistocles spend a year learning Persian "as best he could" (1. 138. 1); Nepos has to go this one better: "Themistocles devoted all that time to the literature and language of the Persians, in which he became so well versed that he is said to have spoken in much better style before the king than those could who were natives of Persia."[37]

It is difficult to evaluate what access Nepos may have had to a tradition for information not found in Thucydides and how reliable that tradition could have been. The usual technique, highly unsatisfactory though it is, is to evaluate any

34. "He was no less active in carrying out his plans than he had been in devising them, because, as Thucydides expressed it, he judged present events with great exactness and divined the future with remarkable skill" (Nepos, *Them.* 1, trans. J. C. Rolfe [Loeb Classical Library] = Thuc. 1. 138. 3).

35. *Them.* 7, trans. Rolfe.

36. A fairly glaring error in view of Thucydides 1. 136. 2, and those editors who insert "⟨non⟩ erat" may be correct.

37. *Them.* 10, trans. Rolfe. The absurdity is repeated by Quintilian ("quem unum intra annum optime locutum esse Persice constat," *Inst. Orat.* 11. 2. 50).

individual item which he may offer on grounds of internal plausibility. Thus, the detail at the beginning of the *Life* that Themistocles' mother was "an Acarnanian who enjoyed the rights of citizenship" is generally accepted in preference to the other accounts, which seem to stem from a hostile tradition bent upon blackening his name, that she was a Thracian or Carian slave-courtesan.[38] In chapter 8 Nepos remarks that after he was ostracized, Themistocles removed to Argos, where he lived *magna cum dignitate*, which may be merely an inference, yet a safe enough one. Nepos states firmly (and he is our only authority for it) that after his death Themistocles was honoured by the Magnesians with two memorials, "a tomb in which he was buried near the city, and statues in the marketplace."[39]

Even more difficult to evaluate properly are chapters 2 and 3 in which Nepos discusses the Naval Bill and the evacuation of the city. Setting aside the error mentioned above regarding the war with Corcyra, we may turn to the figures for Xerxes' invading force: 1,200 warships (the canonical figure, as early as Aeschylus' *Persians* 341–42), with 2,000 transports, 700,000 infantry (these are reductions from Herodotus' figures of 3,000 transport ships and 1,700,000 men), and the absurdly large number of 400,000 cavalry (Herodotus had given 80,000). The tradition is clearly non-Herodotean, but its nature and value cannot be estimated. There is a further discrepancy between the number of *new* ships built before Salamis, but this may be more apparent than real; at the beginning of chapter 2 Nepos says 100 ships were built, on Themistocles' advice, with the "money from the mines which was being wasted by annual distributions by the magistrates." Herodotus (7. 144) had given the figure of 200, and it may be in an effort (perhaps by Nepos' "source") to reconcile the discrepancy that Nepos relates how, after Themistocles had persuaded the people to accept his interpretation of the oracle of the wooden walls, "they added to the fleet mentioned above an equal number of triremes and moved what they could of their possessions, part to Salamis, part to Troizen" (chap. 2, fin.).[40] The figure of 200 ships is repeated again in chapter 3. A further point needs to be brought out: Nepos' narrative reads as if he or his source believed that the evacuation of the city actually took place before the battles of Thermopylae and Artemisium, which are described in chapter 3. Although this is unhistorical, it may indicate that the tradition here followed is the same as that reflected in the Troizen Decree, which implies that the evacuation is to take place *and then* the fleet is to be sent to Artemisium; the partition of the Athenians' families and movable possessions is also emphasized in the decree (lines 8–10), and the figure of 200 ships occurs, although the decree calls for sending only 100 of them to Artemisium (line 41).[41] A final detail in this section of the *Life* calls for comment. Nepos relates that the battle of Artemisium was "indecisive" and that the Greeks withdrew from there, "because there was reason to fear that, if a part of the ships of their opponents

38. See Jacoby, *FGrHist* III b, Komm. p. 87 (on Idomeneus 338 F 4), with n.44.

39. *Them.* 10. The text is usually altered from the plural to the singular, "statue," on what appear to be no very strong grounds; for an effort to interpret "oppidum" as referring, not to Magnesia, but to Athens, see C. Wachsmuth, *Rh. Mus.* 52 (1897), 141.

40. The figures for the increment to the fleet as a result of Themistocles' Naval Bill are discussed in Appendix B.

41. Further discussion of the Troizen Decree is in chapter 8.

should round Euboea, they would be exposed to attack on both sides" (chap. 3, trans. Rolfe). The motivation is strikingly different from the Herodotean picture of panic and despair setting in when news comes to the troops at Artemisium of the débâcle at Thermopylae. But, since the Troizen Decree has called forth a rethinking of the strategy of 480, the tradition (if it is that) preserved in Nepos ought not to be rejected out of hand.[42]

The historical content of the relevant sections of Diodorus of Sicily's *Bibliotheca* has been discussed in the preceding chapter, where the assumption was made explicit that, for affairs in mainland Greece in the first part of the fifth century at least, Diodorus relied heavily (perhaps solely) on Ephorus.[43] The question arises of what this Augustan workhorse, who comments that he spent thirty years collecting material for his forty-book *Bibliotheca* (1. 4), himself contributed, over and above what he found in his source. It is generally assumed that what Diodorus did was parcel out the events he treated according to an annalistic, year-by-year chronological scheme on some basis known only to himself.[44] His method (if it deserves to be called that) has one obvious and glaring defect: he lumps together, under one archontate/ consulate/Olympiad, events which other sources or plain common sense indicate must have taken more than one calendar year to accomplish. The most flagrant example of his manner of proceeding in the career of Themistocles is in book 11, chapters 54 to 59, where, under the archonship of Praxiergos (471/70 B.C.), he relates Themistocles' ostracism, condemnation for treason, escape to Asia, later career, and death. Which (if any) of these events Diodorus had actually found good chronographic evidence for is disputed; it is generally assumed that it is the ostracism which is to be dated to this year.[45] In 11. 41–43 he tells an elaborate and too circumstantial story of Themistocles' fortification of the Peiraeus under the year 477/6, although Thucydides makes it clear that the project had been begun in Themistocles' year as archon—on any hypothesis before 480[46]—and leaves vague when exactly the scheme was brought to fruition: Thucydides (1. 93. 3–7) merely places it after the city fortifications and the Greek capture of Cyprus. Had Diodorus independent—and, more important, trustworthy—evidence for the date? The uncertainty is particularly annoying in regard to a measure of Themistocles which Diodorus mentions at the end of this section (11. 43. 3): his proposal for the annual addition to the Athenian fleet of twenty new triremes. Diodorus may have found this somewhere in Ephorus, and it may be a fact, but it would be more natural to connect it, as some scholars have done, with the Naval Bill of 483. Or does it come from some source (for example, an *Atthis*) which had access to good epigraphic or other documentary evidence?

Similar to the case of the preservation of Ephorus' account embedded in the later

42. As is done by Macan, *Herodotus, Books VII–IX*, II, 83.

43. For Ephorus, see chapter 4, pp. 92 ff.

44. For a recent scholarly opinion on the matter, see M. Sordi, *Diodori Siculi Bibliothecae Liber Sextus Decimus*, vii–viii, and the work by G. Perl cited by her at vi, n.4.

45. "[Diodorus] more frequently relates the sequel of an event under the year in which it commenced than the contrary," F. Clinton quoted by Dindorf in the Teubner edition (Leipzig, 1867), vol. III, p. xx. Cf. Gomme, *Commentary*, I, 400–401.

46. For the chronological problems involved, see Appendix A.

work of Diodorus is that of Pompeius Trogus, who, about 20 B.C., wrote forty-four books of *Philippics* which have come down only in a Latin epitome by a certain Justin (perhaps of the fourth century A.D.) and in excerpts in a collection of *Stratagems* by Frontinus (late first century A.D.). As with most of the other of these late accounts, the work is valuable only for what it preserves from earlier sources. Trogus' treatment of Themistocles comes in book 2, chapters 12 to 15, of the *Epitome*, and it follows Herodotus for the main outlines and for many of the details; he is the only later writer to agree with the Herodotean figure of 200 ships for Themistocles' Naval Bill. Chapter 12 opens with Themistocles' appeal to the Ionians, basically an expansion of Herodotus (8. 22), proceeds to the unsuccessful Persian attack on Delphi (Herodotus 8. 37, with variations), Themistocles' interpretation of the wooden wall oracle (7. 144) and his message to Xerxes (8. 75), Queen Artemisia (8. 87–88), and ends with a distinct departure from the Herodotean version: "While the result of the battle was still doubtful, the Ionians, according to the admonition of Themistocles, began gradually to withdraw from the contest; and their desertion broke the courage of the rest."[47] This contribution of the Ionians in Xerxes' fleet to the Greek victory—in explicit contradiction to Herodotus' statement that the majority of the Ionians did not accede to Themistocles' urgings that they malinger (8. 85)—is called by Macan Trogus' "most plausible addition or development"; and yet, Macan himself believes that "it can hardly be ascribed to genuine tradition: it is more like a rationalistic suggestion to account for the victory."[48] Or perhaps it is no more than a simple transference to Salamis of the motif of Ionian defection at the battle of Mycale, as related by Herodotus (9. 98, 103).

In chapter 13, Xerxes' retreat and Themistocles' second message are narrated. Trogus again takes much from Herodotus: the detail that Themistocles a second time sent to Xerxes the "same servant" as carried the first message (Hdt. 8. 110), the harrowing hardships of the return march (8. 115). What is new is a suppression of the motif so prominent in Herodotus of Themistocles' about-face on the subject of the bridges. Herodotus has him first suggest destroying the Hellespontine bridge, then, as a result of opposition from Eurybiades, assuming the opposite side and pretending in his message that he was responsible for detaining the Greek troops (Hdt. 8. 109–10); in Trogus, Themistocles is unable to persuade the Greeks that Xerxes' troops ought to be allowed to return, else they might "take courage from despair, and open by their swords a passage not to be opened by other means."[49] Of the alternate stories which Herodotus presents (8. 117–20) of how Xerxes himself finally returned, Trogus chooses that which took the king from Abydos by ship, but he heightens the pathos of the event by having him return in a "small fishing boat"; this allows a lengthy disquisition on the *sors humana* which reduced the former master of so many men and ships to this, him "whom shortly before the whole ocean could scarcely contain," now

47. Justin 2. 12. 25, trans. J. S. Watson (Bohn's Library, 1853).

48. Macan, *Herodotus, Books VII–IX*, II, 81. Trogus may have "expanded" on a hint in Ephorus (Diod. 11. 17. 3–4).

49. Justin 2. 13. 6, trans. Watson. Similar arguments are used by Herodotus' Eurybiades in order to dissuade Themistocles, who takes them over and presents them to his men (Hdt. 8. 108–9).

"shrinking down in a little boat" (2. 13. 10, trans. Watson). There follows an account of the battles of Plataea and Mycale in chapter 14, which closes with the statement that, among cities, Athens received the award of merit, among individuals, Themistocles.[50] Chapter 15 is devoted to Themistocles' rebuilding of the city walls. Trogus' account follows Thucydides (1. 90–91) closely, with one or two insignificant embellishments: Thucydides says that when he got to Sparta, Themistocles "did not approach the authorities, but kept delaying and making excuses" (1. 90. 5), which in Trogus becomes, "feigned ill health due to travelling," and Themistocles' orders to detain the Spartan ambassadors are carried "by the hand of a slave." After the account of the walls, Themistocles simply disappears from Trogus' pages; no mention is made of his downfall in connection with that of Pausanias, which is narrated at the end of chapter 15.

Macan's comment that "if it be asked whether Trogus has fished up any forgotten pearls of genuine tradition, or adds anything of real history to our materials, the answer must be in the negative,"[51] appears to be completely justified. It seems unprofitable to speculate on what other authorities Trogus may have used.[52]

Finally, the continuous narrative that has been preserved under the name of Aristodemus may be examined here.[53] His date can only be matter for conjecture, and all attempts to identify him with other known individuals of the same name have proven futile.[54] It is now generally believed that his work, apparently a universal history along Ephorean lines, was composed as late as the fourth or fifth century A.D. but contains embedded within it a genuine early tradition (Thucydides is relied on almost exclusively for the rebuilding of the walls and the end of Themistocles' career), with an admixture of a rhetorical, pro-Athenian account of the fourth century, perhaps from Ephorus. The fragmentary narrative opens with Themistocles' asking (presumably the other generals) for a delay of "just one more day," then sending his children's tutor Sicinnus to Xerxes. The king, believing that Themistocles has "medized," sends his troops to encircle the Greeks. The project of the mole across to Salamis is dated before the battle, as in Ctesias,[55] and the spot from which Xerxes viewed the battle is situated "on Mt. Parnes." The actual fighting (begun, as in Herodotus 8. 84, by Ameinias, though Aristodemus specifies that he was brother of the poet Aeschylus) is perfunctorily narrated, with special prominence being given to Aristeides' exploit on Psyttaleia.[56] The remainder of this first chapter is Herodotean:

50. 2. 14. 10–11, in clear contradiction to Herodotus (8. 123); the error can be found again in Aelius Aristeides, Or. 13, I, 224 Dind. (sec. 118, Oliver).

51. Macan, Herodotus, Books VII–IX, II, 80.

52. Herodotus and Ctesias have been suggested ("used through a later intermediary") by A. Gutschmid (Kl. Schrift. V [1894], 19 ff.), cited by A. Klotz, RE 21 (1952), col. 2309; not, apparently, Ephorus, according to Jacoby, RE 11 (1922), col. 2068.

53. Text at Jacoby, FGrHist 104, and Hill's Sources for Greek History² (Oxford, 1951), 17 ff. There is a useful summary of the new

material added to the tradition by Aristodemus in Macan, Herodotus, Books VII–IX, II, 81–82, n.1. There is a full commentary (in Latin) in Müller, FHG, V, 1 ff.

54. See the full discussion (in Latin) by Müller, FHG, V, "Prolegomena," xxii–xxxiv.

55. This version reappears in Strabo. Herodotus (8. 97) places it after the battle.

56. FGrHist 104. 1(4). Aristodemus gives Aristeides his soubriquet, dikaios (cf. 2[4]), and appears to make Psyttaleia the first cooperative venture between the former enemies (thus tacitly contradicting Herodotus 8. 79, 82).

Queen Artemisia, Dikaios' vision from Eleusis; but Aristodemus follows a pro-Themistocles tradition for the incident of the Greek failure to destroy the Hellespontine bridges.[57] Themistocles' name does not reappear until chapter 5, where his rebuilding of Athens' fortification walls is narrated; the account is manifestly based on Thucydides, perhaps along with Ephorus, since the motif of Themistocles "out-generalling" the Spartans on this occasion is found in Aristodemus and Diodorus, not in Thucydides.[58] There is another discrepancy with Thucydides, the figures given for the length of the Peiraeus circuit wall: Thucydides' figure is sixty stades, while Aristodemus gives eighty, a figure which seems closer to the truth, so far as the archaeologists have been able to ascertain.[59] The close link between Themistocles' fall and that of Pausanias is emphasized in chapter 6, although the somewhat abbreviated version of Thucydides 1. 138. 1 is here expanded: Themistocles' ostracism is ascribed to jealousy of his "outstanding intelligence and *arete*."[60] After a colourful account of the last years of Pausanias' career, Aristodemus returns in chapter 10 to Themistocles' escape from Argos to Persia via Corcyra and Epirus; the route and almost all the details are Thucydidean, the only divergences being the nature of Themistocles' threat to the captain on whose ship he made his escape and Aristodemus' preference for the version which had Themistocles, feeling himself unable to fulfil his promise to bring Greece into the king's dominions because he "thought he ought not to be making war against kinsmen," commit suicide by drinking the blood of a bull which he was sacrificing to Artemis.[61] Although the wording of chapter 11 is slightly confused and may have suffered textual corruption, what Aristodemus seems to have had in mind is that Themistocles' attack against Greece was in the very act of being withstood by a Greek armament (probably led by Cimon), when they learned of his death and "campaigned against Artaxerxes, and the Athenians immediately set about freeing the Ionian and remaining Greek cities [sc. of Asia]" (11. 1). This story, which rests on no earlier ancient authority, can safely be disregarded, especially since Aristodemus compounds confusion by conflating Cimon's earlier victory at the Eurymedon River in Pamphylia and the later, Athenian attempt to assist the revolutionary Egyptian prince Inarus, this latter confusion with the Egyptian revolt recurring in Plutarch (*Them.* 31. 4).

Last in this assorted group of late accounts should be mentioned the work *On Famous Men* by a certain Amphicrates, who may be identical with the Athenian rhetorician of that name active in the first century B.C.[62] From it Athenaeus quotes a two-line epigram which purports to refer to Themistocles' mother:

Abrotonon, by birth a woman of Thrace, but
to have borne Themistocles, great among Greeks.

57. 1 (7), verbally very close to Trogus-Justin.
58. *FGrHist* 104. 5 (1) = Diod. 11. 40. 4.
59. 104. 5 (4) with Müller's note, *FHG*, V, 8–9; cf. Thuc. 2. 13. 7, where Gomme's defence of Thucydides' figure seems to me untenable (*Commentary*, II, 40). For a discussion of the walls, see chapter 10.

60. 104. 6 (1); cf. Diod. 11. 54, fin. (though there the link with Pausanias had already been introduced) and Plut. *Them.* 22. 1.
61. 104. 10 (5). This version of the story, as Müller notes, is followed by the scholiast on Aristophanes, *Knights* 84.
62. Müller, *FHG*, IV, 300.

This "epitaph" is clearly a late invention which is preserved, with variants, also by Plutarch (*Them.* 1. 1) and the *Palatine Anthology* (7. 306). It is not altogether clear whether Athenaeus' reference to Themistocles' mother as a prostitute also comes from Amphicrates, or whether it is Athenaeus' own inference from the lady's name.[63] How extensive Amphicrates' account may have been can now only be conjectured (the epigram and one reference in Diogenes Laertius to another section of it are all that survive), but it may, to judge from the title, have followed in the Peripatetic tradition of deeds and sayings of outstanding figures. The recurrence of the "epitaph" in Plutarch (where Amphicrates is not named) suggests that the work may have contributed significantly to the anecdotic tradition regarding Themistocles which took seed in the Roman literary world of the first century B.C. and grew to outlandish proportions later—its best representative was Plutarch—but any such ascription of influence must remain of course hypothetical.

References in Nonhistorical Writers

The renewed interest that Romans of the first century B.C. began to feel in the great figures of their common Hellenic heritage pervades the works of a writer who was not an historian, but who had an acute sense of the historical tradition of which he felt himself to be an important part. Cicero was clearly intimately familiar with many aspects of Themistocles' career and refers to him frequently,[64] not only for the standard items with which most educated Romans would have connected the name of Themistocles, but also for more recondite information which can only have been the result of special research. References in the speeches are surprisingly few, being far outweighed by occurrences in the letters and philosophical works. One of the facts of Themistocles' life which made a deep impression on Cicero, perhaps because of the parallel with his own career, was his exile at the hands of an ungrateful populace. He is linked in this regard with Miltiades in *de Republica*, as "instances of the fickleness and cruelty of Athens toward her most eminent citizens."[65] In the *pro Sestio* Cicero remarks that Themistocles, the "Saviour of his country," was not deterred by the examples of Miltiades and Aristeides from defending the state in spite of the rash ingratitude of her citizens;[66] and when, at the end of this section, Cicero refers to Rome as "that State, whose worth is so great that to die in its defence is more to be desired than by fighting against it to attain supreme power,"[67] he may have in mind the story of Themistocles' choice to commit suicide rather than to lead a Persian force

63. Abrotonon (or Habrotonon) is not uncommon, and is borne by characters in Menander's *Epitrepontes* and *Perikeiromene*.

64. Macan counted "upwards of three dozen passages [in Cicero] in which Themistocles is named" (*Herodotus, Books VII–IX*, II, 60, n.7, with synopsis there of the most important references) and commented, "Cicero is deeply versed in the Themistoclean legend and Themistocles fills a larger place in his writings than is

taken by any other Greek statesman" (60). See also H. Berthold in *Klio* 43–45 (1965), 38–48.

65. *de Repub.* 1. 5, trans. C. W. Keyes (Loeb Classical Library).

66. Cicero ignored, or was unaware of, the story that made Themistocles responsible for Aristeides' ostracism.

67. *pro Sest.* 47. 141, trans. R. Gardner (Loeb Classical Library).

against Greece. His suicide is alluded to briefly at *pro Scauro* (3. 3), where he is obliquely compared to the tragic Ajax, but Cicero was also aware that the matter was in some doubt. In the course of a comparison between Themistocles and a figure much closer to home, Coriolanus, in the rhetorical treatise *Brutus*, Cicero remarks that these men, for all their prominence in their respective states, were expelled by their ungrateful fellow citizens, and "quieted the impulses of their anger" with death (92). Cicero then half-humorously alludes to a variant version of Coriolanus' death in Atticus' *Liber Annalis*,[68] thus giving Atticus a chance to retort that historians like Cleitarchus and Stratokles have "embellished Themistocles' death in rhetorical and tragic fashion";[69] Atticus clearly states his own preference for (and incidentally manifests Cicero's knowledge of) Thucydides' soberer account. Themistocles and Coriolanus are compared again in the treatise *de Amicitia* (12. 42) and juxtaposed in a letter to Atticus, where Coriolanus is said to have "basely sought aid from the Volsci," while Themistocles "rightly preferred to die" (*ad Att*. 9. 10. 3). In another letter to Atticus, Cicero quotes (probably from memory) Thucydides' appreciation of Themistocles' intelligence and foresight (1. 138. 3), and yet, says Cicero, this intelligence failed him, or he would have seen how to escape the jealousy of the Spartans and his own citizens and how to avoid making promises to Artaxerxes which he could not fulfil (*ad Att*. 10. 8. 7).

What above all struck Cicero about Themistocles was that he combined ability at public speaking with a touch for practical politics ("cum prudentia tum etiam eloquentia" [*Brutus* 28]), Cicero's ideal of the statesman which he constantly strove to emulate in his own public life. Cicero names Themistocles at the head of a list of figures who combined "faciendi dicendique sapientiam."[70] Another aspect which seems to have caught Cicero's interest was Themistocles' alleged mnemonic ability, and he frequently mentions the connection in this regard between Themistocles and Simonides, who was said to have perfected a technique for improving the memory. Four times Cicero reports the incident of Simonides' promise to teach him the "Art of Memory," to which Themistocles replied, "I prefer the art of forgetting, for I remember what I should prefer to forget, and forget what I wish to remember."[71] In the speech *pro Archia* (9. 20), where Cicero is illustrating the point that all men are willing to have their own accomplishments celebrated in verse, an anecdote is related of Themistocles' reply to a question about whose voice he most liked to hear: "His who best celebrates my accomplishments." The story, whether true or not, implies that Themistocles had in mind specifically *poetic* memorialization of his deeds, and if a name were to be given, it would be most appropriate to mention Simonides in this connection, for he had, indeed, enshrined Themistocles' achievements at Artemisium and Salamis in verse.[72]

68. The evidence for Atticus' historical work is collected and discussed by Douglas in his edition of *Brutus*, Introd., sec. 39, pp. lii–liii.

69. *Brutus* 43, with Douglas' note.

70. *de Orat*. 3. 59. Themistocles' name occurs in other such lists at *de Fin*. 2. 21. 67, 2. 35. 116; *Tusc*. 1. 15. 33, 1. 46. 110, 4. 25. 55; *de Off*. 1. 30. 108, 2. 5. 16.

71. *de Fin*. 2. 32. 104; *de Orat*. 2. 351; Simonides is not named at *Acad*. 2. 1. 2, and at *de Orat*. 2. 299. The offer is ascribed to a certain "doctus homo atque in primis eruditus." (See H. Blum, *Die Antike Mnemotechnik*, 41–46 for Simonides; 43, n.32 for Cicero.)

72. The relations between Themistocles and Simonides are discussed in chapter 1, pp. 49 ff.

Cicero recounts several anecdotes from Themistocles' life which are also recorded elsewhere: Themistocles lay awake nights, his rest disturbed by thoughts of Miltiades' trophy for Marathon and how he might equal the achievement (*Tusc.* 4. 19. 44); his response to the man asking for advice regarding the impending marriage of his daughter to "look for a man without money rather than money without a man" (*de Off.* 2. 20. 71); his refusal to play the lyre at banquets which earned for him a reputation for boorishness (*Tusc.* 1. 2. 4; quoted by Quintilian, *Inst. Orat.* 1. 10. 19). The fact that these all crop up again in Plutarch[73] (who was familiar with Cicero's works) suggests they may have been drawn from a common store of similar tales, which, whenever they began to be circulated, seem to have been added to in ever-increasing numbers from the first century B.C. on. Of potentially greater importance is Cicero's vague reference in a letter to Brutus to the "poverty of Themistocles' children" (1. 15. 11). Behind this may lie a version which contradicted the more usual account according to which some, at least, of the children were sent from Athens and lived with Themistocles in Asia (Plut. *Them.* 24. 6, from Stesimbrotus). The story known to Plutarch of Themistocles' suggestion for burning the Greek fleet at Pagasai Cicero narrates again with a variant: it was merely the Spartan fleet at Gytheum which Themistocles proposed to burn;[74] this is a much more plausible version, but may only be an unhistorical reflection of the exploit actually carried out by Tolmides in 455 B.C. (Thuc. 1. 108. 5). In a letter to the historian L. Lucceius, in which Cicero asks him to write a monograph on his career, there is a reference to Themistocles' "exile and return" (*fuga redituque*), which has been taken to indicate that Cicero was familiar with a story, like that found in the *Constitution of Athens*, of Themistocles' return from exile to assist Ephialtes in his attack on the Areopagus in 462 B.C.[75] If this is what Cicero meant (and not, for example, simply the "exile" at the time of the city's capture by the Persians, which Cicero alludes to elsewhere),[76] it seems to conflict with Cicero's own time scheme in the *de Amicitia* (12. 42), where he remarks that Themistocles "did the same thing as Coriolanus" had done some twenty years earlier, that is, went into exile sometime around 471 B.C. Cicero reflects the conservative tradition regarding the victory of Salamis when he says that "while Themistocles could not readily point to any instance in which he himself had rendered assistance to the Areopagus, the Areopagus might with justice assert that Themistocles had received assistance from it; for the war was directed by [its] counsels."[77]

The geographer Strabo, who lived during the last part of Augustus' reign and the opening years of Tiberius', mentions Themistocles but rarely. He says (erroneously)

73. Miltiades' trophy: *Them.* 3. 4, *Thes.* 6. 9, *Mor.* 84 B, 92 C, 185 A, 800 B; a man without money: *Them.* 18. 9, *Mor.* 185 D (this may go back to Ephorus, Diod. 10, fr. 32); refusal to play the lyre: a variant of a story told by Ion of Chios, *Them.* 2. 4, *Cim.* 9. 1.

74. *de Off.* 3. 11. 49; cf. Plut. *Them.* 20. 1–2, *Arist.* 22. 2–4.

75. *ad Fam.* 5. 12. 5, *Const. of Athens* 25. 3–4. The connection is made by P. N. Ure in *JHS* 41 (1921), 176, following a suggestion of E. R. Dodds.

76. *ad Att.* 7. 11. 3, where possibly Cicero is to be interpreted as saying that, in abandoning Rome before Caesar's advance early in 49 B.C., Pompey quoted Themistocles' dictum that "walls do not make a city" (Hdt. 8. 61). Elsewhere Cicero calls Pompey's plan to win through mastery of the sea "Themistoclean" (*ad Att.* 10. 8. 4).

77. *de Off.* 1. 22. 75, trans. W. Miller (Loeb Classical Library). This version is reflected in the *Constitution of Athens* (23. 1) and may go back to Androtion.

that "Xerxes gave Lampsacus to Themistocles to supply him with wine" (13. C 587; Myus and Magnesia are added at 14. C 636). He adds one new item: there was a temple of Dindymene, "Mother of the Gods," at the old site of the city of Magnesia; in this temple "one tradition has it that Themistocles' wife served as priestess, another that it was his daughter."[78] Themistocles is somewhat surprisingly never mentioned by Strabo in connection with the battle of Salamis, but Strabo here, as elsewhere, shows almost no indebtedness to Herodotus; he follows a contrary tradition (preserved also by Ctesias) for the report that Xerxes' project of building a mole or causeway from the mainland to Salamis was interrupted by the battle (9. C 395).

Dio of Prusa in Bithynia, a rhetorician and philosopher who lived in the latter part of the first century A.D. and who was on friendly terms with the emperors Nerva and Trajan, wrote "discourses" (philosophical treatises in the form of orations), eighty of which are extant. In two of these Themistocles' career is briefly sketched. He was exiled on a charge of treason, not only after having restored the Athenians to their land and homes, which they had been forced to evacuate, but also after having made them leaders of the Greeks, a position which the Spartans had held from the beginning but which Themistocles had divested them of (Or. 73. 5). In another place Dio compares Themistocles with Pericles, both of whom he calls *daimones*, or "guiding spirits," of the Athenians; Themistocles, he continues, "compelled the Athenians, who had been foot-soldiers before, to fight on the sea...and stake all their fortunes on their fleet, and afterwards to fortify the Peiraeus with walls of more than ninety stades in length and enjoined upon them by his orders other measures of the same kind, some of which they continued to carry out...even when he was in banishment and after his death."[79] Whether Dio had any particular measures in mind is unclear, but his implication seems to be that the naval policy of Pericles (for whom he does not narrate any specific accomplishments in the section which follows) was merely a prolongation of Themistocles'.

By the second century the interest shown by learned Greeks in their past history and antiquities (an interest which seems to have had largely escapist motives)[80] was in full tide. Aelius Aristeides, mystic, hypochondriac, and friend of the later emperors Marcus Aurelius and Commodus, continued with the genre of rhetorical discourse on a variety of subjects, but his interest and researches in earlier Greek history went much deeper than Dio's. Fifty-one of his orations survive, and two of these are of the utmost importance for the Themistocles tradition.[81] In the *Panathenaicus*, whose inspiration goes back to Isocrates, Xerxes' attack against, and capture and sack of, Athens, and

---

78. 14. C 647. In the version which Plutarch recounts it was unequivocally the daughter, whose name is given as Mnesiptolema (*Them.* 30. 6).

79. Or. 25. 4, trans. J. W. Cohoon (Loeb Classical Library). The figure of ninety stades for the Peiraeus circuit is half again as much as Thucydides' of sixty.

80. See an interesting article by E. L. Bowie, "Greeks and Their Past in the Second Sophistic," *Past and Present*, no. 46 (1970), 3 ff., esp.

28–31.

81. Information about this rather inaccessible writer is most easily obtained in Macan, *Herodotus, Books VII–IX*, II, 103 ff. There is a new, full edition with translation and commentary of Oration 13, the *Panathenaic Discourse*, by J. H. Oliver (*Transactions of the American Philosophical Society*, 1968). A similar study of Oration 46, *For the Four*, is badly needed.

his repulse at Salamis, are narrated very fully in sections 94 to 135,[82] but since this is a panegyric primarily of the city, Aristeides is very careful not to mention any individual by name. Such references to Themistocles as there are occur only in elaborate and somewhat artificial circumlocutions. "It was this city which provided the man who gave the good advice...that was destined to save them" (sec. 103).[83] "I do not mention the leader who was so superior to all the rest that he as one man was worth all the rest, he who alone expounded like a prophet which were the right places and times, and what were the secrets of the King, and what the future would be" (sec. 111). And, as an example of the rhetorical conceits which this type of writing encouraged, "All that did not meet with the approval of a certain man of Athens was invalid, so that the admiral of the Lacedaemonians commanded the admirals from the various states, but the man of Athens commanded the commander of the commanders" (sec. 117; cf. Or. 46, vol. II, p. 252 Dind.). This same "man of Athens," Aristeides mistakenly says, won the first prize for valour (sec. 118). Credit for instigating the decisive battle is reassigned from Themistocles to "the Athenians" generally, but Aristeides redeems himself by ascribing the disaffection among the Ionian contingents in Xerxes' fleet to "foresight on the part of a general" (sec. 124). The rewards which Athens received for the victory were due to her "first because of what the city as a community carried out so famously, secondly because of what she accomplished through her general" (sec. 128). But all reference, even oblique, to Themistocles is absent where it seems natural and might have been expected: the yielding of hegemony to Sparta in order to secure unity (sec. 108),[84] the anonymous hypothetical speech telling the other Greeks that Athens had "transferred the entire city to the triremes" (sec. 110). The absence of mention of Themistocles which has potentially the greatest significance is from Aristeides' account of how the Athenians "passed a decree to entrust the city to the goddess who keeps the city, to deposit women and children at Troizen and themselves...to make the sea their wall" (sec. 122), where there can be no doubt that the words paraphrase the evacuation decree, an epigraphic copy of which was found at Troizen explicitly naming Themistocles as mover.[85] Aristeides' self-imposed restriction on using proper names seems not to have intended to be prejudicial to Themistocles, for when he comes to mention the exploit of his own namesake on Psyttaleia, which he introduces merely as a "fillip" or "bywork" (*parergon*), he ascribes it to "a man of Athens, a volunteer" (sec. 126).

This neglect Aristeides makes up for in large part in Oration 46, the "Second Platonic Oration," *For the Four*, in which he presents a defence against the charges which Plato in the *Gorgias* aims at Miltiades, Themistocles, Pericles, and Cimon. A long central section of the work is devoted to the life and career of Themistocles,

82. Oliver's numbering, where there are references in the margin to the standard edition by Dindorf.

83. The translations from the *Panathenaicus* are Oliver's.

84. The agency of Themistocles is attested by Plutarch (*Them.* 7. 3), but not by Herodotus (8. 3).

85. Oliver accepts Jameson's suggestion that Aristeides' familiarity with the text is further manifested at section 126, where he states that the men who crossed over to Salamis were over fifty, a detail preserved in no other literary account, nowhere else, in fact, but the Troizen Decree.

extended passages of straight narration being punctuated by polemizing comments directed against Plato's criticisms.[86] Aristeides knows intimately, and draws abundantly upon, the accounts of Herodotus, Thucydides, and, surprisingly, Plutarch.[87] He also shows reasonable historical sense in using the primary authorities when they are available (for example, Herodotus for Themistocles' reception at Sparta, Thucydides for the exile) with this exception: the panegyric tendency of his work occasionally makes him choose the more honorific account of Plutarch, especially when it is a question of attributing specific measures, which the earlier authorities say were taken by the Athenians collectively, to the individual agency of Themistocles. Thus, for the composition of quarrels among feuding Greek states in order to present a united front to the invaders, left vague by Herodotus (7. 145), Aristeides (p. 248) gives credit specifically to Themistocles, just as Plutarch had done (*Them.* 6. 5).[88] Both authors attribute to Themistocles by name the statesmanlike act of yielding hegemony to Sparta (*Them.* 7. 3; p. 252 Dind.). Aristeides refers casually to the "decrees," *dogmata*, of Themistocles, passed "at the very time when Greece stood on the razor's edge, whether it would exist or not" (p. 246).

Among these Themistoclean decrees, one would have been tempted, perhaps, to list the mobilization decree, of which Aristeides gives a fairly full and close paraphrase (pp. 256–57). This might have been dismissed as part of the same eulogistic tendency had the actual inscription not been discovered at Troizen, which shows that this very measure was, indeed, attributed to Themistocles at least as early as the third century B.C.[89] It can now be seen that this text, which Plutarch merely summarizes (*Them.* 10. 4), Aristeides knew in a fuller form, perhaps even in its entirety, if the phrase which he appears to quote from it, "to have confidence in the gods" (p. 256), can be taken as a reference to the list of gods at lines 38–40 of the epigraphic text.[90] This reference to the gods is of some importance; Aristeides remarks that in proposing the decree "some god spoke through Themistocles' mouth" (p. 257), that the Athenians who were forced to evacuate their city "clung to his voice as to a sacred anchor" (p. 258). He was "truly born through some divine fate [*theai tini moirai*] and to the advantage of all of Greece" (p. 252). Before Artemisium, he "held his hand over events like some god from the machine and prevented disaster" (p. 254). The wooden wall oracle was "the common prophecy of Pythian Apollo and Themistocles" (ibid.). The clauses of the evacuation decree were "the behests of the *daimon*, but the counsel of Themi-

86. Pp. 238–318 in volume II of Dindorf's edition (1829, rpt. 1964), to which reference is made in the notes which follow.

87. There is a valuable example of the now somewhat outmoded technique of *Quellenforschung* by Alfred Haas, *Quibus fontibus Aelius Aristides in componenda declamatione, quae inscribitur* ΠΡΟΣ ΠΛΑΤΩΝΑ ῾ΥΠΕΡ ΤΩΝ ΤΕΤΤΑΡΩΝ, *usus sit*; cf. Adolf Bauer, *Themistokles* (1881), 144 ff. A selection of material is presented by Macan, *Herodotus, Books VII–IX,* II, 104–6. (That Plutarch himself was used directly by Aristeides cannot be doubted in view of the similarity of wording

and parallel imagery of *Them.* 3. 5 and p. 251 Dind.: "believing that Marathon had been, as it were, merely a prelude for the Athenians, that it was not the finish and completion of the entire war, but rather the beginning and a preparation for other, greater struggles." See Bauer, *Themistokles* [1881], 146, with n.1.)

88. Haas, *Quibus fontibus*, 38–39; Bauer, *Themistokles* (1881), 148.

89. The Troizen Decree is discussed fully in chapter 8.

90. It is generally maintained (on what seem to me insufficient grounds) that Aristeides knew only the first eighteen lines of the decree.

stocles" (p. 256). "At such a critical moment, when matters were all in such a bad way and in such confusion, he stood forth, unchecked, unflinching, and did not pray that the earth should open up for him, nor call upon the happy fate of those long dead, nor do what the majority did, but came forward as Greece's lucky *Daimon*" (p. 243).[91] Aristeides indicates what may be his ultimate source for this theme when he says elsewhere that if one were to ask, "Who was responsible for the salvation of Greece?", a complete answer would be, "First, the gods; next, as far as human agency goes, one city—Athens, and the intelligence of one man—Themistocles" (pp. 248–49); it is precisely this divine agency that Herodotus portrays Themistocles as emphasizing to his men after the battle when the Greek fleet had given up pursuit of Xerxes at Andros (8. 109).

Aristeides' own contributions to the story, even if mere inferences, are at least sensible ones. Themistocles' three great services which saved Greece he lists as (1) his advice to build a fleet, "before any of the ordinary citizens expected that the barbarians would come"; (2) "his persuading them to fight at sea when war was actually at hand"; and (3) "his foresight of where on the sea it would be beneficial to them to hold the battle" (p. 281). Some add a fourth service, "that he advised not only the place but also the time, determining that the sea fight should take place when the wind was blowing downstream,"[92] but Aristeides seems sceptical. Themistocles is convincingly, if somewhat rhetorically, contrasted with Miltiades: "The one defeated the king's lieutenants, the other the king himself" (p. 239); Miltiades' office was "generalship against the barbarians," Themistocles', "true statesmanship [*politeia*] among all the Greeks" (p. 240).[93] Pindar's phrase, already oft-quoted by Plutarch, praising the Athenians for "laying the shining foundation-stone of freedom" at Artemisium, is here applied to Themistocles alone (p. 251). Aristeides' larger theme of polemic against Plato involves him in an incidental correction of Herodotus: "Themistocles not only devised [the building of] the triremes for the Athenians, nor—what is more important —used them opportunely and in a common just cause for all the Greeks, but also single-handedly accomplished and achieved in addition community of purpose [*homonoia*] among the cities, which saved Greece no less than the ships themselves" (p. 253; contrast Herodotus 7. 144). This remarkable feat, Aristeides argues, was "an example of moderation and perseverance such as no Spartan had ever shown."[94] Themistocles alone was the real leader, the leading admiral in all but name; his relationship to Eurybiades was of master to pupil, of one who had to hold up in his own arms another who was unable to swim (p. 253). Aristeides sees, and says, that

---

91. My translation; an interesting echo of Dio Chrysostom, Or. 25. 4, where Themistocles and Pericles are called the *daimones*, "spirits," of the Greeks.

92. P. 281 Dind. One would like to know what basis (if any) there might be to the scholiast's reference here to the love of Boreas, the North Wind, for Oreithyia, "an Athenian maiden" (in fact, daughter of Erechtheus). The scholiast's comment that Boreas "cooperated with the Athenians" looks like a (misplaced?)

reminiscence of Herodotus 7. 189. Cf. also Libanius, *Declam.* 9. 40, 43.

93. There is an extended comparison between Themistocles and Miltiades, on the one hand, and Cimon, on the other, which reads like a specimen set piece for declamation (pp. 260–62), and a further comparison with Dion (268 ff.).

94. P. 253 Dind. Aristeides elsewhere lists among Themistocles' virtues "courage, intelligence, magnanimity, cleverness, mildness, perseverance, amenability" (239–40).

Themistocles' retort, "not stones, or wood, or joiners' products are what make cities but wherever there are men who know how to save themselves, there are walls and cities" (compare Herodotus 8. 61), goes back to Alcaeus (p. 273). If the passage that follows has any authority behind it, Themistocles went on to use another figure: leaving the city was merely "changing costume for the next scene," and if they were leaving the land and taking to the sea, they "would again find both land and city on the sea, and get no worse service from them" (p. 274).

Not the least of Aristeides' contributions is the long passage which he quotes verbatim from the Socratic Aeschines' dialogue, *Alcibiades*.[95] When he provides a totally new fact, as, for example, that after the war Themistocles prevented the Spartans from "removing from the alliance," that is, annihilating, over thirty cities which had sided with the enemy (p. 290), his independent witness may be treated with some scepticism.[96] But on the whole, when he fills in his authorities, he does so in an intelligent and wholly credible way: the Spartans were eager to involve Themistocles in Pausanias' disgrace, not only because misery loves company, but also because "they feared that, if he were left in Athens, they would have in him an intractable adversary at every turn, and in addition they held a grudge against him for his deception concerning the walls" (p. 318). Guesswork this very probably is, but it carries conviction nonetheless.

At about the same time that Aristeides was composing his discourses, Pausanias, a native of Lydia, published a *Tour of Greece*, an annotated guidebook to the main sites and monuments of antiquity. Pausanias thus comes at the end of a long line of writers of this genre, who included Diodorus in the late fourth and early third, and Polemon and Heliodorus in the second, centuries B.C.; not only the wide range of his tour, but the evident care which he took to ascertain and record the facts, makes the preservation of Pausanias' work a happy accident of survival. Twice he mentions dedications by Themistocles' sons: in his description of the Peiraeus and its fortifications and a building "near the largest harbour," which he calls the "grave of Themistocles,"[97] he introduces a note, based on Thucydides, of the report that Themistocles' relations recovered his remains from Magnesia and brought them back to Attica,[98] and he proceeds to add that the sons themselves "obviously did return and set up a picture in the Parthenon in which Themistocles is portrayed" (1. 1. 2). On the Acropolis itself, there stood "a bronze statue of Artemis surnamed 'Leukophryene,' dedicated by Themistocles' sons, for the Magnesians, over whom Themistocles ruled as a gift from the king, hold Artemis Leukophryene in honour" (1. 26. 4). This testimony of Pausanias has sometimes been doubted,[99] perhaps unjustifiably, but Frazer illustrates an Athenian coin of the second century B.C. which has been held to picture this dedication.[100] On Salamis, Pausanias noted "both a sanctuary of Artemis and also a

---

95. Pp. 292–94 (= fr. 1 Krauss); see p. 78.
96. It may be a simple misunderstanding of Plutarch (*Them.* 20. 3).
97. For attempts to identify this building, see chapter 10.
98. Taken almost verbatim from Thucydides 1. 138. 6, with the slight variant that the Athenians had "repented" of their treatment of Themistocles. (Thucydides had said that the reburial was done "in secret.")
99. For example, by U. Kahrstedt, in *RE* 5.A (1934), col. 1696.
100. *Pausanias' Description of Greece*, II, 329. There is a good illustration in Margaret Thompson's *New Style Silver Coinage of Athens*, cat. 713 b, pl. 76 (142/1 B.C.).

trophy erected for the victory for which Themistocles was responsible" (1. 36. 1; this trophy also figures in the twelfth of the so-called Themistocles Epistles, where it is described as "of stone and surpassingly large" [p. 752 Hercher]). No archaeological remains have been discovered which answer to the description of a "sanctuary to Artemis," but the trophy for the victory was described by travellers as recently as the early nineteenth century. The monument apparently stood on the peninsula known as Kynosoura (although very little can actually be seen today),[101] and there was another trophy erected on the island of Psyttaleia, which Plutarch mentions (*Arist.* 9. 4). Pausanias also reports "statues of Themistocles and Miltiades" near the Prytaneion in the Agora; these, he says, "have had their inscriptions changed into 'a Roman' and 'a Thracian'" (1. 18. 3). When the statues were erected is unknown, but there is no need to assume that it was as early as the fifth century or that they were portrait likenesses. Nor does the change of inscription imply any *damnatio memoriae*; the practice, Frazer notes, "appears to have been common under the Roman dominion."[102] Pausanias also relates two anecdotes concerning Themistocles: how the audience at Olympia rose to applaud him (8. 50. 3, a longer version of the same story as that told by Plutarch at *Themistocles* 17. 4);[103] and a suspiciously detailed account of how Themistocles' attempt to dedicate at Delphi part of the Persian spoils was rudely rebuffed by the Pythia (10. 14. 5–6). Pausanias' further report of various explanations for the Pythia's attitude, one of which involves Apollo's foreknowledge that Themistocles would one day become a suppliant of the Persian king, suggests that the incident may be unhistorical. Elsewhere, Pausanias mentions a Themistocles who was a grandson of the "great" Themistocles (descended from him in the female line), who married into a prominent family and whose grave along the Sacred Way bespeaks the importance of his family connections.[104]

The satirist Lucian of Samosata (*c.* A.D. 125–180) comments in his essay *On Slander* that for all his probity even Aristeides "sided against Themistocles and joined in whetting the people's anger against him, since, they say, he was to some extent pricked by the same political ambition" (*Calumn.* 27). Whether there is any basis to Lucian's remark is unknown, and it conflicts with Plutarch's statement in the *Aristeides* that "when Alcmeon and Cimon and many others were attacking and bringing accusations against him, only Aristeides contributed no base deed or word, nor took advantage of his enemy's misfortune" (25. 10). In fact, this tradition in Plutarch may be the more suspect, as it may be thought to have little basis other than an attempt to exaggerate Aristeides' nobility in taking the side of his old political rival when the latter found himself in an increasingly dangerous situation. It is curious that both traditions are represented in the so-called Themistocles Epistles, which were perhaps being com-

101. Paul W. Wallace, "Psyttaleia and the Trophies of the Battle of Salamis," *AJA* 73 (1969), 293–303, esp. 299 ff. Prof. Wallace writes, "Around Ambelaki Bay where Salamis town was probably situated...I found nothing specific enough to suggest a shrine of Artemis" (letter to the author, August 28, 1969). The trophy is also mentioned in *IG* II², 1035, line 33.

102. *Pausanias' Description of Greece*, II, 174.
103. If the historicity of the event be accepted, the likeliest date is that suggested by Macan, *Herodotus, Books VII–IX*, II, 99, Olympiad 76 (476 B.C.).
104. 1. 37. 1 (= Kirchner, *PA*, 6654). A still later Themistocles was archon in 347/6 B.C. (*PA*, 6650, with refs. there).

posed at about the same time as Lucian's works.[105] In the dialogue *Zeus Tragoidos* Lucian notes that the ambiguous phrase in the wooden wall oracle, "O Divine Salamis, thou shalt destroy the children of women," could apply to Greeks or Persians (sec. 20), and later an oracle is given whose meaning is so clear that it "will not need a Themistocles" to interpret it (sec. 31).

Among the favourite themes for rhetorical exercises in the schools of the Roman period were events, real and imaginary, taken from the life of Themistocles. An example of such a set piece for declamation survives in the fifth oration of the fourth-century rhetorician Himerius of Prusa, a fictitious address of Themistocles before the Athenian Assembly in opposition to a motion to conclude a peace treaty with the Persian king. (A similar fictitious situation occurs in the fifth *Suasoria* of the elder Seneca: the Athenians deliberate whether to take down the Persian War trophies after receiving a message from Xerxes who threatens another invasion if they do not remove them.) Himerius, whose rhetorical flourishes are extremely forced and without natural fire, for the most part did little to improve on Aelius Aristeides, whom he admired and drew on heavily.[106] At times he even spoils what he borrows: Themistocles' famous retort to Adeimantus that "men, not walls, make a city" is turned into iambic trimeter and (seemingly; the text is here in doubt) ascribed to Xerxes (Or. 5, sec. 32, Colonna). Occasionally he scores an effective point: Athens' walls may be down, but "if you seek to discover her boundaries, survey in your thoughts the whole inhabited world— land as much as may be traversed and sea sailed; such are Athens' boundaries under Themistocles" (Or. 5, sec. 41, Colonna).

Among the large number of extant works of the orator Libanius there is a pair of orations which represent a speech by Themistocles' father, Neokles, who repents of having disinherited his son and now tries to reclaim him after the victory of Salamis (his action was motivated, Neokles says, by a desire to turn the young Themistocles from his loose living to the path of virtue), and Themistocles' speech in reply.[107] The tone is flat and the theme overelaborated; the content, a mere patchwork of earlier accounts.

Professors of rhetoric composed the *Arts of Rhetoric* and *Progymnasmata*, or "Preliminary Exercises," for their pupils, from the Hellenistic period on, and some examples by Theon and the famous rhetorician Hermogenes in the second century A.D. still survive.[108] The language of the wooden wall oracle was used to illustrate metaphor

105. Aristeides friendly to Themistocles: Epistles 3 (p. 742 Hercher, *Epistolographi Graeci*), 18; Aristeides among Themistocles' accusers: Epistle 8 (an Aeginetan Alcibiades is mentioned in Epistle 11); cf. Epistles 9 and 12. These dubious Epistles are discussed more fully at the end of the present chapter.

106. For example, the point that Themistocles yielded to Eurybiades merely the *schema* of being generalissimo, while retaining the substance for himself, which occurs twice in the extant works of Himerius (Or. 42, sec. 4, and Or. 48, sec. 29, Colonna), comes from Aelius Aristeides (II, 252 Dind.).

107. *Declam.* 9, 10 (vol. 5, Foerster [Teubner]). The same pseudohistorical example clearly lies behind Seneca, *Controversiae* I. 8, although Themistocles and Neokles are not named. The theme of *exheredatio* is apparently anachronistic for fifth-century Greece; see Michael Wurm, *Apokeryxis, Abdicatio, und Exheredatio*, 11 ff. and 42.

108. See George Kennedy, *The Art of Persuasion in Greece*, 270, with refs. there; idem, *The Art of Rhetoric in the Roman World*, 615–16 for Theon, 619 ff. for Hermogenes.

(Theon, II, 81, Spengel).[109] Various fictitious and totally improbable situations were chosen to illustrate points like logical consequence: Themistocles had been able to persuade the Athenians to abandon their city; next, suppose he tries to persuade them to go the whole way and keep the city from falling into the enemies' hands by burning it.[110] Utterly contrived techniques of refutation were exemplified in hypothetical situations: the Athenians, returning to Athens without funds in the public treasury, contemplate selling their ships; Themistocles counters with a suggestion that they condemn him for having proposed the building of the fleet in the first place; if his opponents are right now, they were right then and "clearly the ships had been of no use—it was the infantry which had saved the city."[111] Themistocles' sons answer the charge of treason against their father by demanding that the Athenians take down their fortification walls on grounds that "the man who had engineered this could not be suspected of treason."[112] Or, more innocently, hints in the received account are developed at greater length: Themistocles counsels his men *not* to flee to Sicily,[113] or Themistocles advises the Athenians not only to evacuate the city, but to "hold the mysteries aboard ship."[114]

Some of the most interesting of these *Progymnasmata* on Themistoclean themes are by a certain Nikolaos the Sophist of Myrai in Lycia, who lived in the latter part of the fifth century A.D. He composed a "Comparison of Themistocles and Pericles" (*Progymn.* 10. 11; Walz, I, pp. 373–74) in the tradition of earlier such exercises by Theon, who had set for his pupils a comparison of Themistocles and Artemisia in respect of bravery (Walz, I, p. 234), and Aelius Aristeides.[115] "What Themistocles might have said" when he heard that Xerxes had altered the form of land and sea (by the canal and pontoon bridge) is another of Nikolaos' themes (*Progymn.* 11. 8; Walz, I, p. 388), and there are some slight traces that the rhetoricians did not resist the temptation to fill in the outlines of two momentous scenes in Themistocles' career: his comparison of himself with Pausanias[116] and the speech in his own defence during his trial for treason, of which specific mention is made as early as Ephorus.[117] Among these *Progymnasmata* there is also an *Encomium of Themistocles* (chap. 8, no. 7; Walz,

109. Quintilian provides an interesting analogy. "Themistocles is thought to have urged the Athenians [that is, in the evacuation decree] to 'deposit' their city with the gods, because it would have been harsh to say 'to abandon' it" (*Inst. Orat.* 9. 2. 92).

110. *ta tois proterois* [that is, the evacuation] *hepomena*, Maximus Planudes' *Prolegomena* to Hermogenes' *Heureseis* (Walz, *Rhetores Graeci*, V, 368), Apsines' *Techne Rhetorike* (Spengel, *Rhetores Graeci*, I. 2, 218). The motif seems to be borrowed from Pericles (Thuc. 1. 143. 5).

111. Hermogenes, *Peri Ideon* (pp. 366–67 Rabe; an illustration of *barytes*, "gravity," of which irony seems to be an important constituent), with John the Sicel's scholia ad loc. (Walz, *Rhetores Graeci*, VI, 442–43).

112. Walz, *Rhetores Graeci*, V, 44; cf. IV, 102, 122.

113. Scholiast to Ael. Arist. *For the Four*

(III, 674 Dind.); cf. Hdt. 8. 62.

114. Hermogenes, *Peri Heureseos*, p. 146 Rabe; perhaps a development from Herodotus 8. 65, for Dikaios' vision of the cloud from Eleusis was a favourite *topos* (cf. Libanius, Or. 30. 32).

115. See my suggestion at note 93.

116. Nikolaos' *Peri Synkriseos*, p. 61 Felten (Teubner, 1913).

117. From Longinus' *Peri Heureseos* (Walz, *Rhetores Graeci*, IX, 548–49). It must have contained some stirring oratory: "If you put me to death, let there be inscribed on my grave each of the achievements which have brought me jealousy and condemnation; let there be written 'Artemisium and Salamis, the King's forces and the Athenian fleet' and each of the others" (cf. also Walz, *Rhetores Graeci*, IV, 591, and IV, 122, top).

I, pp. 338–41), which recapitulates many of the familiar themes but adds some new ones. Themistocles was "equally practised in arms and words" (p. 338). In enjoining war with Aegina he was "the gods' ally," for the Aeginetans had appropriated some sacred statues which should have been common to both states and removed them to their own territory.[118] The Athenians "had no knowledge of naval matters before; it was Themistocles who taught them this skill and persuaded them to practise" (a suspicious similarity, here, with Dionysius the Phocaean before the battle of Lade). He "filled Euboea with trophies and made Artemis a witness of her own victory" (p. 340). There is the conventional comparison between Themistocles and Miltiades, "who fought only the king's lieutenants,"[119] and Cimon, "who learnt from Themistocles how to pursue the Persians" (pp. 340–41).

Collections

Although it cannot be determined how early Themistocles' deeds and sayings began to be collected and read for their own intrinsic interest (certainly Herodotus' account of him looks as though it may already have drawn on such a collection), this type of collection became a popular genre in the Roman period. A work entitled *On Memorable Deeds and Sayings* in nine books from the first century A.D. has survived under the name of Valerius Maximus. These short narratives seem to be classified under various headings, but with no determinable overall plan. Themistocles' name occurs along with others as an example of "ingratitude" shown him by his fellow citizens (the motif is as old as Ephorus);[120] he, "the victor, had to grasp the knees of his vanquished enemy" (5. 3, ext. 3). His suicide before the altar at which he had been sacrificing, "like some glorious victim to [his own] *pietas*," shows Greece that "it does not need another Themistocles" (5. 6, ext. 3). Several of these stories Valerius shares with Cicero before him and Plutarch after (thus giving rise to the suspicion that they may all be drawing upon the same *Collection*): it is the version found in Cicero that is followed regarding Themistocles' advice, mediated through Aristeides, to burn the fleet.[121] The advice to the man looking for a son-in-law to seek a man without money rather than the reverse is found in all three authors,[122] as is the comment upon Themistocles' extraordinary powers of memory.[123] Miltiades' trophy keeping Themistocles awake nights also finds a place, and to it is joined an anecdote found elsewhere only in Cicero's *pro Archia* of Themistocles' answer to the question, "Whose voice do you most enjoy hearing?": "The man who gives the best account of my achieve-

118. Walz, *Rhetores Graeci*, I, 339. Perhaps a garbled echo of Hdt. 5. 83 ff.; cf. the grievances between Athens and Megara before the Peloponnesian War (Thuc. 1. 139. 2; Plut. *Them*. 30. 2).

119. Cf. Ael. Arist. II, 238–39 Dind.

120. *P. Oxy*. 1610, frs. 3–5, lines 18–31, and Diod. 11. 58. 4–59.

121. Val. Max. 6. 5, ext. 2, an example of *prudentia* = Cic. *de Off*. 3. 11. 49, the Spartan

fleet at Gytheum. Plutarch (*Them*. 20. 1–2, *Arist*. 22. 2–4) makes it the fleet "of the Hellenes" at Pagasai.

122. 7. 2, ext. 9 (Valerius adds that she was an "only" daughter) = Cic. *de Off*. 2. 20. 71; Plut. *Them*. 18. 9, *Mor*. 185 D. Cf. Diod. 10, fr. 32.

123. 8. 7, ext. 15 = Cic. *de Sen*. 21, *Acad*. 2. 1. 2, and elsewhere; Plut. *Them*. 5. 6.

ments."[124] Valerius retails the conventional story of Themistocles' learning Persian in preparation for his audience with the king (8. 7, ext. 15), and he follows the account already found in Nepos (*Them*. 1) that Themistocles' father disinherited him, adding that his mother, "driven by the spectacle of her son's dissolute life," committed suicide by hanging (6. 9, ext. 2)—both of which stories Plutarch strenuously objects to (*Them*. 2. 8).

Frontinus, thrice consul and governor of Britain under Vespasian, composed, among other works, a book entitled *Stratagems* in which were included four manoeuvres by which Themistocles had outwitted his opponents: his decree to evacuate the city, remove the wives and children, and "transfer the scene of the war to the water"; his first message to Xerxes by which he "pretended to be turning traitor" (the false message, as Frontinus sensibly remarks, had the double effect of wearing out the Persian sailors who had to row all night and of leaving the Greeks to fight in a favourable spot with their strength unimpaired); his reaction to the Athenian plan to destroy the Hellespontine bridge, namely, restraining his own men and sending a second message urging the king to hasten his retreat; his delaying tactics at Sparta while the walls were being rebuilt, which involved feigned illness, outright denial of the reports of construction at Athens, and a secret message telling the Athenians at home to hold the Spartan ambassadors hostage.[125] On the basis of several close similarities in wording between Frontinus and Justin, it appears that Frontinus knew, and used directly, the author whom Justin preserves in epitome, Pompeius Trogus.[126]

About the middle of the second century A.D., a similar collection of *Stratagems*, classified by historical individuals, was produced by a Macedonian rhetorician named Polyaenus. Book 1, chapter 30, is Themistocles', whose whole career is here surveyed in outline: the building of the fleet (Polyaenus follows the tradition first found in the *Constitution of Athens*, which probably goes back to an *Atthis*);[127] the correct interpretation of "wooden walls" and "divine Salamis";[128] the appeal to the Ionians: "You do not act rightly in fighting against your fathers"; the two messages to Xerxes; the embassy to Sparta; his escape to Persia. Polyaenus has the sense generally to follow the best authority: the motive ascribed to Themistocles in appealing to the Ionians follows Herodotus closely (1. 30. 7 = Hdt. 8. 22),[129] and Themistocles' threat to the captain of the ship on which he is escaping comes straight from Thucydides (1. 30. 8 = Thuc. 1. 137. 2). Once he shares with Plutarch a detail found nowhere else: most of the other accounts, beginning with that of Herodotus, report that Themistocles again dispatched Sicinnus with the second message to Xerxes, while Plutarch (*Them*. 16. 5, *Arist*. 9. 6) says it was one of the Persian captives, a eunuch named Arnakes, and this is the version given by Polyaenus, with the unimportant

124. 8. 14, ext. 1 (Valerius adds that Themistocles was "entering the theatre") = Cic. *pro Arch*. 9. 20. The story of Miltiades' trophy is ubiquitous (e.g., Cic. *Tusc*. 4. 19. 44; Plut. *Them*. 3. 4, *Thes*. 6. 9, etc.).
125. These passages are, respectively, *Strat*. 1. 3. 6, 2. 11. 14, 2. 6. 8, and 1. 1. 10.
126. E.g. (Themistocles at Sparta) *simulato morbo* (Frontinus 1. 1. 10), *infirmitate simulata*

(Justin 2. 15. 6). See the parallel passages in Otto Seel, *Pompei Trogi Fragmenta*.
127. See chapter 4 and Appendix B.
128. One notes the simple and effective (οἱ Ἀθηναῖοι) ἐπείσθησαν, ἐνέβησαν, ἐναυμάχησαν, ἐνίκησαν (1. 30. 2).
129. The story of Chileos at Polyaenus 5. 30 is likewise based on Herodotus (9. 9).

variant "Arsakes" (1. 30. 4). Polyaenus tells, at greater length and in greater detail than other sources, a story of how Themistocles and Aristeides made a compact to put aside their long-standing hostility until the Persian threat should have passed (1. 31).[130]

A miscellaneous collection of fact and anecdote under the title *Poikile Historia* (more familiar in its Latin form, *Varia Historia*) has been preserved, probably in an abridged form, from the pen of Claudius Aelianus, a Hellenized Roman who lived and wrote about A.D. 200. Many of the stories he tells about Themistocles are merely part of the tradition, as can be seen from their appearance also in Plutarch,[131] but Aelian occasionally lifts the veil on Plutarch's (direct or indirect) source: the figures for Themistocles' fortune growing from 3 to 100 talents during his tenure of office (Plut. *Them.* 25. 3) Aelian ascribes to Critias (10. 17). The converse process can be observed at *Varia Historia* 9. 5, where the story of Themistocles' prohibition against Hieron's competing in the horserace at Olympia (*Them.* 25. 1) Aelian tells in a slightly different form without naming the source, whom Plutarch cites as Theophrastus. The other Olympic story, of Themistocles' own reception by the assembled audience, is also here,[132] as well as the oversimplified antagonism between Themistocles and Aristeides (13. 44; Plut. *Them.* 3. 1, *Arist.* 2. 2). Occasionally, a traditional story is enlivened by a bit of dialogue which may well be Aelian's own contribution. When he was removed from and then recalled to public office, an event whose claims to being historical are clearly not high, Themistocles remarked, "I do not think much of men who use the same vessel as a wine-jug and a chamber-pot" (13. 40). He has Themistocles quote a phrase of Euripides to the effect that "the man who seeks admiration, really seeks jealousy—a vain thing" (2. 12). Themistocles illustrated the determination which he tried to inspire in his fellow Athenians as they faced the invaders with the example of fighting cocks who "fought not for country, or ancestral gods, or glory, or freedom, or children—but merely not to be beaten one by the other, or yield one to the other" (2. 28). The road which led to Hades he said he found far preferable to that which took him to the speaker's platform (9. 18). One of the more ridiculous of Aelian's stories (whether it was his own, or his source's, invention cannot be determined) involves Themistocles' being told by his tutor to make way for the tyrant Peisistratus (3. 21), who died in 528 B.C., probably well before Themistocles was born. (Themistocles retorts, "Why, isn't this enough road for him?"—an example, Aelian says, of "nobility and magnanimity.") In a passing reference in another work, the *Characteristics of Animals*, Aelian reports that Themistocles "told the Athenians to sacrifice to the winds" (7. 27). This may be an inference, but a plausible one, by

130. J. Melber, "Über die Quellen und den Wert der Strategemensammlung Polyäns," *Jahrb. für Phil.*, supp., n.F. 14 (1885), 436, believes this to be an elaboration of an incident described more briefly by Plutarch, *Mor.* 186 B (cf. *Mor.* 809 B).

131. Themistocles' Thracian mother (*V.H.* 12. 43; Plut. *Them.* 1. 1); disinheritance (2. 12, criticized by Plut. *Them.* 2. 8); his profligate youth reformed and ending in greatness (2. 12

= *Them.* 2. 7). Two of the anecdotes told by Plutarch, *Them.* 18, recur in Aelian, *V.H.* 13. 40 (the gold jewellery on the [Persian] corpses) and 9. 18 (Themistocles' comparison of himself to a tree).

132. 13. 43; cf. Plut. *Them.* 17. 4; the "Themistocles Epistles" (to be discussed below) 8, p. 748 Hercher; Ael. Arist. Or. 46, II, 289 Dind.

Aelian or his source from Herodotus (7. 189), where it is reported that the Athenians before Artemisium prayed to Boreas in accordance with an oracle and later built a temple in his honour near the Ilissus.[133]

The third-century Egyptian writer Athenaeus produced a long and diffuse collection of miscellaneous information on, among other things, food and cooking entitled *Deipnosophistae*, "Sophists at Dinner." The value of the entries on Themistocles depends entirely on their sources, which range from Amphicrates and Neanthes on Themistocles' low birth and Idomeneus on his profligate youth (13. 576 C–D), to the valuable references to the comic writer Telekleides' *Prytaneis* (12. 553 E = fr. 22 Edmonds: life in the time of Themistocles was "luxurious," *habron*) and the local historian Possis, for Themistocles' institution of the festivals of Panathenaea and Choës at Magnesia (12. 533 E). Athenaeus also records, without naming a specific source, some of the standard items from Themistocles' last years in Persia: he learned the Persian language (12. 535 E), and the king gave him (in addition to Lampsacus, Magnesia, Myus, Perkote, and Palaiskepsis) Gambreion for raiment and "bade him no longer wear Greek, but Persian, dress" (1. 29 F).[134] Aristophanes' lines are quoted (*Knights* 83–84), but their author is not named, for Themistocles' suicide by bull's blood (3. 122 A).

The "Themistocles Epistles" and "Themistocles Epigrams"

Discussion has been deferred until last of two works which fall entirely outside the above classifications. The so-called Themistocles Epistles are a collection of twenty-one letters ostensibly written by Themistocles to his friends and associates from various stops along his escape route. Their authenticity was first called into question by the Chiote scholar Leo Allatius in the early part of the seventeenth century and more systematically by Bentley in his famous *Dissertation* of 1697. Still unanswered are the questions, When were they fabricated? Why? By whom? The form in which we now have them can be shown, on grounds of linguistic usage, to date only from the late first or second century A.D.,[135] but their actual literary antecedents may be far older. It could be argued that the lead to future forgers was given by Thucydides, who quotes *in extenso* from Themistocles' letter to Artaxerxes (1. 137. 4).[136] Certainly by the Roman period this kind of imaginative composition of letters by and to important figures of the past was a usual component of the syllabus in rhetoric and

---

133. See note 92.

134. The sixth town, Gambreion, is new and unwelcome, since it is listed by Xenophon (*Hell.* 3. 1. 6) among the towns given to Gongylus of Eretria by Xerxes for having acted as courier between the Persian king and Pausanias, the Spartan regent (Thuc. 1. 128. 6). Phanias of Lesbos, whom Athenaeus has just cited, added Perkote and Palaiskepsis to the three towns named by Thucydides, and he was followed in this by Neanthes (Plut. *Them.* 29. 11).

Phanias is also quoted by Athenaeus for a later visit to the Persian king by a Cretan from Gortyn "in emulation of Themistocles" (2. 48 D).

135. N. A. Doenges, "Letters of Themistocles: A Survey," 31. The fundamental modern study is W. Niessing's *De Themistoclis epistulis*.

136. Charles Huit, "Les épistolographes grecs," *REG* 2 (1889), 107 (an interesting survey).

has obvious affinities with the fictitious speech put into a character's mouth on a specified, more or less improbable, historical occasion. Whether there was a single author (perhaps a better word might be editor) or what his purpose may have been are still disputed points. Doenges puts forward a case for a single author composing a kind of "novelette or short story in epistolary form written either to delight or to inform the reader,"[137] and basing his work on a single early and basically trustworthy source, such as Hellanicus.[138] Nylander, noting discrepancies of detail among certain of the letters, rejects the unitarian theory of authorship: "What we have here is rather a more or less loose and superficially arranged collection of letters circulating—for different reasons and in various contexts—in the name of Themistocles"; but he somewhat strangely believes at the same time in a single early source, perhaps Charon of Lampsacus.[139] Frost accepts Doenges' view that they are "a Themistocles-romance in epistolary form," but rejects his unitary-source theory.[140] An older view which it may yet be worthwhile resuscitating is that the collection represents a kind of essay in letters on the subject of exile, for Themistocles was a favourite example of this theme in Stoic circles.[141] Whatever the ultimate verdict on the Epistles may be, there is clearly too much uncertainty surrounding all the important aspects of authorship to allow any use at all to be made of their contents; questions of how conscientious the author (or authors) may have been, and his (their) possible access to reliable sources, are clearly unanswerable until the more basic one of identity is decided.

It is of hardly more than literary interest, then, to notice the identity of the recipients of "Themistocles'" letters. Epistle 1 is addressed, naturally enough, to the dramatist Aeschylus; Epistles 3, 13, and 20, more surprisingly, to Polygnotus (almost certainly the painter of that name). That the Spartan Pausanias should receive Epistles 2 and 14 is understandable enough, likewise that 4 and 10 should go to Themistocles' close associate Habronichus; but mystery surrounds the name of Leagros, son of Glaukon, who receives Epistle 8 (an important letter in that it contains a good deal of otherwise unattested information). He is known to have been a general who was later killed in Thrace (Hdt. 9. 75), but his name is not connected with Themistocles' elsewhere in the sources, although the letter writer calls him "my con-

137. "Letters," 22. J. Sykutris classes the letters as a *Briefroman* (*RE*, supp. 5 [1931], cols. 213–14).

138. Doenges, "Letters," 183–84.

139. Carl Nylander, *Opuscula Atheniensia* 8 (1968), 134, following R. J. Lenardon, *Phoenix* 15 (1961), 39, for Charon. The quotation is from pp. 132–33. His arguments against unity of authorship are two: "No compiler, however inept, with any ambitions to create a kind of unit out of these epistles, would give such a position to such a letter" (viz., Letter 21 at the end, which he believes to exhibit knowledge, difficult to obtain and impossible to forge, of an official script change in Persia about 520 B.C.) (132, n.53); and secondly there are the internal inconsistencies such as "the wholly varying accounts in Letters 5 and 20 of Themi-

stocles' stay with Admetos; the divergent attitudes to Aristeides in Letters 3, 18 and 4, 8, 9, 12, and those to Pausanias in 2, 14, 16. Letters 8 and 20 give different versions of Themistocles' meeting with the Great King" (132, n.55). Niessing, too, had maintained multiple authorship, but he saw coherence in Epistles 1–3 and 14–20 (*De Themistoclis epistulis*, 15 ff.).

140. Bauer, *Plutarchs Themistokles*, 2d ed. by F. J. Frost, 111–12, with note.

141. W. von Christ, W. Schmid, and O. Stählin, *Gesch. griech. Lit.* II. 1, 483. Themistocles was a favourite example of this theme in Stoic circles: Teles (3d century B.C.), p. 22 Hense; Musonius, p. 46 Hense; Plutarch *de Exilio* 601 F, 602 A, 605 E; Cassius Dio 38. 26. 3 (cited by Niessing, *De Themistoclis epistulis*, 4).

temporary and fellow ephebe." Believers in the basic trustworthiness of the letter's contents may derive some support from the recent discovery in the Cerameicus of eighty-three ostraka bearing Leagros' name.[142]

New items of information for Themistocles' career must be treated with the utmost circumspection: his father, Neokles, had lived long in Argos, and this accounts for his friendly reception there after his ostracism (Ep. 1, p. 741).[143] The agent who gets Themistocles' wife and children out of Athens is apparently to be Sicinnus (4. 744; a contrary tradition is quoted by Plutarch [*Them.* 24. 6] from Stesimbrotus). Epistle 11 contains the information (which may be no more than conjecture) that Themistocles helped to gain for Ameinias the first prize for valour (11. 751). This letter is of potential importance as adding to the list of Themistocles' known enemies: Alcibiades, Stratippus, Lakratides, and Hermokles at Athens, Aristeides the Aeginetan,[144] Dorkon at Epidaurus, and Molon of Troizen; a problem is, however, created by its reference to the charge of treason brought against Themistocles in connection, not with his dealings with Pausanias, but with his generalship. (This may reflect a version in which a charge was laid against Themistocles in relation to the message—or messages—he was alleged to have sent to Xerxes in 480.) Epistle 8 adds further names of accusers to the already known Leobotes (Plut. *Them.* 23. 1): Lysandros of Skambonidai, Pronapes of Prasiai (p. 747), Aristeides, Phaidrias, Tisinikos, and Alcmeonides (p. 748). For his expertise at interpreting the oracle, Themistocles was dubbed Pythios. The story told by Pausanias (8. 50. 3) of Themistocles' standing ovation at Olympia is repeated here (p. 748), but with the addition that it was as he entered the stadium to watch the gymnastic contest. An otherwise unknown uncle, Themistocles, is mentioned, and the writer asks his friend Leagros to pray for "a safe return" for him, this apparent hope of restoration to favour in the eyes of his countrymen being in contradiction to the reference later in the letter to a service, which the writer is ashamed to speak of, that Themistocles proposes to do the Great King. Epistle 18 mentions Themistocles' fear of being tried before a Synedrion, or General Congress, of the Hellenes, a detail which is mentioned also by Diodorus (11. 55. 4) and perhaps derives from Ephorus.

The long and circumstantial Epistle 20 (a favourite quarrying ground of modern scholars in search of "useful information") contains a detailed account of Themistocles' journey from Argos to Persia. The letter is addressed to Polygnotus, who had sent a messenger to warn Themistocles to flee Argos. Accompanied by two of his hosts, Nicias and Meleagros, Themistocles made his way to Cyllene, the harbour of Elis, where bad weather detained him for three days before he could set sail for Corcyra (p. 758; the details, save for the length of the delay at Cyllene, are repeated in Epistles 1 and 4). The Corcyraeans' unwillingness to give him refuge leads Themistocles to contemplate a trip to Sicily to Gelon, tyrant of Syracuse, in a Leukadian ship which is about to depart for the West. Themistocles is deterred from carrying

---

142. R. Thomsen, *The Origin of Ostracism*, 94.

143. Page numbers refer to R. Hercher's

Epistolographi Graeci (1873).

144. Or is this merely a misunderstanding of Herodotus 8. 79. 1?

out this plan by news of Gelon's death and Hieron's accession to the throne.[145] So he sails to Epirus to Admetus, king of the Molossi, instead. (The circumstantial account given in Epistle 5 of the absence of Admetus, who was away visiting the Chaonians, his return "8 or 9 days later," and Themistocles' appeal for asylum with the king's young son Arybbas in one hand and a sword in the other, is either unknown to, or at least ignored by, the writer of Epistle 20.) There is a stirring exchange of speeches between the Athenian and Spartan pursuants of Themistocles on the one side and Admetus on the other, who respects Themistocles' supplication and sends him (as in Thuc. 1. 137. 1) to Alexander at Pydna. The account of the voyage to Ephesus via Naxos is Thucydidean, containing as it does Themistocles' threat to the captain to tell the Greeks that he had bribed him to take him aboard (Thuc. 1. 137. 1); only the episode involving Diopeithes of Bargylia, a "friend of the captain," whom Themistocles had rescued at Artemisium, is added as a gratuitous embellishment. Themistocles makes contact first with Artabazus in Phrygia (who may be the same person as the Artabanus mentioned by Plutarch [*Them.* 27]), who sends him along with thirteen Persian attendants on camels to the court of Artaxerxes;[146] Themistocles admires the scenery en route and learns Persian from his companions (p. 761; the short Epistle 10 is written to Habronichus "from the carriage" in which he rides). The confrontation with the king is skilfully managed. How do you dare to show your face before me? Artaxerxes demands in effect, in a speech not preserved elsewhere; to which Themistocles replies, "My good offices to your father, namely my message to him announcing that the Greeks were about to withdraw from Salamis and my preventing them from destroying the Hellespontine bridges, have led to my own fall from favour and their attempt to punish me" (p. 761; Themistocles specifically calls his response an *apate*, a "deception," but this may help to explain the otherwise puzzling reference in Epistle 11 to the charge of treason being brought somehow in connection with Themistocles' generalship). Themistocles' mention of an Erinys, or "Avenging Fury," with whose help he will do harm to the Greeks, is taken by Artaxerxes as a promise to "restore Greece, of which we were deprived through you." Themistocles is treated with great honour, has gifts lavished on him, including a gold akinake and woven robe, and is continually interrogated about things Greek. The three traditional cities are mentioned, but a novel detail added that Themistocles "freed Lampsacus, which had previously been weighed down under a heavy burden of tribute."[147] The letter ends

145. P. 758. The chronological confusion is absolute. Hieron's accession is generally dated to 476, only the Parian Marble (as Doenges, "Letters," 73, remarks) placing it late enough (472/1) to fit with Themistocles' flight. Epistle 7. 746 contains an allusion to an otherwise unattested grain ship from Gelon heading for Peiraeus.

146. Themistocles' stated intention had been to see Xerxes (p. 760), but his actual meeting is with Artaxerxes, as his words at 761 make clear ("my good service to your father"). The letter writer may thus be taking into account Thucydides' report that "Artaxerxes had recently

come to the throne" (1. 137. 3).

147. P. 761, bottom. Doenges ("Letters," 94–95) accepts L. I. Highby's suggestion that it was for this remission of tribute that Themistocles and his descendants received special honours at Lampsacus (*The Erythrae Decree*, 48–49). Doenges himself puts forward the attractive theory that Cleophantus (who is mentioned in Epistle 4, p. 744) "may in fact have been governor of Lampsacus for Themistocles" and that "Kleophantus and the others were recalled [to Athens; he is mentioned by Plato at *Meno* 93 D] because Kleophantus was responsible for the entrance of Lampsacus into

on a sour, indeed, an ominous, note. Themistocles' new wealth has brought surfeit; his friends are not there to enjoy it with him. "How could we tolerate such substance as Greeks? I consider what I have to have brought me, not good fortune, but risks and the inevitability of Fate [*Ananke*]. The king is raising an army which I am expected to lead. Am I to make war on Athens and do battle with an Athenian admiral? Much else may happen, but never this" (p. 762). It is generally, and probably rightly, supposed that the author here intends a foreshadowing of the story of Themistocles' suicide when faced with the prospect of having to make good on his alleged promise to lead the king's forces against his former countrymen.

We may feel constrained to rate the credibility of the new material contained in the Epistles at a relatively low level, but there can be no doubt that as literary compositions they are often of a moderately high order and continue to stimulate questions. Part of the fascination is that these questions will probably never be finally answered.

The estimate to be placed on the literary merits of the "Themistocles Epigrams" must be less high. Five "epitaphs" are preserved in the *Greek Anthology*, which, in fact, make no serious claims to authenticity; they are mere literary exercises composed by poetasters in the Augustan period or later.[148] The most successful of these is by Tullius Geminus, suffect consul in A.D. 46, who specialized in epigrams on works of art:

> In place of a simple tomb put Hellas, and on her put
> Ships significant of the destroyed barbaric fleets,
> And round the frieze of the tomb paint the Persian host
> And Xerxes—thus bury Themistocles.
> And Salamis shall stand thereon, a pillar telling of my
> Deeds. Why lay you so great a man in a little space?[149]

There is no need to suppose that Geminus actually saw Themistocles' "tomb" in Magnesia (about which in any case there are difficulties),[150] or that terms like "frieze," or "base" (*krepis*), in line 3 and "pillar" (*stala*) in 5 refer to actual features of this particular monument; they are standard architectural terms which the author introduces to carry through his image of Themistocles' glorious achievements serving to embellish (metaphorically) an otherwise simple grave. The motif is in fact similar to that used by Longinus in the fictitious speech which he has Themistocles deliver in his own defence, in which Themistocles bade his jurors inscribe on his tomb the achievements which had earned him the jealousy of his fellow countrymen.[151] The reference in the last line of the epigram to a great man now reduced to small circumstances has caused some trouble. A. S. F. Gow and D. L. Page believe that the words

---

the Delian League" (though Doenges feels that, in default of supporting evidence, this latter theory "must be rejected" ["Letters," 95]).

148. *Anth. Pal.* 7. 73, 74, 235, 236, 237 (printed together by Bauer and Frost, *Plutarchs Themistokles*, 128); discussed by M. Rubensohn, "Themistokles-Epigramme," *Neue Jahrb.*

2 (1894), 457–61.

149. *Anth. Pal.* 7. 73, trans. W. R. Paton (Loeb Classical Library, *The Greek Anthology*, II).

150. This "tomb" is discussed in chapter 10.

151. See note 117.

are "alluding to the small and ill-furnished grave in which Themistocles was re-buried in Attica."[152] If the author intended that meaning, he has veiled his thought in unnecessarily obscure language; a likelier interpretation is that Themistocles' achievements are now, in death, reduced to the confines of the plot of ground which is his grave—wherever it may be.

A further reference to the "cenotaph" has been detected in an epigram by Diodorus of Sardis, whom Strabo mentions (13. C 628):

> This is the ——— monument raised to Themistocles by Magnesia's
>   Folk. He, after saving his country from the Medes,
> Went beneath a foreign land and stone. Such was the will
>   Of envy, which is held in higher esteem than courage.
>
> (*Anth. Pal.* 7. 74)

The text is in doubt in the first line; the epithet for "monument" is restored as *kenon* ("empty") or *xenon* ("foreign"), but the latter is the more probable reading and is in fact that accepted by most editors. The reference to "envy," *phthonos*, in line 4 is of interest, for it is one of the themes emphasized by Plutarch in his *Life of Themistocles*, composed some two generations after this epigram was written. The same motif is the whole point of a two-line epigram by Antipater of Thessalonika:

> I, this Magnesian tomb, am not that of Themistocles, but I was built
>   As a record of the envious misjudgment of the Greeks.
>
> (*Anth. Pal.* 7. 236)

The above translation, by W. R. Paton, brings out the sense of the opening phrase which, more literally, is "I am not the tomb of Themistocles [but my more important function is as a monument to Envy...]." Once again, Gow and Page give a different and far less natural emphasis to the negative when they write, "The couplet is perhaps meant to imply that the tomb at Magnesia does not contain the bones of Themistocles (which are in Athens)."[153] Finally there is a rather conventional epigram by a Diodorus, who may be the same as the above-mentioned friend of Strabo:

> Measure not by this Magnesian tomb the greatness of the name,
>   Nor forget the deeds of Themistocles.
> Judge of the patriot by Salamis and the ships, and
>   Thereby shalt thou find him greater than Athens herself.
>
> (*Anth. Pal.* 7. 235, trans. Paton)

152. *The Greek Anthology: The Garland of Philip*, II, 295.

153. *The Greek Anthology: Hellenistic Epigrams*, II, 103.

6 PLUTARCH

PLUTARCH WAS BORN in the Boeotian town of Chaeronea some time between A.D. 45 and 50 of a long-established and well-to-do local family.[1] He went to Athens for part of his education, was at some stage in his career made an honorary Athenian citizen, and probably revisited Athens many times, thus gaining a thorough familiarity with her monuments and topography.[2] Above all he acquired a deep respect for her history and traditions, and an admiration for the record of her accomplishments, for the "humanity and benevolence, of which the city still gives illustrious examples even in my own day, [and for which] she is justly admired and lauded" (*Arist.* 27. 7).

The *Life of Themistocles* figured in the first group of paired lives (there seem to have been twenty-three pairs in all), which was published probably in the period soon after A.D. 100.[3] It consists of thirty-two chapters, of medium length, longer than *Cimon*, *Aristeides*, and *Nicias* but shorter than *Pericles* and *Alcibiades*. Its structure may be analysed as indicated on pages 136–37.

It becomes clear on reading the *Life* that the unifying conception which Plutarch has of Themistocles' career is based on his view of the dominant quality of his character, his ambition,[4] both in his personal affairs and, in a larger sense, in his

1. The fullest treatment of Plutarch is by Konrat Ziegler, *Plutarchos von Chaironeia*[2] (Stuttgart, 1964) [= *RE* 21 (1951), cols. 636–962, with additional material]. The evidence is conveniently collected by J. R. Hamilton, *Plutarch: Alexander*, Introduction, xiii–xxiii, xxxiii–xlix; cf. also A. J. Gossage, "Plutarch," in *Latin Biography*, ed. T. A. Dorey, 45–77, and, especially for a survey of the less-known works, R. H. Barrow, *Plutarch and His Times*. Plutarch's life and intellectual milieu have recently been discussed by D. A. Russell, *Plutarch*, chap. 1, and C. P. Jones, *Plutarch and Rome*, pt. I.

2. Ziegler, *Plutarchos* (1964), cols. 17–21.

3. Hamilton, *Plutarch: Alexander*, xxxvii; Ziegler, *Plutarchos* (1964), col. 265; C. P. Jones,

JRS 56 (1966), 66 ff. (*Them.-Cam.* "after A.D. 96," p. 69).

4. H. L. Martin, Jr., "The Character of Plutarch's Themistocles," *TAPA* 92 (1961), 326–39, analyses the *Life* in terms of *synesia* ("practical intelligence") and *philotimia*, but the former, taken over, as Martin shows, from Thucydides, can for our purposes be subsumed under the latter. Of the minor characteristics Martin analyses (334 ff.) the most important is *tolma*, "bold initiative," again part of the Thucydidean picture. For a recent schematic analysis of the virtues and vices which Plutarch allots to his characters, see B. Bucher-Isler, *Norm und Individualität in den Biographien Plutarchs* (58–59 for *philotimia*).

Public Events		Personality, Personal History, and Anecdote ("Eidology")[5]
		CHAPTERS
		1–2 Themistocles' parentage, tribal affiliation, early years (heavily anecdotal; Neanthes and Phanias cited)
		CHAPTER
		3 political ambitions
		3. 16 Plutarch's theme, "Right from the beginning he strove to be first"; rivalry with Aristeides and (the memory of) Miltiades
CHAPTER		3. 5 foresight of the Persian threat, leading to →
4 naval policy		
		CHAPTER
		5 Themistocles' competitive ambitiousness (*philotimia*)
	5. 7, fin. Aristeides removed	
6. 3–5 first (undated) moves against Persia	**CHAPTER** 6. 1–2 rivalry with Epikydes	
CHAPTERS 7–17 (7. 1 the campaign of 480 B.C. Themistocles' concern for naval matters echoes chapter 4 and →		7. 4 Athens' *doxa* increases with Themistocles' own.)
		7. 6–7 anecdote from Phanias
CHAPTER 8 Tempe, Artemisium		
CHAPTER 9 Thermopylae		
CHAPTERS 10–17 Salamis		**CHAPTER** 11. 3–6 anecdotes (11. 3, 11. 5 from Herodotus)

CHAPTER
17. 2–3

Account of Themistocles' honours reminds Plutarch (*legetai de*, 17. 4) of the →

popular acclaim accorded him at Olympia (undated), which leads to

CHAPTER
18

further anecdotes and *bons mots* illustrative of *philotimia*.

CHAPTERS
19–20

With the Persian threat removed, Themistocles moves to secure supremacy for Athens over Sparta.

(19. 3–20. 1

Account of the Peiraeus fortifications, which echoes **Themistocles' naval policy in** chapters 4 and 7. 1.)

CHAPTERS
20. 4–22. 3
20. 4
21
22. 1–3

Themistocles loses popularity: with the Spartans, who support Cimon; with Athens' allies; with his fellow Athenians.

CHAPTERS
22. 4–5
23
24–25

Themistocles ostracized, condemned for treason, escapes.

CHAPTERS
27–31. 3

31. 4–7
32

Themistocles in Asia (heavily anecdotal) meets his end (heavily anecdotal) his family and place of burial

5. The terms derive from F. Leo, *Die griech.-röm. Biographie*; see Gossage, "Plutarch," 57. But the distinction should not be pressed, for, as Gomme remarks, Plutarch "'knew that a man's *eidos* is seen in his actions'" (*Commentary*, I, 57). The debt modern scholarship owes to Gomme's penetrating analysis of Plutarch's historical aims and methods (pp, 54–84 of his Introduction; 61–63 for the *Themistocles*) is measured by Hamilton's reference to it as the "*locus classicus* on the subject."

6. Sections of Plutarch's chapters are numbered as in Ziegler's Teubner text.

political projects for his native Athens. From obscure, not to say dubious, beginnings (chap. 1), through contact with a man imbued with Solonian "political acumen and practical intelligence" (chap. 2),[7] Themistocles was inflamed, almost overmastered, by a strong desire to "win first place," to acquire *doxa*, "reputation," through political activity (chap. 3). From the anecdote told at the end of chapter 2, regarding the triremes left to rot upon the beach, it is clear that in Plutarch's view Themistocles' plans are to be realized in action by Athens' becoming a naval power against her opponents, first Persia and then Sparta. The unfolding of Themistocles' plan to turn Athens towards the sea is one of the dominant themes in the *Life*, which Plutarch has taken from Thucydides but has placed in a much more central position. But, paradoxically, and it is a paradox Plutarch savours, it is this very trait, his ambitiousness for himself and for Athens, which, the threat of Persia removed, makes Themistocles obnoxious to his fellow Athenians, some of whom side with his external enemies, the Spartans, to engineer his expulsion. The last years in Persia are glamorous but (Plutarch makes us feel) rather empty. Themistocles' *philotimia* is gratified: we hear of new privileges, "*timai* such as no other foreigners had ever received" (Herodotus 8. 124 uses similar language of his reception at Sparta after Salamis), for which he incurs the *phthonos*, "jealousy," of the Persian nobles (29. 5–6).[8] He is honoured "equally with the best Persians" (31. 3), and he wants to show the Athenians "how great was his honour and power in the king's councils" (31. 1), but none of this seems to be able to compensate for the esteem he had enjoyed among his fellow Greeks and has now lost. The promise of new honours to be had from leading the Persian armies against Greece (31. 5) could not match "the reputation of his own achievements and the trophies of those early days" (31. 5, trans. Perrin), the position of prominence he had won among free people and through political means (*en politeiais kai hegemoniais*, 31. 6). Ambition at the last gives way to patriotism, and so, when faced with the choice of winning new honours only at the price of betraying his country, Themistocles chooses death by his own hand. It is an "honourable" end, as Plutarch makes clear (*prepousan*), in a deeper sense than the incessant pursuit of external *timas* which had been such a driving force in his life, and it may be with a certain gentle irony that Plutarch remarks that King Artaxerxes, "on learning the cause and the manner of his death, admired the man yet more" (31. 7, trans. Perrin) and that the Magnesians, his former subjects, erected a "splendid" (*lampron*; cf. 29. 10) tomb for him in their marketplace (32. 4).

It is a powerful and, to a very laige extent, unified conception that Plutarch has of his leading character. The dominant motives are *tolma*, *philotimia*, *time-doxa*, and their attendant, *phthonos*. The story he tells is one full of dramatic incident and colouring: Themistocles' rise to greatness, against obstacles both personal and national (especially the life-long opposition of Aristeides, a theme which is greatly overplayed); the reversal he suffers through that very dominant characteristic by which he had risen to the pinnacle of success; his fall and the emptiness of exile, redeemed at the end by true wisdom (*arista bouleusamenos*, 31. 5~22. 2) and the nobility of his death.

7. Scott-Kilvert's translation of δεινότητα πολιτικὴν καὶ δραστήριον σύνεσιν (2. 6).
8. It was *phthonos* which prevented his being given first prize at the Isthmus, according to both Herodotus (8. 124) and Plutarch (*Them.* 17. 1).

Themistocles' characteristics are not by any means unique in Plutarch's pages—he has close analogies with Plutarch's Alcibiades[9]—but the portrait is none the less memorable for that. How *historical* the picture may be is another matter.

To say that Plutarch is only as good as his sources is no doubt an oversimplification,[10] but, as with most such, there is some truth in it. "He quotes from," Perrin informs us, "some two hundred and fifty Greek authors, eighty of whom are known to us only by name, and many more by the citations from them which he makes."[11] Of these "no fewer than 150 [were] historians (in the wider sense) including forty who wrote in Latin."[12] But Plutarch was no mere compiler or excerptor of earlier historical accounts. He had the sense and the judgement to cite contemporary (or near-contemporary) writers who were not historians, even in the wider sense, when they might have some light to throw or could be used to illustrate a point Plutarch wished to make: Aeschylus, Simonides, Timocreon of Rhodes, all poets but contemporary with Themistocles and so potentially valuable witnesses. The amount of reading these citations attest to was clearly enormous. Few modern analysts any longer believe that Plutarch lifted his material whole from a predecessor (for example, the shadowy Hermippus) who had done all the research for which Plutarch tacitly takes credit. But "research" may be misleading: Plutarch reads, records or remembers, and writes; the result is partly derivative, partly his own, but wholly unsystematic. As Gomme put it, "He *selects* from a mass of material, as he says more than once..., and arranges it himself."[13]

At the beginning of the *Demosthenes* (a passage often cited), Plutarch talks of the necessity which confronts a historical writer of residence in a famous and populous city (such as Athens or Rome) "that he may have an abundance of all sorts of books" (2. 1). Elsewhere he writes, "I have tried to collect other details which have escaped most writers, or have been mentioned only by some here and there, or are found in ancient votive offerings or public decrees" (*Nicias* 1. 1).[14] Books and personal investigation: a quite respectable way of proceeding; the second element was not disdained by Herodotus. (In *Themistocles*, the details regarding the choregic inscription quoted at 5. 5, the shrine to Artemis in Melite [22. 2–3], the dedications at Artemisium

9. For example, *anomalia* (roughly, "instability"), *Them.* 2. 7, *Alc.* 16. 9; *philotimia*, *Them.* 3. 4, 5. 3, 5, *Alc.* 6. 4, 27. 6, 34. 3, and recrudescence of patriotic feelings at the end of both men's lives. For a useful analysis of Plutarch's *Alcibiades*, see D. A. Russell, *PCPhS* 192 (1966), 37–47.

10. The fundamental discussion of Plutarch's use of his sources is Gomme's (*Commentary*, I, 54 ff.); see also Hamilton, *Plutarch: Alexander*, xliii–xlix, and Ziegler, *Plutarchos* (1964), cols. 273–91. The edition of A. Bauer (1884), which is useful for its citation of parallel passages, has been reissued with additional material by F. J. Frost (1967). Much useful information is also contained in the introductions and notes to the editions of the *Themistocles* by H. A. Holden (3d ed., 1892) and R. Flacelière (Paris, 1961), and the translation by B. Perrin (New York

and London, 1901; translation only in Loeb Classical Library, 1914). Flacelière has recently published a school edition, with brief French commentary (Paris: Presses universitaires de France, 1972). Flacelière also presents a useful survey of recent work in *Actes du VIIIᵉ Congrès de l'Association G. Budé* (Paris, 1969), 483–506.

11. *Plutarch's 'Themistocles' and 'Aristeides,'* 10. The references are collected by W. Helmbold and E. O'Neill, *Plutarch's Quotations*.

12. Hamilton, *Plutarch: Alexander*, xliii, citing Ziegler, *Plutarchos* (1964), col. 273.

13. *Commentary*, I, 82. That Plutarch had certain principles of arrangement has been shown by D. A. Russell in "On Reading Plutarch's *Lives*," *G&R*, 2d ser. 13 (1966), 139–57, esp. 148 ff.

14. Cited and translated by Gossage, "Plutarch," 54.

[8. 3–6], perhaps also the bronze water-girl mentioned in 31. 1, as well as the personal contact with one of Themistocles' descendants [32, fin.], all clearly fall into this category.) To these must be added a source of far inferior value, the tales "told in the Schools of philosophy."[15]

We hear, too, of collections of notes, *hypomnemata*, which Plutarch says he made (*Mor.* 457 D, 464 F), which would certainly have included, but are by no means to be exclusively identified with, the *apophthegms*, "collections of sayings of famous men," from which he drew repeatedly in the *Themistocles* as in the other *Lives*.[16] These collections are referred to as the "*Mnemoneuomena*," or "*Apomnemoneuomena* of Themistocles," at 11. 3 and 18. 1, and a sample of them appears among the *Moralia* as "Sayings of Kings and Commanders."[17] Apart from the notes he must have taken when he had occasion to use the libraries in the great cities, it is inconceivable that Plutarch could have achieved the quantity and variety, which his writings clearly manifest, without the aid of a prodigious memory, and the comment he allows himself in the *Pericles*, "These things coming to my recollection as I write, it were perhaps unnatural to reject and pass them by" (*Per.* 24. 12, trans. Perrin), could certainly have stood at countless other places in his work.

However much Plutarch may have transformed his material (consciously or unconsciously) in achieving the purpose which he avows to be his primary one, the portrayal of *ethos*, "character," he nevertheless represents an authentic tradition which can properly be called *historical*, and which, for the fifth-century *Lives*, goes back to the great initiators of that tradition, Herodotus and Thucydides. It is comforting, then, to see these two authors quoted by name (Herodotus at 7. 6, 17. 1, 21. 1; Thucydides, 25. 2, 27. 1) and often relied on even when they are not named. For the rest,[18] Plutarch is, it must be admitted, rather undiscriminating in the authors he cites, for they range from the valuable early testimonies of Simonides (1. 4, 15. 4) and Timocreon (21), through the early but anecdotal Ion of Chios (2. 4; cf. *Cimon* 9. 1) and Stesimbrotus (2. 5, 4. 5) of whose reliability even Plutarch is dubious (24. 7), to the thoroughly untrustworthy Ariston (3. 2) and Phanias, cited five times (1. 2, 7. 7, 13. 5, 27. 8, 29. 11), but drawn on, one suspects, by Plutarch far too often elsewhere in the *Life*.

Plutarch's chief value lies in the large number of details about Themistocles which he had unearthed, in sources named by him or left unnamed, which have some claim to authenticity and which, but for Plutarch's citation of them, might have been lost to us forever. Whether or not Plutarch had read these authors directly is a problem which will probably never be solved.[19] Fortunately, it is not one which affects the issue at

---

15. *Per.* 35. 2, *Phil.* 2. 3.

16. Details at Gossage, "Plutarch," 58–59, with n.36.

17. *Mor.* 172 A–242 D (184 F–185 F for Themistocles'). Whether these are a genuine and original collection by Plutarch has been doubted. It is now generally maintained that they are (Gomme, *Commentary*, I, 78–79, n.1; Hamilton, *Plutarch: Alexander*, xliv, and n.4; P. A. Stadter, *Plutarch's Historical Methods*,

138, n.27).

18. There is a convenient alphabetical listing of the authors whom Plutarch cites by name in the editions of Perrin, p. 68, with discussion at 29–49; Holden, xxxviii–xlvii and 214; and a brief analysis by Gomme, *Commentary*, I, 61–62.

19. See Hamilton, *Plutarch: Alexander*, xlv–xlvi, for a clear statement of the issues and an attempt to resolve them.

hand, what Plutarch contributed to our knowledge of Themistocles, for even if the authorities he cites had all been cited before him in some *Collection* (in whose existence I find it extremely difficult to believe), we are nevertheless in Plutarch's debt for having recorded, and thus preserved, them.

The named authorities Plutarch cites must be judged on the same criteria of historical evaluation as are applied to such extant authors as Herodotus and Thucydides. One of the most important touchstones is obviously the chronological one: how close in time was the author to the events he narrates? If he was not a contemporary (as will be the case with most of them, even Herodotus), of what quality was the tradition he records? Does it go back to a reliable earlier authority, document, or monument? These questions have been asked separately in preceding chapters for the more important authors Plutarch cites, and an attempt has been made to give reasoned answers to them.

But what of Plutarch's unnamed sources? Most modern commentators agree that he had a prodigious memory. How are we to know, however, that it did not, on some crucial occasion or other, fail him, or, more important, that the nameless source of some detail in the *Themistocles* can itself be trusted? The doubt is a critical one with regard, for example, to the whole collection of anecdotes and sayings which Plutarch had (probably himself) made elsewhere under the heading "Themistocles" and some of which he incorporated into the *Life*.[20] Much of this anecdotal material appears also in later writers like Athenaeus and Aelian, who sometimes name their source. Theories as to lines of transmission must remain mere hypotheses until new solid evidence comes to light. But a comparison of some of the anecdotal material which Plutarch shares with other authors has suggested that their mutual source, which cannot, and indeed need not, be given a name, was "a Thesaurus of Anecdotes, which included famous statesmen...extracts from the learned industry of the Alexandrian period."[21] Can the inquiry be pushed back any further? Had the hypothetical Alexandrians any basis for their compilation? There was no shortage of anecdotes, many relatively "early," associated with the outstanding figures of the fifth century. Stories and *bons mots* had begun to cluster around the personality of Themistocles almost from the earliest years, as is shown by the fact that similar examples are recorded in Herodotus. The mere fact that they find a place in Herodotus' pages does not, of course, guarantee their authenticity, for the imaginations of even contemporaries with regard to the acts and sayings of famous men are notoriously overactive. All we can say is that some of them, whether recorded as early as Herodotus or only as late as Plutarch, *may be* true. No very weighty conclusion can be made to depend on any of them, but if we are content to take them for what Plutarch, like Herodotus before him, intended them to be, illustrative of certain facets of Themistocles' character, they are harmless enough and may even prove to be enlightening.

Plutarch's single most important contribution to the historiographical tradition regarding Themistocles remains the fact that drawing upon the best available authori-

20. For the "Sayings of Kings and Commanders," see note 17.

21. W. G. Uxkull-Gyllenband, *Plutarch und die griechische Biographie*, 33.

ties, Herodotus and Thucydides, for his basic framework,[22] he added to them numerous details from other authors of the fifth and later centuries, who themselves may have had access to a tradition which had some chance of being authentic. Besides this class of literary evidence, Plutarch contributed a certain amount of valuable inscriptional, topographical, and even iconographical evidence which he himself took the trouble to inspect and critically evaluate, as well as the oral tradition which was alive, and therefore potentially accurate, in the schools of Athens and among circles of Themistocles' own descendants.

From all of this there emerges a clear, strong image—the moral shadings Plutarch imparts to it one may wish to disagree with—of a statesman and general, and, above all, an individual.

22. On this point modern scholarship is agreed; see, for example, Hamilton, *Plutarch: Alexander*, xlvii, and Gomme, *Commentary*, I, 61–62.

7 THE OSTIA PORTRAIT

IN 1939 THERE WAS discovered in excavations near the theatre of ancient Ostia a portrait bust, or herm, which is inscribed with the name of Themistocles. Its style of execution and the letter forms of the inscription show it to have been carved in the second century A.D., when the merchants and shippers who populated Rome's harbour town frequently satisfied their artistic inclinations by commissioning or acquiring copies of Greek originals. If the statue is a copy of an authentic original, it is supremely important as showing us how Themistocles looked to his contemporaries. Unfortunately, almost from the day of its discovery, controversy has raged about the work, and scholars continue to be divided in their opinions. Not even the date or provenience of the original from which the Ostia herm may have been copied can be considered settled, for scholarly opinion has dated that original to within, or just shortly after, Themistocles' lifetime, the fourth century B.C., or as late as the Roman period.[1] On stylistic grounds the model has been attributed to a sculptor of the Attic, Argive, or Ionian school, or even a late Roman archaizer. Parallels have been found with Myron's *Diskobolos*, the metopes of the Zeus temple at Olympia, and the "tyrannicides" of Critius and Nesiotes.[2] Mrs. B. S. Ridgway in her recent study of

1. The discovery and original publication were by Guido Calza, "Il ritratto di Temistocle scoperto a Ostia," *Le Arti* 18 (1939/40), 152–61; final publication by R. Calza, *Scavi di Ostia*, V. 1, 11. The statue has had a full-length treatment by Andreas Linfert, "Die Themistokles-Herme in Ostia," in *Antike Plastik*, VII, 87–94, and a good, brief description of the statue and discussion of the issues by Helga von Heintze in Wolfgang Helbig and Hermine Speier, *Führer durch die öffentlichen Sammlungen klassischer Altertümer in Rom*, IV, 27–31. Various opinions about it are discussed by H. Sichtermann in *Gymnasium* 71 (1964), 348–81; see also

Bauer and Frost, *Plutarchs Themistokles*, 136–37. I wish to express my thanks to E. Vanderpool and J. Frel for discussing the statue with me (Professor Frel called my attention to several recent studies of Greek portraiture), and to Dr. F. Eckstein of the Deutsches Archäologisches Institut in Rome for permission to reproduce several photos from the Linfert study mentioned above.

2. Argive school: H. Drerup in *Marburger Winckelmann-Programm* (1961), 24 ff., rejected by Linfert, *Antike Plastik*, VII, 91, who believes in an Ionian original of the 460s. Werner Gauer has recently theorized that the original

the Severe Style of sculpture, which she dates *c.* 480–450 B.C., has concluded that the Ostia bust "shows a very consistent brand of Severe style, such as would be difficult to re-create at a much later date. Not only the general structure of the head, with its cubic geometry, but also the close adherence of the hair to the skull, the rendering of the locks over the nape, the few surviving curls with drilled centers in the beard, and the large bulbous eyes, are well in keeping with a Severe date."[3]

Let us assume for the moment that the statue is a genuine likeness. What might its antecedents have been? In the shrine which he had built near his house in Melite in honour of Artemis, Lady of Best Counsel, which Plutarch says was one of the measures of self-advertisement by which Themistocles merely succeeded in antagonizing his fellow citizens further, there stood an *eikonion* (a word meaning "image," by which either a painting or, more probably, a small portrait statue might be meant), which could still be seen in Plutarch's day. Although Plutarch does not explicitly state that Themistocles commissioned and set his portrait in the shrine, this seems a likely inference from his active agency in building the shrine and in designating the cult title which its goddess was to have. Greek portraiture has in fact been seen as developing from statues such as this and the earlier group of Harmodius and Aristogeiton, which public figures in this period were erecting for propaganda purposes.[4] On the basis of this statue Plutarch remarks further that "he was plainly an heroic man, not only in spirit but also in appearance" (*Them.* 22. 2), a description which may seem to be justified by the Ostia bust. Many supporters of its authenticity therefore believe that it derives ultimately from this early portrait.[5]

But there are other possibilities. Pausanias mentions a dedication by Themistocles' sons on the Acropolis, "a picture in the Parthenon in which Themistocles is portrayed" (1. 1. 2),[6] and "statues of Themistocles and Miltiades" near the Prytaneion in the Agora, which he says "had their inscriptions changed into 'a Roman' and 'a Thracian'" (1. 18. 3). A similar pair of statues apparently stood near the two *parodoi*, or "side entrances," of the theatre of Dionysus, according to a scholiast on Aelius Aristeides (III, 535–36 Dind.). Both these groups have had their champions as models for the

---

was commissioned by Themistocles while in Magnesia from an Athenian sculptor ("Die griechischen Bildnisse der klassischen Zeit als politische und persönlichen Denkmäler," *JDAI* 83 [1968], 118 ff., 148–50 for the Ostia herm; I owe this reference to Professor Frel). G. Becatti in *La Critica d'Arte* 7 (1942), 76 ff., dates the original to the Hadrianic period. Dominant parallels with Myron's *Diskobolos*: L. Curtius, *Röm. Mitt.* 57 (1942), 82; with Harmodius and Aristogeiton: G. Calza, *Le Arti* 18 (1939/40), 156, and G. Zinserling, *Klio* 38 (1960), 104 and 109, who believes that Critius and Nesiotes sculpted Themistocles' portrait.

3. *The Severe Style in Greek Sculpture*, 99.
4. Gauer, *JDAI* 83 (1968), 139 ff.
5. Most recently, Dieter Metzler, *Untersuchungen zu den griechischen Porträts des 5. Jhrdt. v. Christ*, 1–17 (a reference I owe to

Professor Frel) = Metzler's *Porträt und Gesellschaft*, 182–207.
6. Compare the description of the picture which Philostratus says he saw in Naples in the third century A.D., which portrayed Themistocles, "a Greek among barbarians, a man among non-men...his head held in a pose like that of other speakers, but his eyes wandering out of a realization that he is speaking a language he has only just learnt" (*Imagines* 2. 31, Westermann's Didot ed., 390); this is an obvious allusion to the story told by Thucydides (1. 138. 1). E. Kalinka and Otto Schönberger (*Philostratos, Die Bilder*, 26 ff., 470 ff.) follow F. Steinmann, *Neue Studien zu den Gemäldebeschreibungen des älteren Philostrat* (diss. Zurich, 1914), 100, in arguing from Philostratus' uncertainty about details of the portrayal (he twice uses *oimai*, "I suppose") that he is describing a real picture.

Ostia bust.[7] A stronger candidate than any of these is the memorial erected in Themistocles' honour by the Magnesians, which included "a statue [or 'statues'] in the
forum," according to Nepos, whose testimony is confirmed by Magnesian coins of
the Antonine period on which a statue of Themistocles appears to be portrayed.[8]

One of the staunchest believers in the Ostia portrait, however, prefers to reserve
judgement as to possible models; G. M. A. Richter writes, "Whether the Ostia-head
can be identified as reproducing any of the recorded portraits is doubtful."[9] Besides
the literary testimonies to ancient representations of Themistocles (of which she gives
a convenient list), Miss Richter notes the existence of three headless herms, only one of
which is now extant, which bear the identification "Themistocles." The tension of the
neck muscles of the one now in Berlin, it has been argued, shows that both it and the
Ostia statue derive from the same lost original, but so little is left of the Berlin statue
as to make decision in the matter impossible.[10]

The Ostia head itself is somewhat smaller than life size: 52 centimetres (20·47 in.)
in total height and 30 centimetres (11·81 in.) in width, the head alone being 27 centimetres (10·63 in.) high and 20 centimetres (7·87 in.) wide.[11] The overwhelming
impression made from the frontal view (plate 1) is of squareness and of a total harmony
of conception which brings the individual characteristics, forehead, eyes, nose, and
lips, into a satisfying balance. This effect of order and symmetry overlaid upon an
apparent uniqueness of individual elements the sculptor seems to have achieved
mainly through his rendering of the hair, moustaches, and beard, which frame the
face in front and cling to the back of the head in a sort of skullcap, or cowl, extending
down to the neck. The head portrays not a type but an individual, square- even bull-
headed, with large, deep-set, slightly unevenly aligned eyes beneath a deep brow, and
a surprisingly wide mass of lower cheek, jaw, and chin. Miss M. Bieber comments on
"the big, ugly, and brutal mouth" (although her further remark that the mouth
"encourages the belief that he was an energetic leader, but one not scrupulous in the
choice of means at his disposal" seems to me too subjective to be of much value).[12]
What even a casual viewer would find difficult to deny is that the effect is one of
physical strength, of decisiveness and determination—of a unique personality—totally
unlike that of the idealized "generals," whose individual names are belied by a same-
ness of conception, which line the corridors of the Vatican and other museums.

It is precisely this uniqueness of total effect that believers in the portrait's authenticity point to to refute the contention that true portraiture, in which the artist depicts,

7. G. Calza (*Le Arti* 18 [1939/40], 161) selects
the Prytaneion statues, M. Bieber those in the
theatre (*AJA* 58 [1954], 283; 74 [1970], 89).
Both suggestions seem to me to be ruled out
by the fact that an official dedication at Athens
(as opposed to a private memorial) ought to be
later than 352 B.C., the date at which Demosthenes decried the absence of a public memorial
to Themistocles and Miltiades (*Against Aristocrates* 196).

8. Nepos, *Them.* 10. 3. The Magnesian coin
is discussed in chapter 9.

9. *Portraits of the Greeks*, I, 99; see also Miss

Richter's monograph, *Greek Portraits: A Study
of Their Development*, 16–21.

10. The relationship between the Ostia statue
and the herm found in the Villa Negroni in
Rome, now in Berlin (Berlin K 128), was suggested by R. Calza, *Scavi di Ostia*, V. 1, 13;
further bibliography and comments by Zinserling, *Klio* 38 (1960), 89, n.2.

11. I take these measurements from R. Calza,
Scavi di Ostia, V. 1, 11.

12. In *AJA* 58 (1954), 283. R. Calza talks of
"la durezza quasi brutale" (*Scavi di Ostia*, V. 1,
13).

not class or occupational characteristics, but specific items of facial and cranial detail often in such a way as to bring out the dominant features of the subject's personality as well, could not have developed as early as the 470s or 460s. Indeed, its very failure to fit the pattern of assumed development, in which even later in the century artists were turning out high-headed, austere generals and bald philosophers—Pericleses and Socrateses, but not Pericles or Socrates—seems to me to count heavily in favour of its being a true likeness.

8 THE "THEMISTOCLES DECREE" FROM TROIZEN

Text and Interpretation

———

[GODS]

It was decreed by the Council and People
on the motion of Themistocles, son of Neokles, of Phrearrhioi:
to entrust the city to Athena, Athens'
5 guardian, and all the other gods, for safekeeping
and to resist the barbarian for the land's sake. The Athenians
themselves and those aliens who live in Athens
shall deposit their children and wives in Troizen
[?under the protection of . . .], founder of the land,
10 and deposit the old men and possessions in Salamis.
The temple-treasurers and priestesses shall stay on the Acropolis
to protect the property of the gods. All the other Athenians and aliens who are of age shall em-
bark on the two hundred ships which have been prepared and shall
15 fight the barbarian both for their own freedom
and for that of the rest of the Greeks, with the aid of the Spartans and Corinthians and Aeginetans and any others who are willing
to share the danger. The generals shall also appoint
two hundred trierarchs, one for each ship,
20 beginning tomorrow, from those who
possess land and a house at Athens and who have legitimate children
and are not more than fifty years of age,

and shall allot the ships to them. They shall also enrol
ten marines for each ship from those above twenty
25   and below thirty years of age, and four archers;
and they shall assign the petty officers among the ships
at the same time as they allot the trierarchs.
The generals shall also post up the other crew members, ship-
by-ship on the white notice-boards, Athenians from the deme-
30   registers and aliens from those listed with
the polemarch. They shall post them up allocating
them by companies into two hundred ———* and write at the top of
each company the name of the trireme, the
trierarch and the petty officers, so that each company may know on
35   which trireme it will embark. When all the
companies have been apportioned and allotted to the triremes, the Council and the generals shall have the crews embark on
all the two hundred ships, after making propitiatory sacrifices to Zeus
the Almighty, and Athena, and Nike, and Posei-
40   don the Preserver. When the ships are manned,
with a hundred of them they shall make sortie to the temple of Artemis
in Euboea, and with a hundred take up station around Salamis and the rest of Attica and guard
the land. In order that all Athenians may present a united front
45   in repelling the barbarian, those who have withdrawn from the country
for ten years are to go to Salamis and remain there until
a decree is passed by the people about them, while those who have been condemned[1]

[an indeterminable number of lines lost]

* Text and meaning in doubt.

The inscription, first discovered apparently in 1847 by Pittakes, was then lost for over
one hundred years until it was rediscovered by Prof. Michael Jameson "in the summer
of 1959, at which time it was in a collection of inscriptions and minor antiquities
housed first in a kapheneion ['coffee-house'] in the village of Troizen";[2] it has now

1. The translation of the decree is my own but is based on those of Michael H. Jameson (*Hesperia* 29 [1960], 200–201, with improvements at *Hesperia* 31 [1962], 314); J. S. Morrison and R. T. Williams, *Greek Oared Ships*, 126–27; and A. R. Burn, *Persia and the Greeks*, 364–65. What the term *hyperesiai* designates in lines 26 and 34 is not certain; it has been thought to cover those eight or so individuals who make up a ship's "trained sailors" or "petty officers,"
like the pilot and coxswain (see M. Amit, *Athens and the Sea*, 29), but B. Jordan has argued that it means "trained rowers" (*Calif. Studies Class. Ant.* 2 [1969], 183 ff., 201–2 for the Troizen Decree).

2. Jameson, *Hesperia* 29 (1960), 198, n.1. Jameson's article (*Hesperia* 29 [1960], 198–223) is the *editio princeps* and contains very full references to the ancient sources, a discussion of the major issues raised by the discovery, and

been deposited in the National Epigraphical Museum in Athens where it is numbered EM 13330. The stone is of what is said to be Pentelic marble, but it is streaked and of poor quality. It is unprepossessing in size and in the first impression it makes; it is just under 0·60 metres (23·62 inches) high, 0·34 metres (13·38 inches) wide at the top, widening in a gradual taper downwards to 0·375 metres (14·76 inches) at the bottom. The top is flat; the stone lacks the pediment, or triangular decorative panel, which surmounts many of the more important inscriptions from antiquity. It is relatively thin, $2\frac{1}{2}$ to $3\frac{1}{2}$ inches, and, as is clear even from plate 2, slightly asymmetrical: the upper left corner makes a right angle, the upper right a more normal obtuse angle. From a careful study of the physical characteristics of the stone and its carving, Sterling Dow concluded that the inscription shows unmistakable signs of "cheapness or haste."[3] The left side of the inscription is badly worn and seems to have been intentionally gouged and roughened up to serve perhaps as a doorsill.

Jameson's discovery was a momentous one, not only for fifth-century history, but also for the light it may throw on a wide range of other subjects: the processes by which our knowledge of the Persian Wars has been transmitted, the use made of inscriptional evidence by ancient literary sources, and, not least, the whole question of forgery of documents in antiquity. Almost from the moment of its discovery—and in this respect it is akin to the Ostia herm—the decree has been condemned as a fake. The number of studies which Jameson's find has generated is, as might be expected, enormous, nor are there signs of the flood's abating; scholarly opinion on the question of authenticity seems about evenly divided.[4]

What the stone purports to be is a later copy (experts now say it was carved in the third century B.C.)[5] of an actual decree calling for the mobilization of the Athenian forces to meet the threat of Persian invasion in 480 and the evacuation of Athens itself. That the forces were mobilized and the city evacuated is clear from Herodotus' narrative, where, however, these two operations are clearly separated in time: the first taking place in the late summer of 481; the second, the actual evacuation, in the following summer. It is worth citing the passages in full, for Herodotus' words are so close to the decree as to preclude their being independent of each other.

It was decreed by them, upon deliberation following the oracle, to receive the barbarian, who was coming against Hellas, in the ships, the whole people,

the photograph of the stone by Miss Alison Frantz, which I reproduce as plate 2 through the courtesy of Miss Frantz. Some of Jameson's restorations have been improved on by later editors; see *SEG* 22 (1967), no. 274, and R. Meiggs and D. Lewis, *A Selection of Greek Historical Inscriptions to the End of the Fifth Century B.C.*, no. 23. For the early history of the stone, see Mitsos in *AAAth* 3 (1970), 246–48.

3. "The Purported Decree of Themistokles: Stele and Inscription," *AJA* 66 (1962), 355.

4. Full bibliographies are given by M. Chambers in *Philologus* 111 (1967), 166–69, and L. Braccesi, *Il problema del Decreto di Temistocle*, 13–15. The modern studies are

arranged in categories by I. Calabi Limentani, *Parola del Passato*, 22 fasc. 115 (1967), 264–65, n.1. Of the thirty-two scholars (who account for seventy-one separate items) mentioned by Chambers, sixteen seem to be more or less firmly against the authenticity of the decree.

5. The most popular epigraphical criterion, that of letter forms, is not here conclusive. Dow (*AJA* 66 [1962], 353–68) adduces other testimony to a third-century date: profile of the decorative top moulding, the gaps of two spaces in lines 23 and 40, and the fact that the margins taper with the stone (the text, that is, is trapezoidal to fit the stone, not rectangular).

trusting the God, and with those of the Hellenes who were willing. (Hdt. 7. 144. 3)

> After their return [from Artemisium] they made a proclamation that each of the Athenians was to save his children and slaves in any way he could...; they hastened to deposit them...because they wished to obey the oracle. (Hdt. 8. 41. 1–2)

There are phrases here which clearly echo the decree: compare Herodotus' term *hypekthesthai* in the second passage quoted with "deposited" (*katathesthai*) in lines 8 and 10 of the inscription; Herodotus' phrase "those of the Hellenes who were willing" is paralleled in line 17 of the decree; while the words in the first passage, "it was decreed...to receive the barbarian...in the ships, the whole people," read like a paraphrase of lines 5–6 and 12–15 of the decree. But certain difficulties are created by the fact that, as Hignett remarks, "Herodotus clearly indicates two stages, a decision in principle made on the motion of Themistokles by the Ekklesia to evacuate Attica if it should be in danger by the Persian army...and a proclamation, which must have been issued on the basis of the decree by the magistrates [that is, the generals], that the emergency had arisen and that the evacuation must begin at once."[6] Like most critics of the Troizen inscription, Hignett proceeds to assimilate it to the second of Herodotus' two contexts, the "proclamation," on grounds that "there is no indication that the [Troizen] decree is a precautionary measure which is not to come into force until the need arises."[7] It is then pointed out that lines 41–42 of the inscription indicate that the battle of Artemisium has not yet been fought, and so the Troizen Decree "contradicts" Herodotus' account. But such dogmatism is hardly justifiable in view of the fact that, as we have seen, Herodotus presents two possible contexts into which the Troizen Decree might be fitted. And even some of his supporters have had their doubts: "If this alleged decree [Herodotus' proclamation] is authentic," writes Hignett, "it must have been carried earlier with the proviso that it should not come into force until the emergency arose."[8]

It must be admitted, however, that on any interpretation there will be certain unresolved difficulties in trying to fit the data of the inscription into Herodotus' narrative. As Hignett observed, the Troizen Decree carries no indication that it is merely provisional, or precautionary, and in any case the specific clauses regarding the sending of ships to Artemisium and evacuation of residents are unlikely to have been worked out in detail as early as the summer of 481 (Hdt. 8. 144. 3, after the oracles but before the Congress at the Isthmus in the autumn). If on the other hand all the provisions of the decree be thought to refer to the proclamation of spring 480 (Hdt. 8. 41. 1), the fact that in Herodotus' narrative the battle of Artemisium has already been fought creates serious problems. Why, it might be asked further, does the decree call for the sending of only 100 ships to Artemisium (line 41), whereas Herodotus says 127 were actually present (8. 1. 1)? The inscription implies that the city is to be evacuated immediately, and yet Herodotus again says the evacuation actually took place after

---

6. *Xerxes' Invasion*, 464.   7. Ibid.   8. Ibid., 199.

the fleet had returned from Artemisium. What caused the delay? And why are only Troizen and Salamis mentioned in the inscription as places where the refugees are to be "deposited," when Herodotus says some were sent to Aegina as well? Had hostilities with Aegina been settled in the meantime?

Once the decree had been properly studied, it became clear that part of it, at least, must have been known to other ancient authors. Plutarch, writing in the first century A.D., paraphrased the first part of it in his *Life of Themistocles*:

> His [that is, Themistocles'] opinion prevailed, and he framed a decree that they should deposit the city to the safekeeping of Athena, Athens' guardian [the wording is identical with line 4 of the Troizen Decree] and that the men of military age should embark on their ships, and save their children, wives, and slaves as best they could. When the decree was ratified.... (10. 4)

Aelius Aristeides, a rhetorician of the second century of our era, is even closer to the actual wording of the stone, for he includes, in addition to an almost verbatim rendering of line 4, references to the sending of the wives and children to Troizen and the old people to Salamis (lines 8, 10–11), "and that the rest embark in the triremes to contend in behalf of freedom," which is close to the wording of line 15.[9] It has been suggested that since both Plutarch and Aelius seem to put the decree after Artemisium, which is explicitly contradicted by lines 41–42 of the text, neither knew as much of the text as the stone preserves; it has further been pointed out that there seem to be no literary references of any kind to anything in the decree beyond line 18. In that case, it can safely be assumed that Plutarch's source (and so probably Aelius', too) was an earlier written version of part of the decree. Who that earlier author may have been must remain an open question; Craterus the Macedonian, who compiled a *Collection of Decrees* towards the end of the fourth century B.C. and whom Plutarch quotes by name elsewhere, has been a favourite candidate.[10]

That the decree was known in antiquity—the first unequivocal reference to it is in Demosthenes' speech *On the False Embassy* (Or. 19. 303), delivered in 343 B.C.—is of course no guarantee of authenticity. What is it about the Troizen inscription that has aroused suspicion? While it is not possible here to analyse, or even to list, all the objections which have been raised to specific points of wording in the decree, the most important criticisms (for the most part restricted to the opening sections) seem to be the following.[11]

9. Ael. Arist. Or. 46 (II, 256 Dind.). Aelius refers to the decree again in Oration 13 (I, 225–26 Dind.), but the wording there is less close to the text of the inscription.

10. On Craterus (cited by Plut. *Cim.* 13. 5, *Arist.* 26. 1), see F. Schachermeyr, "Die Themistokles-Stele und ihre Bedeutung...," *Oester. arch. Inst. in Wien*, Jahreshefte 46 (1961–63), esp. 159 ff. Other possible candidates might be sought amongst the later "periegetic" writers like Diodorus and Heliodorus who wrote a treatise entitled *On the Acropolis at Athens*, and might, for example, have recorded the inscription in connection with a discussion of the statue of Artemis Leukophryene said by Pausanias (1. 26. 4) to have been dedicated on the Acropolis by Themistocles' sons.

11. The fullest attack remains that of C. Habicht, "Falsche Urkunden zur Geschichte Athens im Zeitalter der Perserkriege," *Hermes* 89 (1961), 1–35; the fullest rejoinder that of H. Berve, "Zur Themistokles-Inschrift von Troizen," *SB Bayer. Akad. der Wiss.*, phil.-hist. Kl., Munich (1961), Heft 5.

Objections have been made to the style of the formal introductory clause, or pre-script, which seems to be at variance with those found on epigraphic texts of the fifth century. But the evidence from those few early decrees which survive points to a certain variety of usage. Thus the earliest extant Athenian decree, which apparently sets out regulations for a colony of recent Athenian settlers on Salamis, begins simply, "It was decreed by the demos,"[12] although a reference to the Boule has been restored in line 12. Meiggs and Lewis point out in their discussion of this decree that "the standard developed form of the preamble...was not reached for more than a genera-tion after Cleisthenes,"[13] and they call attention to *IG* I², 3/4, a decree (perhaps of 485/4) regulating the cult of Athena Polias, in which the prescript is restored as "It was decreed by the demos," with the archon's name being given later in the text (3, lines 16–17; 4, line 26). *IG* I², 5, which specifies the sacrifices to be offered at the Eleusinian festival and which perhaps dates from this same period, shows the more developed form, "It was decreed by the Boule and Demos," and names the secretary of the Council later on. Finally, *IG* I², 16, a decree specifying judicial procedure be-tween Athens and one of her allies, Phaselis, which dates from the 460s, follows the full "official" form in naming the prytanizing tribe (one of the ten Attic tribes which was allotted the function of providing the steering committee for the Assembly in that month), the secretary for the session, and the *epistates*, or "president," of the day's session. In place of this information, which would have, in effect, dated the decree, our inscription merely gives the usual first clause of the formal opening, "It was decreed by the Council and People," and proceeds to identify the mover, "Themistocles, son of Neokles, of Phrearrhioi." Here, too, the phrasing has been questioned: "It seems in the highest degree improbable that any official copy of a fifth-century decree ever gave the patronymic and demotic of the proposer," writes D. M. Lewis.[14] It has further been argued that the mention of Athena with the formal title "Athens' guardian" (*medeousa*) in lines 4–5 is inappropriate at so early a date, that "the epithet presupposes the existence of the Athenian naval league."[15] "The title is basically East Greek,...Athena Polias looked at from outside Athens."[16] Use of the term "Acropolis" in line 11 has aroused suspicion, for, according to Thucydides, Athenian practice down to his own time (late fifth century) was to call the Acropolis simply "polis" (2. 15). "Tomorrow," with no further indication of date, in line 20, has been thought strange.

Critics of the content of the inscription concern themselves mainly with the long central section, from line 18 on, which deals with the specific procedures to be followed

12. *IG* I², 1 (cf. *SEG* 10. 1, 23. 1), Tod no. 11, Meiggs and Lewis, *Selection*, no. 14. (The fragmentary state of *SEG* 24. 1, side A, frs. 1, 2, precludes secure restoration, but what re-mains suggests a decree of the Boule only, followed by the archon's name; B. D. Meritt proposed to restore a reference to the Areo-pagus, and to date the decree to the years of that body's "ascendancy" after Salamis [*Hes-peria* 36 (1967), 74–75].)
13. *Selection*, p. 27.
14. "Notes on the Decree of Themistocles,"

CQ, n.s. 11 (1961), 61–66. Some of his obser-vations are repeated, others modified, in Meiggs and Lewis, *Selection*, pp. 50–52.
15. Habicht, *Hermes* 89 (1961), 4.
16. Lewis, *CQ*, n.s. 11 (1961), 62, citing E. Preuner, in *Ath. Mitt.* 49 (1924), 31–34. But B. D. Meritt, on the basis of a similar use in Aristophanes, *Knights* 763–64, neatly turns this argument in favour of authenticity ("Greek Historical Studies," in *Lectures in Memory of Louise Taft Semple*, 1st ser., 125–28).

in manning the fleet. Some have raised a general objection to the very detailed nature of this part of the decree· "The elaborate provisions...are hardly credible in the Athens of 480; they are typical rather of the radical democracy," writes Hignett.[17] Specifically, the qualifications for trierarchs spelled out in lines 20–22 have been objected to on grounds that the first does not follow the Solonian property classification, and the third, possession of legitimate children, seems to look forward to Pericles' citizenship law of 451/50. Apart from lines 22–23 and 26–27 of this document, there is no reference to allotment of ships or officers until well into the fourth century. The figure of ten marines to each ship in line 24 is in conflict with the figure of fourteen given by Plutarch (*Them.* 14. 2). The "registers" referred to in lines 29–30, when they are mentioned again later in the century, seem to be employed for a totally different purpose, as a register of knights and hoplites eligible for a tax-offering to Apollo.[18]

At first sight, these objections appear impressive, indeed decisive, in the cumulative effect of the indictment they contain against the decree's authenticity. But do apparently conflicting, purported parallels in late sources, whether fourth-century inscriptions or historical accounts like Plutarch's, really prove that similar terms could not have been used in an early fifth century decree, or used in a different sense from that which they would later bear? And certain of the objections raised to matters of detail have been countered, often decisively. Thus, as Morrison and Williams have pointed out, there is little force to Burn's objection that "one would expect better of Themistokles' Athens than this last-minute, deliberately fortuitous assembly of ships' companies which are to meet for the first time at the point of embarkation."[19] The allotment which is unequivocally being referred to in lines 22–23 and 27 is of *ships* to trierarchs (the supplement in line 26 is uncertain, although this may be a reference to a separate allotment of "officers"); there is no reason to exclude the possibility that a trierarch and his crew had previously trained together.[20]

The hardest argument of all to answer is one which turns parallels in other sources for matters of phrasing or content in the decree *against* the latter's authenticity, on grounds that such similarities betray the hand of a careful forger. In lines 38–40, the section of the inscription which lists the gods to whom the generals are to make "propitiatory sacrifices," there are mentioned (apparently) four distinct divinities: Zeus Almighty (*Pankrates*), Athena, Nike, and Poseidon Preserver (*Asphaleios*). The epithet of Zeus occurs several times in Aeschylus, as Jameson notes,[21] which seems to indicate that a mention of Zeus under this title is at least not unsuited to an early fifth century context. Moreover, one of these occurrences, as Jameson points out, is in "a passage with a strong patriotic tinge." The obvious inference from the appropriateness of the epithet was not allowed to go unchallenged. Amandry remarked that "the existence of an official cult rendered to Zeus Pankrates is nowhere attested in the Greek world," and, on the basis of late fourth century archaeological evidence

---

17. *Xerxes' Invasion*, 462.

18. *IG* I², 79, line 6. Habicht's objections on this point are answered (satisfactorily, to my mind) by Meritt, "Greek Historical Studies," 123–24.

19. Burn, *Persia and the Greeks*, 366.

20. Morrison and Williams, *Greek Oared Ships*, 124–25.

21. *Hesperia* 29 (1960), 220. The Aeschylean passages are collected and discussed by Wolfgang Kiefner, *Der religiöse Allbegriff des Aischylos*, 105–15.

for a shrine along the Ilissus to Pánkrates as a separate hero, he tried to discredit the testimony of the decree: "Nothing indicates any relation between this hero and Zeus."[22] But, we may object, a forger might have been expected to know that. So critics make the next obvious move: "L. Moretti...suggests that 'the forger' derived it, as a piece of period colour, from his reading of Aeschylus."[23] Clearly, both explanations cannot be correct and may be thought to cancel one another out. With the cult title of Poseidon the case is slightly different, for the epithet does not seem to be used of Poseidon elsewhere until Aristophanes' *Acharnians*, and this very fact might be thought to prove that its use in the decree is an anachronism. But Lewis has shown that the passage in Aristophanes really seems to point back to the period of the Persian Wars, for the epithet is used by the chorus of "old men [who] have all fought the Mede.... Old men remember many things about the Persian Wars."[24] Again, if the phrase points anywhere, it is to authenticity rather than away from it.

All the details mentioned above, vehemently attacked by some, have found other scholars to defend them, often passionately, and the usual line of defence is to find a parallel, the earlier the better. But, as we have seen, a move always open to the critic at this point is recourse to the "cunning forger." Thus, the whole game of parallel-hunting soon reaches a logical impasse, well summed up by Burn: "In dealing with details the discussion runs into great difficulties; nearly all the arguments are double-edged. If a detail is consistent with Herodotos, it can be used (a) as evidence of genuineness or (b) as ground for suspicion that a forger has used the current tradition; if it is awkward and anomalous, it can nevertheless be used as an argument for genuineness, on the ground that no forger would have done *that*."[25] The match must be declared a draw.

Let two final examples suffice. In the section we have been discussing, the list of gods to be placated, Athena *and* Nike are mentioned separately. To this separation critics have objected that what sparse evidence there is points to an identification between them in the early period when Nike seems to have been one of the many cult titles of Athena. As the text stands, then, it seems to be the work not of a clever, but of a clumsy, forger, who inadvertently fell into standard fourth-century ways in dividing the two and setting up Nike as a separate divinity. It is no use for the defenders to suggest that the "and" between the two substantives is intrusive, an understandable mistake by a stonemason who carved the word three times in line 39 but should only have done so twice (so Meiggs and Lewis: "There may be some misplacing of the καὶ's.").[26] Although that seems to be the easiest solution to an admittedly knotty problem, then we leave ourselves open to the objection that "the lettering shows that [the mason] was a professional, and very painstaking; neither erasure nor error has been detected."[27] Whether the true text read "Athena and Nike" or "Athena...

22. "Thémistocle: Un décret et un portrait," *Bull. de Fac. des Lettres, Univ. de Strasbourg* 39 (1961), 418, with n.7. Meiggs and Lewis have apparently been persuaded: "Pankrates is certainly normally a hero distinct from Zeus" (*Selection*, p. 51).

23. Burn, *Persia and the Greeks*, 370, citing

L. Moretti in *Riv. di fil.* 88 (1960), 397.

24. *CQ*, n.s. 11 (1961), 65.

25. *Persia and the Greeks*, 369.

26. *Selection*, p. 51 (so also Meritt, "Greek Historical Studies," 125).

27. Dow, *AJA* 66 (1962), 358.

Nike," critics will not allow the detail to count in any other way than against the decree's authenticity. But the evidence for Athena–Nike versus Athena ‖ Nike in the fifth century is by no means consistent or easy to interpret. As Lewis noted, Nike occurs as a separate divinity in the "oracle of Bacis" quoted by Herodotus:

> ...then the day of freedom for Hellas
> The wide-seeing son of Cronos and Lady Nike bring on.
> (8. 77, lines 7–8)

Potnia Nike occurs again several times in Bacchylides (XI [XII] 5–6; cf. the beginning of X [XI]). At Aristophanes, *Knights* 589 we read: "Come, Pallas...bringing Nike," and, as Lewis remarks, "she stands by herself at *Lysistrata* 317."[28] If the inscription said by the author of *On the Malice of Herodotus* to have been set up on the altar of Zeus Eleutherios ("Bringer of Freedom") at Plataea after the victory, τόνδε ποθ' Ἕλληνες Νίκης κράτει, ἔργῳ Ἀρήος κτλ.[29] could be verified, we should have inscriptional evidence to add to the literary references. In any case, there is more than a little room for doubt whether the evidence is secure enough to allow a dogmatic assertion that identification of Athena and Nike was the rule in the early fifth century; it is conceivable that the process by which an aspect of Athena was separated and set up into an independent, personified divinity might have begun much earlier than most scholars had supposed.

In an earlier section of the decree, lines 14–18, there are phrases for which, as we have seen, parallels can be found in Herodotus. But these very expressions Habicht turns against the decree by calling them "literarische Ausdrucksweisen."[30] "Scholars have objected," remarks Burn, "to its 'rhetoric,' to phrases such as 'sharing the danger' and 'defence of freedom against the barbarian,' which are reminiscent of fourth-century patriotic oratory."[31] "I should be sorry to think that Themistocles was incapable of a little rhetoric on this occasion," replies Lewis.[32] And, once again, although a parallel is ready to hand, it may be dangerous to take refuge in it. When Aeschylus, writing in 472 B.C., turned into iambic verse the battle cry he had heard as a participant in the battle of Salamis in 480, it read as follows:

> "O sons of Greeks, go on,
> Bring freedom to your fatherland, bring freedom to
> Your children, wives, and seats of your ancestral gods,
> And your forbears' graves; now the struggle is for all."
> (*Pers.* 402–5)

No proof can be adduced that these are Themistocles' own words that Aeschylus is here echoing (although that possibility must remain open), but the similarities of phrasing, particularly the double emphasis on freedom and the recognition that this is a battle being fought for all the Hellenes, are enough to show that the Athenians did not need to wait until the patriotic oratory of the fourth century to describe Salamis

28. *CQ*, n.s. 11 (1961), 65.
29. *Mor.* 873 B (the emendation is virtually certain).
30. *Hermes* 89 (1961), 7.
31. *Persia and the Greeks*, 368.
32. *CQ*, n.s. 11 (1961), 62.

in glowing terms; such descriptions certainly go back, if not to the day of the battle, at least to soon afterwards.[33]

If we allow that the arguments from parallels cancel each other out, there remains a residue of strong support on both sides. In favour of authenticity are certain phrases or usages which, it seems, would have been beyond the abilities of even the most ingenious forger. For example, in line 7, instead of the almost invariable technical word "metic," the stone has merely "aliens," and in line 45, in place of the technical-sounding but apparently late term "those ostracized," we have the euphemistic but demonstrably early and perhaps official phrase, "those who have withdrawn." On the other hand, Hignett makes a vigorous case for the unlikelihood that so many seemingly separate provisions would have been contained in a single decree: "They constitute a jumble of disparate measures, what the Romans called a *lex satura.* . . . no true parallel to this decree can be found in the extant Athenian inscriptions from the fifth century."[34] But cannot a later forger be expected to have known this and to have avoided so obvious an anomaly? And parallels to such a multiple enactment have been adduced.[35]

It must be admitted that if, or however much of, the decree is authentic (and one hardly need doubt that there *was* a decree authorizing mobilization), we have no knowledge of when it may have been inscribed, where it was deposited, or how it was preserved. The existence of an official archives or records office in the early part of the fifth century has been questioned. If such did exist (perhaps in the *Bouleuterion*), the official copy, on wood or papyrus, would have been deposited there either before the city was evacuated or, more probably, immediately after the Athenians returned in 479. On the other hand, it has been maintained that a true records office was not set up until the last years of the fifth century, and that in the *Metroön*, when the democracy was restored after the oligarchic interludes of 411 and 404.[36] If this latter view is the correct one, then there would have been no official copies which were not inscribed on stone in the first instance, and it seems rather improbable that the Athenians had an opportunity to have it inscribed before they left their city in the summer of 480. Obviously the longer the interval between passage of the decree and its inscription, the greater the chance for editorial revisions and alterations. When the Athenians returned home, they may have decided to make a permanent record of the momentous decree by which, paradoxically, their city was both temporarily lost to them and ultimately saved. A number of separate enactments may have been gathered together under one heading, and it is not beyond imagining that Themistocles himself might have commissioned, or at least encouraged, the inscribing of a decree (complete with his own

33. Meritt, "Greek Historical Studies," 129, who adduces the *Persians* passage, also mentions a similar phrase in the so-called Marathon epigram: "[The fallen soldiers] kept all Greece from seeing its day of slavery." Meiggs and Lewis cite Hdt. 5. 64. 2, 7. 144. 3, and 7. 178. 2 (*Selection*, p. 50).

34. *Xerxes' Invasion*, 463.

35. W. Ripper, *Gymnasium* 74 (1967), 136, citing W. Larfeld, *Handbuch der griechischen Epigraphik*[3], 122.

36. U. Kahrstedt, "Das athenische Staats-

archiv," *Klio* 31 (1938), 25–32 ("Es gab also vor 403/2 kein Staatsarchiv in Athen. Vorher hat der Staat auf Holz, Stein oder gar nicht geschrieben" [31]). This view was supported also by A. R. W. Harrison, *JHS* 75 (1955), 26 ff., esp. 27–29. Carl Curtius reconstructed the complex procedures involved in recording, storing, and reproducing official documents (*Philologus* 24 [1866], 112–13). See, most recently, Alan L. Boegehold, "A Central Archive at Athens," *AJA* 76 (1972), 23–30, esp. 28–29.

name and patronymic), whose erection would certainly have redounded to his personal glory.

One of the most difficult of all the problems raised by the text found at Troizen is that of the relation of this decree with the so-called amnesty decree mentioned by the Aristotelian *Constitution of Athens*. In chapter 22. 8 of that treatise we learn that those individuals who had been ostracized in the course of the preceding decade were recalled in the archonship of Hypsichides, "in the fourth year" after the ostracism of Aristeides, that is, in the Athenian year July 481 to July 480. The Troizen Decree breaks off in the middle of what seems to be a provision for these persons. They are treated in two groups, lines 45–47 dealing with "those who have withdrawn" (as we have seen, the apparently official designation of those who had been ostracized), line 47 beginning a new provision for a second group. On the basis of a reference in the late fifth century orator Andocides, Jameson suggested that the clause continued with a provision restoring political rights to the *atimoi*, men who had been deprived of those rights, and his suggestion has found general favour.[37] But the troublesome fact is that lines 45–47 seem to indicate that *final* disposition of the case of the ostracized has not yet been made: "Those who have withdrawn from the country for ten years are to go to Salamis and remain there until a decision is reached [or, in technical language, 'decree is passed'] by the people about them"; in other words, the amnesty decree, if there was a separate one, has not yet been passed. Matters are made more complicated still by the statement in Plutarch that it was Themistocles who moved the decree that "those temporarily removed be allowed, upon their return, to do and speak the best for Hellas with the other citizens" (*Them.* 11. 1). If A. E. Raubitschek is right in arguing that the clause in the Troizen Decree can be fitted into the sequence of events given by the late writer Cornelius Nepos, according to whom the ostracized were recalled by a decree before the battle but their banishment was legally repealed only by a separate enactment after the battle had taken place, a case could perhaps even be made for maintaining that Plutarch's comment at *Themistocles* 11 can best be seen as a reference, not to a separate decree by Themistocles for recall of the exiles, but to precisely this clause in the Troizen Decree.[38] Of course, unless the missing end piece is discovered, we shall never be certain how the decree concluded (and, if Dow is right, it is unlikely that it can have continued beyond more than a line or two),[39] but it is worth considering Raubitschek's further suggestion that the Troizen Decree may have continued, as the *Constitution of Athens* does (22. 8), with a reference to the geographical restrictions to apply to those ostracized henceforth.[40]

37. *Hesperia* 29 (1960), 221–22, on the basis of Andocides, 1. 107.

38. "A Note on the Themistocles Decree," in *Studi in onore di Luisa Banti*, 285–87; cf. idem, *Class. et Med.* 19 (1958), 103–5. S. M. Burstein has recently argued on the basis of ἀπιέναι in line 46 of the Troizen Decree that "the ostracized are in fact included in a plan for evacuating Athens and not being recalled" (*Calif. Studies Class. Ant.* 4 [1971], 103), although I think he overstates the degree of "hostility and suspicion" to the exiles which these clauses bespeak (p. 109).

39. *AJA* 66 (1962), 355.

40. The matter is, however, complicated by a doubtful reading in the MS. at *Const.* 22. 8. Raubitschek follows Kenyon, the *editor princeps*, in accepting the papyrus' ἐντός; others emend to ἐκτός.

Suggested Contexts for a Forgery

Sceptics of the authenticity of the Troizen Decree have attempted to discover plausible ' historical circumstances in which the decree might have been forged. As all the suggested dates are in the fourth century, and the inscription itself is now dated by most scholars to the third century, the theory that it is a forgery has to be modified to this extent: the Troizen inscription may be a copy on stone of a fourth-century forged original, itself either on stone or (more likely) a literary transcription purporting to go back to the fifth-century inscription.

Those who favour this approach have not had to look beyond the circumstances in which a reference to the Themistocles Decree first appears in our sources. Demosthenes mentions it in a speech delivered in 343 B.C., in which he attacks the conduct of Aeschines several years earlier (348/7) in "reading out the Decree of Miltiades and ⟨that of⟩ Themistocles..." (Or. 19. 303). Demosthenes does not here accuse Aeschines of having forged these documents, but they have all been called into question by scholars in modern times. Although we shall return in the next section to consider some of the other alleged forgeries, what interests us here is the political situation at mid-century which may have given rise—indeed, may even have encouraged—the wholesale forging of fifth-century decrees. M. Guarducci believes that such a setting can be found during the so-called Social War, 357–355 B.C., "the only period in Athenian history of the fourth century in which [the allegedly forged documents] fit wonderfully well."[41] She sees in this period a convergence of three conditions which she deems conducive to such a spate of forgeries: friendship of Athens and Sparta, enmity of Athens and Sparta towards Thebes, and renewed hostility to Persia. This last point Guarducci believes to be a decisive consideration for dating the alleged forgeries. There arose at Athens a new wave of anti-Persian feeling directed towards King Artaxerxes III, *Ochos*, and his satrap of Caria, Mausolus, whose encouragement had led to the revolt of Chios, Cos, Rhodes, and Byzantium from the Second Athenian Confederacy; "in just this period of renewed anti-Persian fury, which reached its culmination in the summer of 355, the false documents relative to the Persian Wars find their most worthy framework."[42] There was fear of a new alliance between Artaxerxes and Thebes, and the days of united resistance to Persia and the glories of Marathon and Salamis may well have been recalled.

Now there can be no doubt that Guarducci has shown that this would have been a *possible*, even an apt, time for forging documents which would remind the Athenians of their past resistance to Persia, and, as she recalls, Athens and Sparta fought side by side in the summer of 355 against Thebes; but what exactly can her arguments be said to prove? She points out that "the Decrees served as instruments of propaganda" for Aeschines,[43] but that does not *by itself* prove them false. And, more recently, another —apparently equally plausible—context has been suggested. Lorenzo Braccesi, in a

41. "Nuove osservazioni sul 'Decreto di Temistocle,'" *Riv. di fil.*, n.s. 39 (1961), 69.
42. Ibid., 72. The name Cleidemus has re- cently been given to the alleged forger (G. L. Huxley, *GRBS* 9 [1968], 315).
43. *Riv. di fil.*, n.s. 39 (1961), 74.

short monograph on the Troizen inscription, suggests that the decree was forged by "a member of Demosthenes' circle working in Troizen...ready to make use of the false inscription as an instrument of political propaganda."[44] According to him, the decree is to be dated to "the last period of the orator's exile, certainly later than the arrival in Greece of the news of Alexander's death [that is, in the summer of 323]."[45] The final clause in the decree, he argues, is "substantially extraneous to the spirit of the document [and] was intentionally introduced...to bring again to general attention, with a note of complete verisimilitude, a particularly pressing problem: that of the position of Demosthenes, an exile in Troizen, on the eve of the Lamian War."[46] Support for this theory is found in the reference in the second *Epistle* (II.24) ascribed to Demosthenes to his own position as *atimon*.[47] The appropriateness of Troizen as the origin of such a forgery at just this time stems from the renewed close relations between Athens and Troizen during this period. It seems that Troizenian internal politics in the 330s polarized between a pro-Macedonian party and a group of "anti-Macedonian pro-Athenian democrats," in Jameson's phrase;[48] the former, led by an Athenian metic, Athenogenes, gained the upper hand and forced the latter into exile in Athens. By a kind of reciprocal process, Demosthenes sought refuge in Troizen later in the decade. It was this circle of pro-Athenian democrats that took pains to revive the memory of the Troizenians' benefactions to the Athenian refugees before the battle of Salamis some one hundred and fifty years earlier.

Now, one can certainly accept such a reconstruction of the internal political situation at Troizen at this time on the basis of one or two (admittedly fragmentary) pieces of ancient evidence,[49] without having to concede the further hypothesis that the Themistocles Decree was forged just at this time and in this situation. For an alternate hypothesis is Jameson's, that an authentic original was *copied* at Troizen at about this time.[50] The epigraphic text which we possess, seemingly to be dated to the third century, could just as easily be a copy of a fourth-century copy of an earlier (authentic?) original as of a fourth-century forgery.

If these specific reconstructions of possible contexts in which the Troizen Decree was more or less plausibly forged should prove unsatisfying, doubters can take refuge in a general feeling of uneasiness to which Burn gives voice: "It is Aischines, a leading orator of Euboulos' party, who is recorded to have read the decrees of Themistokles and Miltiades; and in fact, if we are to ask, was there a man in fourth-century Athens who was well placed and well qualified either to invent them or to discover them, we need look no further."[51] It should be noted, however, that no reconstruction which

44. *Il problema del Decreto di Temistocle*, 46–47.

45. Ibid., 51.

46. Ibid., 54–55.

47. On the Demosthenes *Epistles*, see J. A. Goldstein, *The Letters of Demosthenes*; he accepts the authenticity of Epistles 1–4.

48. *Hesperia* 29 (1960), 207, where the evidence for the 330s in Troizen is collected. See also Goldstein, *Letters of Demosthenes*, 233–45,

for the Troizenian background.

49. Hypereides' speech *Against Athenogenes* 32–33; Demosthenes (?), *Epistle* II. 18–19.

50. Although, of course, part of Jameson's hypothesis, that this copy and our stone EM 13330 are identical, will have to be abandoned if an epigraphic date in the third century is accepted.

51. *Persia and the Greeks*, 376.

has so far been proposed for a fourth-century context of forgery attempts to answer the question, Why was the decree copied in the third century?

Guilt by Association

Attempts to discredit the Troizen inscription usually involve placing it in a larger pattern of other documents which purport to go back to the Persian War period but which scholars, ancient and modern, consider spurious. Thus the Troizen Decree is judged, and condemned, by the company it keeps.

It must be admitted that the manner in which it makes its first appearance does not inspire confidence. As we have seen, it is mentioned by Demosthenes in 343 B.C. as having been read out before the Athenian assembly by Aeschines several years before, probably in the summer of 348 B.C.: "Who was it," Demosthenes asks rhetorically, "who harangued you with those long and fine speeches, reading out the Decree of Miltiades and ⟨that of⟩ Themistocles, and the oath which the ephebes swear at the shrine of Aglaurus?" (*On the False Embassy* 303). To the last of these, the Ephebic Oath, we shall return in the following section, but what of the other, the "Decree of Miltiades"? The two decrees do not deserve to be mentioned as on an equal footing, for what few references there are to the so-called Miltiades Decree in the ancient sources are somewhat lacking in their credibility. On the basis of a scholiast's note on the reference in Demosthenes mentioned above (Or. 19. 303), a fleeting and obscure reference in Aristotle's *Rhetoric* (1411 a 9–10, a discussion of metaphor in which the Miltiades Decree fits rather uncomfortably), and a (probably irrelevant) passage in Pausanias (7. 15. 7), N. G. L. Hammond has confidently reconstructed a complete decree whose clauses are both numerous and specific.[52] But so far from guaranteeing the authenticity of the Miltiades Decree, these references point in the opposite direction: a late attempt to fabricate a mobilization decree before Marathon and provide Miltiades with the honour of having initiated a piece of legislation to equal Themistocles'—no doubt with Themistocles' as its model. The process can be detected in a scholiast's comment on a passage in Aelius Aristeides, who, in his eulogy of Miltiades in the speech *For the Four*, mentions in passing a *psephisma* (II, 219 Dind.). The scholiast explains the reference thus: "This is in the decree mentioned by Demosthenes in 'On the False Embassy' [19. 303 as above]; for when the Persians were attacking, he proposed 'that the Greeks not wait for them, but *leave the city to the god*, the old men and women to guard the walls, and all the young men to run to Marathon'" (III, 542 Dind.). The phrase which I have italicized has been transferred bodily from the Themistocles Decree.

It should have become clear that in the Miltiades Decree we do have (*pace* Hammond) precisely the kind of documentary *parvenu* that critics of the Themistocles Decree see behind that decree: an oral tradition that the decree calling for mobilization

52. "The Campaign and Battle of Marathon," *JHS* 88 (1968), 33–34. This somewhat credulous view is also taken by A. Garzetti, "Erodoto e il Decreto di Milziade ΔΕΙΝ ΕΞΙΕΝΑΙ," *Aevum* 27 (1953), 18–21.

before Marathon was moved by Miltiades (perhaps little more than an inference from the fact that it was considered to be uniquely Miltiades' victory) was at some later stage expanded into a full decree, complete with prytany date.[53] It is no wonder, then, that the two decrees could not be kept separate: the scholiast on the Aristotle passage, quoted by Cope, glosses the Miltiades Decree as calling for "no deliberation: Miltiades, without allowing for deliberation, marched out *against Xerxes*" (my italics).

Another mate for the Troizen Decree has been sought by some of its modern critics in the so-called Decree against Lykides, the councillor who, tradition maintained, had presented before the Athenian Boule, in emergency session on Salamis, a motion to accept the peace terms proposed by Xerxes' general Mardonius. According to the story which Herodotus tells (9. 4–5), the Athenians were so infuriated that they stoned the man to death on the spot, while his wife and children received the same treatment at the hands of the Athenian women. The story appears again in the fourth century, but with certain alterations and embellishments. What was summary execution in Herodotus becomes, in Lycurgus, "the *psephism* concerning the man who was put to death on Salamis" (*Against Leocrates* 122 and 71), and it is clearly the same affair that Demosthenes is alluding to in his oration *On the Crown*, although he gives the man's name as Cyrsilus and apparently dates the incident *before* the battle of Salamis (204).[54] Although Lycurgus seems to have had a text of the *psephisma* read into the record during his speech, it does not survive, and the variants in Demosthenes' version seem to show that there was no "official" text. There are clearly no grounds for holding up this *psephism* as being in parallel case with the Themistocles Decree, as Habicht does.[55]

Another, more popular, candidate is the Decree of Nicagoras, whose substance Plutarch gives as follows:

> When [Themistocles'] decree was ratified, most of the Athenians conveyed their families and wives for safekeeping to Troizen, and the Troizenians vied with one another to receive them hospitably. Indeed, they passed a public decree of support [for the refugees], granting them two obols each and allowing the children to pick the fruit wherever they liked, and, in addition, paying the salaries of their teachers. The decree was proposed by Nicagoras. (*Them.* 10. 5)

A number of points raise suspicions: the similar motif of ad lib. fruit-picking in Plutarch's account of how Cimon courted popular favour in rivalry with Pericles (*Cim.* 10. 1);[56] the well-omened name of the proposer; chiefly, though, the exclusiveness of Plutarch's account, in which the refugees go only to Troizen and the Troizenians respond with benefactions. This should give us pause, for Herodotus makes perfectly

53. Plutarch (*Quaest. conv.* 1. 10, 628 E) says it was passed "while Aiantis was the prytanizing tribe"—when was this detail added? The confused passage in Aristotle mentioned above (*Rhet.* 1411 a) shows that the orator Cephisodotus made political capital of Miltiades' Decree in the mid-fourth century.

54. A. W. Verrall, "The Death of Cyrsilus, *alias* Lycides," *CR* 23 (1909), 36–40, attempts,

not with complete success, to resolve the conflicts in the various accounts. P. J. Rhodes comments that "there is nothing unlikely in the statement. . .that the boule met on Salamis" (*Athenian Boule*, 35).

55. *Hermes* 89 (1961), 18, 21–22.

56. This apparently goes back to Theopompus, *FGrHist* 115 F 89 (cf. *Const. of Athens* 27. 3).

clear that some refugees went to Aegina and Salamis as well (8. 41). It is strange that the decree should make its first appearance at just this time; it is first mentioned (apparently; the papyrus is mutilated and the reference is not quite beyond dispute) in Hypereides' speech *Against Athenogenes*.[57] The Troizenian generosity is mentioned again in the second *Epistle* ascribed to Demosthenes (II. 18–19), and the public monument described by Pausanias as being situated in a stoa in the agora at Troizen, "stone statues depicting the wives and children whom the Athenians sent to the Troizenians for safekeeping" (2. 31. 7), may also have been erected at this time. Partly on the basis of the earlier benefaction, Athenian citizenship was granted to a certain Troizenian named Telesias in 139 B.C.[58] There are grounds enough then, perhaps, to justify Habicht's listing of this decree among his "falsche Urkunden."[59]

Defenders of the Themistocles Decree have sometimes felt called upon to prove the authenticity of these and other alleged forgeries, which critics have lumped together with the stele from Troizen. But neither is it possible, nor would it even be desirable, to do so. At most, it can be shown that one or another of them *need not* have been forged, as critics contend; that is, historical arguments can be adduced to prove at most that such-and-such a measure *could have been* (or, conversely, *probably was not*) passed at the time and in the circumstances in which it purports to originate. Furthermore, it is logically conceivable that every one of the alleged parallels can be shown beyond shadow of a doubt to have been forged (and we have not yet reached even this happy state of certainty), without affecting in any way the question of the Troizen Decree's authenticity. Supporters of the Troizen Decree, then, should not let themselves be drawn into a defence of more or less suspicious documents which really have nothing to do with the point at issue, namely, whether this particular text, carved on stone and set up at Troizen probably in the third century B.C., is what it claims to be: a later copy of an original document dating back to the period of the Persian invasion. The frantic search for parallels among the allegedly false documents in our literary sources has distracted scholarly energies from what could be a really useful, perhaps decisive, investigation of other epigraphic texts with which the Troizen Decree might be compared and against which it might be evaluated.

Epigraphic versus Literary Texts

To return first to the other item which Demosthenes says Aeschines had read out before the Assembly in 348 B.C., "the oath which the ephebes swear at the shrine of Aglaurus." In 1932, in the vicinity of the old Attic deme of Acharnae, excavators from the French School discovered a marble stele on which were inscribed, first a text of the Ephebic Oath, followed by the "oath which the Athenians swore when they were

---

57. Secs. 32–33; the words τὴν Τροιζηνίων μαρτυρίαν are taken by most scholars to refer to the "Nicagoras Decree." See Colin's Budé ed. (Paris, 1946), 215, n.3, and Jameson, *Hesperia* 29 (1960), 207, n.26.

58. *IG* II², 971, lines 13 ff.

59. *Hermes* 89 (1961), 20–21; so, too, *FGrHist* III b (Supp.) i. 82. E. Meyer, on the other hand, believes that the notice in Plutarch, *Them*. 10. 5, contains "details which go back to the relevant decree" (*RE* 7.A [1939], col. 640).

about to fight the barbarians."[60] The authenticity of the second oath had been called into question even in antiquity, by the fourth-century historian Theopompus,[61] and most modern scholars follow him in considering it spurious (but there are some exceptions).[62] Of greater interest for our purpose is the first, so-called Ephebic Oath, which is contained in lines 5 to 26 of the inscription. Here the balance of modern opinion is in favour of authenticity and, what is of even greater significance, there exist several ancient literary versions of this same oath: a summary in Lycurgus' speech *Against Leocrates* (76), and purportedly complete versions by the late excerptors Pollux and Stobaeus. M. N. Tod, who tabulated the discrepancies among the three versions, concludes that "Stobaeus and, to a lesser degree, Pollux have preserved a genuine, *though not verbally accurate*, transcription of the oath formula."[63] G. Daux gives what is the natural, and surely correct, reaction to the variations among the different versions of the Ephebic Oath: "Most of the variants. . .are insignificant. The ancients never worried about accuracy in minutiae, and the 'approximate' is almost the rule in matters of editorial detail."[64] To those who are overly concerned about "Athena [?and] Nike" in line 39 of the Troizen inscription, it might be pointed out that the list of eleven gods in the Acharnae stele (Agraulos, Hestia, Enyo, Enyalius, Ares and Athena Areia, Zeus, Thallo, Auxo, Hegemone, and Heracles) "is omitted by S[tobaeus], whose quotation ends Ἵστορες θεοὶ τούτων, and is drastically curtailed by P[ollux]."[65]

What emerges from a comparison of the various literary and epigraphic versions of the oath is a useful distinction between accuracy of substance and verbatim accuracy. There is little doubt that the Ephebic Oath is older (some would say considerably older) than the earliest recorded version of it. Literary testimonies of the fourth and later centuries show verbal discrepancies among themselves and with the inscribed text, but these in no way suggest that any of them is a forged document or that any one version is more authentic than any other. Slight variations and divergencies of the type exhibited in the different versions arise, naturally and almost inevitably, in the very course of transmission over an extended period of time.

An even more interesting case of variation between the literary and epigraphic records of a document—and one strangely ignored by writers on the Troizen Decree[66]—is to be found in the versions of the decree of the Athenian people honouring Lycurgus in 307/6, which is contained both in the treatise *On the Ten Orators* erroneously assigned to Plutarch (*Mor.* 852 A–E) and in *IG* II², 457 (= Dittenberger, *Sylloge³*, no. 326). It is hardly necessary to catalogue all the discrepancies between the

60. The original publication was by L. Robert in *Études épigraphiques et philologiques*, 292–316. An improved text of lines 23–51 is given by G. Daux in *Studies Presented to David M. Robinson*, II, 777–78. For the Ephebic Oath, see also C. Pelekidis, *Histoire de l'Éphébie attique*, 11–13.

61. *FGrHist* 115 F 153.

62. Notably A. E. Raubitschek, in *TAPA* 91 (1960), 178 ff., and G. Daux, in Χαριστήριον εἰς Α. Κ. 'Ορλάνδον (Athens, 1965), I, 86–87.

See, most recently, P. Siewert, *Der Eid von Plataiai*.

63. *A Selection of Greek Historical Inscriptions*, II, p. 305, my italics; full texts at Pollux 8. 105 f. and Stobaeus, *Florilegium* XLIII. 48.

64. *Studies to Robinson*, 781.

65. Tod, *Greek Historical Inscriptions*, II, pp. 305–6.

66. Lewis, *CQ*, n.s. 11 (1961), 61, is a conspicuous exception.

two texts,[67] but certain of the more significant ones, which may be instructive for a proper evaluation of the Troizen inscription, should be mentioned. In the prescript, in addition to the archon's name and the name of the proposer, the literary text adds that the decree was passed "in the sixth prytany, of the tribe Antiochis." When the stone was first discovered, Carl Curtius remarked with surprise on the absence of any sign that the inscription had ever contained a reference to at least the prytanizing tribe.[68] Curtius' solution was that this might have been a *private* copy, set up by Lycurgus' sons who, as his descendants, were their father's beneficiaries.[69] Lewis, who mentions the inscription, remarks of the literary version that "there is no reason to doubt the prytany-indication. Both prescripts are formally incomplete; they have made different selections from the official text."[70] Lines a 5–12 are almost completely obliterated from the stone, but the lines following 63 in the inscription are either preserved or can be restored satisfactorily, and this section offers secure ground for comparison. It deals with Lycurgus' building programme in Athens and Peiraeus, his completion of the shipsheds, arsenal, theatre of Dionysus, Panathenaic stadium, gymnasium at the Lyceum,

καὶ ἄλλαις δὲ πολλαῖ[ς κατασκευαῖς	καὶ ἄλλαις πολλαῖς κατασκευαῖς
ἐκόσμησεν] ὅλην τὴν πόλιν	ἐκόσμησε τὴν πόλιν
(*IG* II², 457. b 8–9)	(*Mor.* 852 C)

This comparison is of great interest and importance. The presence of such stylistic niceties as δέ, ν-*ephelkystikon*, and ὅλην in the stone, and the corresponding absence of these features from the literary text, should warn us of the dangers of using similar features in the Troizen inscription to argue to a forged literary exemplar.[71] The succeeding sections (lines b 9–23 of the stone; *Mor.* 852 D) deal with Lycurgus' patriotism in a more general way and the Athenians' refusal to surrender him to Alexander's demands in 335 B.C. In addition to a colossal blunder in the literary version, where Alexander's demand for Lycurgus' surrender comes "after he had subdued all of Asia," the epigraphic text is considerably fuller and more detailed.[72] Again we find differences of word order and emphasis between the epigraphic and literary versions. The stone has δι[ετέλει ἐναντιούμενος (sc. Ἀλεξάνδρωι) ὑπὲ]ρ τοῦ δήμου, ἀδιάφθορον κ[αὶ ἀνεξέλεγκτον αὐτὸν ὑπὲ]ρ τῆς πατρίδος καὶ τῆς τῶ[ν Ἑλλήνων ἁπάντων σωτηρίας] διὰ παντὸς τοῦ βίου παρ[έχων καὶ ὑπὲρ τοῦ τὴν πόλιν] ἐλευθέραν εἶναι καὶ αὐτ[όνομον πάσηι μηχανῆι ἀγωνι]ζομενος (lines b 12–17), which is reduced in the literary version to διετέλεσεν ἀνεξέλεγκτος καὶ ἀδωροδόκητος τὸν ἅπαντα χρόνον. The noble sentiments on "democracy and freedom," although similar to those found in the inscription, are applied to those who are being exhorted to take Lycurgus as their example (852 D). The obvious moral to be drawn

---

67. The literary and epigraphic texts are printed in parallel columns by N. C. Conomis in his edition of *Lycurgus, Oratio in Leocratem*, 13–17.

68. *Philologus* 24 (1866), 86.

69. Ibid., 90–91.

70. *CQ*, n.s. 11 (1961), 61.

71. Such an argument is used by, for example, L. Moretti, who calls in as evidence against the Troizen inscription, "l'uso costante del *ny* efelcistico, la regolare contrapposizione di μὲν e di δέ, ecc." (*Riv. di fil.* 92 [1964], 120).

72. This was pointed out to me by D. M. Lewis *per litt.*, and is noted by Conomis (*Lycurgus, Oratio in Leocratem*, 15), following Dittenberger: "sive inscitia sive neglegentia temporum ordinem pervertisse."

from this is an extension of Lewis' comment: the writers of both versions "have made different selections (and, be it added, have freely rearranged what they selected) from the official text."

Two final possible parallels may be worth citing. The document, which contains what purports to be the original agreement of the founders of the seventh-century B.C. colony of Cyrene in North Africa, exists only in a fourth-century version.[73] But a foundation document is precisely the kind of sacrosanct text whose memory might be preserved, along with the founders' names and "date" of foundation, from generation to generation; or it might even have been considered important enough to be inscribed in the seventh century and copied (perhaps repeatedly) later. We should probably allow for changes of phrasing and modernization, but there is no reason to suppose that the gist of the whole, and even a good deal of the wording, may not be, in a very real sense, authentic. Two recent studies of the inscription have independently arrived at similar conclusions: "If some of the wording probably belongs to the fourth century, but the document in general seems genuine, then the evidence points to the conclusion that we have a genuine document edited in the fourth century."[74] "I think it not impossible that c. 637, when the colony was decided upon, some kind of document was in fact drawn up and inscribed on wood or stone or bronze...[and] in the fourth century Demis had it inscribed again.... The anachronistic words in it may have been substituted then or in an earlier renewal."[75] And some of the treaties which are given in a literary version by Thucydides, and for which epigraphic texts have since come to light, show how casual ancient practice was in this matter, even when access to the "official" documents, and so verbatim transcriptions of them, were theoretically possible. For example, at 4. 119. 2 Thucydides lists the signatories of the one year's truce of 423 B.C. between Athens and Sparta with their patronymics only, which, as Gomme notes, "is in accord with *Thucydides*' normal manner, but not with that of official documents, especially Athenian documents."[76] The aorist verbs in the heading of the treaty at 5. 18. 1 show that what Thucydides gives is "not strictly the heading of the treaty itself."[77] Although no epigraphic text exists for comparison, some half-dozen "emendations" are suggested by Gomme to bring the document into line with facts known from elsewhere or reasonably to be inferred.[78] Some of these may as easily be considered "corrections" in Thucydides' version as emendations of the manuscripts in which Thucydides' text has been transmitted.

With Thucydides 5. 47 we are on firmer ground for comparison. The literary version of this treaty between Athens and Argos, and the Argive allies, concluded in 420 B.C. through the machinations of Alcibiades, is also preserved on an inscription, *IG* I², 86 (Tod 72). Between the literary and epigraphic versions there exist certain

73. *SEG* 9 (1944), no. 3. This parallel is cited by Berve, *SB Bayer. Akad. der Wiss.*, 5, n.7, and 43; text and translation by A. J. Graham, *Colony and Mother City in Ancient Greece*, 223–26; full discussion by Graham, *JHS* 80 (1960), 94–111, esp. 99 ff., L. H. Jeffery, *Historia* 10 (1961), 139 ff. Meiggs and Lewis, who present a text of this document as number 5 in their collection, "prefer to assume a long

and complex moulding of a genuine original within the tradition of Thera" (*Selection*, p. 9).
74. Graham, *JHS* 80 (1960), 109.
75. Jeffery, *Historia* 10 (1961), 142. Miss Jeffery lists the anachronisms at 141, n.7.
76. *Commentary*, III, 605.
77. Ibid., 666.
78. See Gomme's notes ad loc. (ibid., 667–80).

discrepancies (most of them minor matters of phrasing) which cannot be explained away as textual (that is, scribal errors in the manuscripts of Thucydides): the consistency with which Thucydides names the Argive allies as "Eleians and Mantineans," where the stone reverses the order in lines 7–8 and gives precedence to the Argives themselves in 14; Thucydides' omission of certain phrases contained on the stone; above all, an abridged version in Thucydides of the phrase which appeared in lines 24–25. These differences between the two texts point either to Thucydides' use of one of the copies set up outside Athens (for example, at Argos where Thucydides may have spent some time after his exile), which will have diverged in these minor respects from the "official" Athenian text, or to a casualness on Thucydides' part in giving what purports to be a verbatim transcription of a public document. In either case, absolute fidelity to the exact words of the original, a pedantic literalness, seems not to have been a high desideratum in fifth-century Athens. Tod drew the obvious conclusion: "Verbal divergencies were tolerated even between two copies of a decree engraved for public and permanent exhibition."[79]

The existence of multiple versions of ancient documents, all of them "authentic" in content but not necessarily identical in phrasing, suggests that we may have to adjust our expectations of what constituted an "official" text in fifth-century Athens. Verbal accuracy does not seem to have counted for much. Even when this could in theory be achieved, it often was not, and when a document went through several stages of copying, literary or epigraphic, the copyist seems to have felt no compunction in departing from the exact wording of his original. Selectivity and even minor adaptation always seem to have been allowed, even (apparently) in duplicates on stone. It follows, then, that discrepancies of phrasing in public documents of which several copies exist, or which have gone through stages of transmission which cannot now be traced, do not in themselves constitute grounds for suspecting forgery. We must be willing at least to entertain the concept of authenticity of substance, which need not have been impaired by the (conscious of unconscious) tendency of any later writer, from the mere scribe to the most artful man of letters, to "modernize" the phrasing of what he saw before him, even to substitute usages and turns of phrase which were more familiar to him.

Conclusion

What makes the Troizen Decree unique is that it exists, tangibly, on stone. This puts it far beyond the class of forgeries (if they were such) which were read out to the Athenian Assembly during debates in the fourth century, beyond even the inscriptions which Theopompus claimed to have seen but which can no longer be examined by modern epigraphists, who might be able to confirm his evaluation. There is no denying

---

79. *Greek Historical Inscriptions*, I², pp. 177–78, approved by A. Andrewes in Gomme, Andrewes, and Dover, *Commentary*, IV, 62. Andrewes adds the comment that "it is possible that...strict verbal identity of the several official copies, on papyrus and on stone, was not aimed at, any more than, apparently, in the copies of the English *Magna Carta*" (55). (Further bibliography at H. Bengtson, *Die Staatsverträge des Altertums*, II, no. 193.)

that opportunities and motives for forgery existed in the fourth century, but those who claim that our inscription falls within this category have to contend with its apparently third-century origin. It is at least in theory possible that the mason worked, not from a forged fourth-century original, but from a literary source which, even allowing for modernisms and other alterations in the text, ultimately derived from a reputable (if not "official") fifth-century original. It seems entirely possible that the ancestor of the Troizen stele was a commemorative copy, or even a reconstruction, of the original decree, set up by Themistocles himself or by his descendants after the Athenians' animosities towards him had died down. The dedications which Pausanias mentions of a statue of Artemis Leukophryene (1. 26. 4, in apparent imitation of the cult statue at Themistocles' Ionian base, Magnesia) and a "painting" in the Parthenon (1. 1. 2) would have provided an opportunity for the inclusion of a memorial to their ancestor's crowning achievement. Pausanias also makes clear that there was a construction near the largest of the harbours in Peiraeus which was thought to be Themistocles' "tomb": "for they say that the Athenians had a change of heart about their treatment of Themistocles, and that his relatives recovered his bones from Magnesia and brought them home." That the monument in Peiraeus was actually a tomb seems unlikely in view of Thucydides' testimony (1. 138. 6), but the passage in Pausanias shows at least that there was a rehabilitation of Themistocles' memory at Athens, and to the dedications he mentions may be added a "Themistokleion," the exact nature of which cannot be discovered, to which Aristotle refers.[80] At any one of these it is conceivable that Themistocles' descendants may have set up a copy in stone of the famous mobilization decree, in much the same way as Lycurgus' sons kept their father's memory alive with a memorial dedication of *IG* II[2], 457. This modification of the official text would then have been on public view for later "periegetes" like Diodorus or Heliodorus to transcribe, or for a delegation from Troizen in the third century to copy for a memorial of their own.

Whether or not some such pedigree as this be accepted, we must rule out absolutely any argument which attempts to reject the data of the Troizen inscription on grounds that it conflicts with the reconstruction of Persian War strategy given by Herodotus. It is undeniable that Herodotus is a primary source of our knowledge about the period, but he is hardly infallible or even exhaustively complete. He was not a contemporary of the events he records, and the interviews with eyewitnesses to the battles which he is thought to have carried on while composing his *Histories* were clearly, on one or another specific point, subject to the same kind of error as any other eyewitness report. What is more, as has been remarked above, there even seem to be traces of alternate (and conflicting) traditions in Herodotus' version of events preceding Salamis, so that the substantially different picture of the strategy of the engagement off Artemisium and the timing of the decision to evacuate Athens, which the Troizen Decree presents, may well turn out to be correct.[81]

80. *Hist. Anim.* 6. 15, 569 b 12. (This is sometimes identified with the "tomb" in Peiraeus; see chapter 10.)

81. I wish to express my thanks to Mr. D. M. Lewis for reading an early draft of this chapter and suggesting numerous corrections and improvements in it. Profs. A. E. Raubitschek and A. Momigliano also contributed advice on several points.

9 COINS

AS DYNAST IN MAGNESIA, Themistocles would have had the right to issue in his own name coinage whose value he undertook to guarantee; he was thus following the lead of other Persian satraps, or local governors, who coined silver to support troops in their own provinces.[1] Several examples of this "personal" coinage of Themistocles survive.[2] Three didrachms of Attic weight have long been known. These coins show on the obverse what appears to be a statue of Apollo, perhaps, as Weil suggested, a representation of the statue in the temple of Apollo Pythios at Magnesia (see plate 3a). The figure is nude except for a *chlamys*, or "cloak," slung over the left shoulder; he is standing and leaning on a long staff from which there springs a laurel branch. Around the outside circumference of the coin runs the inscription, in Greek characters, THEMISTOKLEOS (that is, "[The coinage] of Themistocles"). On the reverse there appears a bird, variously described as an eagle, raven, or hawk, with outstretched wings, in an incuse square, and the letters *MA* (for "Magnesians'"). Numismatists point out that in all three specimens not only the obverse but also the reverse are from different dies. Of the three, those in Paris and Berlin are of solid silver, while that in the British Museum is plated.[3] The fact that it is plated seems to indicate that it is an ancient forgery, and Hill expressed the view that what Themistocles may have been doing was "swindling...his subjects by issuing plated coins,"[4] but, as Dr. Colin M.

1. Herodotus (4. 166) reports that Aryandes was in trouble with Darius for issuing competitive coinage in Egypt, and coins of Pharnabazus and Tissaphernes survive from the end of the century; see E. S. G. Robinson, *Amer. Num. Soc. Museum Notes* 9 (1960), pl. I, no. 7 (Tissaphernes), and G. M. A. Richter, *The Portraits of the Greeks*, I, fig. XXXIVa–b.

2. See Barclay V. Head, *Historia Numorum*², 581; discussed fully by R. Weil in *Corolla Numismatica*, 305, more briefly by G. F. Hill,

Historical Greek Coins, 45 ff., and A. Bauer and F. J. Frost, *Plutarchs Themistokles*, 135. Hill mentions a second plated specimen, "of the corresponding drachm," reported to him as in a private collection in Aidin, but of this nothing more was apparently ever heard (*Historical Greek Coins*, 46, n.2).

3. W. H. Waddington in *Revue numismatique*, n.s. 1 (1856), 47–52; B. V. Head, *Brit. Mus. Cat.*, *Ionia*, 158.

4. *Historical Greek Coins*, 48.

Kraay has pointed out to me, "A minor dynast is not likely to make an already un-familiar coinage still less acceptable by issuing plated pieces."[5] Percy Gardner drew a further conclusion from the fact that these coins are of the Attic standard (8·56–8·59 grams), which is said to be "exceptional in Asia": "Even in exile Themistocles regards Athens as his mother city, or else wishes to remain on terms with the Attic coinage,"[6] motives which are not, of course, mutually exclusive.

Until quite recently, this was all that was known of Themistocles' Magnesian coinage, but in 1963 Dr. Kraay published a most intriguing coin in the collection of the Ashmolean Museum, Oxford. It is a quarter-obol, with an owl with folded wings facing right on the obverse, and on the reverse the large letters ΘE inscribed in a beaded, incuse square. I reproduce it as plate 3b through the generosity of Dr. Kraay, who provided a copy of the photograph.[7] Kraay assigned it to Themistocles on the basis of its find-spot at Colophon, less than 50 kilometres from Magnesia; the augury of the owl reported by Plutarch (*Them.* 12. 1) to have appeared to Themistocles before Salamis; and especially the letters *THE* on the reverse (which, if they are not an abbreviation of Themistocles' name, have no other ascertainable significance). Kraay suggests that this coin of small denomination was perhaps issued by Themi-stocles to pay soldiers in his personal employ. What appears to be another specimen of a similar coin has recently been noted as part of a collection in Athens. It is said to contain "on the obverse a helmeted head with beard and crest, on the reverse a ligature of the letters Θ and E."[8]

In addition to these examples of what seem to be Themistocles' own coinage, there exists a Magnesian coin dating from the period of Antoninus Pius (A.D. 138–161), whose bust appears on the obverse. The reverse is of more interest; it portrays a "nude man of stately presence, with short beard, wearing on the head a wreath or fillet, the ends of which fall into the neck. He stands, toward the left, before a blazing circular altar. In his right hand, which is stretched out over the altar, he holds a saucer (*patera*), from which he makes a libation.... With his left hand he grasps the hilt of a sword, which hangs in a sheath at his left side. At the foot of the altar lies the slain victim of the sacrifice, with outstretched head and open mouth,—an Asiatic bison (zebu) [plate 3c]."[9] The coin bears two inscriptions: one, encircling the field, identifies the Magnesian imperial official who had the coin issued, a certain Dios-kourides (otherwise unknown); the other, in rather smaller letters, running above and below the outstretched hand in the left of the field, reads

---

5. By letter July 30, 1969.

6. "Coinage of the Athenian Empire," *JHS* 33 (1913), 165.

7. His original publication is in *Revue suisse de numismatique* 42 (1962/63), 5–14.

8. Richter, *Portraits*, 1, 98. It has since been partially published by Mrs. Varoucha, then Curator of the National Numismatic Museum, Athens, in *Arch. Delt.* 18 (1963), 7, sec. XIII. 3, with an illustration of the reverse only at *Pinax* 2, no. 26. (Richter seems to be in error

in calling it a "quarter of an obol," for its weight is given as 0·41 grams, which, as Dr. Kraay points out to me, although "it is a bit heavy for a half-obol, which ought to weigh about 0·36 [grams]..., is probably a half-obol on the Attic standard.")

9. The description is from B. Perrin, *Plu-tarch's 'Themistocles,'* xvi. The illustration is reproduced from Richter, *Portraits*, I, fig. 410C, by kind permission of Phaidon Press Limited.

ΘΕΜ
. .
ΙΣΤΟΚΛΗ
Σ

Its original editor, A. Rhousopoulos, proposed that the figure on the coin represents a "heroized" Themistocles, copied from the statue which, it is alleged, was set up in his honour in Magnesia.[10] What action is the figure of Themistocles supposed to be performing? Rhousopoulos maintained, on the basis of a story which circulated at least as early as 424 B.C. to the effect that Themistocles committed suicide by drinking bull's blood (Aristoph. *Knights* 83), that the monument portrayed a stylized version of Themistocles in the act of doing precisely this: having just slain a bull during a sacrifice, he is about to drink its blood from the *patera* he holds in his right hand. Percy Gardner and others have postulated a reverse process and maintained that the story in Aristophanes "probably arose from a misunderstanding of this statue, which in reality commemorated Themistocles as oikist and hero, to whom an annual sacrifice was to be brought."[11] Several considerations count against the bull's blood story and in favour of the latter explanation. First, bull's blood is not, apparently, fatal if swallowed (although Aristophanes' audience and the ancients generally must have thought it was). Secondly, there were other versions of how Themistocles met his end: Thucydides says it was from disease (*nosesas*, 1. 138. 4), and the popular account was that he had taken a drug (ibid.). Finally, is it reasonable to suppose that the Magnesians would have commemorated Themistocles in the act of committing suicide? In fact, Gardner's theory of a heroized Themistocles is supported by several examples of coins from Asia Minor which show Apollo holding a *patera* and making a sacrifice before an altar.[12] Such a common divine or "heroic" statuesque pose is likely to have been used by the Magnesians when they commissioned the Themistocles memorial, although it would not follow therefrom that the bull's blood story arose from precisely this confusion.

A final piece of numismatic evidence concerns two specimens of Athenian bronze coins of the Roman period. According to Miss Richter, the first group represents, on the reverse, "a helmeted warrior standing on a warship and holding a *tropaion* and a wreath (on some directed to the right, on others to the left)," which "has generally been thought to represent the monument erected to Themistocles in Salamis."[13] She rejects this identification on the grounds that the description of the Salamis monument which Pausanias gives (1. 36. 1) mentions only a trophy, not a statue, and suggests

10. "Das Monument des Themistokles in Magnesia," *Ath. Mitt.* 21 (1896), 23.

11. P. Gardner in *Corolla Numismatica*, 109; cf. Gardner in *CR* 12 (1898), 21–23. This theory, first put forward by C. Wachsmuth in *Rh. Mus.* 52 (1897), 140–43, is accepted by Hill, *Historical Greek Coins*, 47–48.

12. For example, one from Side *c.* 350–306 B.C. (*Brit. Mus. Cat., Ionia,* 145–46; ibid., p.

145, no. 14 from "Lycia, Pamphylia, Pisidia," with pl. xxvi, nos. 7–11).

13. *Portraits*, I, 98, item a; a good illustration in Perrin, *Plutarch's 'Themistocles,'* pl. 3(*c*) (facing p. 254). Cf. also F. W. Imhoof-Blumer and P. Gardner, *Ancient Coins Illustrating Lost Masterpieces of Greek Art,* p. 153, and pls. EE, xxi, xxii; Bauer and Frost, *Plutarchs Themistokles,* pl. nos. 6, 5–6.

that the coin type showing the figures from right to left (that is, facing left) represents the statue of Themistocles, which was said by a scholiast on Aelius Aristeides to have stood near the right *parodos* of the theatre of Dionysus at Athens.[14] Richter ventures the guess that "they belong to the fourth-century B.C. when it became customary to set up memorials to the great men of the past."[15]

14. Ael. Arist. III, 535 Dind.; cf. Imhoof-Blumer and Gardner, *Ancient Coins*, 151, with pls. EE, vii, viii; Richter, *Portraits*, I, figs. 393–401; fuller discussion in her monograph *Greek Portraits IV, Iconographical Studies*, 9–11.

15. *Greek Portraits IV*, 11.

10 BUILDINGS AND WALLS

OUR INFORMATION about the telesterion, or "initiation place," of the Lykomidai at Phlya, a deme of the tribe Cecropis, comes from Plutarch: "It is clear that Themistocles was connected with the family of the Lycomidae, for he caused the chapel-shrine at Phlya, which belonged to the Lycomidae and had been burned by the barbarians, to be restored at his own cost and adorned with frescoes, as Simonides has related."[1] The site of ancient Phlya cannot be called quite certain. On the basis of somewhat scanty inscriptional evidence, it has been identified with the modern Athenian suburb of Chalandri, some five miles northeast of Syntagma Square in downtown Athens.[2] The main divinities worshipped there were Earth, under her title "Great Goddess" (whose son Phlyus was the eponymous hero of the deme), Demeter and her daughter Persephone; there is also mention of the "Bacchic rites of Orpheus" in this connection.[3] How large the chapel was is unknown, but it was probably smaller than the initiation house at Eleusis itself, a square structure of just over 50 metres (164 feet) to a side.[4] It was decorated with frescoes (as Plutarch's description indicates), and other art objects may have been placed inside. There is archaeological evidence for a pre-Periclean telesterion at Eleusis, which has been dated to the period of Cimon's ascendancy.[5] Themistocles' rebuilding of the initiation house in Phlya may have been his architectural rejoinder to these grandiose projects of Cimon's, for both men were engaged in this period in a bitter propaganda battle which extended even to artistic compositions.

Besides the telesterion at Phlya, Themistocles' name has been associated with an early odeion, or recital hall for musical performances. Vitruvius, the Roman writer on architecture, has this brief comment: "As you leave the theatre, on the left stands

1. *Them.* 1. 4, trans. Perrin.
2. See J. G. Frazer's discussion (*Pausanias*, II, 411–12), with references there.
3. Pausanias 4. 1. 5, 8; Hippolytus, *Refu-tation of Heresies* 5. 20.
4. George E. Mylonas, *Eleusis and the Eleusinian Mysteries*, 115, 117.
5. Ibid., 107–13.

the Odeion, which Themistocles had roofed over with stone columns at intervals and ships' masts and yard-arms from the Persian spoils" (5. 9. 1). The Odeion is usually assigned to Pericles, as part of his extensive programme to beautify the city, on the basis of a reference in Plutarch (*Per.* 13. 8–10), and Vitruvius may simply have blundered in substituting Themistocles' name for Pericles'. But if there is anything to the story that *something* in the Odeion was intended to serve as a relic of the Persian victory, whether its shape or some of the actual timbers from the Persian shipwrecks, then the probabilities are slightly in favour of associating it with Themistocles rather than Pericles, although no very firm conclusion can be drawn from such meagre evidence.[6]

Plutarch mentions a temple of Artemis which Themistocles "had built and fitted out near his house in Melite; [the goddess] he surnamed Aristoboule, 'Best Counsellor,' on the grounds that his counsel was best for the city and for Greece.... In fact, a portrait of Themistocles stands in this temple of Aristoboule, down to my own day" (*Them.* 22. 2–3). By a stroke of good fortune there was discovered in the summer of 1958 "a small temple just west of Theseion Square in Athens...[which] can be identified with virtual certainty as the temple of Artemis Aristoboule founded by Themistokles near his home in the deme of Melite."[7] The building was situated near what is now the corner of the modern Herakleidai and Neleus streets and was described by the excavators as follows: "It faces west and consists of a cella about 3·60 m. [11·8 feet] square and an open porch between antae 1·85 m. [6·06 feet] deep."[8] Some 9½ feet in front of the temple were discovered two blocks which served as a foundation for the altar, and the altar itself, "sadly damaged," was found nearby. "There were no columns, and no steps," the excavators continue; "the walls of the cella are not very well preserved. They are about 0·45 m. [1·48 feet] thick and are built in places of rubble, in places of larger blocks some of which are re-used."[9]

The excavators were able to assign a date to the sanctuary on the basis of fifth-century potsherds found in the earth beside the foundation wall on the south side of the porch, and the style and workmanship of the foundation blocks themselves, as well as a group of black-figure *krateriskoi*, obviously votive in character, which may be dated by their style to the period just after the Persian Wars. Since these vases "are of an unusual form" and since "vases of this type have been found in considerable numbers in the sanctuary of Artemis at Brauron, though they are rare elsewhere,"[10] it may safely be inferred that what we have here is a sanctuary of Artemis. The evidence which clinches the identification (and, incidentally, shows that the temple was rebuilt

6. J. A. Davison argued for a Themistoclean Odeion, "Notes on the Panathenaea," *JHS* 78 (1958), 34. Themistocles' name has also been connected with an early theatre building, either, it has been suggested, incorporating ship timbers salvaged from the Persian wrecks (E. O'Neill, Jr., *CP* 37 [1942], 425–27) or modelled on Xerxes' tent captured from Mardonius (O. Broneer, *Univ. Calif. Publs. Class. Arch.* 1 [1944], 305–11).

7. J. Threpsiades and E. Vanderpool, "Themistokles' Sanctuary of Artemis Aristoboule,"

Arch. Delt. 19 (1964), 26.

8. Ibid., 28.

9. Ibid.

10. This connection is confirmed by L. G.-Kahil, "Autour de l'Artémis attique," *Antike Kunst* 8 (1965), 24, who remarks, "le témoignage de Plutarque, qui avait été mis en doute, se trouve ainsi confirmé archéologiquement, car ces exemplaires, exécutés en figure noire très tardive, doivent dater des environs de milieu de Vᵉ siècle."

about 300 B.C.) is an inscribed votive pillar set up by one "Neoptolemus, son of Antikles, of Melite, to Artemis," who may have been responsible for rebuilding the temple in the fourth century.

The identification of this temple as Themistocles' dedication to Artemis has recently been questioned (to my mind unsuccessfully) by Pierre Amandry.[11] "If it is true," writes Amandry, "that the discovery of the *krateriskoi* ['votive jugs'] attests the existence of a cult to Artemis at the time of Themistocles, nothing proves that the older sherds do not also come from offerings to the goddess."[12] (The "older sherds," mentioned by Vanderpool, were "geometric and Orientalizing sherds found in the earth immediately overlying bedrock in the few spots where it was tested.")[13] Amandry's statement may be true, but there is nothing in the sources to indicate that Themistocles started from scratch, and the excavators make no such claim; Themistocles might well have chosen a spot traditionally connected with rites in honour of Artemis as a site for his new temple. "Neither the situation of the altar, backing against the wall, nor its oblique orientation in relation to the building, corresponds to the usual placing of an altar which is organically connected with a temple."[14] But it may have been precisely the originally existing temenos wall, whose location was probably determined by the ancient street directly outside of it (part of the ancient terracotta drain was discovered in the excavations), which determined the location of the altar. The altar may have been erected directly in front of the wall as a kind of backdrop, or to give it additional support; or (for all we know) the fifth-century altar may have replaced a much more ancient sacrificial area, the reasons for whose situation are now beyond discovery. The large southern orthostate block of limestone had, even to the excavators, the look of being *de remploi*; but there is no evidence to justify the phrase which Amandry appends, "provenant d'un autre monument."[15] Amandry stills his own doubts based on the temple's dimensions (which he calls "faibles") by noting that two public shrines, the Nike temple on the Acropolis and the small shrine dedicated to (?) Zeus and Athena in the sanctuary of Apollo Patroos on the west side of the Agora, "were hardly larger than the structure in Melite."[16] The somewhat unusual westward-facing emplacement is, as Amandry notes, not without parallels, the most significant being the later temple of Artemis Leukophryene at Magnesia, with whose cult Themistocles' name is also connected. The novelty of the cult title Aristoboule is hardly reason to suspect Plutarch's testimony, for Amandry himself presents evidence for worship at Athens of Artemis under the similar title Boulaia; Themistocles may have purposely chosen a unique title to reflect what he believed to be the extraordinary nature of his contribution to the victory.[17] Amandry suggested that the building excavated was merely a treasury and that the main shrine to Artemis was situated

11. "Thémistocle à Mélitè," *Charisterion eis Anastasion K. Orlandon*, IV, 265–79. I am grateful to Prof. R. E. Wycherley for calling my attention to Amandry's views; Wycherley's own rejection of them now appears in *Phoenix* 24 (1970), 287–89.

12. Amandry, *Charisterion eis Anastasion K. Orlandon*, IV, 269–70.

13. *Arch. Delt.* 19 (1964), 28.

14. Amandry, *Charisterion eis Anastasion K. Orlandon*, IV, 270.

15. Ibid., 271.

16. Ibid., 271–72, n.10.

17. It seems illogical to argue, as Amandry does (p. 279), that Plutarch connected the temple with Themistocles by inference from the bust, and then invented an explanation for the surname Aristoboule.

elsewhere, but, as R. E. Wycherley has remarked, "This building is sufficient, and it is not very likely that such a local shrine and cult would have required two temple-like buildings."[18] Amandry's doubts about Plutarch's further statement (*Them.* 22. 3) regarding the *eikonion* which he says he saw in this temple may, or may not, be justified, but that is a matter which must be settled independently of the temple's identification.

Themistocles' name is perhaps also to be linked to the temple of Artemis Proseoia, "Dawnward-facing," which stood near Cape Artemisium. A personal visit to the site of the victory in 1965 revealed little, for even the temple's location cannot be called certain.[19] There is a small modern chapel standing on a rise at some distance from the coast (perhaps the ancient coastline has receded here, as at Thermopylae), and what appear to be traces of marble cuttings nearby. Lolling thought he saw the remains "near a chapel of St. George," and this may, indeed, be the site. The local residents, when I inquired of them, disclaimed any knowledge of an ancient shrine; one farmer pointed to some rough foundations some way from the above chapel which showed no signs of being either ancient or suitably situated. A full modern account of the remains, with measurements and diagrams, is yet to be written.

From Plutarch's account at *Themistocles* 8, it is clear that he personally visited the spot, where he read a four-line dedication in honour of the Athenians who fell in the battle:

Motley races of men from the land of Asia
  Sons of Athenians once on this stretch of sea
Overwhelmed in a battle with ships—a host of Medes perished—
  And set up this monument for virgin Artemis.

(Them. 8. 5; de mal Her. 867 F)

In the light of what is emerging as Themistocles' special devotion to Artemis, it may be suggested that he was the sponsor of this dedication in her temple in Euboea. Pausanias (1. 31. 4) mentions that she was worshipped at the Lykomid centre Phlya under the title "Light-bringing," Selasphoros, which is very close to her appellation "Dawn-facing" at Artemisium; there is inscriptional evidence for a public cult to her under the equivalent title Phosphoros both at Peiraeus and in the Agora, where she was also worshipped as Artemis Boulaia, "Counsellor,"[20] a title which, as we have seen, Themistocles may have adapted for his shrine in Melite. Pausanias saw a sanctuary to Artemis on Salamis and what he thought was the trophy for Themistocles' victory nearby,[21] and, according to Plutarch (*Mor.* 349 F), the anniversary of the victory was celebrated at the shrine of Artemis Munychia at Peiraeus. A memorial dedication by Themistocles in the temple which stood on the cape named for his

18. *Phoenix* 24 (1970), 287–88, n.14.

19. The first—and last—excavation report is (so far as I know) that of H. G. Lolling in *Ath. Mitt.* 8 (1883), 7–23, 200–210. There is a brief discussion by W. K. Pritchett in his *Studies in Ancient Greek Topography*, 12–13, with fig. 2 on p. 15.

20. The material is conveniently assembled by R. E. Wycherley, *The Athenian Agora, III*, 56–57.

21. 1. 36. 1. For a possible identification of the trophy on Salamis, see P. W. Wallace, "Psytteleia and the Trophies of the Battle of Salamis," *AJA* 73 (1969), 293–303.

Plate 1 (and Frontispiece). The Ostia herm (Ostia Museum, Inv. 85). Photograph courtesy of Dr. F. Eckstein, Deutsches Archäologisches Institut, Rome.

Plate 2. The Troizen Decree (Athens, Epigraphical Museum, EM 13330). Photograph courtesy of Miss Alison Frantz.

a

b

c

Plate 3. Coins
a, Magnesian didrachm of Themistocles (Paris, Bibliothèque Nationale). Approximately $2\frac{1}{2}$ times actual size. Reproduced from B. Perrin, *Plutarch's " Themistocles" and " Aristeides,"* facing p. 254.
b, Quarter-obol found near Colophon (Oxford, Ashmolean Museum). Approximately 4 times actual size. Photograph courtesy of Dr. Colin M. Kraay.
c, Magnesian bronze coin of Antoninus Pius. Approximately $1\frac{1}{2}$ times actual size. Reproduced from G. M. A. Richter, *The Portraits of the Greeks*, I, fig. 410C, by permission of Phaidon Press Limited.

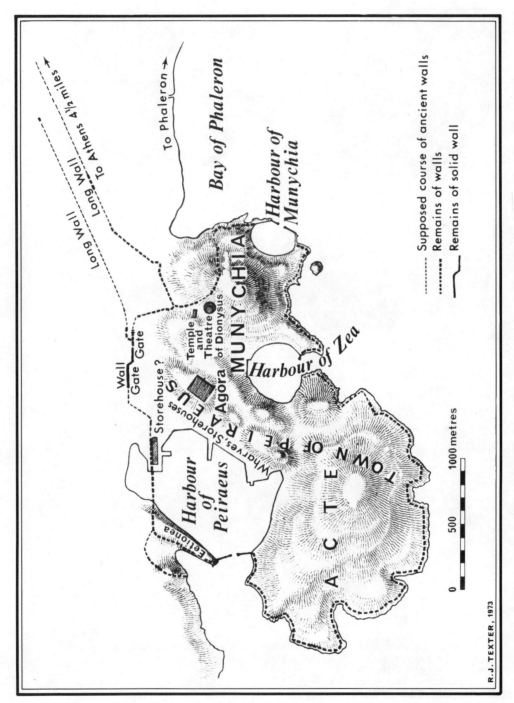

To Phaleron →

Bay of Phaleron

Long Wall
Long Wall
To Athens 4½ miles

Harbour of Munychia

Wall

Gate Gate

Storehouse?

Temple and Theatre of Dionysus

Harbour of Munychia

MUNYCHIA

Harbour of Zea

Agora

Wharves, Storehouses

P E I R A E U S

A C T E

T O W N   O F   P E I R A E U S

Eetionea

Harbour of Peiraeus

. . . . Supposed course of ancient walls
━ ━ ━ ━ ━ Remains of walls
──────── Remains of solid wall

0   500   1000 metres

R.J. TEXTER, 1973

Plate 4. Plan 1: Themistoclean circuit wall of Peiraeus. Drawing by Mr. R. J. Texter, based on W. H. Forbes, *Thucydides Book I*, facing p. 79.

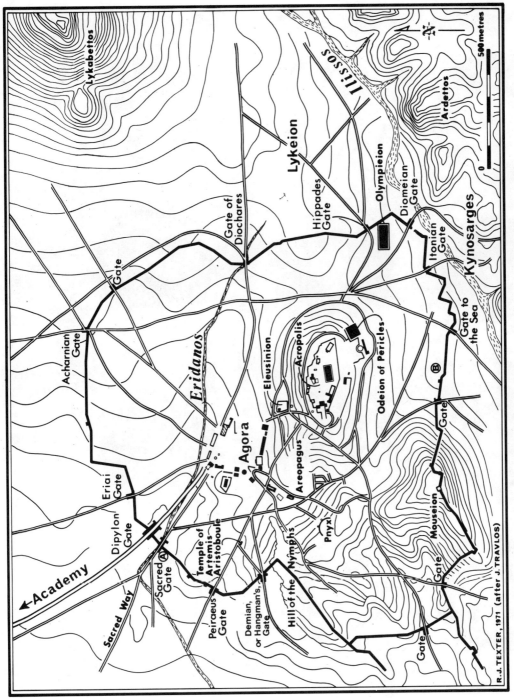

Lykabettos

Ilissos

Lykeion

Ardettos

Gate of Diochares

Gate

Hippades Gate

Olympieion

Diomeian Gate

Itonian Gate

Kynosarges

Acharnian Gate

Eridanos

Eleusinion

Acropolis

Odeion of Pericles

Gate to the Sea

Ⓑ

Eriai Gate

Agora

Areopagus

Dipylon Gate

Mouseion Gate

Academy

Sacred Ⓐ Gate

Temple of Artemis Aristoboule

Pnyx

Gate

Sacred Way

Peiraeus Gate

Demian, or Hangman's, Gate

Hill of the Nymphs

500 metres

0

R.J. TEXTER, 1971 (after J. TRAVLOS)

Plate 5. Plan 2: Themistoclean circuit wall of Athens *c.* 450 B.C. Drawing by Mr. R. J. Texter after J. Travlos, courtesy of Mr. Travlos.

Plate 6. Ostraka from the Athenian Agora, well M (Agora Excavations, AK 1173). Photograph courtesy of Prof. O. Broneer.

From upper left:
AO 68, Group A; AO 38, Group A; AO 52, Group B; AO 5, Group B;
AO 49, Group B; AO 42, Group B; AO 77, Group C; AO 64, Group C;
AO 4, Group D; AO 78, Group D; AO 112, Group E; AO 11, Group E.

a

b

c

Plate 7. Ostraka from the Athenian Agora: *a*, P15577; *b*, P5959; *c*, P9950. Photographs courtesy of the American School of Classical Studies at Athens.

■■■■ = 1 centimetre

a

b

Plate 8*a*, *b*. Ostraka from the Cerameicus in Athens discovered in 1966. Reproduced from *Archaiologikon Deltion* 23 (1968), B, "Chronika," plate 9a, c.

patron goddess, at the scene of his first encounter with the Persians, is therefore not beyond the bounds of possibility.

In about 400 B.C. the Magnesians moved from their original settlement on the Ionian coast slightly inland to the site of their sanctuary to Artemis Leukophryene, "White-browed," the goddess to whom, according to one account, Themistocles was sacrificing when he committed suicide. According to a recent investigator, "Artemis had a temple there from at least the sixth-century B.C., for remains of that date were found under the present building,"[22] but time and the elements have long since covered over the results of the excavations by French and German archaeologists in the last century.[23] My visit to the site in 1965 proved disappointing.

According to numerous later writers, Themistocles had a sepulchral monument of some kind in the agora of the (original) Magnesia. Plutarch calls it a "magnificent tomb" (*Them.* 32. 4), but Thucydides carefully calls it a "memorial" (1. 138. 5). Diodorus' account (11. 58), although it uses Thucydides' term "memorial," implies that it was a real sepulchre, "which is still in existence today"—an unhelpful comment, since this may merely have been copied from Diodorus' fourth-century source, Ephorus. Nepos is the only author to refer to *two* monuments, "a tomb, where he is buried, on the outskirts of the town, and a statue (or 'statues') in the marketplace of Magnesia" (*Them.* 10. 3). Whatever this structure may have been (and it may be with reference to it that some of the "Themistocles Epigrams," composed in the Roman period, were written), it would have been erected some time after the town was relocated.

A reconciliation of the conflicting traditions might be attempted along the following lines. There were two main accounts of where Themistocles was buried: (old) Magnesia or somewhere in Attica. Whichever story is correct (and it seems impossible to decide between them), the Magnesians would clearly have been unwilling to surrender the honour of providing the final resting place for this great figure from their past, and when the town was moved, it would obviously have been easy to obliterate the technical difference between "tomb" and "cenotaph." What was shown to travellers in later times was no doubt *called* Themistocles' tomb, and would clearly have been an imposing structure, decorated with the statue, or statues, which Nepos mentions.

An early version of the story of Themistocles' death, given by Thucydides, was that "his bones were brought home again as he had ordered and were buried unbeknownst to the Athenians." There seem to be echoes of this version in the account contained in a scholium on Aristophanes' *Knights* 84 of an attempt by the Athenians to secure the return of Themistocles' remains from the Magnesians; when they refused, the Athenians "dug up the bones secretly and took them away."[24] At the end of his *Life* Plutarch alludes to a description given by Diodorus the topographer: "Near the

22. George E. Bean, *Aegean Turkey*, 250.

23. C. Humann et al., *Magnesia am Maeander*, summarized in *Arch. Anz.*, 1894, 76–84. There is a recent discussion of the temple by H. Drerup, "Zum Artemistempel von Magnesia," *Marburger Winckelmann-Programm* (1964), 13–22, who follows A. von Gerkan in

dating the extant construction to *c.* 150 B.C. (*Arch. Anz.*, 1923/24, 348).

24. Schol. Aristoph. *Eq.* 84b. (II), in Koster et al., *Scholia in Aristophanem*, I. 2 (1969), 31. (How the strange variant ascribed by Plutarch to Andocides at *Them.* 32. 4 relates to this story remains uncertain.)

large harbour of the Peiraeus a sort of elbow juts out from the promontory opposite Alcimus, . . . as you round this and come inside, where the water of the sea is still, there is a basement [*krepis*] of goodly size" (*Them.* 32. 5, trans. Perrin). Although Diodorus called this the "tomb" of Themistocles, Plutarch expresses serious doubts about the identification. Milchhöfer, who excavated in the Peiraeus in the last century, found what he thought were remains answering to Diodorus' description,[25] but what Milchhöfer saw is now within a secret installation of the Greek Navy and can no longer be viewed except by special and seldom-granted permission. A visit to the naval base in the summer of 1968 to examine the monument proved fruitless, but Prof. Paul W. Wallace has kindly provided the following first-hand description.

A column, probably erected to mark the entrance to the Peiraeus, stands about 10 feet south of the Tomb and is about 30 feet tall. It stands on a modern foundation, but many of the drums, or part of the drums, are ancient. The missing sections have been filled in. At the south end of the modern level space separating the Tomb and column from the Naval offices is a copy of the famous bust of Themistocles, and beneath it is inscribed the passage from the *Persians* [of Aeschylus] 402–405.

I estimated the Tomb at about 15 feet square. A modern ramp connects it with the higher ground on the shore. The wall of the Tomb is ashlar isodomic and about 4 courses can be seen. The interior of the Tomb reveals the encroachment of the sea, for it now has about two feet of water in the bottom of it. There are holes dug to receive sarcophagi in the SW and NW corners. Part of a sarcophagus can perhaps still be seen in the SW hole. There is an inscription in the second course of blocks (from the top) in the inner side of the west wall in the SW corner. It reads

ΘΕΜΙΣΤΟΚΛΕΣ ΝΙΚΟΚΛΕΟΣ
ΦΡΕΑΡΡΙΟΣ

The inscription strikes me as modern, but it seems remarkable that the modern Greeks would have written his father's name wrong. . . .

This structure is certainly ancient, but it would be difficult to say of what period. It was certainly built before the sea began its encroachment, but that may not have occurred until Roman times or even later. . . . The masonry of the Tomb could belong to almost any period, but Hellenistic would be a good guess.[26]

In the *History of Animals* (569 b 9 ff.), Aristotle refers to a "Themistokleion," which he says was located in a "shady and marshy spot," and this may in fact be the same structure as that which Diodorus described. In an inscription dating from the Augustan period, there is mention of a structure (probably a shrine or sanctuary) to a divinity, only the last half of whose name is preserved, -*kane*, "which Themistocles set up before [or, in thanksgiving for] the battle around Salamis." Although J. K. Davies

25. A summary of the results of Milchhöfer's investigations is given by Frazer at *Pausanias*, II, 21–22.

26. Letter to the author dated August 28, 1969. (See his preliminary note, "The Tomb of Themistokles in the Piraeus," *AJA* 76 [1972], 224. See now *Hesperia* 41 [1972], 451–62.)

has recently suggested that this is to be identified with the so-called tomb of Themistocles, it seems likelier to have been a separate structure, whose identity remains a mystery.[27]

In a valuable but troublesome passage Thucydides discusses Themistocles' fortification of the Peiraeus.

> He persuaded them to finish building up the Peiraeus.... And they built the thickness of the wall around the Peiraeus according to his plan, as can be seen even now, for two wagons brought up the stones opposite one another. Inside the wall was neither mortar nor rubble, but large stones were cut to fit together squarely and were fastened to one another on the outside with iron and lead. But as to the height, it was completed to only about half of the height he had intended. (1. 93. 3–6)

There is no way of knowing how extensive Themistocles' original constructions in the Peiraeus were or why they were left incomplete. It is also frustrating that, in the present state of our archaeological knowledge at least, we are unable to confirm or to contradict Thucydides' testimony regarding the method of construction of the Peiraeus walls. T. Lenschau, whose account of the history and archaeology of Peiraeus is the most recent and comprehensive, wrote in 1938: "At the beginning of the last century there were still in existence considerable remains of the fortifications which surrounded the peninsula; now they have for the most part disappeared due to the expansion of the modern city."[28] The situation has deteriorated still further since Lenschau wrote. One or two, and, in some places, more, courses of ancient wall are visible as one drives along the coast, but these are generally assigned to the later rebuilding by Conon (395–392 B.C.). In fact, there is some doubt whether the Cononian wall was an exact successor to the Themistoclean in Peiraeus (their courses in the city circuit were certainly identical). On the basis of the figure given by Thucydides of sixty *stadia* for "the whole circuit of Peiraeus with Munychia" (2. 13. 7), it has been maintained that the Themistoclean circuit, whose measurements Thucydides seems to be giving, fell considerably short of those of the later wall, whose measurements Gomme gives as "some 78 stades long."[29] There are traces of two separate walls in the northwest sector, the area known in antiquity as Eëtioneia, but what has been called Themistoclean here is the outer, longer wall, so this does not help to resolve the discrepancy between Thucydides' figures and the actual measurements.[30] A more drastic expedient was attempted. Some remains of what appeared to be ancient wall were seen and recorded in the last century near the church of St. Basil, in the southwest part of the semicircular peninsula known as Akte, on the basis of which it was maintained that the Themistoclean wall cut diagonally across and over the top of Akte Peninsula from

27. *IG* II², 1035, line 45; J. K. Davies, *Athenian Propertied Families*, 215–16. I am not sure how much faith should be put in the apparent reference by Ammonius, a late writer of a work *On Altars*, to a sanctuary of Aphrodite which Themistocles is alleged to have set up in the Peiraeus after Salamis (*FGrHist* 361 F 5; Judeich, *Topographie*², 73, n.5).

28. *RE* 19 (1938), col. 83.

29. *Commentary*, II, 40.

30. T. Lenschau, *RE* 19 (1938), cols. 84–85; W. Judeich, *Topographie von Athen*², 145–46.

southeast to northwest.[31] W. Judeich, who, in the first edition of his *Topographie von Athen* (1905) accepted the identification, later (1931) recanted, arguing that "apart from the fact that the course of the wall is vulnerable as a fortification—it gives the enemy too much room to get a foothold—difficulties are created especially by remains of an older (Themistoclean?) polygonal wall, noticed by Noack but which can now no longer be confirmed, on the steep shoreline to the south along the line of the Cononian wall."[32] It seems inadvisable then to trace the line of Themistocles' wall across Akte on the dubious basis of 200 metres of seemingly ancient wall, which has, in any case, apparently since been built over (it certainly did not yield to the searches of Professor Vanderpool and myself in the summer of 1968). Plate 4 accordingly shows a plan of Peiraeus with the most probable restoration of the line of Themistoclean wall on the basis of the best available (and no longer available) evidence.

Some doubts have been felt by Thucydides' most devoted modern expounder about the historian's description of the way Themistocles built his Peiraeus wall. A. W. Gomme writes:

> Thucydides goes on to describe [at 1. 93. 5, second sentence] what was the normal Greek method of erecting buildings, such as temples, that were meant to be beautiful and imposing: closely fitted squared blocks of stone or marble, clamped together with iron clamps in molten lead....
>
> The existing remains of the Peiraeus walls are for the most part of those restored in 395–391...and are built generally exactly as Thucydides says the Themistoclean wall was not built, namely with the two outerfaces of squared stone and the interior filled with rubble; moreover, the beds cut in the rock to receive the foundations show that there never had been solid ashlar wall; and a good part of the circuit at least had its upper courses built of crude brick.[33]

Gomme's misgivings, if they were well founded, would indeed be serious. But how strong is an argument based on archaeological silence, that is to say, the absence of visible remains to verify a statement in a reliable ancient author? And Gomme himself admits that "the exception to this is the small stretch of the wall on the land-side northwest of Mounychia hill, the only part of this wall now preserved; it was built of stone throughout."[34] Personal examination of the part of the wall which survives in the vicinity of the gate, generally identified as the Asty- or City-Gate, near the place where the Peiraeus circuit is joined by the North Long Wall (see plate 4) confirmed that it had been built exactly as Thucydides describes; the overwhelming impression was one of massive solidity. It would be risky, though, on the basis of poor or now nonexistent evidence to argue, with Gomme, that "*only* the land-wall of Themistokles' peribolos can have been built of stone throughout."[35] Still less should we acquiesce in Forbes' verdict: "Thucydides examined, after the overthrow of Themistocles' wall, only the most important part of it, which was solid, and erroneously concluded that

31. Judeich, *Topographie*[2], 147, with n.1.
32. Ibid. The reference is to F. Noack, *Ath. Mitt.* 33 (1908), 36–37.
33. *Commentary*, I, 263–64.

34. Ibid., 264; confirmed by W. H. Forbes: "It is of solid stone and over 25 feet thick" (*Thucydides Book I*, 79).
35. *Commentary*, I, 264, my italics.

it was all solid."[36] What we are justified in concluding is merely that it can be shown that *at least* the land portion of the Themistoclean fortification wall in Peiraeus was built of stone throughout. Of course there is always hope that fresh excavations,[37] or (what is in any case badly needed) careful re-examination of those segments of the wall uncovered long ago, may help to settle the matter.

It remains to make some additional comments on Thucydides' account of the Peiraeus fortifications. We shall probably never be certain what Thucydides meant when he wrote "two wagons brought up the stones opposite one another" (1. 93. 5). Gomme argues that since what is being illustrated is the wall's extraordinary thickness ($\pi\acute{\alpha}\chi o\varsigma$), the wagons are to be pictured as coming up from opposite directions onto the wall along its length and passing each other. Alternatively, the sentence might be interpreted as "two transport-wagons, coming up opposite one another [that is, transversely to the wall], brought up the stones."[38] Other interpretations are no doubt possible. And Thucydides' comment concerning the wall's thickness, "as can be seen even now" (1. 93. 5), need not be taken to indicate that Thucydides was writing after the destruction of the Peiraeus and Long Walls by the Spartans in 404 B.C. (the city walls were in fact left standing): "The thickness, width, breadth, of the wall must have been at least as obvious while it stood as after it had fallen.... As far as this sentence goes [the passage] is at least as likely to be earlier as later than 404."[39] By far the best solution, however, is to bracket the phrase (with Gomme and others) as a later note which has intruded itself into the text, a theory which is given some support by the scholiast on the passage, who seems not to have found the words in *his* text.

There is, in addition, a dedicatory epigram preserved by the lexicographer Harpocration, who claims to be reporting it from Philochorus:

These men first began to build the wall, and dedicated
In compliance with the decrees of Council and Demos.[40]

The lines should naturally be taken as referring to the initial building scheme, $\pi\rho\tilde{\omega}\tau o\iota...o\H{\iota}\delta\varepsilon$, and the demonstrative implies that a list of the nine archons followed. Themistocles' name, then, "should have headed the list," Gomme remarks, and the inference is accepted by Lenschau.[41] But, Gomme objects, the epigram "reads like a tasteless parody of the Thermopylae epigram;...some record of a dedication connected with so famous a policy we should have expected to reach us."[42] Others wish to ascribe it to the Cononian programme of the 390s,[43] which seems impossible. The emphasis on the *primacy* of the act shows that we must either assign it to 493 (or perhaps the 470s, as Lenschau suggests), or reject it as utter fabrication. Certainty in the matter cannot at present be attained.

36. *Thucydides Book I*, 80.

37. Part of the city wall was uncovered in 1967 in the harbour of Zea; "At one point part of a tower, said to be of the fifth-century, is preserved" (*Archaeological Reports for 1968–69* [supp. to *JHS* 89 (1969)], 6).

38. S. P. Widmann in *Bursians Jahresbericht* (1923), 215–16, cited, but rather harshly rejected, by Gomme.

39. E. Harrison, *CR* 26 (1912), 248.

40. Harpocration, s.v. $\pi\rho\grave{o}\varsigma$ $\tau\tilde{\eta}$ $\pi\upsilon\lambda\acute{\iota}\delta\iota$ Ἑρμῆς.

41. *RE* 19 (1938), cols. 87–88.

42. *Commentary*, I, 262.

43. Most recently, E. B. Harrison, *The Athenian Agora, XI: Archaic and Archaistic Sculpture*, 113, with n.50.

The general outline of the peribolos wall surrounding the city has long been known, and excavations in recent times have exposed new sections of it almost yearly. Its extent is given by Travlos at 43 stades or 6,450 metres (1 stade = 150 metres). Thucydides seems to take delight in recounting how skilfully Themistocles distracted the Spartans during the winter of 479/8 when the fortifications were being constructed (1. 89. 3–93. 2). Thucydides comments explicitly that although some sort of circuit wall had existed previously, Themistocles' wall was much more extensive (1. 93. 2). Thucydides further remarks that even in his own day it was evident how hastily Athens' wall had been constructed: "The lower bases are of varied stones and in places not fitted together, but put in just as they were carried up, and many grave markers and worked stones were put into the wall. The circuit wall of the city was extended in all directions, and for this reason they hastily used everything they could get their hands on" (1. 93. 2). Thucydides' accuracy on this point has been confirmed by excavations in the 1920s in the vicinity of the so-called Peiraeus Gate, where archaeologists discovered in the core of the earliest, "Themistoclean," wall several fine sculptured pieces, including the statue bases with reliefs of "hockey" players (National Archaeological Museum 3477), a dog-and-cat fight and young wrestlers (3476).[44] The most recent finds of this type come from the inner-west (that is, southwest) tower of the so-called Dipylon Gate in the Cerameicus, excavated by members of the German Archaeological Institute. The surviving towers excavated here are of Hellenistic date, but inside them the excavators discovered what they believe to be, and what they in fact call, an inner, "Themistoclean," core. The archaic material (the sculpture dates from 560 to 510 B.C.) seems to justify this identification, and even more important, if the archaeologists' inferences are correct, some kind of Dipylon or double gate here seems to have been part of Themistocles' original construction, and not, as had previously been supposed, a later modification.[45] The striking similarity between two statue bases used in this "inner" tower and the material discovered in the Themistoclean wall in the 1920s is rightly emphasized by the excavators.[46]

Many remains of the ancient city wall itself have been discovered in the course of modern construction in recent years,[47] and there are several stretches where visible remains have been assigned with some degree of confidence to Themistocles. The section which has been longest known and is still most easily viewed is in the Cerameicus, west of the Sacred Gate (point A on plan 2, plate 5). This section of the wall received its first extensive and systematic publication by Noack in the early part of this century,[48] and it was he who pointed out that there is a substantially different type of construction in the top row of blocks, which are larger and squarer than the lowest three rows: the limestone of which this top layer is built has a blue tinge, whereas the next two lower rows are redder in hue. The foundation level is of ashlar type

44. See A. Philadelpheus, *JHS* 42 (1922), 104–6, pls. VI, VII.

45. G. Gruben and K. Vierneisel, "Die Ausgrabungen im Kerameikos," *Arch. Anz.*, 1964, 384 ff., esp. 395–98.

46. Ibid., 397–400, figs. 10, 11.

47. See E. Vanderpool, *AJA* 58 (1954), 231,

233; 60 (1956), 267; 61 (1957), 281–82; 62 (1958), 321. Recent discoveries mentioned by M. Ervin, *AJA* 73 (1969), 342, and P. M. Fraser in *Archaeological Reports for 1968–69*, 4–5.

48. *Ath. Mitt.* 32 (1907), 123–60, 473–566.

(squared blocks of poros). It is assumed that the uppermost layer dates from the Cononian rebuilding of 395–393, and that the lower three are therefore Themistoclean. The dimensions of this base given by Judeich are 1·70 metres (5·58 feet) high, with a cross-cut thickness of 2·50 metres (8·20 feet).[49] "On this foundation," Judeich wrote, "there was set a superstructure of mud-brick, whose height cannot be ascertained. This type of construction explains above all how the Themistoclean city-walls could have reached a height sufficient to be defended within a few months."[50] At that it must have required an unparalleled display of cooperative energy on the part of the Athenians, as Thucydides implies.

A new and most impressive stretch of the early circuit wall came to light in excavations carried out by the Greek Archaeological Service in 1966.[51] The location is almost directly south of the Odeion of Herodes Atticus on the southern slope of the Acropolis (marked B on plan 2, plate 5). Again, the assumption is that the lower courses only are Themistoclean, the uppermost level dating from a later, probably Cononian, rebuilding of the walls.[52]

49. See the diagram, with description, at Judeich, *Topographie*[2], 133–34.

50. Ibid., 134.

51. See *Arch. Delt.* 22 (1967), B.1, "Chronika," 76–78, with figs. 30–32, and *Pinax* 77; Ervin in *AJA* 73 (1969), 342, with pl. 85, fig. 3.

52. I wish to thank Prof. Eugene Vanderpool for examining this and other sections of the city wall, as well as the elusive Peiraeus fortifications, with me in the summer of 1968, and Mr. John Travlos for discussing the fortifications with me and allowing me to adapt his excellent plan 2.

11 OSTRAKA

The Institution of Ostracism

CHAPTER 22 OF THE *Constitution of Athens* attributed to Aristotle specifically includes "the law concerning ostracism" among "new laws which Cleisthenes enacted to win popular support" (22. 1). It was not, however, until two years after the victory of Marathon, the treatise continues, that, "the demos growing bold, they then for the first time used the law concerning ostracism, which had been enacted because of suspicion against those in power. . . . The first man to be ostracized was Hipparchus, son of Charmos, one of [Peisistratus'] relatives, on account of whom especially Cleisthenes had enacted the law; for Cleisthenes had wanted to drive Hipparchus out of the city" (22. 3–4). By placing the law within the sphere of Cleisthenes' legislation, and dating the first ostracism to (as it appears) 488/7 B.C., the author interposes a gap of at least thirteen, and perhaps as many as twenty, years between the institution of the procedure for ostracism and the first successful implementation of that procedure. The contrast which he draws between "Cleisthenes enacted" and "they [that is, the people] first used" shows that he was aware of the time lag. It has been objected that "such a weapon is not forged to be left for twenty years in the sheath."[1] An alternative to this date was presented by Androtion, the fourth-century writer of a *History of Athens*, as reported by Harpocration, a lexicographer writing in the second century A.D.; Androtion seems to have dated the enactment of the law to just before its first employment.[2] We would, then, seem to have a straightforward disagreement over the date were it not that the language used by the two fourth-century authorities is very close and that Androtion is believed to have been among the sources of the Aristotelian *Constitution of Athens*.[3] In that case, it may be that Aristotle is really correcting one of his sources. Various ways out of the apparent impasse have been suggested:

---

1. K. J. Beloch, *Griech. Gesch.*[2], I. 2, 332, quoted by C. Hignett, *Athenian Constitution*, 160.

2. Harpocration, s.v. Ἵππαρχος.

3. Cf. Hignett, *Athenian Constitution*, 160: "Its author certainly consulted the Atthis of Androtion."

(1) the law was indeed Cleisthenic, but Cleisthenes must have lived into the 480s and had it enacted in the early years of that decade;[4] (2) Harpocration or his source may have misunderstood, or misrepresented, what Androtion actually wrote;[5] (3) a late Byzantine account of ostracism may indicate that the law was introduced in two stages: (a) an earlier one by Cleisthenes in which voting took place in the Boule and a simple majority was sufficient to ostracize, and (b) the later mechanism described by Philochorus and Plutarch.[6] None of these proposed solutions is completely satisfying.

We are on firmer ground in determining the actual technique used and in identifying its first victims. The citizens were asked, at a regular meeting of the Assembly in the sixth prytany of the Attic civil year which began in July (roughly, therefore, January), whether they wished to hold an ostracism that year; if the vote was affirmative, the actual *ostrakophoria* was held at an extraordinary assembly meeting some time before the eighth prytany. Both votes seem to have been of the type which did not allow the possibility of debate.[7] The voting procedure is described by the late fourth century writer Philochorus: "The agora is fenced off with wooden planks, and ten entrances are left open, through which they enter by tribes and deposit the ostraka, turning down the inscription as they do so. The nine archons and the *boule* are in charge of the voting."[8] How many votes the "successful" candidate had to have is a matter of dispute. Philochorus says that a majority of 6,000 was required, while Plutarch makes the figure of 6,000 a quorum within which a simple majority was presumably sufficient to ostracize—if less than 6,000 votes were cast, the ostracism was invalid (*Arist.* 7. 6). This head-on disagreement between ancient authorities has not been resolved, although parallels of other Athenian laws which required a quorum of 6,000 have been adduced, and Jacoby sides firmly with Plutarch: "The fact that 6,000 was a kind of normal number for the total of the Athenian people qualified to vote decisively favours the version of Plutarch."[9] On the other hand, the astonishingly large number of ostraka in the new Cerameicus finds cast against Megacles (R. Thomsen reports a "provisional" total of 4,647) may be thought to count against easy acceptance of the Plutarch/Jacoby view. The person ostracized had ten days in which to leave Athens for ten years (the geographical limits of exclusion were officially set in 481/80 B.C.), but could, according to Plutarch, continue to enjoy the income from his property (*Arist.* 7. 6). There was no loss of political rights (*atimia*), and, apparently, little dis-

4. A. E. Raubitschek, "The Origin of Ostracism," *AJA* 55 (1951), 221–29.

5. K. J. Dover, "Androtion on Ostracism," *CR*, n.s. 13 (1963), 256–57. An attempt has been made to resolve the contradiction by emending the text of Androtion fr. 6 (J. J. Keaney in *Historia* 19 [1970], 1 ff.).

6. J. J. Keaney and A. E. Raubitschek, "A Late Byzantine Account of Ostracism," *AJP* 93 (1972), 87–91.

7. Hignett, *Athenian Constitution*, 164–65.

8. Philochorus, *FGrHist* 328 F 30. The details are further refined by E. Vanderpool: "Tribal and deme officials must have been stationed at each gate to identify those who presented them-

selves as being members of the tribe and as citizens eligible to vote. The voters...presumably were required to remain within the enclosure until all the votes had been cast as a precaution against double voting" (*Ostracism at Athens*, 4; this work will be cited hereafter as Vanderpool, *Ostracism* [1970]. It is particularly valuable in that it illustrates eight Themistocles ostraka which had not previously been published [figs. 7, 14, 15, 16, 23, 24, 26, 34]).

9. *FGrHist* III b (Supp.) i. 317 (commentary on Philochorus, 328 F 30). See also R. J. Bonner, *CP* 8 (1913), 223–25.

grace involved in the penalty. Athens was not the only ancient state to practise ostracism; we hear of a similar system in effect at Miletus, Megara, Argos, and Syracuse, where it was in effect for a short period in the middle of the fifth century and was called petalism (the names apparently being written on olive leaves).[10]

The *Constitution of Athens* implies that Cleisthenes enacted the law to guard against a revival of tyranny at Athens, and it states that the very person against whom it was first used, Hipparchus, son of Charmos (whose name betrays his connection with the Peisistratid family; Peisistratus' son Hippias was said to have married a daughter of Charmos),[11] was the victim against whom Cleisthenes had originally intended to use it. Needless to say, some or all of this may be mere inference and unsupported by any evidence (although not necessarily for that reason untrue), and a modern interpretation sees in the law, not an attack against tyranny, for which purpose other, severer laws existed, but rather a tool for achieving legislative efficiency. A popular leader whose programme was being blocked by a powerful opponent could, if he mustered enough popular support behind him, effect the temporary and relatively harmless removal of the opposition leader for a specified time. Vanderpool has expressed this view well: "The idea was rather to clip the wings of the too ambitious man than to ruin him permanently."[12] Others think that Cleisthenes intended to arm the *demos* with a weapon which would enable it to stifle any nascent attempt by the aristocrats to play the game of family politics, with groups of personally committed supporters behind them, which seems to have beset the Athenian political scene in the last years of the tyranny of Hippias and immediately after its downfall. In any case, Cleisthenes' (if he indeed was the law's author) intention need not have been identical with that which accounts for the law's first successful use in the 480s—and we must leave open the possibility that there were unsuccessful attempts to hold ostracisms before 487.

In the year which is probably to be identified as 488/7[13] there occurred the ostracism of Hipparchus, who, as we have seen, was connected with the Peisistratid family and had been archon in 496/5. He is described by the *Constitution of Athens* (on what evidence we are not told) as "leader and chief of the 'friends of the tyrants.'" In the following year, 487/6, Megacles, son of Hippocrates, of the great Alcmeonid family, was ostracized. "For three years," the treatise continues, "they ostracized the friends of the tyrants, for whom the law had been passed, but in the fourth year after that, they 'removed' any of the others if he appeared to be outstanding. The first to be ostracized of those not connected with the tyranny was Xanthippus, son of Ariphron" (22. 6). Although it is not specified when the three-year period begins, it is generally assumed that it is to be reckoned with the first ostracism, so that the early ostracisms can be dated in tabular form as follows:

10. Miletus and Megara: schol. Aristoph. *Knights* 855; Argos: Arist. *Pol.* 1302 b 18; Syracuse: Diod. 11. 87.

11. Cleidemus, *FGrHist* 323 F 15 (= Athenaeus 13. 609 C). J. K. Davies follows J. Kirchner, *PA*, 15520, in suggesting that it was Charmos who married a daughter of Hippias (*Athenian Propertied Families*, 451).

12. *Ostracism* (1970), 3.

13. "At an interval of two years after the victory [of Marathon]," *Const.* 22. 3. Because of the doubts regarding the presence or absence of "inclusive reckoning," there is some possibility that the year may really be 487/6.

$$
\left.
\begin{array}{ll}
488/7 & \text{Hipparchus} \\
487/6 & \text{Megacles} \\
486/5 & \text{unknown} \\
485/4 & \text{Xanthippus}
\end{array}
\right\} \quad \text{"friends of the tyrants"}
$$

Towards the end of the chapter we learn that "Aristeides, son of Lysimachus, was ostracized about this time, and in the fourth year after, in the archonship of Hypsichides, all the ostracized were recalled" (22. 7–8). Although ancient authorities disagree about the year of Aristeides' ostracism, of the two possible years, 484/3 and 483/2, the latter year seems preferable.[14] The usual picture of antagonism between Aristeides and Themistocles is doubtless much exaggerated, but it seems clear that it was Aristeides' opposition to Themistocles' Naval Bill that caused Themistocles to engineer his opponent's removal through ostracism.[15] The point is made explicitly and repeatedly in our sources. It would not be hard to derive from this last ostracism of the eighties a hypothesis that Themistocles was behind the manipulation of this political tool even earlier in the decade, when he might well have used the slogan "friends of the tyrants" against his political enemies, who included the Alcmeonids and their leader Megacles, as well as men like Xanthippus, who were related to them by marriage. Such a theory has the strong support of Hignett: "The programme of the anti-Persian party in these years evinces a fertility in expedients and a brilliance in the adaptation of means to ends which point to Themistokles as its originator. By the device of ostracism he and his collaborators eliminated their chief opponents one by one."[16] Although I have elsewhere expressed my adherence to this view,[17] it must be stressed that its strength derives from a convergence of circumstances—frequent and successful use of ostracism, which would clearly have demanded energetic canvassing by someone to muster sufficient votes against the intended victim; exploitation of the anti-Alcmeonid (and false) version of the "tyrannicide" of Hipparchus in 514; perhaps also the electoral reform of 487/6 (as Hignett also believes)—but not one of these by itself can be shown to be directly attributable to Themistocles. What we have is ancient literary testimony that Themistocles secured the removal of his political opponent Aristeides through ostracism and ancient archaeological evidence that he himself was also a candidate as early as the year in which Megacles was ostracized, 487/6; the picture must be filled out by inference.[18]

14. See Hignett, *Athenian Constitution*, 185, 336–37. The Aristotelian *Constitution of Athens* is in this respect (as so often) self-contradictory: its suggestion at 22. 7 that the ostracism took place in the archonship of Nicodemus (483/2) is cancelled by the reference at 22. 8 to the archonship of Hypsichides (481/80) as "the fourth year" afterwards.

15. Plutarch, *Them.* 5, fin., 12. 6; *Const. of Athens* 22. 7, mentions Aristeides' ostracism in the context of Themistocles' ship-building operations.

16. *Athenian Constitution*, 188–89. So, too,

D. W. Knight (*Some Studies in Athenian Politics in the Fifth Century B.C.*, 29), although I find no evidence for his view that the ostracisms (much less the archonship law of 487/6) were engineered by "Themistokles and Aristeides combined."

17. *Historia* 15 (1966), 129–41.

18. The sceptic's position regarding Themistocles', or anyone's, manipulation of events during this period, especially the introduction of allotment of archons in 487/6, has now been restated by E. Badian, "Archons and *Strategoi*," *Antichthon* 5 (1971), 1–34.

Ostraka

One of the most exciting of all direct archaeological links with Themistocles' career is the discovery in recent years of fragments of potsherds with names of candidates for ostracism inscribed on them. The two major find-spots have been the Agora and the cemetery in the district known as Cerameicus, or Potters' Quarter, northwest of the Agora. A recent account lists "1,658 ostraka, 1,238 from the Agora excavations, the rest mostly from the German excavations in the Kerameikos,"[19] which we shall label group i; to these must now be added a very large new find in the Cerameicus in 1965 and 1966, here called group ii.[20]

Group i

Until these most recent finds have been fully published, our knowledge of the ostraka is confined to observable facts or inferences that can be drawn from this earlier group. Obviously, conclusions may need to be modified in the light of future publication of the Cerameicus material. One conclusion which is not likely to be overthrown, however, is that Themistocles was statistically one of the most popular candidates during the early years in which ostracism was employed. Meiggs and Lewis give a total of 1,658 pieces, out of which 568, just short of one-third of the total, were cast against Themistocles (373 from the Agora, 195 found elsewhere).[21] It would obviously be of great importance to be able to assign some of these to particular years in which Themistocles was a candidate, but there seems to be little hope of achieving certainty in such a project. The nature of the find-spots—wells, ditches, or other dumps for waste material—would seem to preclude any but the roughest chronology. "The kind of evidence we should most like to have," remark Meiggs and Lewis, "would be sealed deposits of ostraka, of which we could say with confidence that they all came from one ostrakophoria, with no intrusive evidence, earlier or later, and large enough in number to be statistically significant.... Such evidence is still in very short supply."[22] In addition, it became clear to the excavators that they were dealing, some of the time at least, with re-deposits, "ostraka [which] were not dumped here immediately after the ostrakophoria in which they were cast but were originally dumped elsewhere and only reached the place where we found them a generation or two later."[23]

In 1959 A. R. Hands surveyed the then known ostraka and assigned them to groups, which he discussed in terms of evidence for stratification or other indications of date.[24] In deposits which can confidently be assigned to the period before the sack of Athens

19. R. Meiggs and D. Lewis, *Selection*, 40. There is a selection of ostraka in M. Guarducci's *Epigrafia Greca*, II, 524–34.

20. Preliminary notices by F. Willemsen, *Ath. Mitt.* 80 (1965), 100–126; A. H. S. Megaw, *Archaeological Reports for 1966–67* (supp. to *JHS* 87 [1967], 4–5); M. Ervin in *AJA* 71 (1967), 295; F. J. Frost, *Calif. Studies Class. Ant.* 1 (1968), 124; Georges Daux, *BCH* 92 (1968), 732–33. A tentative inventory is published by

Willemsen in *Arch. Delt.* 23 (1968), B, "Chronika," 28–29, and a further "provisional" count has recently been published by R. Thomsen, *Origin of Ostracism*, 93 ff.

21. *Selection*, 46.

22. Ibid., 43.

23. Homer A. Thompson, *Hesperia* 17 (1948), 193.

24. "Ostraka and the Law of Ostracism," *JHS* 79 (1959), 69–79.

in 480, the levels at which ostraka bearing different names were found tend to substantiate the chronological sequence given in the literary sources. Thus, the single Themistocles ostrakon in Meiggs/Lewis group A (= Hands group F) occurs with three ostraka of Aristeides and substantially above (that is, later than) three against Megacles, son of Hippocrates. This suggests, as the excavators remark, that "votes were cast against Themistokles"[25] in the year in which Aristeides was banished, 483 or 482—exactly what we might have expected on grounds of general probability. In the five remaining groups discussed by Meiggs and Lewis, B through F (= Hands A–D, F), all of which contain significant percentages of Themistocles ostraka, they detect "a noticeable shift of votes away from the Alkmeonids, Kallixenos and Hippocrates, against Aristeides."[26]

A study of the ostraka and the names they bear throws interesting light on various aspects of Themistocles' career. First, among the names that seem to be assignable to the period before 480, there are a large number of Alcmeonid names, both already known and otherwise unattested. Second only to Themistocles in total votes received (263 in Meiggs and Lewis' table) was Kallixenos, son of Aristonymos, of Xypete, "shown by his Sicyonian patronymic (Hdt. VI. 126) and one ostrakon reading [Ἀλκ]-μεον[ιδōν | Καλ]λίχσεν[ος | Ἀρ]ιστο[νύμο] to be an Alcmeonid, descendant of the marriage between Megakles and Agariste of Sicyon."[27] Another unknown Alcmeonid is Hippocrates, son of Alcmeonides, of Alopeke, who ranks third with a total of 125 ostraka. There is another Hippocrates, son of Anaxileos, represented by 10 ostraka, who may also be an Alcmeonid.[28] Archaeological evidence thereby confirms the picture of a struggle during this period between Themistocles and the Alcmeonids, each side using whatever propaganda weapons it could find (such as the Marathon shield signal and the "tyrannicide" story) against the other.[29] It is probably in this context that we should interpret the elegiac couplet on the ostrakon cast against Xanthippus, Pericles' father, who had married an Alcmeonid and was ostracized in 484: "This ostrakon says that Xanthippus son of Ariphron / does most wrong of all the cursed leaders."[30]

Secondly, it seems to be significant that the names of several individuals who are either known to have been associated with Themistocles, or for whom such an association has been plausibly conjectured, are represented in the ostraka. Habronichus, son of Lysikles (see Hdt. 8. 21, Thuc. 1. 91. 3), 4 ostraka; Melanthius (presumably the same as the Athenian commander sent to aid the Ionians in 498), 3; and from the new Cerameicus finds, Mnesiphilus Phrearrhios (Themistocles' alleged mentor), 14.[31]

Finally, an extremely interesting group of 191 ostraka, all bearing Themistocles'

25. *Hesperia* 15 (1946), 274.

26. Meiggs and Lewis, *Selection*, 44.

27. Ibid., 40–41. See also Vanderpool, *Ostracism* (1970), 18–19.

28. See Vanderpool, *Hesperia* 15 (1946), 272, 275, and A. E. Raubitschek, *AJA* 51 (1947), 259, with n.11.

29. See my article in *Historia* 15 (1966), 129 ff.

30. Meiggs and Lewis' translation (42) of Wilhelm's interpretation; the ostrakon was first published by Raubitschek, *AJA* 51 (1947), 257–62.

31. See Frost, *Calif. Studies Class. Ant.* 1 (1968), 124, and Daux, *BCH* 92 (1968), 732. (The location of the deme Phrearrhioi has now been definitively settled by Vanderpool [*Hesperia* 39 (1970), 50–53].)

name, was discovered in a well on the north slope of the Acropolis and published by Oscar Broneer in 1938. The names are inscribed on pottery of a limited range of types (the most numerous are kylix bases, ten are skyphos bases, and twenty-six are parts of small bowls). As Broneer remarked, "It is obvious that they were all made at one time and for a given purpose, and it is most unlikely that they had been in use before they were inscribed."[32] What points even more strongly in this direction is the fact that Broneer has been able to classify all the inscriptions into only fourteen different hands: "This shows beyond a doubt that they were not inscribed by the voters themselves."[33] In other words, we seem to have here prefabricated ostraka, prepared in advance for distribution to voters who either could not write themselves, or were willing to have a candidate "suggested" to them. "We may credit the opponents of Themistokles with the foresight of having prepared the ostraka on specially attractive material for distribution among the citizens who were not sufficiently well versed in the art of writing or were otherwise unwilling to take the trouble to prepare their own ballots."[34] It does not look as if ballot boxes were emptied of their contents after the voting had taken place; the find-spot, well M, is on the north slope of the Acropolis, at some distance from the actual voting in the Agora, and there are no other names mixed in, as in other deposits of used ostraka. Broneer, therefore, concludes that these prefabricated votes were prepared for distribution by Themistocles' enemies, but, the reason for this is unclear, dumped before they were actually distributed. Meiggs and Lewis concur, "The group presents such uniformity that it is highly improbable that it was ever used."[35] On the basis of similarity in profile and decoration between this material from well M and ostraka from the Agora bearing the name of Aristeides, Broneer suggests that "there is every probability that the ostraka from well M were prepared for the ostracism of 482," the year to which he assigns Aristeides' ostracism.[36] Meiggs and Lewis are more circumspect: "Archaeologically, it seems slightly more likely that the sherds were prepared for an ostracism in the late 480's than for the final successful campaign against Themistocles."[37] Vanderpool has recently discussed these ostraka anew and suggests that Themistocles' enemies were unable to use all the ostraka they had prepared: "The party workers had been over-optimistic and had made more ostraca than they had been able to distribute, perhaps more than they were able to carry with them to the Agora. Some were left over, and I think it is probably these leftovers that were discarded," in well M mentioned above.[38]

Through the kindness of Professor Broneer I am able to reproduce a photograph of some of the material from well M, which illustrates the uniformity of shape and lettering (plate 6).

Before the recent finds in the Cerameicus, the most extensive collection of ostraka was that excavated by the American School of Classical Studies at Athens and housed in the Agora collection. With the assistance of Professor Vanderpool, I was able to examine the collection in the summer of 1968. Much of the information presented

32. *Hesperia* 7 (1938), 230.
33. Ibid., 232.
34. Ibid., 243.
35. *Selection*, 43.

36. *Hesperia* 7 (1938), 242.
37. *Selection*, 43.
38. *Ostracism* (1970), 12. (He illustrates a selection of these ostraka at figs. 30 and 31.)

here was made available to me by him and now appears in his monograph *Ostracism at Athens*. The Agora collection contains 373[39] of the total of 568 Themistocles ostraka known to Meiggs and Lewis.[40] Insofar as this material can be dated at all, on the basis of "stratifications" (with the limitations arising from the nature of the find-spots already mentioned), pre-Persian War material found along with the ostraka, or type of pottery employed, the excavators feel that the bulk of the Themistocles ostraka are "early," rather than "late," or, in more concrete terms, they were cast against Themistocles probably in one of the years before 480 in which he would have been a candidate, but in which one of his opponents was ostracized instead; the year of Aristeides' ostracism has been a favourite candidate.

In the overwhelming majority of Agora specimens (293 out of the then total of 311 in which the letter survives), Themistocles' name is spelt with a theta as the sixth letter. This seems more euphonious, especially in conjunction with the preceding sigma, and may be influenced by the first letter;[41] at any rate, it clearly reflects how the majority of his countrymen pronounced Themistocles' name.[42] The type of pottery which predominates, about 40 per cent of the whole, is unglazed or semiglazed coarse pots (everyday cookware), with semiglazed kraters (mixing bowls) representing about 23 per cent of the whole and fragments of fine black-glazed vases of various shapes—the easiest to read—about 27 per cent.[43] A photograph of the rough type of pottery is reproduced as plate 7a (P15577) which identifies Themistocles by his deme only, "of Phrearrhioi"; 7b (P5959) shows a fragment of black-glazed ware on which is inscribed his name and that of his father, "[son] of Neokles"; while 7c (P9950) gives his full appellation: his own name, followed by patronymic and demotic. It should be noted, too, that there are spelling variants, especially in word ending. Vanderpool's figures are as follows: *Themisthokles* 116,[44] *Themisthoklees* 45; *Neokleos* 69, *Neokleōs* 6, *Neokleous* 3; *Phrearios* 58, *Phrearrios* 21, *Phrearhios* 8, *Phrearrhios* 1. There are, in addition, according to Vanderpool, "some remarkable misspellings." In the early stages of study of the ostraka there was a feeling that variation in respect of patronymic and demotic might have some deeper significance. It had been maintained, for example, that the occurrence of a patronymic indicated aristocratic birth, while use of a demotic only emphasized plebeian origin. But, as Raubitschek pointed out, a likelier determinant is the habitual practice, and perhaps therefore a reflection of the social status, of the writer of the ostrakon, not that of the person against whom it

39. The main finds of Themistocles ostraka are these: 69 Themistocles from the group of 172 ostraka found in 1939 (mentioned in *Hesperia* 9 [1940], 301–2, and *Hesperia*, supp. 8, 395); 172 Themistocles out of a total of 605 from the large 1947 group (*Hesperia* 17 [1948], 193–94, and 19 [1950], 387); 17 Themistocles from the group discovered near the road south of the Tholos (*Hesperia*, supp. 4, p. 33); 23 Themistocles from the Valley Road Group, 85 to 90 metres southwest of the Tholos (Hands, *JHS* 79 [1959], 77).

40. *Selection*, 46. To the overall total of 1,232 known in 1959 were added 6 new ostraka of considerable interest (none of Themistocles) published by Vanderpool in *Hesperia* 37 (1968), 117–20.

41. So K. Meisterhans, *Gram. attisch. Inschrift.*[3], 103, who classifies it as "metathesis of aspiration over two syllables," and cites examples from inscriptions.

42. These figures are presented by Vanderpool, *Ostracism* (1970), 13, with illustrations listed there.

43. These statistics appear in ibid., 5.

44. Vanderpool has now revised this figure upward to "198 instances" (ibid., 14).

was cast.[43] Only 8 of the Themistocles ostraka discovered on the north slope of the Acropolis and published by Broneer have demotics; Vanderpool's figures divide evenly: 148 with patronymic only, 148 with demotic only, 5 with both, and 5 with neither.[46] In the recent Cerameicus finds, those with patronymic only are said to out-number those with demotic only by two to one.

Group ii

Through the courtesy of the staff of the German Archaeological Institute in Athens, I was able to examine the Cerameicus ostraka in the summer of 1968. Although full details must await final publication, enough has already been made known to indicate that the discoveries have much light to throw both on the whole topic of ostracism and on Themistocles' part in it.[47] According to R. Thomsen, the total number of ostraka newly discovered in the Cerameicus "amounted to approximately 9,000."[48] Of these, by far the largest number were cast against Megacles, son of Hippocrates (Thomsen gives a "provisional" total of 4,647),[49] and in second place stands Themistocles, with 1,696 ostraka. The third highest total (760) belongs to a certain Kallias, son of Kratios. On the basis of his designation on 11 pieces as *Medos* or *ek Medon* (that is, a Persian), and a rough illustration of him on the reverse of 1 ostrakon in what seems to be the dress of a Persian archer, it has been suggested that Kallias was the third man to be ostracized in the initial series of votes cast against "friends of the tyrants" (*Const. of Athens* 22. 6). Thus we have a possible new candidate for the ostracism held successfully in 486/5.[50]

Daux pointed out that "the majority of ostraka of Themistocles were collected at the same time as the sherds inscribed 'Megacles' and ought then to be assigned to the ostrakophoria against Cleisthenes' nephew (487/86)."[51] This theory seems to be con-firmed by 3 ostraka, each originally part of the rim of a krater or large wine-mixing bowl, on which are inscribed the names of both Megacles and Themistocles.[52] We thus seem to have proof that Themistocles was a candidate as early as the spring of 486. It is only a short step to the conclusion that even this early a power struggle was taking place between Themistocles and his political enemies. Of great interest and importance are the conjunction of names inscribed on the rim of what seems to be the same black-figure krater: Themistocles, Megacles—and Cimon! This shows that Cimon, too, must have been a candidate as early as 486, although he was then still relatively young; he would undoubtedly have inherited some of his father's political

45. "Ostracism," in *Actes du deuxième Congrès international d'épigraphie grecque et latine*, 69.

46. *Ostracism* (1970), 8. He suggests that "Themistokles must have deliberately cultivated the use of the demotic.... He did this in order to increase his popularity among the common people."

47. See Daux, *BCH* 92 (1968), 732–33; Willemsen, *Arch. Delt.* 23 (1968), B, "Chronika," 24 ff., with the list at pp. 28–29; Thomsen, *Origin of Ostracism*, 69 ff., 92 ff. (additional information has been supplied to

me through the courtesy of Profs. H. Mattingly and E. Badian, to whom I here wish to express my thanks). Prof. Mattingly has now presented his views more fully in *The University of Leeds Review* 14 (1971), 277 ff.

48. *Origin of Ostracism*, 69.

49. Ibid., 93, for these and the following figures.

50. See Vanderpool, *Ostracism* (1970), 21–22.

51. *BCH* 92 (1968), 732, confirmed by Thomsen, *Origin of Ostracism*, 94–95.

52. Vanderpool, *Ostracism* (1970), 11; Thomsen, *Origin of Ostracism*, 95.

quarrels, along with his debts. At the same time, this discovery makes it exceedingly difficult to suggest a firm date for another ostrakon which bears the names of Cimon and Themistocles; it could come from Themistocles' own ostracism of *c*. 471, or from as early as 486. The same uncertainty attends the rest of the 490 ostraka against Cimon discovered in the recent excavations, which could have been cast as early as 486 or as late as the "successful" ostracism of *c*. 461. Plate 8, *a* and *b*, shows some of these momentous finds, the Themistocles/Megacles and Themistocles/Cimon ostraka.

Some final facts. The name Mnesiphilus Phrearrhios occurs on 14 ostraka; he must be the person mentioned by Herodotus (8. 57, 58) and Plutarch (*Them.* 2. 6) as Themistocles' fellow demesman and "mentor," who is thus confirmed as a real person. It is no longer possible to dismiss him (as Macan had done) as a mere figment, although the details of Themistocles' utter dependence on him for the plan to stay and fight at Salamis are not necessarily therefore anything more than anti-Themistocles propaganda. One wonders whether votes may not have been cast against him—we know not when—chiefly for his connection with Themistocles' circle. The same reason perhaps accounts for the 11 ostraka in group ii against a certain Myronides Phlyeus whose deme suggests that he may have belonged to the *genos* of the Lykomidai, with whom Themistocles claimed affinities. The name of Habronichus of Lamptrai also occurs (30 ostraka).[53] It was he who, according to Herodotus (8. 21), brought to the Athenian fleet at Artemisium news of the annihilation of Leonidas' force at Thermopylae, and he was later to serve with Themistocles and Aristeides on the delaying embassy to Sparta while the Athenian city walls were being rebuilt (Thuc. 1. 91. 3). It seems reasonable to assume that his candidacy for ostracism may also have been based on his involvement with Themistocles.[54] Some 83 of the new ostraka were cast against a certain Leagros, son of Glaukon, to whom the fictionalized Themistocles of the Epistles addressed his eighth letter, and who is thus given considerably greater reality as a political associate of Themistocles than he had previously possessed in the late epistolographer's pages.

There is an ostrakon which was mentioned briefly in the preliminary notices and which I was able to examine in 1968.[55] Roughly translated it reads:

> For Themistocles of Phrearrhioi
> This ostrakon—his reward [τιμῆς ἕνεκα].

53. Thomsen, *Origin of Ostracism*, 100.
54. So, for example, Willemsen, *Ath. Mitt.* 80 (1965), 106–7.
55. See *AJA* 71 (1967), 295, and Vanderpool, *Ostracism* (1970), 8–9. (At fig. 19 he illustrates an interesting ostrakon which he translates as "Themistokles, Son of Neokles, out with him!")

APPENDIX A
CHRONOLOGY

TOWARDS THE END of his *Life of Themistocles*, Plutarch remarks, "He died in Magnesia, after having lived sixty-five years, most of them in political life and military commands" (31. 5). Where did Plutarch get the figure? Perhaps from his friend and fellow student, the Themistocles, descendant of the statesman, whom he mentions at the very end of the *Life*. Fixing this sixty-five-year span down to particular dates is a difficult problem. Earlier in the same chapter Plutarch presents a vague synchronism between Themistocles' death and Cimon's "mastery of the sea"[1] and a naval expedition to Cyprus, which Thucydides (1. 112) seems to date to *c.* 450/49. When Plutarch deals with this synchronism in the *Life of Cimon* (18. 1), he dates it firmly after Cimon's return from exile, but, in chapter 17 of the same *Life*, Plutarch accepts Theopompus' account that Cimon had been specially recalled after five, not the regular ten, years on the motion of Pericles. Since Cimon was ostracized in about 461 B.C., it suggests that one ancient account at least placed Cimon's recall, the expedition to Cyprus, and, with it, Themistocles' death all together around 456 B.C. A date in this period also seems to be implied by Plutarch's reference, at the beginning of his story of how Themistocles met his end, to the revolt of Egypt and Athenian assistance to the revolutionaries (*Them.* 31. 4), events which occurred about 459 B.C. Towards the end of his account of Cimon's expedition in the *Cimon*, Plutarch quotes the fourth-century Atthidographer Phanodemus, and it may be his researches which lie behind the synchronism.[2]

1. θαλασσοκρατῶν, *Them.* 31. 4; since the same word is used in a similar context by Diodorus (12. 4. 1), Ephorus, whom Diodorus drew upon, may be among Plutarch's sources here. Plutarch mentions Ephorus twice in his account of Cimon's Eurymedon victory (*Cim.* 12. 5, 6).

2. Elsewhere, the synchronism moves up considerably—to Cimon's Eurymedon campaign (Aristodemus, *FGrHist* 104 F 11. 1, and the Suda lexicon, s.v. Κίμων). E. Meyer has shown that details of the Eurymedon and Cimon's last expedition to Cyprus are often interchanged in the later accounts (*Forschungen* II, 1 ff., *Geschichte des Altertums*[3], IV. 1, 496, n.1).

It is in any case clear that the events narrated by Plutarch in the last section of his *Life*, however much embroidery on the plain facts there has been in the tradition, imply a lapse of some years between Themistocles' arrival in Persia (which probably took place early in 464)[3] and his death. This will give a date of death sometime after 460. On the assumption that Plutarch's figure of sixty-five years is genuine, a date of birth can be fixed roughly in the period from 524 to 520 B.C.

The tradition offers another fixed chronological point: Themistocles' archonship, which is recorded by Dionysius of Halicarnassus (*Rom. Ant.* 6. 34. 1) under the year 493/2. Although numerous attempts have been made to subvert this date, either by claiming that some other Themistocles must be meant,[4] or by maintaining that the archon list used by Dionysius was untrustworthy,[5] these efforts to shake Dionysius' testimony are unconvincing.[6] It can hardly be maintained that Themistocles was never archon, for this is specifically attested by Thucydides,[7] and confirmed by the confused account in the *Constitution of Athens*, where he is described as "of the Areopagites" (25. ?), that is, a former archon. Suspicion of 493/2 as the date for Themistocles' archonship is based on the fact that Herodotus, in introducing Themistocles into his pages in 481 B.C., describes him as "recently having come to the fore" (7. 143. 1). Attempts to dilute Herodotus' meaning here seem doomed to failure;[8] we can only infer that he or his source did not know of (or chose to ignore) Themistocles' archonship of twelve years earlier. Gomme argued that "it does not seem at all probable that Themistokles, whether or not he was archon in 493–492, began a naval policy then which was dropped for ten years,"[9] but we know too little about the internal politics of Athens during this period for this argument to carry much weight. Above all, it seems illogical to reject the only ancient evidence we have, Dionysius, and then postulate a date for Themistocles' archonship in 482/1, the virtue of that year being that it is the only one for which we do not possess an archon's name!

Further help with Themistocles' chronology has been sought in the argument that he must have held the archonship in 493/2 *suo anno*, that is, like magistrates in the Roman Republican period, at the earliest possible date, when he was just thirty (or a year or two over).[10] Although this would fit in well enough with a birth date *c.* 524, it is by no means certain that thirty was the legal minimum age for archons in the

---

3. The evidence for this date is set out below.

4. We hear of an homonymous uncle in the "Themistocles Epistles" (Ep. 8, p. 749 Hercher).

5. This has been maintained most recently by W. H. Plommer, "The Tyranny of the Archon-List," *CR*, n.s. 19 (1969), 126–29.

6. Dionysius' date is vindicated by G. Busolt, *Griech. Gesch.*², II, 642–43, n.1.

7. 1. 93. 3. In spite of the arguments of A. W. Gomme, *Commentary*, I, 262–63, and C. W. Fornara, "Themistocles' Archonship," *Historia* 20 (1971), 534 ff., it is clear that Thucydides meant the annual, and probably also the eponymous, archonship, for he uses an almost identical expression to designate the archonship at 6. 54. 6 (compare the Parian Marble, *FGrHist* 239, Ep. 32, cited by Plommer, *CR*, n.s. 19

[1969], 129).

8. I am not persuaded by F. J. Frost's assertion that "archons and junior Areopagites were not to be considered among the *protoi*" (*Calif. Studies Class. Ant.* 1 [1968], 115), or by R. J. Lenardon's argument that "Herodotos merely states that Themistokles had recently come to the front with the proposal concerning the fleet" (*Historia* 5 [1956], 412, n.57, following R. Flacelière, *REA* 55 [1953], 17, n.5).

9. *Commentary*, I, 262, restating the case he had argued earlier at greater length in *AJP* 65 (1944), 323.

10. Lenardon, *Historia* 5 (1956), 414, n.72, following H. T. Wade-Gery, *BSA* 37 (1936/37), 263, n.1.

early part of the fifth century. The *Constitution of Athens* (30. 1–2) asserts that in 411 B.C., under the Constitution of the 5,000, "the members of the Boule were to be men over thirty who would serve for a year without pay; from these [that is, the *boule* members][11] were to come the generals, the nine archons" and so on. But a legal requirement for which we have evidence from the latter part of the century need not have been in effect at its beginning. There survives an inscription from the early part of the fifth century, setting up procedures for the selection of officials who were to supervise athletic games in honour of Heracles at Marathon, which specifies that they "shall select from the visitors three from each tribe. . .not less than thirty years of age."[12] But it might be argued that religious law is always more conservative and sets the lead in such matters to the civil code, and if one were looking for an appropriate time for the introduction of a minimum-age requirement for the archons, the change which occurred in the selection procedures in Telesinus' year, 487/6, naturally suggests itself. It would be unsafe, then, to use the fact of Themistocles' archonship in 493/2 to argue back to a birth date thirty years earlier.

The most troublesome, and the most discussed, chronological problem in Themistocles' career is that of the date(s) of his ostracism and subsequent condemnation for treason. The lower limit is fixed by Thucydides' report that after his arrival in Asia "he sent a letter to King Artaxerxes, son of Xerxes, who had recently ascended the throne" (1. 137. 3). "Fortunately Xerxes' death and Artaxerxes' accession can be dated by independent evidence to late in the year 465," writes M. E. White in an important article.[13] Themistocles' arrival in Persia can then be dated securely to late 465 or early 464 B.C. Thucydides "quotes" from Themistocles' letter to Artaxerxes to the effect that he wished to spend a year learning Persian before he came into the Royal Presence; "and after a year he came into his presence and achieved a position of prominence at court" (1. 138. 2). Themistocles' arrival in Susa, then, should be dated to *c.* 463 B.C.

The date of Themistocles' escape from Greece following upon his ostracism and condemnation in absentia is much more difficult, some would say impossible, to fix. The only thing approaching "testimony" which we possess is Diodorus' account (11. 54), where the problematic first trial and acquittal, the ostracism, the second move for condemnation, and the flight from Argos to the Molossians are all dated to the archonship of Praxiergos, 471/70. Now Diodorus' method (if method it can be called) seems to have been to collect an assortment of related events and narrate them under a year in which only one of them occurred; the difficulty is in determining which, if any, he had trustworthy evidence for as having taken place in 471. Some have argued for the ostracism, others for the condemnation for *prodosia*, but, as Gomme points out, "The date of either event could have been and was probably recorded. . . .

---

11. See J. E. Sandys' commentary at *Constitution of Athens* 30. 1–2 for this interpretation.

12. *SEG* 10. 2 B, lines 19–26, translated by E. Vanderpool in his edition of the inscription in *Hesperia* 11 (1942), 329–37; I owe the reference to Mr. J. K. Davies.

13. "Some Agiad Dates: Pausanias and His Sons," *JHS* 84 (1964), 140–52; the quotation is from p. 142 (the evidence is cited in n.13).

The difficulty is that Diodorus can mean either."[14] P. N. Ure put rather more pointedly the objection to using Diodorus' chronology: "The fact that [Diodorus] was ignorant of several important dates in the later career of Themistocles is curious evidence for the contention that he must have been certain about one."[15] Help has been sought from another quarter. Aeschylus' *Persians* is generally thought to have been motivated, at least in part, by a desire to recall to the minds of the Athenians their debt to Themistocles, and although it is conceivable that Themistocles may already have been ostracized at the time of its production at the Dionysia held in March 472, "the most suitable moment for Aeschylus' excursion into political propaganda was when Themistocles stood within danger of ostracism but had not yet succumbed to that danger."[16] While admitting the inherent weakness of the argument and the absence of any real evidence, we may essay the following tentative reconstruction:

March, 472:   Themistocles' name mentioned as a "candidate" for ostracism; an unsuccessful attempt to ostracize him?

spring, 471:[17]   Themistocles ostracized; he "had his abode in Argos, but made visits to the rest of the Peloponnese," according to Thucydides (1. 135. 3). To Themistocles' agency has been ascribed the synoecism of Elis and Mantineia, which occurred about this time.[18]

c. 470:   Death of Pausanias, the regent;[19] the "evidence" on which the charge of treason against Themistocles was based was said to have been found among the papers of the dead regent (Thuc. 1. 135. 2).

late 470 or 469:   Themistocles' final condemnation and flight to Corcyra, thence to King Admetus in Epirus. His journey thence took him within range of the Athenian fleet besieging Naxos, says Thucydides (1. 137. 2), an event which occurred in the period between 469 and 467.[20]

14. *Commentary*, I, 401 (and see his comments at 53, n.4); he cites K. J. Beloch, *Griech. Gesch.*[2], II. 2, 192–93, for the view that it was the ostracism (to this may be added White, *JHS* 84 [1964], 146, and W. G. Forrest, *CQ*, n.s. 10 [1960], 241), Busolt, *Griech. Gesch.*[2], III. 1, 112–13, n.2, that it was the final condemnation. Busolt's arguments are restated by Lenardon, "The Chronology of Themistokles' Ostracism and Exile," *Historia* 8 (1959), 24–29.

15. "Themistocles, Aeschylus and Diodorus," *CR* 37 (1923), 64. Similar scepticism has been voiced by P. J. Rhodes: "Honesty surely compels us to admit that the dates of Themistocles' ostracism and condemnation cannot be established" (*Historia* 19 [1970], 398).

16. M. Cary, "When Was Themistocles Ostracized?" *CR* 36 (1922), 162. Gomme accepts this argument as "probable...not certain by any means...but probable" (*Commentary*, I, 401).

17. According to Philochorus, *FGrHist* 328 F 30, the people voted by *procheirotonia* before the eighth prytany (roughly March) to see whether an ostracism should be held (*Const. of Athens* 43. 5 suggests that the preliminary vote was held as early as the sixth prytany). If so, the actual *ostrakophoria* presumably ensued rather quickly, to remove undesirable candidates from the elections to the generalship (cf. C. Hignett, *Athenian Constitution*, 164–65).

18. A. Andrewes, *Phoenix* 6 (1952), 2–3, Forrest, *CQ*, n.s. 10 (1960), 229. Diodorus 11. 54 narrates the synoecism of Elis as the first event of 471/70.

19. I accept, though without any urgent conviction, the apparent testimony of Justin-Trogus that Pausanias held Byzantium for seven years, that is, from 478/7 to 472/1 (see Fornara, *Historia* 15 [1966], 257 ff. and J. D. Smart, *JHS* 87 [1967], 137–38). Against Miss White's arguments that Pausanias must have had time to sire three sons from c. 475, one need only adduce the consideration, which she herself presents, that "the four sons of Anaxandridas...all were born within about five years" (*JHS* 84 [1964], 151).

20. "Naxian war c. 469–468 to 468–467" (Gomme, *Commentary*, I, 408).

Between this and Themistocles' arrival in Ionia in late 465 or early 464, there is a two- or three-year gap during which his whereabouts and activities cannot be accounted for; but such a gap will occur at some stage in his journey on any chronological scheme.

After the year in which he acquired the rudiments of the Persian language, Themistocles went up to Susa (probably, as we saw, in 463) and began his second career as "Greek general in residence" at the court of Artaxerxes. Even if they are largely fictitious, the stories in chapters 29 and 30 of Plutarch's *Life of Themistocles* imply a period of time sufficiently long for Themistocles to have ingratiated himself with Artaxerxes and to have incurred the jealous dislike of the king's other courtiers. Thucydides says that he was given three cities (that is, apparently, their revenues were assigned to his use) and that he actually "ruled over" the third, Magnesia. But inscriptional evidence makes it clear that he had established a branch of the family at Lampsacus, and at Magnesia itself he seems to have busied himself with establishing cults, as well as, it seems not unreasonable to suppose, generally attending to the functions of civic life. Theopompus had him "wandering over Asia,"[21] to which Plutarch takes specific exception: he "had a house in Magnesia, enjoyed generous presents from the King, and was accorded equal honors with the great Persian nobles. In this way *he was able to live for many years without disturbance*, because the King paid no attention to Greek affairs."[22] Furthermore, Themistocles had won his way into the hearts of the Magnesians to the extent that, according to Plutarch (*Them.* 32. 4), he was honoured by them after his death with a "magnificent tomb." All this implies an extended period of time, but the uncertainty as to exactly how long remains.

The present state of the evidence, then, will not permit Themistocles' dates to be specified more closely than *c.* 524–520 to *c.* 459–455.[23]

21. *FGrHist* 115 F 87.

22. *Them.* 31. 3, trans. Scott-Kilvert (my italics). Later in the same chapter Plutarch remarks that "the majority" of Themistocles' sixty-five years were spent in "political life and military commands" (31. 6), which may suggest that Themistocles held certain magistracies in Magnesia.

23. See now the brief, lucid discussion by J. K. Davies, *Athenian Propertied Families*, 214–15, who concludes: "The dates 524–459 are likely to be right to within a year or two" (215).

APPENDIX B
THE NAVAL BILL

WHAT WE KNOW about this important measure comes from Herodotus (7. 144) and the *Constitution of Athens* (22. 7); all the later accounts derive from these and, insofar as they diverge from them, show no signs of having independent authority.[1] Of the differences between them the most serious concerns the number of ships called for by Themistocles' proposal: Herodotus gives the figure 200, the *Constitution* 100. The discrepancy has proved to be intractable. It matters little that only the late and derivative account of Justin follows Herodotus' figure, while the number 100 reappears in Nepos, Plutarch, Polyaenus (whose account is virtually a direct copy of that in the *Constitution*), and Libanius,[2] for truth in such matters is not to be attained by the mere counting and weighing of authorities. Various attempts have been made to reduce the figure in Herodotus (for example, it has been maintained that what he meant to say was, "the navy was increased *up to a total of* two hundred"),[3] but his text as it stands is perfectly unambiguous. Labarbe's approach, to suggest that "in speaking of Laurium, Herodotus, unlike Plutarch, gave to the name its widest significance: it refers to all the mines in operation, to the new galleries of Maroneia as well as to those which resulted from the former exploitation under the Peisistratids,"[4] is methodologically unsound and leads him to the improbable theory that Themistocles sponsored *two* naval decrees: one concerning the extraordinary strike at Maroneia, the income from which was to be turned over to the 100 wealthiest citizens; the other for discontinuance of the "usual" yearly distribution of money which had always taken

1. The ancient passages are collected by J. Labarbe in a useful introduction to his study *La loi navale de Thémistocle*, but his conclusions from the evidence are often conjectural.

2. Justin 2. 12. 12; Cornelius Nepos, *Them.* 2, init.; Plutarch, *Them.* 4. 3; Libanius, *Orat.* 10. 27.

3. So W. W. How and J. Wells in their commentary on the Herodotus passage: "This is H.'s figure for the full strength of the Athenian navy." Legrand in his Budé edition of 1951 suggested the insertion of ⟨ἐς⟩ before the numeral, which seems very suspicious Greek and rests on no manuscript authority.

4. *La loi navale*, 37.

place (presumably since the days of Peisistratus!). Of this alleged double measure, "on conçoit que divers auteurs anciens n'aient été informés qu'à moitié,"[5] which is misplaced confidence in the reliability of "auteurs anciens," whose testimony must always be weighed, and often rejected.

Traces of some early attempt (Ephorus'?) to reconcile the two figures have filtered down to Nepos (*Them.* 2. 8), who says that, in addition to the 100 ships built with the money from the mines (that is, in 483), "an equal number of triremes" was constructed just before the evacuation decree was passed, a more convincing resolution of the difficulty than most of those suggested by modern writers. The fuller account in chapter 22 of the *Constitution* contains some suspicious details: "Themistocles did not tell what he would use the money for, but urged that it be lent to the hundred wealthiest citizens, a talent to each and then if their expenditure of it should be satisfactory, the State would bear the expense, but if not, the State could reclaim the money from the men to whom it had been lent." Parallels exist for this motif of secret schemes. Herodotus tells how Miltiades obtained his 70 ships from the Assembly in 489, "without telling them against what country he was intending to campaign" (6. 132), and Themistocles' plan to burn the Greek, or Peloponnesian,[6] fleet has to be kept from the people and communicated only to Aristeides (Plut. *Them.* 20. 1–2). The mechanism involving the 100 wealthiest men sounds like a proto-trierarchy, a later system whereby wealthy citizens discharged their public obligations by maintaining a trireme and keeping it in repair for a year.[7] We should ask ourselves whether the *Constitution* is not guilty of an anachronism.

What is being dated by the *Constitution* to the archonship of Nicodemus (483/2)[8] is Themistocles' proposal, not the discovery of the new vein at Maroneia, which may have occurred as long as ten or fifteen years earlier.[9] Themistocles may indeed have been biding his time, using information perhaps provided to him by his family in Phrearrhioi, which was on the fringe of the mining district, about the increasing amounts of silver coming out of the state mines, and possibly looking to the example of the Thasians, who, according to Herodotus (6. 46. 2), in the 490s had used the income from their mines to build a fleet and strengthen their fortifications. It is difficult to tell whether Themistocles' proposal involved the discontinuance of a dole which had been going on for some years previous to 483 or whether this was the first occasion on which such a dole was proposed. The numismatic evidence is on this point inconclusive, for the particularly handsome specimens of Attic decadrachms, which, as some scholars have pointed out, seem to fit in very well with Herodotus'

5. Ibid., 50.

6. Cic. *de Off.* 3. 11. 49. The motif is transferred to the fortification of the Peiraeus and considerably embellished by Diodorus (11. 42).

7. See G. S. Maridakis, "La loi de Thémistocle sur l'armement naval," in *Studi in onore di B. Biondi*, II, 193–226, esp. 207 ff.

8. Νικοδήμου ἄρχοντος is the reading of *P. Berol.* IIb and Dionysius of Halicarnassus (*Rom. Ant.* 8. 83); *P. Lit. Lond.* 108 reads Νικομήδους. See T. J. Cadoux, "The

Athenian Archons from Kreon to Hypsichides," *JHS* 68 (1948), 118, with n.257, and Labarbe, *La loi navale*, 83, n.2.

9. This was originally pointed out to me by the late Prof. W. P. Wallace, whose kindness and encouragement at an early stage of this study I would like here to acknowledge. See his article, "The Early Coinages of Athens and Euboia," *Numismatic Chronicle*, 7th ser. 2 (1962), 23 ff., esp. 28–32.

report of a proposed ten-drachma distribution to each citizen, are likelier in fact to have been minted after 480.[10] It is often assumed that a literal interpretation of Herodotus' phrase τῆς διαιρέσιος ταύτης παυσαμένους implies that the distribution had been going on for some time and that Themistocles was now proposing to discontinue it, but this inference is unjustified, for Herodotus' use of the demonstrative shows that he is referring only to the proposed distribution *on this occasion*; nor need the verb παύω imply discontinuance, but simply a *failure to carry out* some contemplated act.[11] We should recall, too, that of the two earliest sources it is only the *Constitution of Athens* which gives a date. Herodotus' phrasing is somewhat vague: "another proposal...before this one" (that is, Themistocles' interpretation of the wooden wall oracle).

In a confused passage Plutarch appears to be reporting a statement by the fifth-century writer Stesimbrotus that Themistocles' ship-building programme was carried out against the opposition of Miltiades.[12] If this is not simply a mistaken substitution of Miltiades' name for Aristeides', it may be that Stesimbrotus actually said that Themistocles' efforts to fortify the Peiraeus in his year as archon (493/2 B.C.) were the first stages in the process of turning the Athenians into sailors, and it was this plan of fortification that Miltiades opposed.[13]

Did Themistocles propose, as part of his bill, a complete overhaul of Athens' naval organization? Cleidemus apparently reported that Cleisthenes, as part of his political reorganization of 508, "divided the ten [new] tribes into 50 parts which they called 'naucraries,'" and some scholars maintain that it was left to Themistocles finally to abolish these obsolete early divisions of the population (apparently for the purpose of supplying ships for a primitive navy) and to reassign their naval functions to the thirty Cleisthenic "trittyes."[14] But the fact that we do not hear of any other specific changes to account for the system in effect in the fourth century is not sufficient grounds for connecting Themistocles' name with such a reorganization.

A final word on the design of the ships. According to Thucydides (1. 14. 3), Themistocles' ships "did not yet have decks throughout their length," that is, their decks were "fore and aft decks, not running the whole length of the ship."[15] Plutarch remarks that the Greek ships at Salamis "lay low in the water and were rather small,"

---

10. The decadrachms connected with the dole in the 480s: Wallace, *Numismatic Chronicle*, 7th ser. 2 (1962), 23, following C. Seltman, *Greek Coins*, 92–94; a date after Salamis: C. M. Kraay, "The Archaic Owls of Athens," *Numismatic Chronicle*, 6th ser. 16 (1956), 57–58, with 58, n.3, and *Numismatic Chronicle*, 7th ser. 2 (1962), 418.

11. For this use of the term, see Plutarch, *Them*. 20. 2, where the Athenians order Themistocles to "desist from" (παύσασθαι) burning the Greek fleet at Pagasai, a plan which he of course has not yet begun to carry out.

12. Plut. *Them*. 4. 5 = *FGrHist* 107 F 2.

13. Labarbe, *La loi navale*, 84–87; Johan Schreiner, "Thucydides I. 93 and Themistokles during the 490's," *SO* 44 (1969), 23–41 (al-

though I cannot agree with Schreiner's interpretation of Thuc. 1. 93. 3–4); E. Gruen, "Stesimbrotus on Miltiades and Themistocles," *Calif. Studies Class. Ant*. 3 (1970), 91–98.

14. F. Jacoby's argument from Cleidemus, *FGrHist* 323 F 8 (*Commentary*, II b. i, 66–67) following Wilamowitz, *Aristoteles und Athen*, II, 165–66, and W. Kolbe in *Philologus* 58 (1899), 522–23; see also B. Keil, *Anonymus Argentinensis*, 218 ff., and M. Brillant in *Dict. des antiquités*, by Daremberg and Saglio, V, 444 (s.v. "trierarchia, trierarchus"). Maridakis believes that Themistocles "side-stepped" the naucraries ("La loi de Thémistocle," 220).

15. Gomme, *Commentary*, ad loc., citing F. Miltner, "Seewesen," *RE*, supp. 5 (1931), col. 932.

as against the Persian ships "with their towering sterns and lofty decks and sluggish movements [*bareias*] in getting under way,"[16] a statement which seems to conflict with Herodotus' comment that the Greek ships were "heavier [*baruteras*] and fewer in number" than the Persian (8. 60. 2, Themistocles speaking). J. S. Morrison and G. T. Williams attempted to reconcile the two statements by pointing out that "the Persians were able to arrive in Greek waters with dry bilges [cf. Hdt. 7. 59. 2–3], while the Greeks, never knowing when the Persians might appear, could not risk taking their ships out of commission for a similar drying-out operation. In the crucial battles, then, the Greek ships were heavy compared with their adversaries."[17]

Plutarch supplies further information about these ships. In the naval encounter with the Persians at the Eurymedon River (*c.* 467 B.C.), Cimon commanded a fleet of 200 ships. "These vessels," according to Plutarch, "had been from the beginning very well constructed for speed and manoeuvring by Themistocles; but Cimon now made them broader, and put bridges between their decks, in order that with their numerous hoplites they might be more effective in their onsets" (*Cim.* 12. 2, trans. Perrin). Morrison and Williams remark that Cimon "seems clearly to be giving up the Themistoclean theory which saw the ship primarily as an oar-powered machine for ramming and sinking the enemy, and adopting the opposing theory by which the ship was merely a platform for the accommodation of as large a force of hoplites and archers as possible,"[18] but his strategy was justified in the event, for the battle of the Eurymedon became Cimon's most celebrated victory.

16. *Them.* 14. 3, trans. Perrin.
17. *Greek Oared Ships*, 135. Other attempts to remove the discrepancy involve emending Herodotus' βαρυτέρας to βραδυτέρας (Stein) or outright rejection of Plutarch's testimony.
18. *Greek Oared Ships*, 163.

APPENDIX C
THEMISTOCLES' FAMILY

THE FAMILY SEAT was in Phrearrhioi,[1] in southern Attica, but of Themistocles' father, Neokles, nothing is known. The eighth of the so-called Themistocles Epistles (p. 749 Hercher) mentions an uncle, also named Themistocles, whose existence has been doubted.[2] Plutarch reports that one of Themistocles' daughters married her cousin, Themistocles' nephew (ἀδελφιδοῦς); although the word more frequently denotes a "brother's son," it occasionally also designates a "sister's son." In fact, a brother, Agesilaus, figures in a romantic tale recorded by Plutarch in his essay *Parallel Tales of the Greeks and Romans* on the authority of the shadowy Agatharchides of Samos: Agesilaus was sent in disguise to slay Xerxes, but having bungled the job and after his plot was discovered, he showed great fortitude in allowing his hand to be cut off in a sacrifice Xerxes was performing to the Sun (shades of Aeschylus' brother Kynegeiros at Marathon!).[3]

About Themistocles' marriages and children our fullest information comes from Plutarch's *Themistocles*, chapter 32, which Plutarch may have derived from the family traditions preserved by Themistocles the Stoic, Plutarch's schoolmate at Athens whom he mentions at *Themistocles* 32. 6. Although Plutarch introduces these children in a rather confusing order, it appears that Themistocles had five sons by his first wife, Archippe, daughter of Lysandros, of Alopeke; of these the eldest, Neokles (named, as was customary, for his paternal grandfather), died in childhood, and the second, Diokles, was adopted by his maternal grandfather. Of the three younger sons, Cleophantus was mentioned by Plato in a context which, as Plutarch points out, suggests that he had acquired a reputation for shiftlessness.[4] The reference in Plato (if it is

---

1. The evidence on Themistocles' family is collected and discussed by J. Kirchner, *PA*, 6669 (pp. 431–35); A. Bauer and F. J. Frost, *Plutarchs Themistokles*, 132–34; J. K. Davies, *Athenian Propertied Families*, 217–20.

2. "Very dubious," comment Bauer and Frost.

3. *FGrHist* 284 F 1. There is an analogous (and probably equally fictitious) sacrifice by Themistocles reported by Plutarch (*Them.* 13. 2 ff.).

4. *Meno* 93 D. Perhaps the "Diophantus" of *Mor.* 1 C should be corrected; in any case, the anecdote told there and repeated at *Them.* 18. 7 and elsewhere is without value.

accurate) indicates, as Davies asserts, that Cleophantus' "activity as hippeus was in Athens and . . . that he had the facilities in Athens, in terms of land, for horse-rearing."[5] In that case, however, I do not find it as easy as Davies to reconcile the testimony of an inscription from Lampsacus of c. 200 B.C., which proves that Cleophantus' descendants were still receiving honours there at that time.[6] It is unknown which of these surviving sons (if any) Pausanias may be alluding to when he mentions two dedications supposedly made by them, a bronze statue of Artemis Leukophryene on the Acropolis (1. 26. 4) and a painting in the Parthenon (1. 1. 2). The story contained in the Suda lexicon that two of Themistocles' sons, having won a competition at certain games connected with a public funeral celebration, were nearly stoned to death when the crowd recognized them almost certainly derives from a late sensationalizing source; the coincidence of the two names given to the boys by the Suda, Neokles and Demopolis, with those in an account by the third-century historian Phylarchus, which Plutarch mentions only to reject at *Themistocles* 32. 4, suggests that it was Phylarchus who invented the story which has found its way into the Suda entry.[7]

Plutarch reports that Themistocles also had "many" daughters, and he proceeds to name five. Of these, Mnesiptolema (already mentioned at *Them.* 30. 2 and 6) is assigned to a second wife, who is unnamed; but as the last girl mentioned, Asia, is described as the "youngest," she, too, must have been born from this second marriage. It is very unlikely that this second wife is to be identified with the lady of extraordinary beauty, virtue, and wealth whom Diodorus mentions (11. 57. 6) as having been among the king's gifts to Themistocles, for her existence has with reason been doubted. Plutarch gives further details about the girls. Mnesiptolema married her half-brother Archeptolis, and, after their father's death, another daughter, Nikomache, was given in marriage by her brothers to Themistocles' nephew Phrasikles, who had sailed to Magnesia to fetch her and who also undertook to raise the "youngest child of all," Asia. Of the remaining daughters, Italia and Sybaris married, respectively, Panthoides of Chios and Nikomedes of Athens.[8]

At *Themistocles* 24. 6 Plutarch cites Stesimbrotus for Cimon's successful prosecution of a certain Epikrates of Acharnae for having "secretly sent Themistocles' wife and children out of Athens" to him in Molossia. It is uncertain whether this was his

5. *Athenian Propertied Families*, 218.

6. H. Lolling, *Ath. Mitt.* 6 (1881), 103–5. The inscription is given in full by Bauer and Frost, *Plutarchs Themistokles*, 97–98. N. A. Doenges suggests that Cleophantus was allowed to return to Athens because of his services in bringing Lampsacus into the Delian League ("Letters of Themistocles," 95), and Davies accepts from the authors of the *Athenian Tribute Lists* (III, 112–13) the theory that "on his return to Athens Kleophantos waived his doubtful title to revenues from Lampsakos— or confirmed his father's alleged action ["Themistocles," in Epistle 20, p. 761 Hercher, is quoted as saying, "I set Lampsacus free and relieved it of all the heavy tribute with which it was burdened"]—and received a benefactor's honours from Lampsakos in return" (*Athenian Propertied Families*, 218).

7. The Suda, s.v. Θεμιστοκλέους παῖδες; cf. F. J. Frost, *AJP* 83 (1962), 419 ff.

8. E. Badian has recently suggested that the Phrasikles or Phrasikleides who was archon eponymous in 460/59 was Themistocles' nephew and son-in-law ("Archons and *Strategoi*," *Antichthon* 5 [1971], 34); this is possible, but by no means certain. (Badian also believes that the archon of 483/2 was Themistocles' son-in-law Nikomedes, but the name of that year's archon is likelier to have been Nicodemus, as given by the Berlin papyrus of *Constitution of Athens* 22. 7 and Dionysius of Halicarnassus, *Rom. Ant.* 8. 83.)

first or second wife, or how many of the children went along with her; Davies thinks it was "no doubt" his second wife and her daughters Mnesiptolema, Nikomache, and Asia.[9] On the other hand, only two of the girls, as we have seen, need have issued from this second marriage, which is as likely to have taken place after, as before, Themistocles left Greece; and Plutarch mentions "brothers" residing in Magnesia. The burning questions regarding the later fortunes of the family are, as Davies further remarks, when they returned to Athens and whether this involved an official "rehabilitation" of their father's name. Davies believes that the children "returned to Athens as and when they wished after 459, no doubt encouraged by the changed political climate of the Ephialtic Revolution."[10] The dedications which Pausanias saw likewise suggest relative freedom of movement in Athens, even to the extent of setting up private memorials in their father's memory. From Thucydides' uncertainty about where his remains were buried, however, and from the accompanying comment about the strictures against burying traitors in Attic soil (1. 138. 6), it seems that at the time Thucydides wrote those words no public decree had yet been passed officially repealing the banishment.

We learn of later descendants who acted in various official capacities in Athens. A Themistocles is mentioned as archon in 347/6 B.C.,[11] and in the mid-second century B.C. a mint official by that name issued coins picturing a trophy on the prow of a trireme, clearly a reference to his famous ancestor.[12] Inscriptions of the Roman period survive to show that the family had by then become related by marriage to the *genos* of the Kerykes, for several individuals named Themistocles are mentioned as *daidouchoi*, "torch-bearers," an official title connected with the cult of Eleusinian Demeter, which was the traditional preserve of the Kerykes.[13] Plutarch closes his *Life* with a reference to a Themistocles who was his "colleague and friend" at Ammonius' school in Athens; this individual, a practising Stoic, also appears as a character in one of Plutarch's symposiac dialogues.[14]

9. *Athenian Propertied Families*, 217.
10. Ibid., 218.
11. Kirchner, *PA*, 6650; Diodorus 16. 56; and schol. Aeschines 1. 109.
12. Kirchner, *PA*, 6651; Margaret Thompson,

New Style Silver Coinage of Athens, 221 ff., 568, 604.
13. Kirchner, *PA*, 6655 and 6656; for the family, P. Roussel in *Mélanges Bidez*, 528 ff.
14. Plut. *Them*. 32. 6; *Mor*. 626 E.

BIBLIOGRAPHY

Adcock, F. E. *Thucydides and His History*. Cambridge: At the University Press, 1963.

Africa, T. W. "Phylarchus and the Gods." *Phoenix* 14 (1960), 222–27.

Agard, W. J. "Boreas at Athens." *CJ* 61 (1966), 241–46.

Alexandre, O. "Athenai: Ephoreia Klassikon Archaioteton." *Arch. Delt.* 22 (1967), B, "Chronika," 37–130.

Amandry, Pierre. "Thémistocle à Mélitè." *Charisterion eis Anastasion K. Orlandon IV. Biblioth. Athen. Arch. Hetaireias* 54 (1967), 265–79.

———. "Thémistocle: Un decret et un portrait." *Bulletin de Faculté des Lettres, Université de Strasbourg* 39 (1961), 413–35.

Amit, M. *Athens and the Sea: A Study in Athenian Sea-power*. Collection Latomus, 74. Brussels, 1965.

Andrewes, A. "Athens and Aigina." *BSA* 37 (1936/37), 1–7.

———. *The Greeks*. London: Hutchinson, 1967.

———. "Sparta and Arcadia in the Early Fifth Century." *Phoenix* 6 (1952), 1–5.

Ardaillon, E. "Metalla." In *Dictionnaire des antiquités grecques et romaines*, by C. Daremberg and E. Saglio, III. 2. 1840–73.

———. *Les mines du Laurion dans l'antiquité*. Bibliothèque des écoles françaises d'Athènes et de Rome, 77. Paris, 1897.

Badian, E. "Archons and *Strategoi*." *Antichthon* 5 (1971), 1–34.

Barrow, R. H. *Plutarch and His Times*. Bloomington: Indiana University Press, 1967.

Barth, Hannelore. "Das Verhalten des Themistokles gegenüber dem Gelde." *Klio* 43–45 (1965), 30–37.

Bassett, Samuel E. "The Place and Date of the First Performance of the *Persians* of Timotheus." *CP* 26 (1931), 153–65.

Bauer, Adolf. *Plutarchs Themistokles für quellenkritische Übungen*. Leipzig, 1884. 2d ed. with additional material by F. J. Frost, Chicago: Argonaut, 1967.

Bauer, Adolf. *Themistokles. Studien und Beiträge zur griech. Historiographie und Quellenkunde.* Merseburg, 1881.

Bean, George E. *Aegean Turkey.* London: Ernest Benn, 1966.

Beazley, J. D. *Attic Red-figure Vase-Painters*². Oxford: Clarendon Press, 1963.

Becatti, G. "Il problema del Temistocle." *La Critica d'Arte* 7 (1942), 76–88.

Beloch, K. J. *Griechische Geschichte*². I. 2, II. 2. Strassburg: Trübner, 1913, 1916.

Bengtson, H. "Themistokles und die delphische Amphiktyonie." *Eranos* 49 (1951), 85–92.

———. *Die Verträge der griech.-röm. Welt, 700–338 v. Chr., Staatsverträge des Altertums.* II. Munich and Berlin: C. H. Beck, 1962.

———. "Zur Vorgeschichte der Schlacht bei Salamis." *Chiron* 1 (1971), 89–94.

Bergk, Theodor, ed. *Poetae Lyrici Graeci*⁴. III. Leipzig: Teubner, 1914.

Berry, E. G. "The Oxyrhynchus Fragments of Aeschines of Sphettus." *TAPA* 81 (1950), 1–8.

Berthold, Heinz. "Die Gestalt des Themistokles bei M. Tullius Cicero." *Klio* 43–45 (1965), 38–48.

Berve, H. "Zur Themistokles-Inschrift von Troizen." *SB Bayer. Akad. der Wiss.*, phil.-hist. Kl., Munich (1961), Heft 5.

Bicknell, P. J. "The Archon of 489/8 and the Archonship of Aristeides Lysimachou Alopekethen." *Riv. di fil.* 100 (1972), 164–72.

———. *Studies in Athenian Politics and Genealogy.* Historia Einzelschriften, 19. Wiesbaden: Steiner, 1972.

Bieber, M. "A Critical Review [of *Antike Plastik*, VI–VIII]." *AJA* 74 (1970), 79–95.

———. "The Entrances and Exits of Actors and Chorus in Greek Plays; Appendix, The Statues of Miltiades and Themistokles in the Theater at Athens." *AJA* 58 (1954), 282–84.

Blackman, David. "The Athenian Navy and Allied Naval Contributions in the Pentecontaetia." *GRBS* 10 (1969), 179–216.

Blum, H. *Die Antike Mnemotechnik.* Spudasmata, 15. Hildesheim: Olms, 1969.

Bodin, Louis. "Histoire et biographie: Phanias d'Erèse." *REG* 28 (1915), 251–81; 30 (1917), 117–57.

Boegehold, Alan L. "A Central Archive at Athens." *AJA* 76 (1972), 23–30.

Boer, W. den. "Themistocles in Fifth-Century Historiography." *Mnemosyne*, 4th ser. 15 (1962), 225–37.

Bonner, R. J. "The Minimum Vote in Ostracism." *CP* 8 (1913), 223–25.

Bowie, E. L. "Greeks and Their Past in the Second Sophistic." *Past and Present*, no. 46 (1970), 3–41.

Bowra, C. M. *Greek Lyric Poetry*². Oxford: Clarendon Press, 1961.

Braccesi, L. "Ancora sul Decreto di Temistocle." *Epigraphica* 30 (1968), 172–79.

———. *Il problema del Decreto di Temistocle.* Saggi di antichità. Bologna: Cappelli, 1968.

Brillant, M. "Trierarchia, trierarchus." In *Dictionnaire des antiquités grecques et romaines*, by C. Daremberg and E. Saglio, V. 1913.

Broneer, O. "Excavations on the North Slope of the Acropolis, 1937: Ostraka." *Hesperia* 7 (1938), 228–43.

Broneer, O. "The Tent of Xerxes and the Greek Theater," *University of California Publications in Classical Archaeology* 1 (1944), 305–11.

Brunt, P. A. "The Hellenic League against Persia." *Historia* 2 (1953/54), 135–63.

Bucher-Isler, Barbara. *Norm und Individualität in den Biographien Plutarchs.* Noctes Romanae, 13. Bern and Stuttgart: P. Haupt, 1972.

Burn, A. R. *Persia and the Greeks.* London: Edward Arnold, 1962.

Burstein, Stanley M. "The Recall of the Ostracized and the Themistocles Decree." *California Studies in Classical Antiquity* 4 (1971), 93–110.

Bury, J. B. "Aristeides at Salamis." *CR* 10 (1896), 414–18.

Busolt, G. *Griechische Geschichte².* II, III. 1. Gotha, 1895–97.

———, and Swoboda, H. *Griechische Staatskunde.* I, II. Munich: C. H. Beck, 1920, 1926.

Cadoux, T. J. "The Athenian Archons from Kreon to Hypsichides." *JHS* 68 (1948), 70–123.

Calabi Limentani, I. "Aristide il Giusto, fortuna di un nome." *Rend. Ist. Lombardo* (Milan), classe di lett., sc. mor., e stor., 2d ser. 94 (1960), 43–67.

———. "Sulla tradizione del consiglio di Temistocle di abbandonare Atene davanti al pericolo persiano." *Parola del Passato* 22 fasc. 115 (1967), 264–86.

Calza, Guido. "Il ritratto di Temistocle scoperto a Ostia." *Le Arti* 18 (1939/40), 152–61.

Calza, Raissa. *Scavi di Ostia.* V. *I Ritratti,* pt. I. Rome: Ist. poligrafico dello stato, 1964.

Carpenter, Rhys. *The Architects of the Parthenon.* Harmondsworth: Penguin, 1970.

Cary, M. "When Was Themistocles Ostracized?" *CR* 36 (1922), 161–62.

Cawkwell, G. L. "The Fall of Themistocles." In *Auckland Classical Essays Presented to E. M. Blaiklock,* pp. 39–58. Auckland: Auckland University Press; London: Oxford University Press, 1970.

Chambers, M. "The Significance of the Themistocles Decree." *Philologus* 111 (1967), 157–69.

Christ, W. von; Schmid, W.; and Stählin, O. *Geschichte der griechische Literatur.* II. 1. Munich: C. H. Beck, 1920.

Clinton, H. F. *Fasti Hellenici: The Civil and Literary Chronology of Greece².* Oxford, 1851.

Connor, W. R. "Lycomedes against Themistocles? A Note on Intra-genos Rivalry." *Historia* 21 (1972), 569–74.

———. *Theopompus and Fifth-Century Athens.* Washington: Center for Hellenic Studies, 1968.

Conomis, N. C. "A Decree of Themistocles from Troezen (A Note)." *Klio* 40 (1962), 44–50.

———. *Lycurgus, Oratio in Leocratem.* Leipzig: Teubner, 1970.

Crahay, Roland. *La littérature oraculaire chez Hérodote.* Bibliothèque de la Faculté de Philosophie et Lettres de l'Université de Liège, 138. Paris: Les belles lettres, 1956.

Croiset, Maurice. *Histoire de la littérature grecque².* III. Paris, 1899.

Croiset, Maurice. "Observations sur les *Perses* de Timothée de Milet." *REG* 16 (1903), 323–48.

Curtius, Carl. "Zum Redner Lykurgos, i. Zwei Bruchstücke vom Dekret des Stratokles." *Philologus* 24 (1866), 83–114.

Curtius, L. "Archäologische Bemerkungen, I: Zum Porträt des Themistokles aus Ostia." *Röm. Mitt.* 57 (1942), 78–91.

Daux, Georges. "Chronique des fouilles, 1967—Céramique." *BCH* 92 (1968), 732–33.

———. "Serments amphictioniques et serment de Platées." In *Studies Presented to David M. Robinson*, II, pp. 775–82. St. Louis, Mo.: Washington University, 1953.

Davies, J. K. *Athenian Propertied Families, 600–300 B.C.* Oxford: Clarendon Press, 1971.

Davison, J. A. "Notes on the Panathenaea." *JHS* 78 (1958), 23–41.

Day, J., and Chambers, M. *Aristotle's History of Athenian Democracy.* Berkeley and Los Angeles: University of California Press, 1962.

Delorme, Jean. *Gymnasion.* Bibliothèque des écoles françaises d'Athènes et de Rome, 196. Paris, 1960.

Diehl, E. "Moschion (3)." *RE* 16 (1935), cols. 345–47.

Diels, Hermann, and Kranz, Walther. *Die Fragmente der Vorsokratiker*[6]. Berlin: Weidmann, 1951.

Dihle, A. *Studien zur griechischen Biographie.* Abhandlungen der Akademie der Wissenschaft zu Göttingen, phil.-hist. Kl., 3. Folge 37 (1956).

Dittmar, Heinrich. *Aischines von Sphettos.* Philologisches Untersuchungen, 21. Berlin: Weidmann, 1912.

Dobson, J. F. "Isocrates." In *OCD*[1], 1949.

Doenges, N. A. "The Letters of Themistocles: A Survey." Diss. Princeton, 1953.

Dorey, T. A., ed. *Latin Biography.* Studies in Latin Literature and Its Influence. London: Routledge and Kegan Paul, 1967.

Douglas, A. E., ed. *Cicero, Brutus.* Oxford: Clarendon Press, 1966.

Dover, K. J. "Androtion on Ostracism." *CR*, n.s. 13 (1963), 256–57.

Dow, Sterling. "The Purported Decree of Themistokles: Stele and Inscription." *AJA* 66 (1962), 353–68.

Drerup, H. "Das Themistoklesporträt in Ostia." *Marburger Winckelmann-Programm* (1961), 21–28.

———. "Zum Artemistempel von Magnesia." *Marburger Winckelmann-Programm* (1964), 13–22.

Ebeling, H. L. "The Persians of Timotheus." *AJP* 46 (1925), 317–31.

Edmonds, J. M. *Lyra Graeca.* III. London: Heinemann; Cambridge, Mass.: Harvard University Press, 1927.

———, ed. *The Fragments of Attic Comedy.* Leiden: Brill, 1957–61.

Ervin, M. "News Letter from Greece." *AJA* 71 (1967), 293–306; 73 (1969), 341–57.

Evans, J. A. S. "Notes on Thermopylae and Artemisium." *Historia* 18 (1969), 389–406.

Ferrara, Giovanni. "Temistocle e Solone." *Maia*, n.s. 16 (1964), 55–70.

Flacelière, R. "État présent des études sur Plutarque." In *Actes du VIIIe Congrès de l'Association G. Budé*, pp. 483–506. Paris: Les belles lettres, 1969.

Flacelière, R. *Plutarque, Vie de Thémistocle*. Paris: Presses universitaires de France, 1972.

——. *Plutarque, Vies II*. Paris: Les belles lettres, 1961.

——. "Sur quelques points obscurs dans la vie de Thémistocle." *REA* 55 (1953), 5–28.

——. "Thémistocle, les Érétriens, et le Calmar." *REA* 50 (1948), 211–17.

Forbes, W. H. *Thucydides Book I*. Oxford, 1895.

Fornara, Charles W. *Herodotus: An Interpretative Essay*. Oxford: Clarendon Press, 1971.

——. "Some Aspects of the Career of Pausanias of Sparta." *Historia* 15 (1966), 257–71.

——. "Themistocles' Archonship." *Historia* 20 (1971), 534–40.

——. "The Value of the Themistocles-Decree." *American Historical Review* 73 (1967), 425–33.

Forrest, W. G. *The Emergence of Greek Democracy*. London: Hutchinson, 1966.

——. "Themistokles and Argos." *CQ*, n.s. 10 (1960), 221–41.

——. "The Tradition of Hippias' Expulsion from Athens." *GRBS* 10 (1969), 277–86.

Fraser, P. M. "Archaeology in Greece, 1968–69." *Archaeological Reports for 1968–69*. Supp. to *JHS* 89 (1969), 3–39.

Frazer, J. G. *Pausanias' Description of Greece*. London, 1898.

Fritz, K. von. *Die griechische Geschichtsschreibung*. I. Berlin: de Gruyter, 1967.

——, and Kapp, E. *Aristotle's 'Constitution of Athens' and Related Texts*. New York and London: Hafner, 1950.

Frost, F. J. "Phylarchus, Fragment 76." *AJP* 83 (1962), 419–22.

——. "Some Documents in Plutarch's *Lives*." *Class. et Med.* 22 (1961), 182–94.

——. "Themistocles and Mnesiphilus." *Historia* 20 (1971), 20–25.

——. "Themistocles' Place in Athenian Politics." *California Studies in Classical Antiquity* 1 (1968), 105–24.

——. "Thucydides i. 137.2." *CR*, n.s. 12 (1962), 15–16.

——. Review of *Plutarchi 'Vita Aristidis,'* by I. Calabi Limentani. *CP* 61 (1966), 216–17.

Fuhrmann, F. *Les images de Plutarque*. Paris: Klincksieck, 1964.

Gardner, P. "Coinage of the Athenian Empire." *JHS* 33 (1913), 147–88.

——. "Copies of Statues on Coins." In *Corolla Numismatica: Numismatic Essays in Honour of Barclay V. Head*, pp. 104–14. London: Oxford University Press, 1906.

Garzetti, A. "Erodoto e il Decreto di Milziade ΔΕΙΝ ΕΞΙΕΝΑΙ." *Aevum* 27 (1953), 18–21.

——. "Plutarco e le sue 'Vite Parallele,' Rassegna di Studi, 1934–1952." *Riv. stor. ital.* 65 (1953), 76–104.

Gauer, Werner. "Die griechischen Bildnisse der klassischen Zeit als politische und persönlische Denkmäler." *JDAI* 83 (1968), 118–79.

Gerkan, A. von. "Der Altar des Artemis-tempels zu Magnesia am Maeander." *Arch. Anz.*, 1923/24, pp. 344–48.

Geyer, Fritz. *Topographie und Geschichte der Insel Euboia I.* Quellen und Forschungen zur alten Geschichte und Geographie, 6. Berlin: Weidmann, 1903.

Gigon, O. *Kommentar zu Xenophons Memorabilien.* Schweizerische Beiträge zur Altertumswissenschaft, 5, 7. Basel: Friedrich Reinhardt, 1953–56.

Gilbert, G. *The Constitutional Antiquities of Sparta and Athens.* English trans. London and New York, 1895.

G.-Kahil, Lilly. "Autour de l'Artémis attique." *Antike Kunst* 8 (1965), 20–33.

Glotz, G., and Cohen, R. *Histoire ancienne, II: Histoire grecque.* Paris: Presses universitaires de France, 1929. Rpt. 1948.

Goldscheider, Klaus. *Die Darstellung des Themistokles bei Herodot.* Diss. Freiburg im Breisgau, 1965. Robert Oberkirch.

Goldstein, J. A. *The Letters of Demosthenes.* New York: Columbia University Press, 1968.

Gomme, A. W. "Athenian Notes, 1. Athenian Politics, 510–483 B.C." *AJP* 65 (1944), 321–31.

———. *A Historical Commentary on Thucydides.* I–III. Oxford: Clarendon Press, 1945–56.

———; Andrewes, A.; and Dover, K. J. *A Historical Commentary on Thucydides.* IV. Oxford: Clarendon Press, 1970.

Gottlieb, Gunther. *Das Verhältnis der außerherodoteischen Überlieferung zu Herodot.* Habelts Dissertationsdrücke, Reihe alte Geschichte, 1. Bonn: Rudolf Habelt, 1963.

Gow, A. S. F., and Page, D. L., eds. *The Greek Anthology: Hellenistic Epigrams.* Cambridge: At the University Press, 1965.

———. *The Greek Anthology: The Garland of Philip and Some Contemporary Epigrams.* Cambridge: At the University Press, 1968.

Graham, A. J. "The Authenticity of the ΟΡΚΙΟΝ ΤΩΝ ΟΙΚΙΣΤΗΡΩΝ of Cyrene." *JHS* 80 (1960), 94–111.

———. *Colony and Mother City in Ancient Greece.* Manchester: University of Manchester Press, 1964.

Gruben, G., and Vierneisel, K. "Die Ausgrabungen im Kerameikos." *Arch. Anz.,* 1964, pp. 384–467.

Gruen, E. S. "Stesimbrotus on Miltiades and Themistocles." *California Studies in Classical Antiquity* 3 (1970), 91–98.

Guarducci, M. *Epigrafia Greca.* II. Rome: Ist. poligrafico dello stato, 1969.

———. "Nuove osservazioni sul 'Decreto di Temistocle.'" *Riv. di fil.,* n.s. 39 (1961), 48–78.

Gülke, Christina. *Mythos und Zeitgeschichte bei Aischylos.* Beiträge zur Kl. Phil., 31. Meisenheim am Glan: Hain, 1969.

Guratsch, Curt. "Der Sieger von Salamis." *Klio* 39 (1961), 48–65.

Guthrie, W. K. C. *A History of Greek Philosophy.* II. Cambridge: At the University Press, 1965.

Haas, Alfred. *Quibus fontibus Aelius Aristides in componenda declamatione, quae inscribitur* ΠΡΟΣ ΠΛΑΤΩΝΑ ῾ΥΠΕΡ ΤΩΝ ΤΕΤΤΑΡΩΝ, *usus sit.* Diss. Greifswald, 1884. Julius Abel.

Habicht, C. "Falsche Urkunden zur Geschichte Athens im Zeitalter der Perserkriege."
    Hermes 89 (1961), 1–35.

Hamilton, J. R. *Plutarch: Alexander*. Oxford: Clarendon Press, 1969.

Hammond, N. G. L. "The Campaign and the Battle of Marathon." *JHS* 88 (1968),
    13–57.

———. "Strategia and Hegemonia in Fifth-Century Athens." *CQ*, n.s. 19 (1969),
    111–43.

Handley, E. W., and Rea, John. *The 'Telephus' of Euripides*. Bulletin of the Institute
    of Classical Studies, University of London, supp. no. 5 (1957).

Hands, A. R. "On Strategy and Oracles, 480/79." *JHS* 85 (1965), 56–61.

———. "Ostraka and the Law of Ostracism." *JHS* 79 (1959), 69–79.

Harrison, A. R. W. *The Law of Athens*. I, II. Oxford: Clarendon Press, 1968, 1971.

———. "Law-Making at Athens at the End of the Fifth Century B.C." *JHS* 75 (1955),
    26–35.

Harrison, E. "To Save the Athenian Walls from Ruin Bare." *CR* 26 (1912), 247–49.

Harrison, Evelyn B. *The Athenian Agora, XI: Archaic and Archaistic Sculpture*.
    Princeton: American School of Classical Studies at Athens, 1965.

Hauser, A. "Literatur zu Plutarchs Lebensbeschreibungen (bis 1934)." *Bursians
    Jahresbericht* 251 (1936), 38–86.

Hawes, Harriet Boyd. "A Gift of Themistocles: The 'Ludovisi Throne' and the Boston
    Relief." *AJA* 26 (1922), 278–306.

Head, Barclay V. *A Catalogue of the Greek Coins in the British Museum, XVI: Ionia*.
    London, 1892. Rpt. Bologna, 1964.

———. *Historia Numorum²*. Oxford: Clarendon Press, 1911.

Helbig, Wolfgang, and Speier, Hermine. *Führer durch die öffentlichen Sammlungen
    klassischer Altertümer in Rom*. IV. Tübingen: Ernst Wasmuth, 1972.

Helmbold, W., and O'Neil, E., eds. *Plutarch's Quotations*. Philadelphia: American
    Philological Association Monographs, 1959.

Herbert, K. B. J. "Ephorus in Plutarch's *Lives*." Diss. Harvard, 1954.

Hercher, R. *Epistolographi Graeci*. Paris, 1873.

Hicks, E. L., and Hill, G. F. *Greek Historical Inscriptions*. Oxford: Clarendon Press,
    1901.

Highby, L. I. *The Erythrae Decree. Klio*, Beiheft 25. Leipzig: Dieterich, 1936.

Hignett, C. *A History of the Athenian Constitution*. Oxford: Clarendon Press, 1952.

———. *Xerxes' Invasion of Greece*. Oxford: Clarendon Press, 1963.

Hill, G. F. *Historical Greek Coins*. London: Constable, 1906. Rpt. Chicago: Argonaut,
    1966.

———, ed. *Corolla Numismatica: Numismatic Essays in Honour of Barclay V. Head*.
    London: Oxford University Press, 1906.

———; Meiggs, R.; and Andrewes, A. *Sources for Greek History between the Persian
    and Peloponnesian Wars*. Oxford: Clarendon Press, 1962.

Holden, H. A. *Plutarch's 'Life of Themistocles'³*. London, 1892.

Homeyer, H. "Zu den Anfängen der griechischen Biographie." *Philologus* 106 (1962),
    75–85.

How, W. W., and Wells, J. *A Commentary on Herodotus.* Oxford: Clarendon Press, 1912.

Huart, Pierre. *Le vocabulaire d'analyse psychologique dans l'œuvre de Thucydide.* Études et Commentaires, 69. Paris: Klincksieck, 1968.

Huit, Charles. "Les épistolographes grecs." *REG* 2 (1889), 149–63.

Humann, C.; Kohte, J.; and Waltzinger, C. *Magnesia am Maeander.* Berlin: G. Reimer, 1904.

Huxley, G. L. "Choirilos of Samos." *GRBS* 10 (1969), 12–29.

———. "Kleidemos and the 'Themistocles Decree.'" *GRBS* 9 (1968), 313–18.

Imhoof-Blumer, F. W., and Gardner, P. *Ancient Coins Illustrating Lost Masterpieces of Greek Art.* Chicago: Argonaut, 1964. Expanded ed. of "A Numismatic Commentary on Pausanias," *JHS* 6–8 (1885–87).

Jacoby, Felix. *Atthis: The Local Chronicles of Ancient Athens.* Oxford: Clarendon Press, 1949.

———. "Herodotos." *RE*, supp. 2 (1913), cols. 205–520.

———. "Ktesias (1)." *RE* 11 (1922), cols. 2032–73.

———. "Some Remarks on Ion of Chios." *CQ* 41 (1947), 1–17.

———, ed. *Die Fragmente der griechischen Historiker.* Leiden: Brill, 1926–.

Jameson, Michael H. "A Decree of Themistokles from Troizen." *Hesperia* 29 (1960), 198–223.

———. "The Provisions for Mobilization in the Decree of Themistokles." In *Akte des IV. intern. Kong. für griech. u. lat. Epigraphik*, pp. 174–79. Vienna: Öster. Akad. der Wiss., 1964.

———. "A Revised Text of the Decree of Themistokles from Troizen." *Hesperia* 31 (1962), 310–15.

———. "Waiting for the Barbarian." *G&R* 8 (1961), 5–18.

Jeanmaire, H. *Dionysos².* Paris: Payot, 1970.

Jeffery, L. H. "The Pact of the First Settlers of Cyrene." *Historia* 10 (1961), 139–47.

Jones, C. P. *Plutarch and Rome.* Oxford: Clarendon Press, 1971.

———. "The Teacher of Plutarch." *HSCP* 71 (1967), 205–15.

———. "Towards a Chronology of Plutarch's Works." *JRS* 56 (1966), 61–74.

Jones, D. Mervyn, and Wilson, Nigel G. *Scholia Vetera in Aristophanis Equites et Scholia Tricliniana in Aristophanis Equites.* Groningen: Wolters-Noordhoff, 1969.

Jordan, Borimir. "The Meaning of the Technical Term *Hyperesia* in Naval Contexts of the Fifth and Fourth Centuries B.C." *California Studies in Classical Antiquity* 2 (1969), 183–208.

Judeich, W. *Topographie von Athen².* Munich: C. H. Beck, 1931.

Kahrstedt, U. "Das athenische Staatsarchiv." *Klio* 31 (1938), 25–32.

———. "Themistokles (1)." *RE* 5.A (1934), cols. 1686–97.

Kalinka, E., and Schönberger, O. *Philostratos, Die Bilder.* Munich: Heimeran, 1968.

Keaney, John J. "The Text of Androtion F6 and the Origin of Ostracism." *Historia* 19 (1970), 1–11.

———, and Raubitschek, A. E. "A Late Byzantine Account of Ostracism." *AJP* 93 (1972), 87–91.

Keil, D. "Der Perieget Heliodoros von Athen." *Hermes* 30 (1895), 199–240.

Kennedy, George. *The Art of Persuasion in Greece*. Princeton and London: Princeton University Press, 1963.

———. *The Art of Rhetoric in the Roman World*. Princeton: Princeton University Press, 1972.

Kiefner, Wolfgang. *Der religiöse Allbegriff des Aischylos*. Spudasmata, 5. Hildesheim: Olms, 1965.

Kinkel, G. *Epicorum Graecorum Fragmenta*. Leipzig, 1877.

Kinzl, Konrad. "Themistokles." *Der kleine Pauly*, in press.

Kirchner, J. E. *Prosopographia Attica²*. Berlin: G. Reimer, 1901, 1903. Rpt. 1966.

Klotz, A. "Pompeius Trogus." *RE* 21 (1952), cols. 2300–2313.

Knight, D. W. *Some Studies in Athenian Politics in the Fifth Century B.C.* Historia Einzelschriften, 13. Wiesbaden: Steiner, 1970.

Köhler, Ulrich. "Urkunden und Untersuchungen zur Geschichte des delischattischen Bundes." *Abhandlungen der Berlin Akad.*, phil.-hist. Kl. (1869), 2. Abt.

Kolbe, W. "De Atheniensium re navali quaestiones selectae." *Philologus* 58 (1899), 503–52.

Koutorga, M. de. "Mémoire sur le parti persan dans la Grèce ancienne et le procès de Thémistocle." *Académie des inscriptions et des belles-lettres* (Paris), 1st ser. 6 (1860), 361–90.

Kraay, Colin M. "The Archaic Owls of Athens." *Numismatic Chronicle*, 6th ser. 16 (1956), 43–68.

———. "The Early Coinage of Athens: A Reply." *Numismatic Chronicle*, 7th ser. 2 (1962), 417–23.

———. "Monnaies provenant du site de Colophon." *Revue suisse de numismatique* 42 (1962/63), 5–14.

Labarbe, Jules. *La loi navale de Thémistocle*. Bibliothèque de la Faculté de Philosophie et Lettres de l'Université de Liège, 143. Paris: Les belles lettres, 1957.

Lammert, Friedrich. "Polyainos (8)." *RE* 21.A (1952), cols. 1432–36.

Lang, Mabel. "Scapegoat Pausanias." *CJ* 63 (1967), 79–85.

Laqueur, R. "Phainias." *RE* 19 (1938), cols. 1565–91.

Larfeld, W. *Handbuch der griechischen Epigraphik³*. Leipzig: Reisland, 1914.

Larsen, J. A. O. "The Constitution of the Peloponnesian League." *CP* 28 (1933), 257–76; 29 (1934), 1–19.

Laskaris, K. A. *Phos eis to Thoukidideion Erebos*. A'. Athens: Vartsos, 1922.

Lenardon, R. J. "The Archonship of Themistokles, 493/2." *Historia* 5 (1956), 401–19.

———. "Charon, Thucydides and 'Themistokles.'" *Phoenix* 15 (1961), 28–40.

———. "The Chronology of Themistokles' Ostracism and Exile." *Historia* 8 (1959), 23–48.

———. "Studies in the Life of Themistokles." Diss. Cincinnati, 1954.

Lenschau, T. "Peiraieus." *RE* 19 (1938), cols. 71–100.

Leo, Friedrich. *Die griechische-römische Biographie*. Leipzig: Teubner, 1901.

Levi, M. A. *Plutarco e il V Secolo*. Milan: Ist edit. Cisalpino, 1955.

Lewis, D. M. "Notes on the Decree of Themistocles." *CQ*, n.s. 11 (1961), 61–66.

Linfert, Andreas. "Die Themistokles-Herme in Ostia." In *Antike Plastik*, ed. W.-H. Schuchhardt, VII, pp. 87–94. Berlin: Gebr. Mann, 1967.

Lolling, H. G. "Das Artemision auf Nordeuböa." *Ath. Mitt.* 8 (1883), 7–23, 200–210.

———. "Mittheilungen aus Kleinasien, I: Ehrendecrete aus Lampsakos." *Ath. Mitt.* 6 (1881), 95–105.

Maas, Paul. "Timokreon." *RE* 6.A (1937), cols. 1271–73.

———. "Timotheos (9)." *RE* 6.A (1937), cols. 1331–37.

Macan, Reginald W. *Herodotus, the Seventh, Eighth and Ninth Books*. London: Macmillan, 1908.

Marg, Walter. "Herodot über die Folgen von Salamis." *Hermes* 81 (1953), 196–210.

Maridakis, G. S. "La loi de Thémistocle sur l'armement naval." In *Studi in onore di B. Biondi*, II, pp. 193–226. Milan: Giuffré, 1965.

Martin, Hubert L., Jr. "The Character of Plutarch's Themistocles." *TAPA* 92 (1961), 326–39.

Marx, Friedrich. "Der Tragiker Phrynichus." *Rh. Mus.*, n.s. 77 (1928), 337–60.

Mattingly, H. B. "Facts and Artifacts: The Researcher and His Tools." *The University of Leeds Review* 14 (1971), 277–97.

Méautis, Georges. "Thucydide et Thémistocle." *Antiquité classique* 20 (1951), 297–304.

Megaw, A. H. S. "Archaeology in Greece, 1965–66." *Archaeological Reports for 1965–66*. Supp. to *JHS* 86 (1966), 3–24.

———. "Archaeology in Greece, 1966–67." *Archaeological Reports for 1966–67*. Supp. to *JHS* 87 (1967), 3–24.

Meiggs, Russell. *The Athenian Empire*. Oxford: Clarendon Press, 1972.

———, and Lewis, D. *A Selection of Greek Historical Inscriptions to the End of the Fifth Century B.C.* Oxford: Clarendon Press, 1969.

Meineke, A. "Über den tragischen Dichter Moschion." *SB Berlin Akademie* (1855), 102–14.

Meister, Klaus. "Zum Zeitpunkt der Einführung des Ostrakismos." *Chiron* 1 (1971), 85–88.

Meisterhans, Konrad. *Grammatik der attischen Inschriften*³. Berlin: Weidmann, 1900. Rpt. 1971.

Melber, J. "Über die Quellen und den Wert der Strategemensammlung Polyäns." *Jahrbücher für Philologie und Pädagogik*, supp., neue Folge 14 (1885), 417–688.

Meritt, B. D. "Greek Historical Studies." In *Lectures in Memory of Louise Taft Semple*, 1st ser., pp. 95–132. Princeton: Princeton University Press, 1967.

———. "Greek Inscriptions." *Hesperia* 8 (1939), 48–90.

———. "Greek Inscriptions." *Hesperia* 36 (1967), 57–101.

———; Wade-Gery, H. T.; and McGregor, M. F. *The Athenian Tribute Lists*. III. Princeton: American School of Classical Studies at Athens, 1950.

Mette, H. J. "Choirilos." *Der kleine Pauly* 1 (1964), 1152–53.

Metzler, Dieter. *Porträt und Gesellschaft. Über die Entstehung des griech. Porträts in der Klassik*. Münster: privately printed, 1971.

———. *Untersuchungen zu den griechischen Porträts des 5. Jhrdt. v. Christ.* Diss. Münster-Westf., 1966.

Meyer, Eduard. *Forschungen zur alten Geschichte*. II. Halle, 1899. Rpt. Hildesheim, 1966.

———. *Geschichte des Altertums*[3]. IV.1. Stuttgart: J. G. Cotta, 1939. Rpt. Basel, 1954.

———. "Troizen (2)." *RE* 7.A (1939), cols. 618–53.

Miltner, Franz. "Seewesen." *RE*, supp. 5 (1931), cols. 906–62.

———. "Des Themistokles Strategie." *Klio* 31 (1938), 219–43.

Momigliano, Arnaldo. *The Development of Greek Biography*. Cambridge, Mass.: Harvard University Press, 1971.

Moretti, L. "Nota al decreto di Temistocle trovato a Trezene." *Riv. di fil.* 88 (1960), 390–402.

———. "Studi sul decreto di Temistocle." *Riv. di fil.* 92 (1964), 117–24.

Morrison, J. S., and Williams, R. T. *Greek Oared Ships, 900–322 B.C.* Cambridge: At the University Press, 1968.

Müller, C., and Müller, T., eds. *Fragmenta Historicorum Graecorum*[2]. Paris, 1878–85.

Mylonas, George E. *Eleusis and the Eleusinian Mysteries*. Princeton: Princeton University Press, 1961.

Natorp, P. "Aischines' Aspasia." *Philologus* 51 (1892), 489–500.

Nauck, August. *Tragicorum Graecorum Fragmenta*[2]. Stuttgart, 1889.

Nenci, Giuseppe. "Per una interpretazione del proemio del *Persiani*." *Parola del Passato* 5 (1950), 215–23.

Niessing, W. *De Themistoclis epistulis*. Diss. Freiburg, 1929. Robert Noske.

Noack, Ferdinand. "Bemerkungen zu den Piraeusmauern." *Ath. Mitt.* 33 (1908), 33–38.

———. "Die Mauern Athens, Ausgrabungen und Untersuchungen." *Ath. Mitt.* 32 (1907), 123–60, 473–566.

Nylander, Carl. "ΑΣΣΥΡΙΑ ΓΡΑΜΜΑΤΑ: Remarks on the Twenty-first 'Letter of Themistocles.'" *Opuscula Atheniensia* 8 (1968), 119–36.

Oliver, James H. *The Civilizing Power: A Study of the Panathenaic Discourse of Aelius Aristides. Transactions of the American Philosophical Society*, n.s. 58, pt. 1. Philadelphia, 1968.

O'Neill, Eugene, Jr. "Note on Phrynichus' *Phoenissae* and Aeschylus' *Persae*." *CP* 37 (1942), 425–27.

Page, D. L. "Simonidea." *JHS* 71 (1951), 133–42.

———, ed. *Poetae Melici Graeci*. Oxford: Clarendon Press, 1962.

Papastravros, J. ΘΕΜΙΣΤΟΚΛΗΣ ΦΡΕΑΡΡΙΟΣ. Athens, 1970.

Parke, H. W., and Wormell, D. E. W. *The Delphic Oracle*. Oxford: Blackwell, 1956.

Pearson, Lionel. *Early Ionian Historians*. Oxford: Clarendon Press, 1939.

———. *The Lost Histories of Alexander the Great*. American Philological Association Monographs, 30. Ithaca: Cornell University Press, 1960.

Pelekidis, C. *Histoire de l'Éphébie attique*. École française d'Athènes, travaux et mémoires, 13. Paris: de Boccard, 1962.

Peppas-Delmousou, D. "Περὶ τοῦ Ψηφίσματος τοῦ Θεμιστοκλέους, καὶ τῆς σχετικῆς βιβλιογραφίας." *AAAth* 2 (1969), 146–56.

Perrin, B. *Plutarch's 'Cimon' and 'Pericles.'* New York: Scribner's, 1910.

Perrin, B. *Plutarch's 'Themistocles' and 'Aristeides.'* New York and London: Scribner's, 1901.

Pfister, F. "Zur Gesandschaft des Themistokles nach Sparta." *Berliner Philologische Wochenschrift* 35 (1915), 381–83.

Philadelpheus, A. "Three Statue-Bases Recently Discovered at Athens." *JHS* 42 (1922), 104–6.

Plommer, W. H. "The Tyranny of the Archon-List." *CR*, n.s. 19 (1969), 126–29.

Podlecki, Anthony J. *Aeschylus, 'The Persians.'* Englewood Cliffs, N.J.: Prentice-Hall, 1970.

———. "Cimon, Skyros and 'Theseus' Bones.'" *JHS* 91 (1971), 141–43.

———. "The Peripatetics as Literary Critics." *Phoenix* 23 (1969), 114–37.

———. *The Political Background of Aeschylean Tragedy.* Ann Arbor: University of Michigan Press, 1966.

———. "The Political Significance of the Athenian 'Tyrannicide-' Cult." *Historia* 15 (1966), 129–41.

———. "Simonides: 480." *Historia* 17 (1968), 257–74.

———. "Themistocles and Simonides, Supplementary Notes." *Historia* 18 (1969), 251.

Pohlenz, Max. *Griechische Tragödie*2. Göttingen: Vandenhoeck and Ruprecht, 1954.

Preuner, E. "ΣΑΜΙΑΚΑ." *Ath. Mitt.* 49 (1924), 26–49.

Pritchett, W. K. *Studies in Ancient Greek Topography, Part II: Battlefields.* Berkeley and Los Angeles: University of California Press, 1969.

Raubitschek, A. E. "The Covenant of Plataea." *TAPA* 91 (1960), 178–83.

———. "Herodotus and the Inscriptions." *Bull. Inst. of Class. Studies, Univ. of London* 8 (1961), 59–61.

———. "Die Inschrift als geschichtliches Denkmal." *Gymnasium* 72 (1965), 511–22.

———. "A Note on the Themistocles Decree." In *Studi in onore di Luisa Banti*, pp. 285–87. Rome: Bretschneider, 1965.

———. "The Origin of Ostracism." *AJA* 55 (1951), 221–29.

———. "Ostracism." In *Actes du deuxième Congrès international d'épigraphie grecque et latine*, pp. 59–74. Paris: Adrien Maisonneuve, 1952.

———. "The Ostracism of Xanthippos." *AJA* 51 (1947), 257–62.

———. "Theophrastus on Ostracism." *Class. et Med.* 19 (1958), 73–109.

———. "Die Verstoßung des Themistokles." *Hermes* 84 (1956/57), 500–501.

Re, R. del. "Gli Studi plutarchei nell'ultimo Cinquantennio." *Atene e Roma*, 4th ser. 3 (1953), 187–96.

Reinach, S. "Les *Perses* de Timothée." *REG* 16 (1903), 62–83.

Rhodes, P. J. *The Athenian Boule.* Oxford: Clarendon Press, 1972.

———. "Thucydides on Pausanias and Themistocles." *Historia* 19 (1970), 387–400.

Rhousopoulos, A. "Das Monument des Themistokles in Magnesia." *Ath. Mitt.* 21 (1896), 18–26.

Richter, G. M. A. *Greek Portraits: A Study of Their Development.* Collection Latomus, 20. Brussels, 1955.

———. *The Portraits of the Greeks.* London: Phaidon, 1965.

Ridgway, Brunilde S. *The Severe Style in Greek Sculpture.* Princeton: Princeton University Press, 1970.

Ripper, Werner. "Bemerkungen zur Themistokles-Inschrift von Troizen." *Gymnasium* 74 (1967), 134–39, 565.

Robert, L. *Études épigraphiques et philologiques.* Bibliothèque de l'École pratique des hautes études, 272. Paris: Champion, 1938.

Robinson, E. S. G. "Some Problems in the Later Fifth Century Coinage of Athens." *American Numismatic Society Museum Notes* 9 (1960), 1–15.

Rogers, B. B. *The 'Knights' of Aristophanes.* London: George Bell, 1916.

Romilly, Jacqueline de. *Thucydide, La guerre du Peloponnèse, Livre I*[2]. Paris: Les belles lettres, 1958.

Roussel, P. "Un nouveau document concernant le génos des KHPYKES." *Mélanges Bidez, Annuaire de l'institut de philologie et d'histoire orientales,* II, pp. 819–34. Brussels: Université libre, 1934.

Rubensohn, M. "Themistokles-Epigramme." *Neue Jahrbücher* 2 (1894), 457–61.

Russell, D. A. "On Reading Plutarch's *Lives.*" *G&R,* 2d ser. 13 (1966), 139–57.

———. *Plutarch.* London: Duckworth, 1973.

———. "Plutarch, 'Alcibiades' 1–16." *PCPhS* 192 (1966), 37–47.

Ste Croix, G. E. M. de. *The Origins of the Peloponnesian War.* London: Duckworth, 1972.

Sandys, J. E. *Aristotle's 'Constitution of Athens'*[2]. London: Macmillan, 1912.

Schachermeyr, F. "Das Bild des Themistokles in der antiken Geschichtsschreibung." *XII*[e] *Congrès intern. des sciences historiques, Vienna. Rapports* IV (1965), 81–91.

———. "Stesimbrotos und seine Schrift über die Staatsmänner." *SB Oesterreiches Akademie,* Vienna, phil.-hist. Kl. 247. 5 (1965).

———. "Die Themistokles-Stele und ihre Bedeutung für die Vorgeschichte der Schlacht von Salamis." *Oester. arch. Inst. in Wien,* Jahreshefte 46 (1961–63), 158–75.

Scherling, K. "Lykomidai." *RE* 13 (1927), cols. 2300–302.

Schreiner, Johan Heinrik. *Aristotle and Perikles: A Study in Historiography. SO,* supp. 21. Oslo: Universitetsforlaget, 1968.

———. "Thucydides I. 93 and Themistokles during the 490's." *SO* 44 (1969), 23–41.

Schwartz, E. "Aristodemos (32)." *RE* 2 (1896), cols. 926–29.

Schweitzer, B. "Das Bildnis des Themistokles." *Die Antike* 17 (1941), 77–81.

Séchan, Louis. *Études sur la tragédie grecque.* Paris: Champion, 1926. Rpt. 1967.

Seel, Otto. *Pompei Trogi Fragmenta.* Leipzig: Teubner, 1956.

Seltman, C. T. *Athens, Its History and Coinage before the Persian Invasion.* Cambridge: At the University Press, 1924.

———. *Greek Coins.* London: Methuen, 1933.

Shear, T. Leslie. "The Campaign of 1939, Section Nu Nu." *Hesperia* 9 (1940), 300–304.

Sichtermann, H. "Der Themistokles von Ostia, seine Wirkung in fünfundzwanzig Jahren." *Gymnasium* 71 (1964), 348–81.

Siewert, P. *Der Eid von Plataiai.* Vestigia, 16. Munich: C. H. Beck, 1972.

Simon, Erika. "Boreas und Oreithyia auf dem silbernen Rhyton in Triest." *Antike und Abendland* 13 (1967), 101–26.

Smart, J. D. "Kimon's Capture of Eion." *JHS* 87 (1967), 136–38.

Smith, Philip. "Phanias." In *William Smith's Dictionary of Greek and Roman Biography and Mythology*, III, pp. 236–37. London, 1880.

Snell, Bruno. *Tragicorum Graecorum Fragmenta*. I. Göttingen: Vandenhoeck and Ruprecht, 1971.

Solmsen, F. "Philiskos (9)." *RE* 19 (1938), cols. 2384–87.

———. "Philostratos (10)." *RE* 20 (1941), cols. 136–74.

Sordi, M. *Diodori Siculi Bibliothecae Liber Sextus Decimus*. Florence: La Nouva Italia, 1969.

Spengel, L. *Rhetores Graeci*. Leipzig, 1853–56.

Stadter, P. A. *Plutarch's Historical Methods*. Cambridge, Mass.: Harvard University Press, 1965.

Stauffenberg, Graf Alexander Schenk von. "Themistokles." In *Macht und Geist*, pp. 122–39. Munich: Callwey, 1972.

Stoessl, Franz. "Die Phoenissen des Phrynichos und die Perser des Aischylos." *Mus. Helv.* 2 (1945), 148–65.

Sykutris, J. "Epistolographie." *RE*, supp. 5 (1931), cols. 185–220.

Taylor, A. E. "On the Date of the Trial of Anaxagoras." *CQ* 11 (1917), 81–87.

———. *Philosophical Studies*. London: Macmillan, 1934.

Theander, Carl. *Plutarch und die Geschichte*. Bull. de la Société royale des lettres de Lund. 1950–51.

Thiel, J. H. "The Inscription from Troezen." *Meded. der Kon. Nederlandse Akad. van Wetenschappen, afd. Letter.*, n.r. 25.8, Amsterdam (1962), 525–41.

———. "Themistokles (een polemiek)." *Tijdschrift voor Geschiedenis* 65 (1951), 1–39.

Thompson, Homer A. "The Excavation of the Athenian Agora, Twelfth Season: 1947: Ostraka." *Hesperia* 17 (1948), 193–94.

———. "Excavations in the Athenian Agora: 1949: Inscriptions and Ostraka." *Hesperia* 19 (1950), 336–37.

———. *The Tholos of Athens and Its Predecessors. Hesperia*, supp. 4 (1940).

———, and Wycherley, R. E. *The Athenian Agora, XIV: The Agora of Athens*. Princeton: American School of Classical Studies at Athens, 1972.

Thompson, Margaret. *The New Style Silver Coinage of Athens*. New York: American Numismatic Society, 1961.

Thomsen, Rudi. *The Origin of Ostracism, a Synthesis*. Humanitas, 4. Copenhagen: Gyldendal, 1972.

Threpsiades, J., and Vanderpool, E. "Themistokles' Sanctuary of Artemis Aristoboule." *Arch. Delt.* 19 (1964), 26–36.

Tod, M. N. *A Selection of Greek Historical Inscriptions*. I², II. Oxford: Clarendon Press, 1946, 1948.

Toepffer, J. *Attische Genealogie*. Berlin, 1889.

Travlos, John. "Τὸ Γυμνάσιον τοῦ Κυνοσάργους." *AAAth* 3 (1970), 6–14.

———. *Pictorial Dictionary of Ancient Athens*. London: Thames and Hudson, 1971.

Ure, P. N. "Themistocles, Aeschylus and Diodorus." *CR* 37 (1923), 64.

———. "When Was Themistocles Last in Athens?" *JHS* 41 (1921), 165–78.

Uxkull-Gyllenband, W. G. *Plutarch und die griechische Biographie.* Stuttgart: Kohl-hammer, 1927.

Vanderpool, E. "A *Lex Sacra* of the Attic Deme Phrearrhioi." *Hesperia* 39 (1970), 47–53.

———. "New Ostraka from the Athenian Agora." *Hesperia* 37 (1968), 117–20.

———. "News Letter from Greece." *AJA* 58 (1954), 231–41; 60 (1956), 267–74; 61 (1957), 281–85; 62 (1958), 321–25.

———. *Ostracism at Athens. Lectures in Memory of Louise Taft Semple*, 2d ser. Cincinnati: University of Cincinnati, 1970.

———. "The Rectangular Rock-Cut Shaft." *Hesperia* 15 (1946), 265–336.

———. "Some Ostraka from the Athenian Agora." *Commemorative Studies in Honor of Theodore Leslie Shear. Hesperia*, supp. 8 (1949), 394–412.

Varoucha-Christodoulopoulou, E. "Athenai-Attike, Ethnikon Archaiologikon Mou-seion; A'. Nomismatike Sylloge." *Arch. Delt.* 18 (1963), B, "Chronika," 4–8.

Verrall, A. W. "The Death of Cyrsilus, *alias* Lycides." *CR* 23 (1909), 36–40.

———. "Two Unpublished Inscriptions from Herodotus." *CR* 17 (1903), 98–102.

Wachsmuth, C. "Das Heroon des Themistokles in Magnesia am Maiandros." *Rh. Mus.* 52 (1897), 140–43.

Waddington, W. H. "Médailles frappées en Ve siècle en Carie et en Ionie, I: Thémi-stocle." *Revue numismatique*, n.s. 1 (1856), 47–52.

Wade-Gery, H. T. *Essays in Greek History.* Oxford: Blackwell, 1958.

———. "Miltiades." *JHS* 71 (1951), 212–21.

———. "Themistokles' Archonship." *BSA* 37 (1936/37), 263–70.

———. "Two Notes on Theopompos, *Philippika*, *X*." *AJP* 59 (1938), 129–34.

Wallace, M. B. "Early Greek *Proxenoi*." *Phoenix* 24 (1970), 189–208.

Wallace, P. W. "Psyttaleia and the Trophies of the Battle of Salamis." *AJA* 73 (1969), 293–303.

———. "The Tomb of Themistokles in the Piraeus." *AJA* 76 (1972), 224.

———. "The Tomb of Themistokles in the Piraeus." *Hesperia* 41 (1972), 451–62.

Wallace, William P. "The Early Coinages of Athens and Euboia." *Numismatic Chronicle*, 7th ser. 2 (1962), 23–42.

Walz, C. *Rhetores Graeci.* Stuttgart, 1832–36.

Webster, T. B. L. *The Tragedies of Euripides.* London: Methuen, 1967.

Wecklein, N. "Über die dramatische Behandlung des Telephosmythus." *SB könig. Bayer. Akad.*, philos.-philol. u. hist. Kl., Munich (1909), 1 Abh.

Wehrli, F. *Die Schule des Aristoteles*[1]. Basel and Stuttgart: Benno Schwabe, 1944–59.

Weil, R. "Themistokles als Herr von Magnesia." In *Corolla Numismatica: Numis-matic Essays in Honour of Barclay V. Head*, pp. 301–9. London: Oxford University Press, 1906.

Weizsäcker, A. *Untersuchungen über Plutarchs biographische Technik.* Problemata, 2. Berlin: Weidmann, 1931.

Wernicke, K. "Artemis *Leukophryene*." *RE* 2 (1896), col. 1392.

White, Mary E. "Some Agiad Dates: Pausanias and His Sons." *JHS* 84 (1964), 140–52.

Widmann, S. P. "Bericht über die Literatur zu Thukydides für die Jahre 1919–1922." *Bursians Jahresbericht* 195 (1923), 193–220.

Wilamowitz-Moellendorff, Ulrich von. *Aristoteles und Athen.* Berlin: Weidmann, 1893. Rpt. 1966.

———. "Panionion." *SB Berlin Akademie* (1906), 38–57.

———. "Parerga XXV." *Hermes* 14 (1879), 183.

———. *Sappho und Simonides.* Berlin: Weidmann, 1913.

———. *Timotheos, Die Perser.* Leipzig: Hinrichs, 1903.

Will, Edouard. *Le monde grec et l'orient.* I. Paris: Presses universitaires de France, 1972.

Willemsen, F. "Die Ausgrabungen im Kerameikos 1966." *Arch. Delt.* 23 (1968), B, "Chronika," 24–32.

———. "Ostraka." *Ath. Mitt.* 80 (1965), 100–126.

Wimmer, Friedrich. *Theophrasti Eresii Opera.* Paris, 1866.

Wörrle, Michael. *Untersuchungen zur Verfassungsgeschichte von Argos im 5. Jhrdt. v. Chr.* Diss. Erlangen-Nürnberg, 1964.

Wrede, Walther. *Attische Mauern.* Athens: Deutsches Archäolog Institut, 1933.

Wurm, Michael. *Apokeryxis, Abdicatio, und Exheredatio.* Münchener Beiträge z. Papyrusforschung, 60. Munich: C. H. Beck, 1972.

Wycherley, R. E. *The Athenian Agora, III: Literary and Epigraphical Testimonia.* Princeton: American School of Classical Studies at Athens, 1957.

———. "Minor Shrines in Ancient Athens." *Phoenix* 24 (1970), 283–95.

Ziegler, Konrat. *Plutarchos von Chaironeia*[2]. Stuttgart: Druckenmüller, 1964.

———. "Der Ursprung der Exkurse im Thukydides." *Rh. Mus.* 78 (1929), 58–67.

Zinserling, G. "Themistokles–sein Porträt in Ostia und die beiden Tyrannenmörder-gruppen." *Klio* 38 (1960), 87–109.

INDEXES

1. *Persons and Subjects*

Themistocles (*cont.*)

mentioned by Aeschines along with Solon and Aristeides, 85–86; lacked true wisdom because he could not impart it to his son, according to Plato's *Meno*, 79; harshly treated by Plato in *Gorgias*, 79; in Thucydides' estimation a forerunner of Pericles, 74; compared to Pericles by Dio of Prusa, 118; compared to Alcibiades by Aeschines of Sphettus, 78; contrast with Aristeides emphasized by *Const. of Athens*, 90–91; interest in his career awakens in Rome in first century B.C., 108; exaggerated rhetorical accounts of his death criticized by Cicero, 116; compared to Coriolanus by Cicero, 116; characterized by ambition, intelligence, and daring, according to Plutarch, 135, 138; famous sayings and anecdotes anthologized in Roman period, 126–27; subject to numerous anecdotes told by Aelian, 128–29; in Hellenistic and Roman rhetorical schools, the subject of contrived and hypothetical accounts, 124–26; praised in an *Encomium* composed in the rhetorical schools, 125–26; basically favourable account of his achievements given by "Aristodemus," 114; subject of eighteenth-century drama, 43

Themistocles (*PA*, 6654), 123

Themistocles (*PA*, 6650), archon 347/6 B.C., 123 n. 104, 207, with n. 11

Themistocles (*PA*, 6651), Athenian mint official in 2d cent. B.C., 207, with n. 12

Themistocles (*PA* 6655, 6656), name of Athenians related to Kerykes in Roman period, 207, with n. 13

Themistocles the Elder, putative uncle of Themistocles, 196 n. 4, 205

Themistocles the Stoic, 205, 207

"Themistocles Epigrams," five late compositions in the *Greek Anthology*, 133–34

"Themistocles Epistles," 129–33; perhaps a romance in epistolary form, or an essay in letters on the subject "exile," 130

Themistokleion: referred to by Aristotle, 80–81, 167, 178–79

Theodorus Metochites, 38 n. 41

Theon, rhetorician, 124–25

Theophrastus: as an historian, 81 n. 19; implies Themistocles enriched himself while in office, 81; records Themistocles' denunciation of Hieron at Olympia, 81; records arbitration by Themistocles between Corinth and Corcyra, 81

Theopompus: perhaps influenced by Isocrates' conservatism, 83; outstanding pupil of Isocrates, 99; gives favourable picture of Cimon in contrast with Themistocles, 99, with n. 42; makes size of Themistocles' fortune 100 talents, 99; reports that Themistocles bribed Spartan ephors (perhaps supported by Andocides), 99, with n. 40; suggested as source for *Const. of Athens*, 90 n. 7; suggested as a source for Trogus, 100; probably wrote a full-scale account of Themistocles, but the remains disappointing, 101; alleged influence on Nepos and Justin, 101; denies authenticity of Ephebic Oath, 163

Theramenes: contrasted with Themistocles by Lysias, 82

Therma, 17

Thermaic Gulf, 38

Thermopylae, 16, 30, 110, 111

Theseion Square (in modern Athens), 174

Theseus: allegedly appears to Miltiades at Marathon, 37; restored to Athens by Cimon, 37; ostracism of (unhistorical), 39 n. 41

Thespiai: grants citizenship to Sicinnus, 22

Thessalians, 5, 16

Thessaly, 8, 15, 16

Thrace, 130

Thucydides, son of Melesias, 99

Thucydides, son of Olorus: emphasizes Themistocles' contribution to saving Greece, 68; possible early date of excursus on Pausanias and Themistocles, 72; apparently "correcting" Herodotus, 72; element of fiction in his account of Themistocles in Asia, 73; probably inauthentic account of Themistocles' correspondence with Artaxerxes, 73, with n. 17; expresses uncertainty about place of Themistocles' burial, 73; accounts of Themistocles and Pausanias truly biographical, 73, with n. 19; analysis of Themistocles' character, 73–74; attributes Themistocles' success to native ability, not formal training, 73–74; analyses qualities of a good leader, 74; passes over Themistocles' character flaws in silence, 75; account of Themistocles' letter to Artaxerxes possibly inspires later forgeries, 129; cited by Plutarch, 140; records decrees with variations from epigraphic versions, 165–66; his measurements for Peiraeus circuit wall difficult to reconcile with actual remains, 179; description of Themistoclean fortifications in Peiraeus, 180–81

2. Passages Cited or Discussed